CW00662357

NO. 7 BOMBER SQUADRON RAF IN WORLD WAR II

NO. 7 BOMBER SQUADRON RAF IN WORLD WAR II

THOMAS G. DOCHERTY

Pen & Sword
AVIATION

First published in Great Britain in 2007 by
Pen & Sword Aviation
an imprint of
Pen & Sword Books Ltd
47 Church Street
Barnsley
South Yorkshire
S70 2AS

Copyright © Thomas G. Docherty 2007

ISBN 978-1-84415-481-4

The right of Thomas G. Docherty to be identified as Author of this Work
has been asserted by him in accordance with the Copyright,
Designs and Patents Act 1988.

A CIP catalogue record for this book is
available from the British Library

All rights reserved. No part of this book may be reproduced or transmitted in
any form or by any means, electronic or mechanical including photocopying,
recording or by any information storage and retrieval system, without
permission from the Publisher in writing.

Typeset in Sabon 10/12pt by
Concept, Huddersfield

Printed and bound in England by CPI UK

Pen & Sword Books Ltd incorporates the Imprints of Pen & Sword Aviation,
Pen & Sword Maritime, Pen & Sword Military, Wharncliffe Local History,
Pen and Sword Select, Pen and Sword Military Classics and Leo Cooper.

For a complete list of Pen & Sword titles please contact
PEN & SWORD BOOKS LIMITED
47 Church Street, Barnsley, South Yorkshire, S70 2AS, England
E-mail: enquiries@pen-and-sword.co.uk
Website: www.pen-and-sword.co.uk

CONTENTS

PREFACE

I served on No. 7 Squadron for a brief period in the late 1980s whilst it was equipped with Chinook helicopters, and at the time I was honoured to meet and talk to many of the veterans of the wartime squadron at a reunion at Odiham. Over ten years later I once again renewed my link with the squadron when crews of 7 and 18 Squadrons, with whom I was serving at the time, were amalgamated in Saudi Arabia for the first Gulf War under the banner of Chinook Squadron (Middle East).

Having served with members of the squadron through this short war I experienced its comradeship and 'can do' spirit and realized that in some ways we must have been very similar to the air and ground crews of those far-off days of the 1940s. As a long time member of the squadron association I maintained my link and through the newsletters read many tales of wartime adventures. It was this link to the past which brought me to the decision to write the wartime history of No. 7 Squadron. I could not have done it without the unstinting support of the 7 Squadron Association membership, who provided so much in the way of reminiscences, documentation and photographs, and the equally enthusiastic assistance of the squadron members themselves, particularly squadron historian Mark Bradley.

All those who assisted me are listed under the acknowledgements but in particular I would like to thank Malcolm Barrass, who provided the aircraft profiles. Wherever possible I have attempted to ascertain the copyright of all images used, though with the passage of years and with images passing through many hands to get to me this has not always been possible. If any are incorrectly attributed then I apologize and hope the owners do not mind their use. With the passage of time photographs of the aircraft and crews of No. 7 Squadron become increasingly hard to find. Many are simply thrown away by relatives who are not aware of their historical value. I have included many photos in the book which are of relatively poor quality, but they are of historical importance and simply the only record of many of these valiant men. I make no apology for their inclusion. It is vital to the story of a great and famous squadron.

Tom Docherty
Forres
October 2005

INTRODUCTION

No. 7 Squadron was formed as a unit of the Royal Flying Corps at Farnborough on 1 May 1914. It was equipped with Longhorns, BE8s and Tabloid 394s but had only a short life in this guise, disbanding on 8 August 1914.

Re-formed on 29 September 1914 the unit operated a wide variety of aircraft types including Vickers FB5s, Bristol Scouts and RE8s. On 1 April 1918 it became No. 7 Sqn RAF at Proven in Belgium. It returned to England at the end of the war and was disbanded at Farnborough on 31 December 1919.

Four years later, on 1 June 1923, it was again re-formed from D Flight of No. 100 Sqn and over the next fifteen years operated the current bomber types, including various marks of Vimy, Virginia, Heyford and Wellesley.

Wireless Operator Ted Brightmore joined the squadron whilst it was operating Heyfords and remained until it was equipped with Hampdens.

The squadron was a heavy bomber squadron and our aircraft were Handley Page Heyfords, big biplanes powered by two Rolls-Royce Kestrels, top speed about 120 miles per hour, range 900 miles. Looking back the state of our front-line squadrons at the time was pretty frightening and archaic. I don't think we realized it; certainly I didn't. I was just fascinated by the whole business of being part of the flying scene.

Vickers Virginia 'M' of 7 Sqn being refuelled. P.S. Foss

Vickers Virginia 'M' with squadron ground crew. P.S. Foss

I was allotted to an aeroplane, 'D for Donald', on which the wireless equipment was to be my personal responsibility – routine inspections, modifications, repairs, calibrations etc. and I was to fly with the aircraft as wireless operator [W/Op]. The usual crew for cross country and other away from base exercises was pilot, co-pilot (who also navigated) and wireless operator. Gunners were carried only if the exercises included air firing. The Heyford had no R/T [Radio Telephony] an no electrical intercom. Gosport tubing was fitted. The usual method of crew communication was by passing notes on small message pads. The wireless operator couldn't use the Gosport tubing anyway, as his helmet was the only one fitted with headphones. W/T [Wireless Telegraphy] was the only means of communication with the ground. Navigation was usually by dead reckoning and by astro when conditions were right. Navigational aids were a bit sparse. We could, with some effort, get W/T fixes on MF D/F [Medium Frequency Direction Finding] and some stations had HF D/F [High Frequency Direction Finding]. They could give bearings only.

Night flying was a hazardous business and not just for those doing the flying. No runways, of course and the duty night-flying crew consisted of a duty pilot, a duty signaller (W/Op) and several other reluctant 'erks'. The most onerous task was to lay out the flare path, using gooseneck paraffin flares. The last job of the night (or early morning) was to take them in again. One's working uniform stank of paraffin for days.

Our squadron CO at the time was W/Cdr Soden, followed by W/Cdr Theak and he in turn succeeded by W/Cdr Nixon. Our flight commander (A Flight) was S/Ldr J.N. Jacques, later replaced by S/Ldr M.H. Kelly.

The NCO in charge of squadron signals was F/Sgt Tam Pearce, an ex-sergeant pilot. He was commissioned into the Signals Branch in the middle of 1939 and

Handley Page Heyford 'K' of 7 Sqn. P.S. Foss

was not replaced by another SNCO [senior NCO]. As I had just obtained my 'props' I was promoted to corporal and took over A Flt signals. Jimmie Green, also an LAC [leading aircraftman] was promoted to take over B Flt.

We were gradually re-equipped with Whitleys during April and May of 1939. I personally was a little sad to see the Heyfords go, as I did and still have an affection for biplanes, but thank God we didn't have to go to war in them.

By 1938 the squadron, commanded by W/Cdr F.O. Soden, was flying Armstrong Whitworth Whitleys and in May took part in mass formation flights over the country's industrial areas. In August it took part in the Home Defence exercises. During this period the RAF was desperately trying to rearm and prepare for war and in September 1938 it faced its first test when the Munich crisis flared up. On 7 Sqn all Whitley flying ceased in order to conserve airframe and engine hours in preparation for war. The squadron markings were removed and replaced with wartime code markings. The crisis passed, however, and normal training was resumed by mid-October. On 21 October the squadron lost Whitley Mk II K7241, when it crashed into a house on approach to Finningley. Ray Curdy recalls the arrival of the Whitley.

The re-equipment with Whitleys took place soon after my arrival in 1938 and the aircraft were painted for night operations; however, day flying was still the order of the day apart from one or two keen types who carried out circuits and very bumpy bumps at dusk! The Whitley was the first bomber type to be fitted with power-operated gun turrets. We were issued with electric talking hats (R/T and intercom had arrived) and limited navigation aids. Retractable gear was certainly new to the squadron and at least one inadvertent wheels-up landing occurred at Finningley. I had the doubtful honour of being the first gunner to land in the mid-under turret, a dustbin-type structure with a bucket in the bottom to accommodate the lower legs. Visibility was virtually zero in this position and we bumped the runway before I could retract. However, I managed to tuck my legs up just before the final impact and watched in dismay bits and pieces of the dustbin bounce down the runway behind me!

Ted Brightmore was still serving as a wireless operator in the Signals Section when the Munich crisis occurred and recalls life on the squadron at that time.

Rumours of war grew during 1938 but the Whitley wasn't really equipped for it. It had no defensive armament. Front and rear turret areas were blanked off with plywood and fabric. Practice bombs could be carried on the wing racks, but that was about all.

Flight commanders would put up a flying programme for the day on the notice board detailing pilots and the exercise but not the aircraft. The Signals Section was usually the last to be informed, very often the 'chiefy' [flight sergeant] sticking his head through the door and shouting 'Who's on "D Donald" – you're off in ten minutes!' Panic! – Dash to the accumulator room, test six 2 volt accumulators and put them in the crate, grabbing two spares if it looked like a long trip. Collect log-book, frequency chart, codebooks etc. Into the crew locker room to don flying kit, grab parachute and stagger out to the aircraft, which by now was being run up, then clamber aboard. The Whitley was not easy to get into. One way was via the hatch under the nose, about 5 feet from the ground. There should be a ladder, but it was never in place, so one had to jump and heave oneself up – not easy in flying kit. The second way was through the door at the side, but to get to the front cabin one had to crawl through a very low, narrow tunnel in the wing centre section, pushing a conglomeration of accumulators and gear in front of you. One arrived at the wireless cabin in a bit of a state. The accumulators still had to be installed and tested. I have, on occasions, had to do this whilst taxiing for take-off. Looking back, I don't know why we put up with it. I'm sure we could have organized things a lot better.

September 1938 – the Munich crisis. We were certainly not in any shape to go to war, but something had to be done. Everybody in the squadron, from the CO down, donned overalls and painted the aircraft in war colours. The roundels were painted out and replaced by blue and red discs. The large white numbers

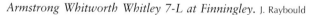

Armstrong Whitworth Whitley 7-L at Finningley. J. Raybould

*under the wings were obliterated with black paint and contractors came in,
working day and night, to fit manually operated turrets fore and aft.*

*I had very little gunnery training up to now. I had fired some rounds from a
Lewis gun on the 25 yard rifle range and had a couple of lectures on how to deal
with stoppages. All of the W/Ops in the section who were not qualified gunners
had been put up for a gunnery course, but none of us ever went. Now it looked as
though we might have to fire some shots in anger. I forget what guns were fitted
in the turrets just installed, I think they were Brownings. They never actually got
the guns in anyway. Chamberlain came back from Munich with his famous bit of
paper and we all breathed a sigh of relief.*

The squadron had been operating Whitley Mk IIs, designated 'heavy' bombers during
this period but these began to be replaced by Mk IIIs in 1938, the first Mk III was
collected from the manufacturers on 29 November. Re-equipment was completed by
19 December. The squadron also received a new CO on 4 December, W/Cdr W.E.
Theak. He, in turn, was replaced by S/Ldr J.N. Jacques on 2 January 1939. Whilst
operating the Mk IIIs K8968 was lost on a night approach to Finningley on 23 March
1939. S/Ldr Jacques was replaced as CO by W/Cdr L.G. Nixon on 29 March and
Handley Page Hampdens began replacing the Whitleys from 22 April. Re-equipment
was completed on 11 May. The Hampden was in the 'medium' bomber class and its
Pegasus engines gave it a speed of 254 miles per hour. It could carry 4,000 pounds of
bombs and had a service ceiling of 19,000 feet. It appeared that this was the aircraft
that the squadron would go to war with, but a change of role was on the horizon.

Joe Raybould was a fitter's mate and air gunner with the squadron whilst
it operated Whitleys and Hampdens. The fitter's mate and air gunner were drawn
from ground crew trades and were expected to carry out their normal duties in
addition to flying. Joe recalls the Whitley days.

*With the Whitley the air gunner entered the rear turret through a hinged door,
you pulled the hinged door up after you. We went to Wolverhampton Airport
once for their open day on 25 June 1938. The aircraft was K7236, flown by P/O
England, a Canadian. At this small airfield we pushed our tail against some poor
old fellow's fence and opened up. I bet he cursed. On brake release we shot
forward, got up to some height then did a dive down towards the watchtower,
followed by a steep climb. I was forced off my tail seat onto the floor. So, the
Whitley could dive and climb, although it looked clumsy. One of the first
Whitleys had to land with its wheels up but F/Lt Norris landed it quite close to
the hangars for repairs.*

*Some church parades were a must – to the local church. Other times a couple
of real church members would come around, open the door slightly and call out,
'Anyone for church?' to receive a barrage of boots and other objects, but it never
stopped them. We had a boxing team. P/O Allen was very good. It still amazes
me that I joined the team. Flare path duty was dirty and sometimes dangerous if
the W/Op forgot to wind his aerial in.*

Ray Curdy was still with the squadron when it re-equipped with the Hampden and
recalls this period.

*In early to mid-1939 the squadron got new aircraft, in this case Hampdens.
Crews were reduced to four bodies per aircraft: pilot, observer, wireless operator*

and air gunner. Again the aircraft were camouflaged for night operations and some night flying did take place. I recall one incident following a night cross-country when one aircraft landed on top of another. Air traffic control did not exist in those days; control consisted of a duty pilot, equipped with an Aldis lamp, a Very pistol and an assortment of cartridges. A particular friend of mine was the wireless operator in the lower aircraft and he suffered severe burns and broken bones. I visited him in hospital some days after the 'prang' and asked him how he had managed to extricate himself. He was rather short in stature and under 8 stone in weight. He had wrenched the aft upper canopy out of its mounting and said he could have lifted the bloody aeroplane off his back if it had been necessary!

Ted Brightmore also recalls the re-equipment, first with newer Whitleys then the Handley Page Hampden. Early flights with the Hampden were to result in numerous accidents and fatalities.

We were re-equipped twice during the next six months with advanced marks of the Whitley fitted with power-operated gun turrets, etc. I fitted my W/T set (the same that I had in the Heyford) in two further marks of 'D for Donald'.

In May 1939 we were re-equipped with Handley Page Hampdens. These machines were faster, more manoeuvrable and carried a bigger bomb load. They were also very deadly from a pilot's point of view; having very little keel surface they could easily get into a flat spin. This coupled with engine teething troubles (Bristol Pegasus) and a large number of airframe problems, resulted in some fatal crashes. The Whitley was a large, lumbering aircraft, built like a tank. We'd had a number of prangs but no one got hurt. When the dust settled one picked up one's parachute and walked away. Most of us had had some experience like that. I myself was involved in one when we were delivering an old Mk I to the MU [maintenance unit] at Kemble. We tried to land in very bad visibility with pouring rain and finished by ploughing the airfield on our starboard side with the port wing sticking up in the air. We walked to the watch office in the rain because the fire tender and rescue truck got stuck in the mud as soon as they left the tarmac. Not the right way to deliver an aircraft, suggested Kemble.

On 20 May the squadron took part in the Empire Air Day display at Doncaster airport, carrying out a low-level bombing attack with four Hampdens. Another Hampden was placed in the Exhibition Park.

The squadron's first Hampden loss came on 23 May 1939 when L4155 was lost in a crash near Newark. The aircraft burst into flames and all five crew members, F/O J.G. McGrail, P/O G. Lloyd, Sgt H.K. Trencham, AC2 E.B. Bretnall and AC1 R. Lumley, were killed. Ted Brightmore recalls the loss of this aircraft and several others.

The Hampden ... was a different kettle of fish. The first casualties occurred in June. Four killed – the aircraft spun in near Newark. Frank Lumley was the W/Op. This was a severe shock to the squadron – the first deaths for nearly two years, possibly longer. By September 1939 the Hampdens claimed three more lives.

The Squadron received eight Ansons similar to this one pictured in Canada on 1 June 1939.
Don Lamb

On 1 June the squadron received eight Avro Ansons to complement the Hampdens and was informed that, along with 76 Sqn, it would become a training squadron for No. 5 Group. On 13 July the new squadron crest was approved by the King. From now on the Squadron would fly under the sign of the seven stars.

Training for the crews was still rather haphazard, even on the brink of war, as Ted Brightmore recalls.

> *The guns on the Hampden were the new Vickers K. We never had the opportunity to do any air firing with them but we did fire a few rounds on the range. The rate of fire was breathtaking. I did, however, have the opportunity to try my skill in the air with a camera gun against a Hurricane, but the film did not come out and the rear sight got squashed when the cupola swung down on top of it. I never did become a qualified air gunner. Pity. It would have brought me an extra sixpence a day on my flying pay, which was, if I recall, one shilling per day at that time.*

By August it was clear that war was imminent and the squadron took part in the Bomber Command Home Defence exercises. This consisted of daylight raids of formations up to six aircraft and composite formations made up of aircraft of both 7 and 76 Squadrons. On the 24th all squadron personnel were recalled from leave. The RAF had a plan, known as the Scatter Scheme, which entailed the dispersal of its squadrons to a wide variety of airfields throughout the country to protect them from the projected massive bombing attacks by the enemy. No. 7 Squadron's scatter airfield was Doncaster, a pre-war grass surfaced civil airfield of quite small dimensions, and the squadron moved in on 1 September. Two days later war was declared.

CHAPTER ONE

TRAINING AND RE-EQUIPMENT SEPTEMBER 1939– DECEMBER 1940

No. 7 Sqn went to war under the command of W/Cdr L.G. Nixon and comprised 251 officers and men equipped with eight Hampdens and eight Ansons. It was tasked with the training, to operational standard, of crews for No. 5 Group squadrons. Doncaster was not an easy airfield to fly from. It was small, it had limited night-flying facilities and the shortage of accommodation for the squadron personnel was acute. Spares for both the Hampden and Anson were also difficult to obtain. Whilst there the squadron had its first wartime loss when P/O Playfair, flying alone, crashed Hampden L4161 at Cockwood Farm, near Cantley on 5 September. On 8 September S/Ldr N.B. Norris, commanding B Flt was replaced by S/Ldr M.H. Kelly. The following day the first five observers were posted in for training.

Ray Curdy went to Doncaster with the squadron.

We moved to Doncaster airport – part of the Bomber Command dispersal programme. Nothing much happened there but I recall rumours were rife about a move to France and the undersides of the aircraft were to be painted 'duck egg blue' for daylight ops. The odd squadron chaps, fitters and riggers, did get marching orders, but the aircraft and crews remained at Doncaster.

Ted Brightmore was among those who moved to Doncaster and he was thrown into a period of uncertainty and chaos.

Then came war, Sunday 3 September 1939. The station tannoy ordered everyone to listen to the PM's broadcast at 11.00 a.m. Consciously we had all been expecting it for months, but subconsciously most of us thought something might happen and all would be well. However, here it was, we were at war and it took time to sink in. Then started the flap! That very afternoon the whole Squadron was transported to Doncaster Airport, our 'scatter' station. There were two squadrons at Finningley, No. 7 and the other, No. 76. Doncaster was not prepared to receive us. The civil airlines had barely moved out. My section was given a workshop in what had been the KLM hangar. They had left in a hurry, leaving all sorts of things behind; including a bundle of clean, white overalls with KLM emblazoned on the back. These were, of course, donned by those who found them.

Doncaster accommodation was non-existent. There were some unfinished huts, intended as offices, which we occupied. Some bedding was brought from Finningley and I made do with a door on two trestles with 'biscuit' mattresses

*and some blankets. Around midnight the air-raid sirens wailed. We tumbled out
of bed thinking, 'This is it.' Having dug slit trenches that afternoon, we now
stood by them, shivering with cold and possibly fright! The trenches had water
lying on the bottom. The prospect of leaping in and lying flat was only slightly
less chilling than that of being blown to pieces! But nothing happened. 'All
'clear' allowed us back to bed.*

*We stayed almost two weeks at Doncaster Airport. A couple of times we were
on standby, once as far as donning flying kit. This readiness lasted almost an
hour and we were walking around in flying kit festooned with gas mask, gas cape
and tin hat. We were supposed to fly with all this stuff, although very soon they
ruled out the gas cape and tin hat, but we still had to take the gas mask.
Eventually we were stood down. The only flying that was done during those few
days was some solo circuits and bumps. We lost another Hampden, however,
engine cut and the usual flat spin. P/O Playfair was killed.*

The difficulties of operating at Doncaster forced a move to Finningley on
15 September, but the squadron was not to remain there long. A week later it was
transferred to No. 6 Group (at that time a training group and not, as later in the war,
a Royal Canadian Air Force (RCAF) group) and moved to Upper Heyford in
Oxfordshire, an air party moving in on the 21st. The rest of the squadron moved by
road and rail.

During September the squadron flew 332 hours despite only having an average
serviceability of three Hampdens and four Ansons. It would remain here in the
training role until 4 April 1940 when it combined with No. 76 Sqn to form
No. 16 Operational Training Unit (OTU). On 1 October it was reorganized into
a flying flight under S/Ldr Kelly and a maintenance flight, commanded by S/Ldr
A.W. Sawyer, the Chief Ground Instructor. WO J.B. McGinn was the NCO in charge
of Maintenance Flight. On 2 November three aircraft were detached to Squires Gate
to work with the Towing Flight at this station until the 6th.

On 25 October the squadron had its first accident at Upper Heyford, when
Hampden L4170 had its port wheel fold up whilst night flying. The pilot, P/O
E.J. Hewitt, was uninjured but the aircraft had to have the port wing and propeller
changed. The first loss at Upper Heyford was on 6 November 1939 when P/O
A.C. Manaton hit a tree on the approach on a training sortie. He escaped unhurt. Just
over two weeks later, on 24 November, P/O C.D.P. Price escaped uninjured after an
accident in Hampden L4158. He had selected the port undercarriage up accidentally.
On 28 November W/Cdr Nixon was posted to No. 52 Sqn and his place was taken by
W/Cdr A.E. Paish.

Ray Curdy was involved in the move to Upper Heyford.

*We all moved to Upper Heyford, still awaiting battle orders. The term OTU was
being bandied about, but whether the squadron was officially disbanded as such,
I don't know. I was a lowly airman at the time and the CO, quite rightly, kept
such information to the higher ranks.*

Ray left his post as a squadron armourer at Upper Heyford to train as an air gunner
and completed a tour of operations on Wellingtons with No. 148 Sqn before going on
to become Gunnery Leader with 467 and 44 Squadrons.

On 13 December S/Ldr Kelly and his crew had a lucky escape when landing in Anson N5013. It touched down on a ridge on the airfield and the port tyre burst, causing a violent swing to port and the port undercarriage collapsed. The crew escaped uninjured. Four days later Sgt M.P. Murray had to make a forced landing at Barnstaple airport in Anson N5015. Approaching to land the port wheel struck a tree stump on the airfield boundary and the aircraft came to rest, with the crew uninjured, on its port wing.

New Year's Day 1940 saw the squadron lose another Hampden. P/O Horace M. McGregor flew into Snaefell on the Isle of Man. The pilot and two of his crew, Sgt Thomas Dennis and Sgt R.J. Bailey, were killed. The only survivor, who was badly injured, was Cpl P. 'Ted' Brightmore. He recalls his miraculous escape: 'I remember a terrific thump and tearing sound, being drenched in petrol and rolling down a slope and into some snow, which must have put out my personal fire and saved my life.' He made his way down the mountain after the crash. Mrs Jessie Cottier walked 2 miles in the snow to raise the alarm. Harry Jacobson, an airman at nearby RAF Jurby, recalls his involvement in the search for the crashed aircraft.

It all came about on New Year's Day, 1940. I was at RAF Jurby, No. 5 BGS [Bombing and Gunnery School], as a flight mechanic on short-nosed Blenheims. Our airfield was shut down on account of snow. It was so bad there was no flying. A 7 Sqn Hampden, P1260, was flying out of Upper Heyford on a navigational exercise. The pilot was Horace McGregor; Sgt Thomas Dennis was navigator and Sgt Robert Bailey a trainee navigator. They left about ten o'clock that morning on a training exercise for the trainee navigator. The crash occurred at around 11.30 a.m.

We were all in the mess at midday and a corporal came rushing in and said, 'All out, as you are.' We only had overalls on. We all baled out into the 3 and 5 ton RAF trucks and made our way up to where the TT course road crosses the railway track. They split us into groups of five and gave us instruction to walk in a straight line, in the snow on the mountainside, for one hour. No matter where we were in one hour we were to turn round and come back. With the mist up there you could get lost. We did not know what we were looking for, nobody knew.

After two hours we finished up back at the trucks. We were stood about; lads were smoking, waiting for the rest to return. We had a small floodlight on the truck lighting up the mountain. As we were about to leave for base a woman came down the railway track and said she thought there was smoke on top of Snaefell. She told us to stick to the railway as we went up, otherwise we would get lost. A group of us set off immediately up the railway track. When we got to the top we saw the burnt-out Hampden on top of the track.

The aircraft was completely burnt out and there were three bodies inside. What happened next made me very sick. The medical orderlies got the bodies out of the aircraft and in order to put them on the stretchers they stood on them, to straighten them out. They were all burnt to a crisp. It was my first experience of burnt bodies and being only eighteen it was a shock.

We returned to camp and three days later I caught pneumonia. I was the only one in a four-bed ward. A medical orderly told me I was soon to have company. This chap came in and I was sick again. It was Ted Brightmore, the surviving crew member. He had virtually no face, his arms were badly burnt and he was being treated with Vaseline about every three hours. Eventually we made friends. Archibald McIndoe spent three years rebuilding his face and he remained in the RAF.

During January the very poor weather had severely hampered the training programme and all of the high-level training exercises had to be cancelled. This forced an extension of the training courses from six to nine weeks in order to complete the syllabus. The training was also hampered by a lack of dual-control Hampdens for instrument training. Night-flying training was also restricted, but despite all the difficulties the squadron was still providing crews trained to pre-war standards.

Flying during February was severely restricted by bad weather and the squadron reported that the standard of the new pilots coming through for training was lower than their pre-war contemporaries. It sent a detachment to Newton on 4 March for air-firing and bombing training, but it was still being reported that standards were lowering and the latest intake had to have their flying hours increased in order to pass the course. On 29 March 1940 P/O J.E. Newton-Clare suffered an engine failure on a training sortie, but he managed to force land the Hampden at Brackley airfield, he and his crew escaping unhurt.

It seemed as though No. 7 Sqn would take no part in the war but it was informed on 4 April that it would re-form as an operational squadron at Finningley. The original squadron was to combine with No. 76 Sqn to become No. 16 OTU on 22 April. In the event it re-formed at Leeming, Yorkshire, on 7 August 1940, equipped with the first of the new four-engined heavy bombers, the Short Stirling. The Stirling was a great leap forward in capability compared to the Hampdens, Whitleys and Wellingtons then in service, but it did suffer from a limitation which would cost the squadron dear in the years to come. Due to a requirement for the aircraft to fit into the standard RAF hangars the wingspan was limited to 100 feet, a limitation which resulted in an aircraft which had a severely limited operational ceiling. The benefit of the short wing was that it endowed the Stirling with excellent manoeuvrability.

With the advent of the Stirling the squadron adopted the code letters MG. The first person to arrive at Leeming on 1 August was P/O Roberts, as squadron adjutant. He was followed two days later by the CO, W/Cdr P.I. Harris DFC. The initial complement of aircraft was to be one flight of eight Stirlings, but this was increased to two flights of eight on 5 August. G/Capt R.W. Cox DSO DFC AFC (Retd) recalls the first Stirlings supplied to the squadron.

During the first part of the war I was posted from the Bomber Performance Testing Squadron at A&AEE [Aeroplane & Armament Experimental Establishment] Boscombe Down and I tested the first Stirling at Oakington. We firstly formed a development flight and then re-formed the squadron in 3 Group. I remember taking a Stirling to RAF Northolt for an inspection by the Prime Minister. After our introduction Churchill said, 'I know a lot about this bitch, but she has to fly.' – It did.

The early days of Stirling operation were to highlight both the improvements over the previous bomber types, but also some of the deficiencies that would plague the aircraft throughout its service. Crew member Roy Jackson recalls the first Stirlings operated by the squadron.

The squadron was re-formed at Leeming and I joined it as part of that process. We had two crews and one aeroplane. My pilot was F/Lt Bradley; the observer was Sgt Griffin. We had finished an operational tour on Whitleys, we had just bombed Turin and Milan and my last Whitley operation was a pretty useless raid on Berlin. As WOp/AG [wireless operator/air gunner] I had the same R1082/ T1083 and TR9 radios as on the Whitley. The engines were radial, whereas we had come to revere our Merlins. However, the big sleeve valves were a long cry from the dreadful Armstrong Siddeley Tigers we had known, the horrible 14-cylinder, 845 horsepower that scorched its ignition harness while idling and blew pots off at the most inconvenient times!

The Stirling seemed to me to be a cross between a flying boat and an erection of scaffolding, but it flew beautifully and very fast. There were no dorsal turrets, but the Blenheims sent to affiliate with us just could not catch us in level flight. Handling was good in the air but on the ground it was ridiculous. With the three-stage undercarriage and the centre of gravity way above the ground the aircraft swung horribly on take-off. We developed a technique that got some 80 miles per hour airspeed before the outer starboard engine was opened up. Landing tail down was the drill, but that gave us a fantastic angle of attack and one always feared that the trelliswork separating us from the wheels would bend! The aircraft was a mass of electrically operated bits; gill motors were a nuisance, I remember. However, the Frazer Nash turrets were to be fitted and this I approved of. The development programme was bedevilled by problems of ancillary failure and a huge modification programme.

With the arrival of the Stirling a new breed of aviator entered service with the RAF – the flight engineer. Essentially a 'pilot's mate' he was responsible for engine handling, fuel-flow maintenance and a host of other engineering responsibilities, thus releasing the second pilot to fill the seat in another bomber. John Prentice was one of the first flight engineers to be trained and arrived at Leeming in August 1940.

After returning from the debacle in Norway and now an LAC, I was posted in August 1940 to Leeming Bar, in Yorkshire, to join No. 7 Squadron, just then re-equipping with Stirlings. Like many ex-Brats [Halton apprentices] I hankered after pilot training, but things were not looking too promising in that direction, so very shortly after joining 7 Squadron when the call came for volunteers from fitters II for aircrew duties I volunteered. We were to be known as fitter II air gunners, soon to be changed to flight engineer. Two other volunteers and I were sent on a course at the Austin factory at Longbridge and on returning to Leeming Bar we were given gunnery instruction, followed by gunnery practice in the air at Stradishall.

The Isle of Man was an unlucky place for the squadron. Having lost a Hampden there in January 1940 they were to lose another aircraft when Stirling Mk I, N3640, flown by F/O T.P.A. Bradley DFC, was hit by anti-aircraft fire over the island on 29 September. The aircraft was crash-landed at Hodge Branding, near Kirkby Lonsdale. Roy Jackson was a member of this crew.

We were at about 10,000 feet and the anti-aircraft gunners thought we were a Focke Wulf Kurier. We fired the colours of the day but that didn't help. I think they damaged the two port engines and we made for base losing height. We were unable to make it and on landing hit a wall and the aircraft was wrecked. Luckily the crew escaped serious injury. We came down wheels up and killed some livestock. The farmer was peeved because he did not get the right price for them – they had not been slaughtered under the prescribed conditions and by approved methods! That was the end of my time with the squadron, very short, not very productive. I never liked the machine, although I admired the engines and the wing looked right, but it was never meant to be anywhere near the ground that aeroplane!

This was the first Stirling to be written off in Bomber Command service.

The squadron moved to Oakington on 29 October and came under the control of No. 3 Group. Six officers and 142 airmen arrived with two Stirlings. The remainder of the Stirlings arrived the following day and on the last day of the month all of the airmen were medically examined. By 1 November the remainder of the squadron had arrived from Leeming. Another accident occurred on 28 November when Stirling N3638 had to make a forced landing near Edinburgh with engine trouble. P/O R.W. Cox managed to land the aircraft, undamaged, on the small Turnhouse airfield.

Teething troubles with the new Stirlings severely hampered the training and development flying during the month. This was exacerbated by continual modifications to the aircraft, which left only two or three available for training at any time. The squadron aircraft strength was now five.

Oakington was perhaps an unusual choice of airfield to operate large Stirling bombers from, as it was grass surfaced and during the winter months the soft surface was to cause many problems for the aircraft's large, ungainly undercarriage. In fact the airfield would be unserviceable so often that the Stirlings often had to fly over to Wyton to be bombed up for operations. Throughout 1940 the situation slowly improved with the installation of a perimeter track and hard standings and the erection of two T2-type hangars on the north-west side of the technical site. Bomb stores were to the north.

James Cantley trained as a flight mechanic at St Athan in 1940 and was posted to join the squadron at Oakington just as it was forming. He recalls the early days of Stirling operation.

I was posted to Oakington, where I met a lot of 'sprogs' who were all from various schools, after all, all types of airmen were required. I think there were only four 'kites' when I arrived and it was a dawdle then for we were all waiting for our aircrews, but it soon got busy with the usual circuits and bumps.

One of the duties we had a turn at was 'kite duty' and all it meant was you slept in the 'kite'. There was a canvas frame attached to the inside of the fuselage on the right-hand side facing the cockpit. I am sure there must have been some 'high jinks' in the dispersal areas. Where 'L' was situated there was a gap in the hedge for easy access to and from the village. Speaking of the village, the bakery was the highlight. We used to nip out after 'kite duty' for jam doughnuts.

Once or twice we, the ground crew, were invited by the aircrews to a 'booze up', but this was before the serious business of operations. Our first drops were leaflets, then came the heavier 1,000 pound bombs which gratified all the crews.

The flight engineers, who had remained in the rank of LAC after training, were all promoted after the move to Oakington, as John Prentice recalls: 'In October 1940 the squadron moved to Oakington. Training proceeded apace and towards the end of the year I was promoted to sergeant, as was now the norm for all aircrew.

Another member of the ground crew was Doug Humphery. He joined the squadron in 1940 and recalls the winter of that year and the problems with the early Stirlings.

I went to Oakington from the training school as a fully blown electrician. We reported to the SWO [Station Warrant Officer] and he told us to find a bed and bed down. In the barrack blocks the residents decided if there was an empty bed for you. If they liked you they found a bed for you.

We reported to the section and I had the impression straight away that the average class of tradesman was above the average at this squadron and it may be a portent of things to come. The Electrical Section was next door to the new Radar Section, which was very secret, with notices on the door and nobody was allowed in. We did not know it but it was Gee [a navigation device with a 350-mile range, which relied on three transmitters sending signals which were picked up by the aircraft on a receiver and displayed on a cathode ray tube providing an accurate navigation fix] and Oboe [Oboe was similar to 'Gee' but had a greater range and only required two transmitters. It was highly accurate but had a limitation of only being useable by one aircraft at a time.] being developed in there.

The hangar was new and it was a brand new camp, all brick built and it was relatively comfortable. A large boiler pumped heat all over the camp, but it was totally inadequate and it was always cold in the barrack blocks. The MO [medical officer] decided that all of the beds in the block would face alternately to avoid transmitting colds. This did not work very well, because the sleeping airmen were sticking out into the room and were far to tempting for the revellers who were coming in in the middle of the night. They would wake them up and ask if they wanted to buy a battleship! The result was that, though the beds were alternate, everyone slept with their heads to the wall. Beds were made up in the morning to reflect the alternation.

Winter 1940 was very cold and there was much snowballing. We had about a foot of snow at Oakington. As the demand on the squadron increased our beds and locations were numbered so we could be called out for sudden panics. Mail was delivered to each block and the NAAFI was very popular, films were shown once a week or so. Chocolate and cigarettes were rationed. I liked chocolate and didn't smoke, others liked to smoke and we used to swap.

Maintenance on the aircraft was always a big problem, because the Stirling was not the most reliable of aircraft. We had all sorts of problems, not least of which was that we were all fitters, electricians and so on, straight from 'civvy street', but we soon learned. As the summer of 1941 came on it got very hot and we would go swimming at Earith. We had a temporary attachment to other stations whilst the runways were being laid at Oakington and we went to Warboys and Newmarket for bombing up and they took off from there. I went up on an air test and flew over Newmarket Heath while the race meeting was on. I commented on what it must be doing to the race meeting with a Stirling circling overhead! The temporary attachment to Newmarket was later cancelled and it was rumoured that the Jockey Club had put a stop to it!

An early Stirling prior to delivery to the squadron. 7 Sqn

As the bombing increased the Radar Section kept their equipment in the section and only installed it just before take-off. Those of us who had bicycles used to go on leave and park them at the railway station, 9 miles away. The parking space was chock-a-block and to get the bicycles out was a nightmare. Sometimes you would have to move twenty bicycles to get at yours.

Some aircrew were in with us in the H block. They were all promoted to sergeant later on and moved to the sergeants' mess, much to our relief, as they were a rowdy lot. Ground staff were encouraged to fly on air tests, electricians especially as they might be able to sort out undercarriage problems. Some aircraft crashed on the drome. It was not unusual to see an aircraft circling with one wheel up and one wheel down. Electricians could usually sort it out by disengaging the gearbox and winding down by hand. The aircrew were also trained to do this. We would jack the aircraft up in the hangar and do retraction tests on the undercarriage.

Early on, our electrical officer F/O Rostran stayed in a tent at the back of the officers' mess, because the mess was not finished. He took it very well. The Station Engineering Officer was S/Ldr 'Pop' Matthews. Both went on to become Group Electrical and Group Engineering Officer respectively. Four erks – I was one – were allocated to work in the bomb department with the armourers. We set up the preselective units before take-off, which determined the sequence in which the bombs were release so as to balance the aircraft. This suited us as we got our leave pass from the electrical section and an early departure chit from the armament WO [warrant officer].

When I was posted in the squadron only had four Stirlings. When one flew, it was an event and we threw our hats in the air! Early troubles were experienced with the undercarriage and exactor controls. Later more aircraft arrived and the squadron became more operational.

I was once working on an aircraft in the hangar and heard the distinctive whine of an undercarriage motor. The aircraft lurched and there were men *running and jumping off maintenance trestles. One even jumped off the trailing edge of the wing! The undercarriage folded up and the wing dropped onto one of the trestles, doing some damage, and hung there. I ran up the fuselage and met one of my fellow electricians, looking at the relay panels. He looked shaky and said that he was tightening the nuts on a relay when the motor started. I looked and found the telltale marks where the spanner had shorted across and welded itself, thus energizing the 'up' circuit on one wheel. The aircraft was unserviceable for weeks.*

Training of airmen as flight engineer/air gunners was started on 5 December and three days later A/Cdre Smartt visited the squadron. On 9 December S/Ldr Lynch-Blosse DFC took over B Flt and the following day the squadron had hoped to commence night-flying training. This was halted by problems with the Stirling's tail unit. The squadron received a lift on the 22nd when S/Ldr J.M. Griffith-Jones and Sgt D.K. Deyck were awarded the DFC and DFM respectively. The next day Deyck was commissioned. On 24 December the Station Commander inspected a fully loaded Stirling, showing off its capability by carrying sixteen 500 pounds bombs. In the last days of the year the squadron ground crew strength was increased by an influx of new corporals and airmen. This, however, did not help the serviceability of the Stirling. Each problem solved was replaced by another and carburettor icing was being experienced by the N3000 series. The squadron hoped that this would be solved by the time it began to receive new aircraft in the N6000 series.

CHAPTER TWO

JANUARY–DECEMBER 1941

The first week of 1941 saw little flying due to the poor weather and poor serviceability of the aircraft. In the following week five of seven aircraft were unserviceable and the two which flew only managed seven hours thirty-five minutes in the air. On 13 January the squadron began training four ATA [Air Transport Auxiliary] pilots to form a pool at Belfast to ferry Stirlings from the Shorts factory.

The King and Queen visited Oakington on 16 January, escorted by AM Sir Richard Pierse and AVM Baldwin. They inspected Stirling N3642. Sgt Jack Roberts, an engineer, was able to provide the Queen with some timely assistance. The red carpet had been laid out and with two hours to go all preparations for the royal visit seemed just right. Suddenly Jack realized that there was no appropriate way for their guests to climb aboard the aircraft. The crew always entered the Stirling through the hatch, but it could not be expected that the Queen would do that. The next two hours were spent finding suitable wood to construct a ladder. The station carpenter finished it just in time. 'I was panicking when she stepped out,' said Jack. 'If it should collapse I had visions of spending the rest of my days in the Tower!'

On 18 January more awards came when P/O J.F. Sach and Sgt A. Watkins were awarded the DFC and DFM respectively.

Their Majesties the King and Queen inspecting target photos during a visit to 7 Sqn on 16 January 1941. 7 Sqn

On 22 January the squadron was ordered to place two crews in readiness for a special duty, the details of which were not disclosed. The following day it was informed that it would not be provided with NCO flight engineers and was to commence with the training of aircraftsmen for this duty.

By the end of the month the weather was again restricting flying, but on the credit side the squadron was greatly overmanned, with ground crew awaiting new aircraft to work on; they would have to wait for these.

The serviceability of the early Stirlings left much to be desired and during the first half of February only two out of the seven aircraft were available to fly. The squadron only managed twenty-nine hours' flying time. Working up to operational readiness was not going to be easy. Frank Wills, who joined the squadron at Oakington, recalls the problems encountered: 'I well remember the "old master's" teething troubles. Bags of belly landings, undercarriage collapses, and lots of manhandling in the mud and working in the open dispersal in snow and ice was no picnic.'

On 2 February the squadron managed to get a few aircraft up but two became bogged down on the waterlogged airfield. The weather was

HM the Queen descends from Stirling N3642 via the steps built at the last minute by the carpenter. N. Colling via 7 Sqn Association

severely hampering flying. Some excitement was generated on the 3rd when instructions were received to send two aircraft to an unspecified 5 Group airfield for sea mining on some nights. Three days later an aircraft was stood by for a 'Gardening' (sea mining) operation but this was cancelled. Three aircraft were stood by for an attack on Boulogne on the 7th, but this was also cancelled. The following day a four aircraft operation to Antwerp was cancelled.

On the 9th F/O Cox made a perfect wheels-up landing in Stirling N6003. After almost five hours of flying during which one undercarriage leg would not lower, the other was raised and Cox made his approach. The aircraft slid for 165 yards before coming to a halt. The crew were uninjured but all were sick due to fumes from an exploding accumulator.

The squadron's first operation with the Stirling came on the night of 10/11 February when three aircraft, flown by S/Ldr J.M. Griffith-Jones DFC, S/Ldr P.W. Lynch-Blosse DFC and F/Lt C Howard-Smith, made up part of a force of forty-three aircraft bombing the oil storage tanks at Rotterdam. Between them the Stirlings dropped fifty-six 500 pound bombs; Lynch-Blosse and Howard-Smith both had a bomb hang up. This raid was flown at the same time as a larger raid on Hanover, on which seven bombers were lost. The Rotterdam force returned with no losses and the pilots returned to Oakington well pleased with the Stirling aircraft.

On 15 February W/Cdr Harris and F/Lt C.W. Bennett took their Stirlings to Boulogne and bombed the docks along with forty-one others. Many fires were seen and there were no losses from the force. Bennett's rear gunner saw their stick burst on the ground and large fires started. Dennis Witt also flew on this operation and his flight engineer, John Prentice, recalls these early operations.

On 15 February 1941 I was airborne on my first operation. It was to Boulogne, with the docks as the target. The flight lasted some three hours. Then followed three operations to Brest in an attempt to destroy the German battleships, Scharnhorst and Gneisenau; a lunchtime daylight solo raid on the port of Emden, which was the first daylight raid by a four-engined bomber on Germany proper; five ops to Berlin of fearful memory and other assorted raids over Germany. My pilot and captain for these operations was Dennis Witt, an ex-Brat of the twenty-third entry. There were two other pilots on the squadron who were ex-Brats – Reg Cox and Gerry Blacklock.

Oakington airfield was not useable for operations during the next few days and the squadron sent aircraft to Newmarket Heath for operations. In the event these were all cancelled. On the night of 24/25 February the squadron sent three Stirlings to Brest along with a further fifty-four aircraft, including six Manchesters on their first sorties. The target was a Hipper class cruiser. The squadron suffered no losses but had an anxious wait for news of S/Ldr Lynch-Blosse, who failed to return. It transpired that he had been forced to abort the sortie due to a heavy snowstorm and landed safely at Boscombe Down, having dropped his bombs 'safe' over Salisbury Plain. Brest would become a regular target for the squadron, particularly with the arrival of the *Scharnhorst* and *Gneisenau* at that port.

That same night a German aircraft dropped bombs on Oakington, creating two large 30 foot diameter craters, 8 feet deep, but no damage was caused. Two days later Oakington suffered an attack from a lone Dornier which bombed and strafed the airfield, dropping nine high-explosive (HE) bombs and incendiaries, but it caused little damage and the only damage to aircraft was to the elevator of Stirling N3652. More awards came on 28 February when F/Lt PR Crompton and F/O Larney received the DFC.

On 2/3 March two Stirlings, loaded with twelve 2,000 pound bombs between them went to Brest to attack the Hipper class cruisers anchored there. F/Lt Best in N3652 landed at Boscombe Down, having jettisoned his bombs. W/Cdr Harris, flying N3653, brought his bomb load back to Newmarket. March also saw several losses, including Stirling Mk I N3653, which failed to return from Brest on the night of 3/4 March. S/Ldr Griffiths-Jones DFC, who had taken part in the squadron's first war operation, was the captain of this aircraft, the first Stirling to be lost on operations by the RAF. The aircraft took off with its load of four 2,000 pound AP [Armour Piercing] bombs and had been given a fix after leaving the target but nothing further was heard from it. F/Lt Pike took N3641 on the same operation but failed to locate the target and jettisoned his bombs in the sea.

The crews were out the following day searching for the missing Stirling. S/Ldr Lynch-Blosse took off in the morning in a borrowed Wellington and F/O Sach and F/Lt Pike followed later. Nothing was found. Several operations were put on, then cancelled, over the next few days. On the 7th, in an unpopular move, the married officers were ordered to move into the mess.

F/O R.W. Cox and crew at Oakington in 1941. 7 Sqn

On the 12th F/O Sach attacked one of the invasion ports, Calais, and three days later A Flt moved to Newmarket once again due to the poor state of Oakington airfield. At this time the U-boat was becoming a serious threat to the country's shipping lifeline and accordingly Bomber Command was directed to target U-boat production, ports and harbours as well as keeping a close eye on the German battleships holed up in Brest. Over the next four months the weight of Bomber Command would fall upon Kiel, Hamburg, Vegesack, Bremen and a host of other targets related to the maritime war.

On the night of 17/18 March the squadron sent out two Stirlings, to Bremen and Rotterdam, flown by S/Ldr Lynch-Blosse and S/Ldr Robertson respectively. The former was the first Stirling to hit a target on German soil. Lynche-Blosse reported bomb flashes in the southern corner of the target with greenish-white explosions rising out of the bursts, developing into a long fire visible from 60 miles away. One bomb hung up in the starboard wing bomb bay. He landed at Boscombe Down. Robertson landed at Wyton on his return from Rotterdam. The following night it was the turn of F/Lt Williams in N3637 and F/O Witt in N3642. Witt bombed oil tanks at Rotterdam but did not observe the results. One bomb hung up but was eventually jettisoned. F/Lt Williams carried the Group Gunnery Officer on his aircraft as an observer. The night of 21/22 March saw a single Stirling, flown by F/Lt E.V. Best, attack the U-boat base at Lorient in conjunction with sixty-five other aircraft for no loss. He landed safely at Swinderby. F/O C.B. Blacklock should have been on the same operation but a taxiing accident prevented him from taking off. In addition to the attack on Lorient two aircraft, N3641 and N3643, set out for Ostend flown by F/O Cox and S/Ldr Robertson respectively. Robertson failed to reach the target, jettisoning his bombs before reaching the coast and suffering a port inner-engine failure. Cox found the target obscured by cloud.

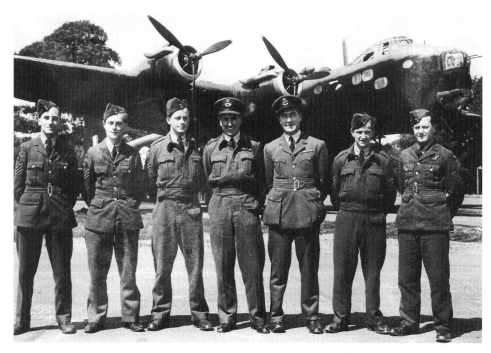

F/O R.W. Cox and crew. This view shows the Stirling's height, due to its stalky undercarriage, to good effect. 7 Sqn

Stirling N3643, captained by S/Ldr Robertson, was hit on the Rotterdam raid on 23/24 March, while the main forces of Bomber Command attacked Berlin, Kiel and Hanover and, returning on fire, the aircraft hit HT cables and then struck the roof of a house crashing at Hazelwood Common near Leiston in Suffolk. All of the crew was killed instantly with the exception of the W/Op, Sgt F.B. White, who died of his injuries later.

Stirling Mk I N3637:MG-K, flown by F/Lt Williams on the Rotterdam raid of 18/19 March 1941. After serving with the AFEE she was written off in February 1945. 7 Sqn

By the 26th A Flt was fully moved in to Newmarket and most of B Flt were also operating from there, as Oakington's surface was in a terrible state and completely unuseable for operations. On 27/28 a single Stirling, captained by F/Lt Best, went to Cologne and returned safely, though the bomb door failed to close after bombing and the undercarriage had to be lowered manually.

Geoff Garner joined the squadron at the end of March 1941 and worked in the Armoury Section until April 1943. During this period he observed many of the difficulties involved in the operation of the huge Stirling bombers.

My memories are of a humble erk trying to remember all the King's Regulations and reading Daily Routine Orders every day. Avoiding the wrath of the Station Warrant Officer, Mr Gibson, and his minions was not easy. It was said that he transferred from a Guards regiment to the RAF when the latter formed. He had a long line of WWI medals and a voice suitable for an RSM of a Guards regiment. He was the best-known person on the station, but perhaps not the most popular one. At times he had orders to provide the names of a certain number of airmen, who were aircraft hand/general duties, for overseas postings. He would lie in wait by the cookhouse door at breakfast time with a 'discip' corporal and would grab as many GDs as he needed when they arrived for their meal. The word soon got round and airmen at risk decided to wait for the NAAFI to open for their first bite of the day.

Unless a crew survived for some time, we ground crews did not get to know them very well. However, if they were lucky and survived, a bond of friendship was formed which, if they failed to return later from an op, made the loss felt even more.

The Stirling was beset with problems at the start; the biggest problem was the undercarriage. It was not unusual to see one circling the airfield with one wheel down and the other up and petrol being jettisoned before it tried a landing on one wheel. It was quite usual to see two or three on the airfield on their bellies, or with one wing in the mud, the other pointing skywards, awaiting recovery.

Those early ops were fraught with dangers and not all from the enemy. There was frustration too, both for the ground and air crews when targets were changed, often at the last moment, or cancelled. Both usually meant a lot of work. Bomb loads might have to be changed and either more petrol put in the tanks or some taken out. For us armourers it was, to say the least, annoying, having sweated buckets winching up the bomb load, having to take them off again. To winch a 1,000 pound bomb to one of the bomb stations at the front of the Stirling bomb bay took some 900 turns of a winch handle; hot work especially if it was a hot day and the aircraft had been in the full sun. One did not find many tubby armourers on a Stirling squadron.

I recall when the first aircraft arrived with the secret H2S [a downward looking rotating radar transmitter giving a visual radar representation of the ground below] *in the autumn of 1942 we were refused admittance into the plane to wind up the bomb load. How that was resolved I cannot recall.*

In those early days there was an armed guard on every aircraft each night, mounted by fitters/airframe or fitters/engines. They were on all night if their aircraft was not flying or mounting guard once it had been bedded down for the night. Not very pleasant in the winter months, but it could be pleasant in the summer. They could lock the door, make themselves comfortable on the rest bed and get some sleep. These guards drew a Sten gun and a magazine of ammunition from the armoury in the afternoon, returning both the next morning. A check by a sergeant armourer found that many magazines were far short of the regulation number of thirty-two rounds. It seems that some of the lads guarding planes out of earshot of the camp were amusing themselves on the long light evenings by trying to knock over a few rabbits. I never did learn if any succeeded. A Sten gun was not the best of weapons with which to go rabbit shooting.

Most of the locals were friendly. Not quite so the local policeman, as some of the lads might have made more work for him on the evenings of pay-days. I have known men in the village, some miles from camp late at night, 'borrowing' a bike from a villager there, riding it back, and then leaving it outside the house of the Longstanton policeman. The locals did have reason for grumbling, beer being in short supply and hordes of thirsty airmen in their pubs drinking what they might consider 'their beer'.

We usually patronized the local pubs if they were not too crowded, the Bull at Longstanton and the Black Bull in Oakington. Another was the Three Tuns at Willingham, a short cycle ride away, where we were befriended by some couples who went there at weekends. Often we were taken back to their homes for supper after closing time. One kind lady I recall getting out a huge pan and doing a huge fry-up. We lads numbered six or eight. It must have been in the autumn as in the pan went tomatoes, mushrooms, as well as sausages and fried bread.

Some of us were also befriended by other, older local couples, who would welcome us to their homes in the evenings for a chat and a game of cards, cocoa and biscuits before we mounted our cycles and returned to camp.

During March the squadron had been detailed to carry out twenty-three sorties. Eleven were cancelled, ten were successful and two aircraft went missing. The squadron dropped 45 tons of bombs on enemy targets. Operating from Newmarket was fraught with difficulty, particularly in the area of bombing up the aircraft, where the soft ground and damage to lifting cranes created problems. Throughout the spring months runway construction was carried out with the squadron operating from the grass strips parallel to the new runways. Eventually the new main runway 05/23, some 1,700 yards long, was completed, but work on the other two, forming a triangle, would not be completed till spring of the following year. The two subsidiary runways were 01/19 at 1,300 yards and 10/28 at 1,400 yards in length. The number of pan hardstanding was also increased to thirty.

On 3/4 April Brest became the focus of attention again when ninety aircraft were sent to bomb the warships. The crews reported that they had been difficult to locate and the lone Stirling from the squadron returned safely. Two more Stirlings were sent to bomb oil tanks at Rotterdam but low cloud obscured the target and F/Lt Cruickshank, in N3642, jettisoned his bomb load into the sea. F/O Sach, flying N6009, took off for the same target but, encountering electrical problems with his aircraft soon after take-off, jettisoned his bombs safe on Lakenheath range. By the 5th it had proved too overcrowded at Newmarket and the personnel of B Flt moved back to Oakington, travelling daily to and from the advanced base.

The largest bomber raid to a single target, Kiel, took place on 7/8 April, 7 Squadron sending three Stirlings. The attack caused widespread damage, particularly to the eastern dock areas. The bright moonlight and excellent visibility aided the crews and a fire in an armaments depot burned for two days. F/O Sach, in N6009, again experienced engine trouble and dropped his bombs on Wangerooge airfield observing bomb burst on the edge of the airfield. F/Lt Cox, in N3652, bombed the target, observing his first stick hitting the aiming point and his second landing close to the railway station. F/O Witt, flying N6012, saw his two sticks hit the target area, starting fires. The force returned to Kiel the following night, the squadron sending a single Stirling, which returned safely. The damage caused this time was mainly to the town, killing 125, wounding 300 and making over 8,000 homeless.

John Prentice had returned from Norway in late 1940 and volunteered for aircrew duties as a flight engineer. On completion of training he joined 7 Sqn and took part in one of the night raids on Brest.

On a night raid to Brest we had an Me109 flying in fairly close proximity. Denis Witt guessed right in assuming that he was relaying our height and speed to the ground gunners and as soon as he peeled off we did a very rapid descent, whilst the German gunners let off a very heavy barrage to where we had been.

Berlin came under attack from the aircraft of Bomber Command on 9/10 April. Eighty aircraft struck the capital. Stirling N6011, flown by F/Lt V.F.B. Pike DFC, failed to return from this, the squadron's first raid on a target that would become familiar to many crews in the coming years. It was attacked by Fw Karl Heinz Scherfling of 7/NJG 1, crashing near Lingen, and Pike and five of his crew were killed. Sgt C. MacDonald survived to become a POW. F/O Sach, the captain of N6009, had engine trouble for the third time and turned back over the Dutch coast. F/Lt Blacklock, in N6005, was attacked by a Bf110 near Lingen but managed to drop his bombs on Emden. From 16,000 feet he saw them burst in the dock area starting a fire which could still be seen twenty minutes later.

The following day F/Lt Best left the squadron, taking N3644 with him, to form No. 15 Sqn, the second Stirling squadron to form. With the surface at Oakington beginning to make a good recovery after the savage winter B Flt returned from Newmarket on the 12th. Two days later W/Cdr H.R. Graham took over command of the squadron from W/Cdr Harris.

Three Stirlings struck a Brest in company with 46 Wellingtons, 25 Hampdens and 20 Whitleys on 14/15 April, but cloud cover safeguarded the *Gneisenau* and *Scharnhorst*, ensuring poor results. The three squadron Stirlings flown by S/Ldr Lynch-Blosse (N6010), F/O Witt (N6012) and F/Lt Williams (N6006) all bombed the target.

The following night it was the turn of Kiel again. Ninety-six bombers, including two from the squadron flown by S/Ldr Lynch-Blosse (N6010) and F/O Sach (N6009), made the attack, but again cloud thwarted attempts to cause significant damage. Sach dropped his bombs on Emden after failing to find the target. The squadron returned to Berlin for the second time in April when, on the night of the 17th/18th, F/Lt Williams took off in N6010. Flying with 117 Wellingtons, Hampdens and Whitleys he dropped five 1,000 pound bombs and seven 500 pounders in a stick, across the city centre. These were the first of many bombs to be dropped by the squadron on the German capital. Bomber Command lost eight aircraft on this raid, but Williams returned safely. Lord Trenchard visited the squadron following the raid and the following day AM Sir Edgar Ludlow-Hewitt inspected it.

On 20 April 75 personnel were transferred to No. 15 Sqn and the squadron began to take on a more normal proportion, having been overmanned for some time. W/Cdr Graham took Stirling N3655 to Hatfield to take part in a display for VIPs. Several new types were on display, but the Stirling was reported to have stolen the show.

On 20/21 April the target was Cologne. Weather conditions were very poor and the raid was not a success. N6009, flown by F/Lt Cruickshank, failed to locate the target. It almost made it home but crashed on a 'Q' site [a dummy airfield used to decoy enemy bombers away from the real airfield] at Stambourne in Essex. The crew were unhurt, but they were almost hit by an enemy aircraft, which had followed them, dropping a stick of bombs on the site.

Two nights later the target was the port of Brest and specifically the battleships hiding there. The squadron sent two Stirlings, N6010 and N6012, captained by S/Ldr Lynch-Blosse and F/O Witt, but the warships were not located due to intense flak and searchlights. Lynch-Blosse dropped his bombs in a stick across the waterfront and Witt dropped his in a shallow dive from 10,000 feet down to 8,000 feet. His rear turret was damaged by flak and the glare of the searchlights prevented him from observing the results. The following night the squadron returned. Two Stirlings attacked alongside sixty-five other aircraft. Hits were claimed by some crews on the *Scharnhorst* and *Gneisenau*, but they were unconfirmed. F/Lt A.L.T. Naish, flying N6013, set out for this target, on his first operation, but developed engine trouble, dropping his bombs safely on Berners Heath.

Kiel was attacked twice in succession on 24/25 and 25/26 April. The squadron sent a single Stirling on the first raid. The original target for three aircraft was Berlin on 24th/25th but only one reached the target, the second turning back and the third bombing Kiel. The attack was very scattered and no serious damage was done. The second raid, in which the squadron did not participate, was also a failure.

S/Ldr Lynch-Blosse set out to bomb a target in daylight on the 27th, but had to return after cloud cover ran out. On the same day A Flt returned from Newmarket.

Bomber Command would take advantage of cloud cover to launch daylight unescorted raids from time to time and on 28 April ten aircraft, including three from 7 Sqn, were sent out. Results were not seen due to the mist. Stirling N6010, flown by F/O Witt, was more fortunate and was the only aircraft to reach a German target, bombing Emden with eighteen 500 pound bombs and machine-gunning the dock area from low level. John Prentice took part in this raid.

We were the only aircraft [from 7 Sqn] taking part. We took off at 1155 hrs and flew low level, only gaining a little height as we approached the target. We bombed from 1,500 feet. This was the first daylight raid by Stirlings on Germany proper. Keith Deyell was our regular navigator. The idea was for us to appear over Emden as everyone was going for lunch and this is what happened.

On 30 April/1 May ten Stirlings went to Berlin, six from 7 Sqn. Three reached the target; three did not due to the cloud and weather. One aircraft ran out of fuel and crashed at Southwold, Stirling N6014, flown by F/Lt N. Williams DFC, a New Zealander, putting down in a field at Wenhaston. Unfortunately the undercarriage collapsed on landing. One of the crew was LAC R.C. Watkins, who was still waiting for his promotion to sergeant to be promulgated.

During April the squadron had sent out seventeen successful sorties of a planned thirty-one. Eleven were aborted, with one aircraft missing, and three sorties were only partially successful. A total of 185,000 pounds of bomb were dropped during the month.

By May 1941 Bomber Command had introduced the 4,000 pound 'Cookie' bomb [a large 4,000 lb bomb similar to a dustbin or oil drum in shape] into service and, as the Stirling's bomb bay was designed in such a way that carriage of this bomb was impossible, the bomb loads became predominantly large numbers of incendiaries. The incendiaries had been found to spread the fires and destruction much more than blast bombs. The combination of the 'Cookie' spreading debris over a large area and the incendiaries setting fire to it all became a potent and destructive force.

The squadron was still hampered by the extremely slow production rate of Stirlings, and losses did not help the situation either.

Hamburg was attacked on the night of 2/3 May by ninety-five aircraft, three of them from the squadron piloted by P/O A.J. Oliver (N3652), F/O J.K. Collins (N3655) and F/Lt R. Cruickshank DFC (N6012). Three aircraft were lost over the target, but none from the squadron. Good bombing results were claimed but Hamburg reported only minor damage and casualties. However, on return to base, F/Lt Cruikshank, was circling the airfield when the Stirling was attacked by a Ju88 intruder. The aircraft quickly caught fire and Cruikshank brought the aircraft in too low on the approach to the airfield and hit some trees. It crashed at Dry Drayton, killing all of the crew. Sgt E. Barratt, the rear gunner, survived the crash but died of his injuries the following day.

That night it was the turn of Cologne and the main force of 101 bombers caused minor damage. The squadron took part in a smaller raid to Brest, with three Stirlings

Form 540 extract showing the Berlin raid flown on the 9/10 April 1941. Harry Rossiter

Aircraft Type and No.	Crew.	Duty.	Time Up.	Time Down.	Details of Sortie or Flight.	References.
	Sgt. Pear.	W/Operator.				
	" Gardiner.	Air Gunner.		1*		
	" Drew.	" " (R)				
	" White.	Engineer.				
Stirling. N. 6012	P/O. Witt.	Captain.	22.45	03.58	KIEL. Two sticks in the target area followed by fires.	
	S/L. Barnes.	1st Navigator.				
	P/O. Blunden.	2nd Pilot.				
	" Dyers.	2nd Navigator.		1*		
	Sgt. Austen.	W/Operator.				
	" Burrows.	Air Gunner.				
	" Savage.	Air Gunner. (R)				
Stirling. N. 6005.	" Prentice	Engineer.				
	F/Lt. Blacklock.	Captain.	20.30	02.53	5/4/41 BERLIN. A.14. Turned back near HANNOVER owing to engine	
	P/O. Saunders.	2nd Pilot.			trouble. Attacked and damaged by ME.110 near LINGEN but	
	Sgt. Stowe.	Navigator.			in spite of this Captain bombed EMDEN from 16,000 ft.	
	" Mossiter.	W/Operator.			flash burst seen in docks which started fire. Which was	
	" ?	Air Gunner.			observed 20 mins. after leaving target.	
	L.A.C. Price.	Engineer.				
Stirling. N. 6009.	F/O. Stook	A/G. (R).				
	F/O. Sach.	Captain.	20.35	22.52	BERLIN. Starboard inner airscrew failed. Captain turned	
	P/O. Sharpe.	2nd Pilot.			back over the Dutch coast and dropped bombs in sea from	
	Sgt. Halles.	Navigator.			18,000 ft.	
	" Glenwright.	W/Operator.				
	" Smithson.	Air Gunner.				
	" Harding	" " (R)				
	" Brown.	Engineer.				
Stirling. N. 6011.	F/Lt. Pike.	Captain.	20.40		BERLIN. One faint signal received asking for instructions.	
	Sgt. Stubb.	2nd Pilot.			Failed to return.	

helping to make up a force of thirty-three bombers. Accurate bombing was claimed by the crews and they returned without loss. A single crew went back to Brest the following night alongside fifty-four Wellingtons, twenty-one Whitleys and twenty-one Hampdens. Once again crew claimed direct hits on the *Scharnhorst* and *Gneisenau* but these went unconfirmed. The force returned with no losses.

On 5/6 May the squadron managed to get four Stirlings airborne for a raid on Mannheim. The crews were greatly hampered in their attempts to navigate to the target by 10/10ths cloud all the way there. One hundred and forty-one aircraft took part in the raid but Mannheim reported only twenty-five bomb loads hitting the city. The casualty report listed the loss of fifty rabbits and chickens! Hamburg was attacked by 115 aircraft on 6/7 May. The squadron dispatched three Stirlings on this raid. Eighty-one crews claimed to have struck the target, whilst twenty-two attacked alternative targets, in poor visibility. Hamburg reported only twelve bomb loads coming down in the city and little damage caused. All of the bombers returned safely to base.

On the night of 7/8 May the main target was Brest but several minor operations were carried out, including 7 Sqn sending three Stirlings to Bremen for no loss. Following the poor raid on Hamburg on 6/7 May the bombers returned on the 8th/9th. The squadron sent a single Stirling. This was a large raid of 188 aircraft and it caused the highest fatal casualty figure on a German target thus far: 185 killed, 518 injured and 1,966 bombed out. The Stirling returned safely to base, though three Wellingtons and a single Hampden were lost.

N6019, flown by S/Ldr W.T.C. Seale, was lost in a take-off crash on 9 May after the starboard outer engines cut out due to fuel pump failure just after the aircraft got airborne, followed by the port outer at barely 100 feet. The Stirling crashed 1 mile north-east of the airfield; the crew escaped injury. On 10/11 May Stirling N6010, carrying a load of five 1,000 pound and seven 500 pound GP [General Purpose] bombs did not make it back from a raid on Berlin. The captain, F/Lt N. Williams DFC, a New Zealander, and his crew were killed when the aircraft crashed at Cloppenburg in Germany. Bomber Command was attacking two targets that night. The larger force of 119 aircraft was sent to Hamburg again and a smaller force of only twenty-three bombers went to Berlin. The Stirling was one of two lost on the raid along with a Manchester.

On the night of 15/16 May the squadron sent a single Stirling to Hanover as part of a

W/Op/AG Sgt John McIntyre of F/Lt Cruikshank's crew who were all killed in a crash at Dry Drayton returning from Hamburg on the night of 2/3 May 1941. D. Miller

force of 101 bombers, whilst another force of fourteen Manchesters and Stirlings raided Berlin. The Stirlings all returned safely. On the night of 23/24 May fifty-one bombers attacked Cologne. Among them were W/Cdr Graham in N6020:MG-B and F/O Witt in N6006:MG-G. Bombing from 13,000 feet the results were recorded for the first time with a camera. The photographs were poor, though, as the photoflashes exploded whilst the camera shutter was still closed. The target itself was cloud covered and bombing results were also poor. Towards the end of May S/Ldr R.D. Speare took over A Flt from S/Ldr Lynch-Blosse.

The night of 2/3 June saw the loss of F/O J. Mitchell, the captain of Stirling W7430, and his crew on a raid on Berlin as part of a small force of eight Stirlings from 7 and XV Squadrons accompanied by three Wellingtons. They were last heard from at 0218 hrs when west of Hamburg. Mitchell was shot down by a night fighter of 2/NJG3 and crashed between Dobbrikow and Hennickendorf near Luckenwalde. The only survivor was the rear gunner, Sgt W.S. Bellow. F/O Cox brought N6006: MG-G back safely.

On the night of 12/13 June eleven Halifaxes and seven Stirlings, including three from the squadron attacked Huls. The target was a chemical works and several fires were started in the target area for no loss. Dusseldorf was raided on the night of 16/17 June by a force of sixty-five Wellingtons and seven Stirlings, three provided by 7 Sqn. Haze over the target prevented many crews from identifying the aiming point and only fifty-eight claimed to have bombed it. Once again there were no losses.

Four Stirlings were sent to Brest again on the night of 18/19 June but haze and an effective smokescreen prevented the bombers from sighting the warships, which were to be the target. None of the sixty-five bombers were lost. Two nights later five crews went to Kiel. Four did not find the target and the fifth, S/Ldr Seal in N6032:MG-T, landed at Newmarket with a failed engine. The target three nights later was Kiel again. Once more five crews set out in a small force of twenty-six Stirlings, Halifaxes and Wellingtons. One Halifax was lost and little damage was done to the target. Five crews set out for Kiel again on the night of 26/27 June. The raid was made by a total of eight Halifaxes, eighteen Manchesters and fifteen Stirlings, but ground haze spoiled the attack and two Manchesters were lost.

On 28 June the squadron lost Stirling N6007:MG-Q, piloted by F/Lt J.K. Collins when it was ditched in the North Sea after being damaged in a fight with Messerschmitt Bf109s from 1/JG52. S/Ldr Speare in N6020, F/Lt Collins in N6007 and F/Lt Blacklock in N3663 were returning from Emden when they were attacked by three Bf109s. During the three-minute fight Blacklock and Collins closed formation, descending to sea level. Unfortunately for the Stirlings, five minutes later more Bf109s appeared and began to attack. One closed to 25 yards but was beaten off smoking by the mid-upper gunner on Collins' aircraft. Collins formated on Blacklock again but was in difficulties, with an unserviceable starboard engine. With reduced airspeed he began to fall behind. Blacklock began circling to try and provide some cover whilst his crew tried to establish contact by Aldis lamp. The Stirling was doomed, however, and Collins hit the sea nose first, breaking off the tail and sinking. None of the crew was seen to escape from the crash. This was not a lucky day for Blacklock and his crew. Having evaded the attacks of the enemy they were set upon by a couple of Hurricanes as they crossed the coast. Quickly firing off the colours of the day the Hurricanes turned away, but not before one of them had opened fire. Luckily no damage was caused and Blacklock landed safely.

The squadron raided Hamburg on 29/30 June losing Stirling Mk Is N3664:MG-V, captained by F/O V.R. Hartwright DFM, and N6001:MG-E, captained by S/Ldr W.T.C. Seale, which failed to return. Hartwright was shot down by Oblt Helmut Lent of 6/NJG1, crashing at Zeven, north-east of Bremen, with the loss of the crew and all of Seale's crew was killed in a second attack by Oblt Lent, crashing at Wesermunde-Bremerhaven. Eight crews briefed for the raid but F/Lt Cox in N6013:MG-A did not take off due to an unserviceable engine. F/Sgt Yardley also failed to take-off. His Stirling, W7433:MG-U, had an unserviceable identification friend or foe (IFF) set. F/Lt Saunders, flying N6003:MG-S had a battle with a night fighter during which he jettisoned his bombs and he crashed on landing. F/O Witt in N6022:MG-D brought his bombs back.

Sgt George Mitchell, an air gunner, was on this raid and was to be awarded the DFM for his actions. His first sortie with the squadron was to Kiel on 26 June and on the 28th/29th he went to Bremerhaven, where he probably destroyed a Bf110 which attacked them north-west of Texel. The citation for his award reads:

> One night in June, 1941, this airman was the rear gunner of an aircraft which was detailed to attack Hamburg. On the return journey an attack was made by a Messerschmitt 110. Despite an intense concentration of cannon and machine gun fire from the attacker, Sergeant Mitchell withheld his fire until the enemy came within close range. He then fired a burst of 600 rounds at the enemy aircraft, which broke away with its port engine aglow. It was subsequently confirmed that this aircraft was destroyed. Sergeant Mitchell displayed great courage and determination and set an excellent example.

George Mitchell would go on to on to complete many sorties with the squadron, including raids on Cologne and Dusseldorf, where his aircraft was hit by flak, Borkum, being attacked by fighters shooting down one and damaging another, a daylight attack on Brest in December, where the pilot attacked in a dive, the aircraft was hit by flak and Mitchell shot down a fighter. He received his DFM at Buckingham Palace on 4 November 1941 but, sadly, was killed in action serving with 75 Sqn on 6 April 1942.

The following day playing 'good Samaritan' was to cost the crew of N6013:MG-A dear. They were last seen circling a dinghy and under attack from enemy aircraft on the return from Borkum. Thirty-nine Blenheims and six Stirlings had been sent out to various targets in north-west Germany. Three of the squadron's Stirlings, captained by F/O J. Kinnane, P/O Denis T. Witt and Sgt B. Madgewick, set out to attack the seaplane base at Borkum. The small group of bombers was set upon by Bf109s from 2/ZG76; Kinnane in N6013 was shot down and all of the crew was killed. P/O E. Bolton's body was washed ashore some time later. The Bf109s continued their attacks and P/O Witts' Stirling came under attack four times, during which one of the gunners, F/O J.L.A. Mills, was wounded. Mills continued to fire throughout the attacks and managed to drive off the enemy fighters. He then left his turret. Flight engineer John Prentice was in the turret when another attack developed; he successfully fought the Messerschmitts off.

> It was a daylight raid and on this occasion it was to Borkum seaplane base. We took of at 1205 hrs. I was standing in the astrodome, which is what the flight engineer had to do on daylight raids. I was thinking to myself that the ground

Date	Aircraft Type & Number	Crew	Duty	Time		Details of Sortie or Flight	References
				Up	Down		
15/5–16/5	Stirling I. N.3655.	F/O. Collins J.K.	Captain	22.30	04.00	BERLIN. Same load (5 x 1000 and 5 x 500 G.P.), bursts seen	
		Sgt. Williams F.	2nd. Pilot.			lighting up cloud. Trouble experienced. (i) Hit by flak.	
		Sgt. Webb G.T.	Air.Obs.			(ii) Altimeter u/s at 12000 (iii) I.F.F. Control panel u/s.	
		Sgt. Kelly C.	W.Op.			(iv) Starboard inner seized over Zuider Zee (v) Rear turret	
		Sgt. Cole A.E.	A.G.			u/s no oil pressure in pump.	
		Sgt. Chapple D.W.	A.G.				
		Sgt. Harding W.	Fit/FEE.				
	N.6006	P/Lt. Faish A.L.T.	Captain	22.01	03.00	BERLIN. Same load (5 x1000 and 5 x 500 G.P.) Primary	
		P/O. Kinnane J.	2nd. Pilot.			abandoned owing to heavy petrol consumption and bombs	
		P/O. Bolton T.E.	Air.Obs.			dropped on Hanover. One long burst being seen under cloud.	
		Sgt. Nichols B.	W.Op.			Aircraft was followed by E.A. which did not attack.	
		Sgt. Ryder T.J.	A.G.				
		Sgt. Huntley K.	A.G.				
		Cpl. Merrells D.S.	Fit/FEE.				
16/5–17/5	N.6022	P/Lt. Blacklock G.B. (DFM)	Captain	22.25	03.10	A.34. KOLN. Load 5 x 1000 and 14 x 500 G.P. seven bursts were	
		P/O. Sanders A.A.J.	2nd. Pilot.			observed in first stick, one small fire seen on arrival had	
		Sgt. Kenny A.J.	Air.Obs.			grown when aircraft left. One 500 hung up on station 23.	
		Sgt. Rossiter H.	W.Op.			Auto controls u/s. Hazy up to 6000 feet.	
		Sgt. Ashton E.J.W.	A.G.				
		Sgt. Brown C.W.D.	A.G.				
		Sgt. Price H.W.	Fit/FEE.				

Form 540 extract showing the sorties flown on the night of 15/16 May. Harry Rossiter

crew had not cleaned the perspex very well and I tried to rub out some of the little specks, but these little specks happened to be six Me109s and they had seen us. We were attacked and the rear gunner was injured and I had to take over as he was given first aid. I stayed in the rear turret until we landed back at base.

An extract from the squadron Form 540 showing the sorties flown on 23 May. Harry Rossiter

Date	Aircraft Type & Number	Crew	Duty	Time		Details of Sortie or Flight	References
				Up	Down		
23/5.	Stirling I. N.6020.	W/Cdr. Graham H.R.	Captain	00.01	05.12	A.35 KOLN. 5 x 1000 14 x 500 G.P. Primary abandoned owing to	
		P/O. Harbright	2nd. Pilot.			various troubles and bombs dropped in two sticks at	
		P/O. Austing H.F. (DFM)	Air.Obs.			Haamstede. Two photos taken reveal second stick undershot.	
		Sgt. Watson R.	W.Op.				
		Sgt. Wheatley R.	A.G.				
		Sgt. Walker	Fit/FEE.				
		P/Lt. Stock S.G.	A.G. (Rear).				
	N.6022	P/O. Blacklock G.B. (DFM)	Captain.	00.49	05.34	KOLN. 5 x 1000 and 14 x 500 G.P. Primary abandoned owing	
		S/Ldr. Speare R.D.	2nd. Pilot.			to electrical earth. Bombs dropped at Rotterdam. Seven	
		Sgt. Kenny A.J.	Air.Obs.			flashes seen in first stick. Some of these green and seven	
		Sgt. Rossiter H.	W.Op.			or eight fairly close together in second stick.	
		Sgt. Ashton E.J.	A.G.				
		Sgt. Brown C.W.D.	A.G.				
		Sgt. Price H.W.	Fit/FEE.				
	N.7830	F/Lt. Mitchell J.	Captain	00.34	04.27	KOLN. 5 x 1000 and 12 x 500 G.P. Bombs seen to burst on	
		Sgt. Smith P.B.E.	2nd. Pilot.			target area. Bank of 10/10 cirrhus over target. North Sea	
		Sgt. Wynne K.N.	Air.Obs.			and Low Countries clear. 9/10 low cloud over Germany W. of	
		Sgt. Clarke E.	W.Op.			Rhine. 2 x 500 hung up.	
		Sgt. Armstrong J.	A.G.				
		Sgt. Spearman A.	A.G.				
		Sgt. Claire D.G.	Fit/FEE.				

Two 7 Sqn crews back from a daylight raid on Borkum. Rear L to R: Sgt George W. Robertson, Sgt Wally Mankelow, Sgt F.J. Lloyd, Sgt ? DFM, P/O G.E. 'Tex' Mitchell DFM RCAF, Sgt A.B. Chambers. Front L to R: Sgt E. Blacklaw, P/O A.J. Low, P/O R. Colwell, F/Sgt R.W. Taylor RAAF, W/Cdr R. Graham DSO DFC, Sgt Eroll Green RAAF, Sgt Mark Roach DFM RCAF, F/Sgt W. Robinson DFM. (Mankelow, Lloyd, Blacklaw, Low and Taylor would all be killed during an unofficial fighter affiliation exercise with a Hurricane on 17 January 1942). R.C. Pointer

Sgt J. McCarley, Sgt E. Blacklaw and Sgt ? in a humorous shot during a lull in ops. R.C. Pointer

The following night a small force of thirteen Halifaxes and four Stirlings went to Magdeburg. The squadron provided the Stirlings but all four returned with their bomb loads.

During this period the RAF began to fly Circus operations – a small force of bombers, escorted by a larger force of fighters, designed to entice the *Luftwaffe* into a battle of attrition. On 6 July 7 Sqn was involved in one such operation to the shipyards at Le Trait. Three aircraft flown by W/Cdr Graham, P/O Denis Witt and S/Ldr Cox carried out the attack but results were poor.

7 July saw yet another daylight raid when four Stirlings went to Meaulte-Albert to bomb an aircraft factory. They dropped 22,500 pounds of bombs and a further 360 incendiaries.

On 8 July the target was Bethune. Two raids were planned by three and five aircraft respectively, but, the second was cancelled. S/Ldr Speare, F/Sgt Yardley, P/O Blunden and P/O R.D. Morley planned to take their Stirlings, N6022:D, W7433:U, N6017:Z and N6034 to Bethune but only Speare and Morley took off. Speare failed to find the target and Morley failed to return. His aircraft was hit by flak in the starboard inner engine over the French coast and caught fire before crashing. Sgt L.N. Chappell and Sgt G.S. Edwards, a Canadian, survived to become POWs.

On the 9th a power station at Mazingarbe and a chemical works near Lens were attacked by three Stirlings. Crossing the French coast on the way to the target near Boulogne heavy flak forced them to turn away. Two managed to bomb at Lens. P/O Witt was attacked by fighters but escaped.

Luck was to run out though on 10 July for F/O C.V. Frazer DFC and his crew. P/O Witt was leading a formation of three Stirlings and after he had rendezvoused with the fighter escort over Rye he set course for target. Nearing Hardelot, *en route* to Bethune, Stirling N6017, piloted by Frazer was hit by flak and, blown to pieces, crashed into the sea. One of the crew, Sgt E.H. Rogers managed to bale out. F/O Rolfe, flying the third Stirling was attacked by a fighter, which damaged his tail. The beam gunner, however, damaged the fighter, driving it off. Witt was to receive a DFC for this action and the citation for the award of the DFM to his bomb aimer, Sgt Mark Roach details the events of that day.

This airman was the air observer of one of a section of three aircraft which was detailed to attack a target near Bethune. When the section crossed the enemy coast it was subjected to intense anti-aircraft fire, one of the aircraft being shot down. On approaching the target the two remaining aircraft were again subjected to anti-aircraft fire. Despite this and the fact that his pilot was taking evasive action, Sergeant Roach carefully and successfully bombed the target. The success of this high level attack under extremely difficult conditions was largely due to the courage and determination of Sergeant Roach.

Roach, a Canadian, would go on to serve with 9 Sqn and later as Bombing Leader with 426 Sqn RCAF.

The squadron attacked French targets again on the 11th before returning to night operations and German targets as Bomber Command swung its focus back to the enemy homeland.

The weather often played a part in the success of a raid and it was poor weather that caused the loss of several aircraft on the night of 14/15 July. The crew of N6022: MG-D, captained by F/O Witt DFM ran out of fuel on the way back from Hanover and abandoned the aircraft, which crashed at Newton Flotman, Norfolk. Sgt Prentice broke his back but made a good recovery, later being commissioned. P/O D.K. Deyell DFM was also injured escaping from the doomed bomber. John Prentice recalls the events of that night.

On 15 July we were briefed for a night raid on Hanover, the target an industrial complex. It was my twenty-second operation and one I remember well! We took off at 2300 hrs. Over the UK it was a dark and cloudy night, but skies cleared as we tested our guns and droned on our way over the North Sea. Crossing the Dutch coast we came under fire from flak and later on more flak. In our efforts to evade these defences we used up far more fuel than planned and we knew, before we reached the target, that we might not have enough fuel to reach Oakington on our return. Nevertheless, Dennis Witt pressed on and we dropped our bomb load on the target, a mix of 1,000 pound and 500 pound bombs plus 420 incendiaries. The bombs were seen to explode across a series of sheds starting a major fire.

Turning for home we once again came under heavy attack from flak and our poor old Stirling sustained more damage. With fuel now dangerously low there was a real risk that we might have to ditch. This did cause me some concern as I couldn't swim and thus had an aversion for water! I breathed a sigh of relief, as I imagine the rest of the crew did, when we finally reached and crossed the English coast near Cromer. But the relief was short lived, for as we headed inland with the fuel gauges reading zero the engines finally cut out. It was eerily quiet. We were around 14,000 feet and, as we gathered around the bottom exit, the clouds seemed to be an awful long way down. Dennis gave the order to bale out and, as one has no choice in such matters, with a quick last check of my 'chute, I went.

Pulled up with a jerk when my chute opened I had the distinct feeling that I was going the wrong way, up instead of down! When I finally broke through the low cloud I started singing 'Roll out the bloody barrel' in a very loud voice, with the idea that this might convince any member of 'Dad's Army' who might be on patrol that I was not a German parachutist! It was very dark beneath the cloud and I really didn't see the ground coming up to meet me, which I hit with an awful thump at an angle of about 45 degrees, breaking my ankle and crushing two vertebrae.

A Land Army girl found me and helped me to a farmhouse. From there I was picked up by an ambulance and taken to Ely hospital. After a couple of weeks at Ely, where I was patched up with plasters to back and ankles and a short spot of leave I was transferred to a specialist establishment at Hoylake, which dealt with broken backs and broken necks. The highlight of my six weeks stay at Hoylake was a soccer match, the broken backs versus the broken necks! I cannot recall who won, but as all players were encased in plaster casts, I do remember that the broken necks had a huge advantage when it came to heading the ball!

After this John Prentice was grounded and sent and posted to 1651 Heavy Conversion Unit (HCU) at Waterbeach in charge of flight engineer training. Nine months later he returned to flying and retired from the RAF as a wing commander in 1971.

A second Stirling, N6033:MG-W, flown by F/Sgt Madgewick was lost on the same raid. The crew of N6033 had circled trying to locate the airfield with no success. They were flying in very poor visibility and the W/T set was unserviceable. After searching for some time the engines cut. Out of fuel, the Stirling crashed at High Street, Northampton. The crew all baled out safely apart from the captain who was killed. Tragically, he slipped out of his parachute harness and fell to his death. The Chief Constable of Northamptonshire telephoned Oakington to register a protest about the crash, which occurred in his county. He is said to have remarked: 'I can't have this.' A third aircraft was written off when F/Lt D.A.J. Saunders diverted in N6036:MG-Y to Bircham Newton, overshot the runway on landing and crashed into a dyke. Two other aircraft were diverted to Waterbeach and Honington respectively, both landing safely.

On the night of 20/21 July three Stirlings from the squadron took part in a 113 aircraft raid on Cologne. The target was the rail network but thick cloud resulted in scattered bombing and little damage to either the railway or the city. All three crews returned safely.

On 23 July the *Scharnhorst* slipped out of Brest and sailed to La Pallice. Bomber Command quickly planned an attack and three aircraft from the squadron were involved. N6037, captained by S/Ldr R.W. Cox, N6035, flown by F/Lt G.B. Blacklock and W7434, captained by the recently promoted F/O Witt. Skilful navigation brought the bombers over La Pallice at 15,000 feet and the bombs straddled the *Scharnhorst*, one of them actually hitting the target. The formation was attacked by six fighters, two of which were shot down by Sgt Chappel, the rear gunner on R.W. Cox's crew, as the Stirlings turned for home. He also managed to damage a third fighter. Cox recalls the raid.

We had a 'daylight' on La Pallice when the Scharnhorst *was there. We got a direct hit with our semi-armour-piercing bomb and took photos, landing at St Eval. We travelled to and from the target at 50 feet, climbing to 10,000 feet to bomb. It was the only time I ever flew in shirtsleeves. We shot down two Me109s. My rear gunner, Sgt Chappel was awarded the DFM and P/O Walker, the bomb aimer, received the DFC.*

Berlin featured on the target list again on 25/26 July; a small force of seven Stirlings and two Halifaxes took part in the raid. The squadron was to dispatch three aircraft, but in the event W7433:MG-V, captained by F/Sgt Yardley, did not take off due to undercarriage problems. Of the two which did leave Oakington that night the crew of Stirling N6035:MG-A, piloted by F/Lt M.C.G. Sherwood, failed to return, crashing at Ouddorp in Holland. All of the crew survived and became POWs. The third bomber, W7434:MG-E, flown by P/O Blunden landed at Manston on its return.

On the night of 30/31 July Bomber Command despatched 116 aircraft to Cologne. The raid was not a success due to the extreme weather. The squadron sent out five Stirlings, of which four found and attacked the city. The returning crews had to contend with thunderstorms, icing and electrical storms. W/Cdr Graham entered one such storm near Bexhill and the Stirling, N3663:MG-H, immediately began to ice up. With a blinding flash it fell out of control from 10,000 feet. All of the cockpit instruments were lost and Graham was not able to recover the aircraft until 4,000 feet. The crew finally landed back at Oakington after a flight using map reading, bearings from ground stations and dead reckoning. Stirling N6029:MG-Q flown by

An aerial view of Oakington taken on 20 July 1941.

P/O C.I. Rolfe encountered storms as well and had his radio burnt out by a lightning strike. He managed to land safely at Martlesham Heath.

On 2/3 August 1941 the target was Berlin. Haze over the target made bombing difficult and Stirling Mk I, N3663:MG-A, captained by F/O C.I. Rolfe failed to return from this raid. Attacked by a night fighter, Sgt Burrows was mortally wounded. The Stirling crashed at Werder and Rolfe, Sgt D.S. Merrells and Sgt C.A. Tout survived to become POWs. On the night of 5/6 August four of the Stirlings were dispatched to Karlsruhe. The bombs dropped mainly in the western side of the city and F/Lt Saunders in N6037:MG-V encountered heavy flak bombing from 5,000 feet.

The squadron had been issued the second production Stirling Mk I, N3636, in 1940 but it was lost in an servicing accident on 7 August 1941 when it fell off supporting jacks at Oakington, damaging the mainplane strut. It was eventually consigned to the role of an instructional airframe, as 3056M, in April 1942. It had only flown one operation with the squadron since delivery.

That night four crews set out to bomb Essen in a force of 106 aircraft. The bombing caused only slight damage to the target and three bombers were brought down.

Six Stirlings took off from Oakington on the night of 12/13 August and in company with forty Wellingtons, twelve Halifaxes, nine Manchesters and a further three

An atmospheric shot of a 7 Sqn Stirling being serviced by the ground crew. R. Thomas

Stirlings raided Berlin. The Air Ministry building on Alexander Platz was the aiming point, but of the seventy aircraft involved only thirty-two reached the target. F/Lt Lay in N3666:MG-Z encountered heavy flak over the target and dropped his bombs early. All six Stirlings returned safely. The following night P/O Astell-Burt set out in W7579:MG-Y to lay mines in the Daffodils mining area. He crashed off Nymindegab in Denmark with only one survivor, Sgt V.H. Sharp, who was captured.

There was another loss at Oakington on 15 August when Stirling N6041:MG-H, flown by W/Cdr H.R. Graham, overshot its landing on return from bombing an

A trio of 7 Sqn Stirlings in formation in August 1942. 7 Sqn Association

airfield south of Hanover after failing to attack the primary target at Magdeburg. That same day N6042:MG-T, piloted by P/O Crebbin, hit an obstruction as the pilot tried to land at Graveley on return from raiding Magdeburg along with fifty-one other bombers. W7434:MG-E, flown by F/O D.T. Witt DFC, who had bombed a secondary target due to 10/10ths cloud over Magdeburg, also suffered an undercarriage collapse whilst landing at Oakington returning from Hanover. The four other Stirlings from the squadron returned safely.

The Bomber Command favourite, Kiel, was attacked again on 19/20 August. The squadron planned to dispatch five Stirlings in a force of 108 bombers to bomb railway targets. F/Lt Lay did not take off and S/Ldr Spiers in N3666:MG-Z failed to find the target. The crews encountered icing and thick cloud cover. The bombs were dropped in heavy rain and little damage or casualties occurred. All of the Stirlings returned safely.

N6020:MG-B, flown by F/O K.O. Blunden, was lost on the Karlsruhe raid of 26 August. Sgt D.A. Lloyd was the only survivor, baling out and being captured. The Stirling had suffered a lightning strike in a storm and was shot down by flak. Thirty-seven Wellingtons and twelve Stirlings, five from the squadron, had struck at the city centre, but storms and thick cloud had prevented accurate bombing. August also saw another aircraft struck off charge when Mk I N3666:MG-Z was attacked and severely damaged by a Messerschmitt Bf110 on the Duisburg raid on the 28th/29th. The squadron sent seven Stirlings on this raid, five of which bombed the target area.

Stirling N3666:MG-Z following the forced landing at Newmarket on 29 August 1941.
G. Pitchfork

N3666:MG-Z was piloted by F/Lt D.J.H. Lay, who had to fight an uncontrollable aircraft which had been severely damaged around the tail area. The rear turret was shattered and Sgt MacRae, the rear gunner, was severely wounded. Whilst Lay and Sgt Tourville struggled to regain control MacRae, thinking the bomber was doomed, baled out. The pilot eventually managed to regain control and selected an alternative target for his bomb load before turning for home. Lay elected to land at Newmarket. The undercarriage was wound down by hand but did not stand up to the landing impact and the port gear failed. The crew walked away from the wreck with only one wounded and the missing gunner. Sgt J.E. Chilvers and the crew of W7438:MG-A were last heard from at 0245 hrs and failed to return, their Stirling coming down near Dusseldorf.

On the night of 30/31 August a single Stirling, N6006:MG-G, took off from Oakington flown by P/O Crebbin to attack Cherbourg docks along with five Wellingtons. The bombers started fires in the target area and all returned.

Another MG-coded 7 Sqn Stirling crash-landed. R. Thomas

Gunner Bob Pointer completed his OTU at Lossiemouth in August 1941 with his friend and fellow gunner Walter (Jimmy) Raven and was then posted to 7 Sqn. He recalls crewing up at Lossiemouth and early days at Oakington.

After eighteen flights with various pilots, on 31 August we were crewed up with our future crews. Jimmy and I stayed together, our pilot a very outgoing sergeant from Australia, older than the rest of us, named Frank K. Lister, but called 'Pop' from then on by the rest of the crew. Our second pilot was Derek Barritt, who wanted to be a fighter pilot (he eventually got his wish after doing a few trips on 7 Sqn as second pilot). Our rear gunner was from Nairn, Fred (Jock) Hay, a very dour bloke, but a good gunner. Our navigator's name was Bob Henley. We flew together from then on, using all our new skills.

We were posted to Oakington and 7 Sqn, but were given leave first. I made my way to my new station by bus and train and finished up at Oakington railway station, which was on the wrong side of the campsite. I had to walk all around the airfield through to Long Stanton, which was the main gate. I started out carrying two kit bags and was about halfway there, looking at the giant Stirlings at dispersal and feeling very excited at the prospect of flying in these great machines, when a small RAF van pulled up beside me and gave me a lift to the main gate.

Our crew met up again in the sergeants' mess. We didn't fly together though; both of the pilots were going to have to fly with seasoned pilots as 'second dickeys' for a few trips. As there was a surplus of WOp/AGs the only way we could get in some flying was to fly as a front gunner. I tried to keep my station, so couldn't get any flights. Meanwhile, the rest of us familiarized ourselves with the airfield. Jimmy Raven got a place on a crew, as did Jock Hay our rear gunner, and they were soon flying on ops. I was attached to Waterbeach, No. 1651 Conversion Unit, for three weeks of further instruction. I was then sent back to the squadron as a supernumerary, getting in plenty of flying, but not on ops.

In the meantime Jimmy was notching up a few trips, to Happy Valley [the Ruhr], Brest, in daylight, to bomb the German battleships, Hamburg and 'Gardening' off the Friesian Islands. It was on one of these raids that Pop Lister, our first pilot, was shot down over Brest. Two of the crew were killed and the rest, including Pop, were taken prisoner of war. Derek Barritt left after a few trips, transferring to Spitfires, was commissioned and survived the war. Bob Henley, the navigator, got in with F/O Jack Davies DFM, was commissioned as a pilot officer and was killed with the rest of his crew on 12 December 1942. They crashed at Jussecourt in France.

Cologne was the focus of Bomber Command's attentions on the night of 31 August/ 1 September. One hundred and three aircraft took part in the raid which included four 7 Sqn crews. The weather was bad and most crews bombed the estimated position of the target. None of the Stirlings were lost.

Four Stirlings from the squadron, flown by P/O Crebbin, P/O Ellis-Brown, P/O Hindstaff and F/Sgt Yardley, took part in a 140 aircraft attack on Brest on the night of 3/4 September. Nos 1, 4 and 5 Groups recalled their aircraft due to worsening weather but the aircraft of 3 Group, including 7 Sqn, proceeded to the target and bombed the estimated position of the German warships anchored in the harbour through a smoke screen. All four crews returned safely.

Stirling MG-E starting up on 31 August 1941 before setting out for Cologne. R. Thomas

Stirling Mk I, N6046:MG-Y, captained by F/Sgt A. Yardley failed to return from a raid on Berlin on 7/8 September when 197 aircraft bombed on three aiming points. Yardley and his crew survived a night-fighter attack to become POWs. The crews claimed good bombing and several areas of the sprawling city experienced damage. Sgt A. Speakman was flying as rear gunner in this aircraft, flown by F/Sgt Yardley. He recalls life at Oakington during this period and the fact that it was not always the enemy who were trying to stop you from flying operations.

I personally did not interact with the local community except to drink in the local pub now and again. Two local children found occasion to interact with me though. I had a .22 rifle with which I used to shoot rabbits and wood pigeons in the surrounding fields (poaching, if you like). These two kids, a girl and a younger boy, learned about this and followed me around, asking if they could have stuff. Naturally, as they seemed to be from a poor family, I agreed. After I was shot down on 7 September the rifle and a camera disappeared from my kit. We would climb over the fence near our dispersal to buy, from the village bakery, the most luscious cream doughnuts I have ever tasted. I believe that many other crews followed the same trail in later years.

In most accounts of the Second World War it is claimed that the nation pulled together as one to achieve victory. It is far from true; apart from the army dodgers and the black marketeers there were some, even in the forces, who did not pull their weight. A good number of the HQ staff at Oakington resented the fact that young aircrew were getting sergeants' stripes that had taken some of them twenty years to earn. This, of course, does not refer to the ground crews, whose contribution is very much underrated.

I was flying as rear gunner with F/Sgt Yardley. Shortly before take-off I found that one of my guns was u/s. Knowing that there was an aircraft undergoing major overhaul, I got a driver to run me back to the hangar, where I took out one of the Brownings and replaced it with the dud. After the op I reversed the procedure. The following morning the Station Armament Officer sent for me (who had informed him I never knew). I was berated for committing such a grievous crime! I explained the circumstances and pointed out that it was my job to protect the aircraft and crew to the best of my ability. I could do it better with four guns than with three. I also said that I would do the same thing again, if necessary, in spite of what the SAO thought. He replied, 'What if you had been shot down?' I laughed in his face. 'If I'd been shot down, the last thing that I'd be worrying about would be a borrowed machine gun.' His reply to this was even dafter than his first remarks. 'While the aircraft was on major overhaul it was on Short's books and not the RAF's.' I said to him, 'Well, what's all the fuss? They expect four guns; they have got four guns.' The answer I got from this was supposed to flatten my argument, 'Ah! But the serial number of the gun would be wrong!' I still find it hard to grasp that a warrant officer, arguing with a scruffy 20-year old gunner could produce such stupid reasons against my actions. He should have been backing me up; after all we were supposed to be on the same

A 7 Sqn crew briefing in late 1941. Second from left is W/Op/AG Sgt Alec Donaldson. R. Thomas

side. This was at a time when we were losing quite a few aircraft, complete with crews. The fact of a gun turning up with the wrong number on it didn't strike me as being at all important.

Six aircraft took off for this raid but P/O Ellis-Brown in W7440:MG-W and WO Fletcher in W7435:MG-V returned early due to engine problems.

The night of 10/11 September saw the first raid by Stirlings to an Italian target. A force of seventy-six aircraft, seven of them 7 Sqn Stirlings, struck Turin. The aiming point was the Royal Arsenal. After a long flight across the Alps, passing close to Lake Geneva, they reached the target. The bombs dropped by W/Cdr Graham and S/Ldr Speare landed in the city centre, with those of F/Lt Lay, F/Lt Sanders and Bayley starting incendiary fires. Ellis-Brown dropped his bombs to the north of the railway station. All of the crews returned safely to Oakington.

Four crews went to Frankfurt on 12/13 September. One hundred and thirty aircraft took part in the raid, bombing through thick cloud. Navigation was still causing problems for the bomber crews and in these conditions, and although large fires were started, the bombing was scattered over Frankfurt and the nearby town of Offenbach. All of the 7 Sqn crews returned.

Two crews, captained by P/O Ellis-Brown in N6049:MG-Z and Sgt Morris in N3669:MG-E, bombed Brest on the night of 13/14 September. One hundred and forty-seven aircraft set out to attack three warships in the harbour. The crews bombed from 15,000 feet through a smokescreen, which was effectively masking the target. No aircraft were lost.

On 15/16 September the railways of Hamburg were once again the aiming point for a force of 169 aircraft. Five Stirlings were dispatched by the squadron and found clear conditions over the target. The clear conditions hampered the bombing, however, as the glare from the searchlights was blinding the crews, making target recognition difficult. The bombing caused widespread damage. F/Lt Lay in N6049: MG-Z was engaged by a night fighter but his mid-upper gunner returned fire and they escaped.

A group photo of 7 Sqn in 1941. Albert Burrows and Albert Chambers are in the third row from the rear, sixth and seventh from right. Second rear row sixth from right is W/Op/AG Sgt John McIntyre. Front row seventh from right is F/Lt Blacklock. R. Thomas

On 19/20 September the bombers made the long haul to Stettin on the Baltic coast. Seventy-two aircraft took part, five from the squadron, but the crews, who had been allocated individual targets, found them difficult to identify. Bombing from 15,000 feet they turned for home, all returning safely.

One hundred and four aircraft were dispatched to Cologne, Emden, Genoa and Mannheim on the night of 26/27 September, but due to a forecast of fog the force was recalled. Most returned but a few, including P/O Ellis-Brown in W7440:MG-W, bombed opportunity targets. Ellis-Brown dropped his bombs on Locobecques near Lille before returning to Oakington.

The Stirlings made the long journey to Stettin once more on the night of 29/30 September, four out of five crews taking off. W7433:MG-U, flown by WO A. Fletcher, and W7441:MG-Y, captained by Sgt C.J. Cobbold, failed to return. All of Fletcher's crew, last heard from 40 nautical miles north-east of Lowestoft when an SOS was sent at 0258 hrs, was killed. Three of the bodies were eventually washed up on the Dutch coast. Sgt Albert Burrows, who had joined up and undergone training with Alec Donaldson on Cobbold's crew was one member of this crew picked up by a boat. Unfortunately he succumbed to the bitter North Sea despite the efforts of the crew to revive him. W7441 was shot down by a night fighter over the Little Belt, Denmark, and Sam Cobbold and three of his crew, Sgt D.Y. Neil, WOp/AG Alec Donaldson and J.J. Copley survived and managed to evade capture until the following day when they became POWs. Three of the survivors, including Donaldson, had dinner with the German who shot them down at the *Luftwaffe* airfield.

German intruders were active over England on 3 October and one of them, a Junkers Ju88, flown by Fw Alforns Koster of 1/NJG2, shot down Stirling Mk I, N6085:MG-H near Bourn as it was returning to base from a bombing sortie to Brest. The squadron was now using Bourn as a satellite and S/Ldr D.I. McCleod was heading for this airfield when he was attacked. He evaded six attacks but the rear gunner had left his turret, leaving the intruder unmolested. Two of the crew, P/O J.R. Alverston and Sgt I. Hunter, a Canadian, parachuted to safety from 700 feet before the Stirling crashed in flames. (Hunter would be killed six weeks later in a take off crash). Sgt

L to R: Alec Donaldson, Albert Chambers and Albert Burrows. Donaldson and Burrows were both shot down on the same raid. Donaldson survived to become a POW; Burrows died in the North Sea. Albert Chambers was killed on a bombing raid on D-Day. R. Thomas

S.G. Matkin tried to intervene by positioning his Stirling so his gunners could fire on the Ju88. They claimed to have damaged it, but the intruder broke off and then bombed Oakington before disappearing into the night.

Three other Stirlings set out that night along with over 100 other bombers to attack Antwerp, Brest and Rotterdam. P/O Handstaff in N6048:MG-J returned early from Brest due to exactor trouble, a common problem with the Stirling. S/Ldr Spiers in W7436:MG-D encountered thick cloud over the target and P/O Ellis-Brown came under heavy flak fire, but both returned safely.

The squadron was to lose some aircraft and experienced crews on 5 October when C Flt was split off to form No. 26 Conversion Flt at Waterbeach. On the night of 15/16 October a small force of twenty-seven Wellingtons and seven Stirlings attacked Cologne. Six of the Stirlings came from the squadron, although P/O Ellis-Brown in W7442:MG-M returned early with engine trouble. Crews reported large fires in the city, but in fact the bombs landed mainly in villages east of the Rhine including Lindenthal and Wesseling.

Bremen was raided on the night of 20/21 October but the 153 aircraft, including five from 7 Sqn started only a few fires and the Bremen authorities only recorded a small raid. Two nights later a single Stirling, W7444:MG-G, piloted by P/O Winch, raided Brest, returning safely. The following night five crews went to Kiel in the company of 109 others but only sixty-nine reached the target. Sgt Taylor in N6089:MG-L returned early and the attack, which was made in two waves, caused much damage to the U-boat yards and naval base.

Towards the end of October the Stirlings carried out their longest flights to date, attacking the Skoda works at Pilsen in Czechoslovakia on the night of 28th/29th.

Sqn crew pictured in front of N6037:MG-V at Oakington. L to R: Harry Kirkland, Alec Donaldson, Pete Whitwell, A.A.J. Sanders, J.J. Copley, D.Y. Neil, Sam Cobbold. R. Thomas

Sgt Sam Cobbold and his crew of Stirling W7441 lost on the night of 29/30 September 1941 pictured in front of Stirling N6037:MG-V at Oakington. L to R: D.V. Neil, Alec Donaldson, Sam Cobbold, A.A.J. Sanders, Harry Kirkland, J.J. Copley and Pete Whitwell. Cobbold, Neil, Donaldson and Copley escaped from the doomed Stirling and were later captured. R. Thomas

Four crews, of a planned eight, set out but the weather forecasters had got it completely wrong and strong winds forced them to drop their bombs on other targets in Germany before turning for home. Two nights later eight crews set out for Bremen. The weather was bad and few crews found the target. W7444:MG-L, flown by P/O N.E. Winch, returned early with oxygen trouble and was crashed on landing. P/O Ellis-Brown in W7446:MG-S, also returned early due to an unserviceable rear turret.

Over the following nights several operations were cancelled and then Berlin was the target again on 7/8 November and Stirling N3677:MG-J, captained by F/O Van Buskirk, failed to return. All of the crew was killed, shot down by a night fighter near Duisburg. N6091:MG-K, piloted by Sgt J.W.C. Morris, also failed to return, shot down by flak and crashing at Hekelingen in Holland. Morris and his crew were all killed. This had been a major effort by Bomber Command after a series of disappointing raids with poor bombing results caused mainly by poor weather. Three hundred and ninety-two aircraft operated that night, 169 going to Berlin, but the poor weather forced two of the Stirlings dispatched by the squadron, flown by S/Ldr Jennings and P/O Pilling, to turn back and four to bomb alternative targets. A total of thirty-eight aircraft were lost by Bomber Command that night.

Two nights later four Stirlings were sent to Hamburg. Fires were started in the docks and the city and all four crews returned safely. After a break of five nights, five crews were briefed for a raid on targets in Germany. It was not a good night for the squadron, though. One Stirling sortie was cancelled due to the weather, one bogged down whilst taxiing, a third, W7445:MG-V, crashed on take-off. Sgt A.C. Bennett's windscreen iced up and the Stirling crashed into a house. Bennett, an Australian, and his second pilot, Sgt I.H. Hunter, were killed. Sgts W.D. Topping,

RAF aircrew in a Luftwaffe *POW camp. Second right is W/Op/AG Sgt Alec Donaldson of 7Sqn.* R. Thomas

T. Bentham, A.J. Ansell and Hudson were all injured. Sgt Helliwell escaped unscathed. N6087:MG-A returned early after encountering heavy icing and the only aircraft to drop its bombs, W7440:MG-W, landed at Manston on return.

The squadron returned to Brest on 18/19 November, losing N6087:MG-A, captained by P/O J.T. O'Brien. On take-off the port outer engine burst into flames and the pilot tried to force land. Unfortunately the Stirling hit some telegraph wires near West Bluntisham and crashed, killing the second pilot, Sgt J.E. Rose,

7 Sqn POWs. Second left Alec Donaldson, fifth left J.J. Copley. R. Thomas

Stirling MG-S. Note the artwork on the nose. R. Thomas

Sgt A. Grant and F/Sgt P. Comroe. Sgt J. Devlin, Sgt T. Ryder and P/O J.A. Lopez, an Australian, were all injured. Lopez died soon afterwards from his injuries. Except for one which bombed through a brief break in the cloud and two which bombed on estimated positions, the other crews found the target obscured by cloud and brought their bombs back. W7446:MG-S flown by F/O M.W. Hardstaff was lost on landing when it overshot. Landing on the wet surface at Oakington, the pilot found the brakes to be ineffective and, in an attempt to avoid a dispersal point, he swung the Stirling round and the undercarriage collapsed. It was not repairable and was written off.

During this period several of the squadron's Stirlings were fitted with early Oboe sets and pilots from 105 Sqn flew sorties with 7 Sqn crews to test the equipment under operational conditions. Their main target would be enemy battleships at Brest and other ports. N6090 was the first 7 Sqn Stirling to be fitted with the equipment.

24 November saw the squadron engaged on yet another small daylight raid. W/Cdr Graham took his Stirling to the Baltic in company with Sgt Taylor and attacked shipping off Borkum. They were set upon by eight Bf109s but fought them off for over twenty-five minutes, absorbing a large number of hits and shooting down two fighters and damaging a third before making good their escape.

That night six Stirlings bombed Brest again, all returning safely. On the last night of November four crews bombed the city and shipyards of Hamburg. Over the target P/O Ellis-Brown, flying N6089:MG-L, had to take violent evasive action, which resulted in a descent to only 500 feet, before escaping.

Two days into December Stirling N3701 was damaged. The crew, captained by S/Ldr J.H. Lay DFC, had been out on a search over the North Sea and on returning to Oakington the pilot landed downwind in very poor visibility. The Stirling hit an obstruction and the undercarriage collapsed.

The squadron was still involved in the highly secret early Oboe trials under the codename Trinity and sent two aircraft thus equipped with two others to Brest with poor results on 7 December. S/Ldr Lay, flying N6094:MG-G, had to take violent evasive action and P/O Heard in N6095:MG-K returned early with engine trouble.

On 9 December the squadron attempted to take advantage of cloud cover to launch a small attack on Ruhr targets but the two aircraft dispatched, W7451:MG-D flown by F/Lt Crebbin and W7440 piloted by F/O R. Ellis-Brown, were forced to choose alternative targets. Finding a tanker and two flak ships of the Dutch coast they turned to attack. The flak ships immediately began to put up a hail of shrapnel and W7451 was hit. The navigator, Sgt H.C. Cotton, was wounded. W7440 was also hit and both aircraft returned to base with damage. Crebbin landed without a tailwheel and Ellis-Brown had his port undercarriage collapse on landing.

Trinity ops were on again on 11/12 December and four Stirlings, N3668:MG-B, N3669:MG-E, N6032:MG-T and N6194:MG-G, bombed Brest. Brest was attacked again on the night of 15/16 December by five crews. N3669:MG-E and N6032: MG-T were forced to take violent evasive action over the target. The following night it was the same target for five crews. W7454:MG-S returned early, the crews of N3668:MG-B, N6094:MG-G and N3669:MG-E were forced to take violent evasive action over the target, and the crew of W7442:MG-M failed to bomb the target.

The Channel ports received regular visits from Bomber Command throughout 1941 and on 18 December the target was Brest. Bomber Command was keeping a particularly close watch on this port in case the German battleships should attempt to break out. The squadron sent nine aircraft on this daylight raid. Accurate bombing and a hit on the *Gneisenau* were claimed by the crews. The bombers arrived early at the target so they turned away to lose time and by the time they were on the bomb run the fighters were up. W/Cdr Graham, flying N3669:MG-E, was attacked by the Bf190s and hit several times as well as being struck by the accurate flak. His rear gunner; P/O G.E. Mitchell scored hits on one fighter, shooting it down. (The damaged Stirling was later repaired and given the maintenance airframe serial 3637M in February 1943.) Stirling Mk I, W7436:MG-D, captained by S/Ldr L.W.V. Jennens, was shot down by the fighters. Jennens and Sgts F.K. Lister, E.V. Smith, F.V. Davis and J.C. Webb survived to become POWs.

N6095:MG-K, captained by P/O G.T. Heard, was struck in the astrodome by flak just after the bomb run. The flight engineer, Sgt Hayward, was badly wounded and the rear gunner, Sgt Inman, was wounded in the shoulder. Inman did not report this to the crew and remained at his guns. Hayward eventually succumbed to his multiple injuries. The Stirling was also attacked by fighters. Stirling N6089:MG-L was

Stirling W7451:MG-D being bombed up at Oakington. W7451 later served with 218 Sqn Conversion Flight and No. 1657 Conversion Flight. G. Pitchfork

No. 7 Sqn ground crew photographed in front of an unidentified Stirling. 7 Sqn

severely damaged by the flak but F/Sgt R.W. Taylor nursed the stricken bomber back to Bourn with leaking fuel tanks and unserviceable turrets for a crash landing at Bourn, landing on one good tyre. The Stirling was repaired and went on to serve with No. 26 Conversion Flt.

Oakington in December 1941 with work on the two subsidiary runways still to be completed.

P/O Matkin bombed successfully from N6121 but badly damaged, he crash landed at Oakington with damaged undercarriage, hydraulics and a fair portion of the rudder blown off. His gunners claimed a Bf109 destroyed and one damaged. The severe battle damage to his Stirling was repaired and the aircraft was transferred to No. 101 Conversion Flt.

N3700 did not reach the target turning back for Oakington. F/Lt B. Parnell and crew in N3680:MG-Y failed to return. They were shot down by Bf109s off the French coast. P/O R.E. Pilling's Stirling, W7454:MG-S suffered severe battle damage on this raid, as did N3668:MG-B, flown by P/O G.C. Bayley. Bayley's rear gunner shot down an Me109 during the fight and the Stirling was repaired and subsequently served with No. 15 Sqn. W7449:MG-J, flown by WO N.I. Tayler, was also damaged but landed safely at Bourn.

On 21/22 December the crews were sent to Munich, but most of the bombing missed the city, possibly attracted by a decoy site. Fraser Barron was attacked over the target by a night fighter and set on fire but managed to return safely after a nine-hour flight.

The Stirlings returned to Brest on the night of 23/24 December as part of a force made up of thirty-eight Wellingtons and nine Stirlings. Six crews from the squadron took part but the target battleships were not hit. All six aircraft returned safely. The last sorties of the year were carried out on small-scale night raids and thus ended 1941.

VIP visits to the squadron were common. In this view the visitors are King Peter of Yugoslavia and AVM Baldwin, AOC No. 3 Group. They are accompanied by the CO, W/Cdr Graham DSO DFC. 7 Sqn

CHAPTER THREE

JANUARY–DECEMBER 1942

The New Year commenced with the award of the DFC to F/Lt W.N. Crebbin and the MBE to F/Lt A.C. Ward in the New Years' Honours List. The raids against Brest using Trinity/Oboe continued into January and the squadron attacked the battleships and the port on the nights of 2nd/3rd and 3rd/4th without loss. Bombing was inaccurate, however, and on the first raid P/O G.T. Heard failed to reach the target, losing one engine and having a second fail on the return. P/O J.D. Hart brought back his bombs, as he could see nothing over the target. On the second raid P/O H.G. Pilling brought his bombs back to drop them on Berners Heath after instrument failure. The squadron was visited by the Secretary of State for Air and AVM J.E.A. Baldwin, on the 3rd. Two days later the squadron was taken off operations to be equipped with a new item of navigation equipment – TR 1335 Gee. This was a British development, which allowed the bomber navigator to fix the aircraft position anywhere within a 400-mile radius of the transmitters. He used a cathode ray tube and a chart with a grid overlay. At the maximum range it was accurate to within 6 miles. The correct designation of the equipment was TR1335, but it was most commonly known to the crews who used it as Gee. Plans for its first use during the month were suspended on the 12th due to a shortage of the necessary equipment.

On 8 January the pilot of Stirling N3668:MG-B dropped a wing on approach at Alconbury and landed on one wheel, collapsing the undercarriage. During this period

No 7 Sqn Electrical Section photographed, some time in 1941 or 1942, in front of a Stirling of No. 101 Conversion Flight. 7 Sqn

Stirling N6120:MG-V, piloted by P/O Tony Hart, which force landed following a 'friendly fire' incident on 17 January 1942. L.C. Young via 7 Sqn Association

many conversion flights were formed and 7 Sqn hived off crews and aircraft to form No. 7 Conversion Flt under the command of F/O R. Ellis-Brown. The role of these flights was to train crews to operational standard, providing a period of more specialized training after leaving No. 1651 Conversion Flt at Waterbeach and prior to joining the squadrons for operations. They were to provide new crew with thirty-five hours of training over a period of two weeks. The flight existed for ten months before being absorbed into No. 1657 CU at Stradishall.

Losses continued in the first weeks of 1942 and Mk I N3672 was damaged when it bounced on landing after attempting to avoid a tractor on 14 January. Taxiing back in, the undercarriage collapsed.

The target was Hamburg on the night of 14/15 January. P/O J.D. Hart in W7454:MG-S and Sgt Green in N6300:MG-A both set out on this raid. Hart had engine trouble and jettisoned his bombs. Green bombed the target but did not see the results. Three days later N6120:MG-V was written off after P/O Hart overshot landing at Oakington and hit the railway embankment returning from a raid on Bremen. The Stirling had been attacked by a 'friendly' convoy 20 miles out in the North Sea and hit in the port outer engine, which was set on fire. P/O Hart jettisoned the bombs but one 500 pounder bomb hung up. Unable to throttle back the Stirling overran the runway and crashed. Les Young was a member of the crew of this Stirling and recalls the convoy and the crash.

> We were on our way to bomb a German airfield at a place called Soesterberg in Holland. On leaving the English coast we passed over a convoy which shouldn't have been there according to Intelligence. We were only at 1,500 feet so they could not miss. Our port outer engine was hit, which caught fire and the prop fell off. We had on board twenty-four 500 pound GP bombs, which were jettisoned, the fire put out and we turned for home, but crashed on landing. There were no injuries. We found out next morning that we still had two bombs left.

Another view of N6120 ,with her back broken, on the railway embankment at Oakington on 17 July 1942. L.C. Young via 7 Sqn Association

Bob Pointer, who had arrived in September, only to have his crew split up amongst other crews, became gunner to F/Sgt Tony Hart, the pilot of N6120, that day. He recalls some of the circumstances of the crash and how he joined the crew.

One of my flights in November 1941 was an air test in W7445:V-Victor with F/Sgt Hart, lasting 35 minutes. This was to be my future skipper. About this time three Royal Artillery lieutenants were seconded to the squadron to fly as front gunners, to observe the German ack-ack. As Tony Hart's front gunner was suffering from LMF [Lack of Moral Fibre] at the time, one of them flew with him. On one sortie they were fired upon by one of our own convoys in the North Sea and hit. They got back to base, but crashed on landing and finished up in half, across the railway track skirting the airfield. I decided there and then to forgo my wireless training and go in for front gunner.

A new aircraft was supplied and I joined the crew. On 4 February we flew for navigation practice for the first time as a crew. On 5 February we flew to Belfast with another crew in W7470:U, to pick up a new aircraft, the first one with an FN50 mid-upper turret. We had to stay for two nights because the weather turned adverse. We had no small kit with us so had to go to a local barber for a shave. This was a little scary because the IRA had been very active at the time.

Tony Hart, by now a pilot officer, was captain of R9305:V-Victor and I was the front gunner. The rest of the crew were: Sgt Bill Green, navigator (Newfoundland); Sgt Jack Davis, 2nd pilot; Sgt Fred (Ginger) Pool, W/Op (Mexico); Sgt Les Young (Blossom), rear gunner; Sgt Dusty Rhodes, flight engineer. We flew on a practice flight called 'Crackers 2' on 19 February, a mock attack on the Isle of Man, lasting three hours, thirty minutes. We did a couple of cross-country flights, some fighter affiliation, formation flying and a little low

N3709:MG-K at Oakington in early 1942. 7 Sqn

flying, during which we took 6 feet off the top of a poplar tree. There were some Gypsy caravans nestling beneath the poplars; it must have shaken them up a bit. It certainly did me, sitting in the front gun turret. It left a huge imprint of a branch on the front of my turret. I kept some of the pieces in the bottom of my kitbag for yonks. We were now ready for anything. Something that frightened me a bit when night flying was the way the engines stood out, glowing white hot when in flight. I was sure enemy aircraft could see them if they flew in front of us.

That same day F/Sgt Taylor was giving dual instruction to S/Ldr J.N. Mahler DFC near Earith when they were rammed by a Hurricane of No. 61 OTU flown by P/O Browne. There were no survivors. The Stirling buried itself 15 feet into the earth and burned for several days. The hole filled with water, making work impossible and preventing the recovery of the bodies of two of the crew.

The first two days of February were spent clearing the runways of snow and all personnel were involved in this task. On the night of 3/4 February the squadron took part in a raid which was to introduce many new techniques to Bomber Command operations. The target was the Renault factory at Boulogne-Billancourt to the west of Paris, which was estimated to be producing 18,000 lorries a year for the German forces. The 235 aircraft sent out was the greatest number sent to a single target thus far in the war and they were dispatched in three waves, the most experienced crews in the first wave dropping their bombs from low level. Wellingtons dropped a large number of flares in the first wave to illuminate the target and 7 Sqn bombed the power station and a gasometer. The factory was severely damaged and only one Wellington was lost.

On 11 February W/Cdr Graham began instructing pilots in the dual control Stirling, and a considerable amount of training flying was done over the following days. The long-awaited breakout of the *Scharnhorst* and *Gneisenau* took place on 12 February and Bomber Command launched Operation Fuller in an attempt to sink them. By the time the squadron was informed the ships had almost made good their escape and though two Stirlings, R9300 captained by P/O S.G. Matkin and R9297 flown by W/O W. Nicholls, were sent out to search, Matkin saw nothing and returned with his bombs. Nicholls briefly saw the ships through a small break in the cloud, but just as quickly lost them again. The pride of the *Kriegsmarine* had escaped.

On 22 February the squadron ground defence troops took part in an anti-invasion exercise with the local Home Guard and Cambridge OTC [Officer Training Corps]. The 'enemy' did not come into contact with the defence troops and a large supply of bricks, which had been accumulated to deal with the opposing tanks, was fortunately not required! Two days later decontamination tests were carried out on a Stirling using a steam generator. Air Ministry and group gas officers observed the tests in very cold weather. The method of decontamination appeared to be effective against the mustard gas used in the trials.

On 23 February a milestone was reached when P/O J.R. Alverson left the squadron after completing twenty-five operations. F/Lt W.N. Crebbin DFC took over the conversion flight, which had been formed in January, from F/O Ellis-Brown on the 25th and three days later W/Cdr J.H.A. Chapman arrived to take over command of the squadron from W/Cdr Graham.

February had been a very quiet month operationally, with a large amount of flying training taking place, including much use of the Link Trainer to practice Gee procedures. On the last day of the month Lord Trenchard visited the squadron again and addressed the crews and ground crew.

On the night of 3/4 March the squadron sent nine Stirlings out of twenty-nine ordered to attack the Renault works at Billancourt. The total force was 235 aircraft. The squadron's Stirlings dropped 100,000 pounds of bombs onto the target. Hits were observed on the power station and the gasometer, which blew up. Most crews reported a congestion of friendly aircraft, very few searchlights and little flak. The squadron ORB [Operations Record Book] noted that it was a perfect party, except for the lack of a traffic cop! F/O V.C. McCauley (R9297:MG-P) did not identify the primary target and bombed Dieppe instead. S/Ldr D.J.H. Lay DFC (W7501:MG-Z) was on the bombing run when his aim was spoiled by having to take evasive action to avoid a friendly aircraft in the congested airspace over the target.

During March the squadron became involved in minelaying operations, known as 'Gardening'. The mines were code-named 'Vegetables' and were dropped by parachute into exact positions laid down by the Admiralty. These operations could be extremely risky as the bomber often had to remain in the target area for some time, pinpointing positions and dropping mines. A squadron member recalls the risks involved in such missions.

Three crews were briefed to go minelaying off the Dutch Friesian Islands. Minelaying was a tricky business and a very exacting exercise for pilots as an aircraft had to be piloted to an exact map reference at sea, and held on a fixed heading at 500 feet until all mines had been dropped at ten-second intervals. This was a nerve-wracking business for all the crew. The gunners had to be ready to open up on any flak ship, which might have sailed into the lane after dark. There was never any intelligence on flak ships, as they were mobile. There was always a chance that you might go swanning into the drink if the instruments were not spot on and, of course, you could get your tail blown off if the mine exploded on impact with the surface. In addition to this, on this particular trip, the crews were warned to stay well clear of Texel as intelligence reports showed it had become a fortress of flak batteries and night fighters. The crews were also briefed to return over or south of Cromer, as an escorted convoy would be anchored north of Cromer on their return. Two of the crews on their mining runs in the

'Trefoils' area saw the third aircraft boxed by flak over Texel and, as it was a clear night, they saw it break away and start heading for home, limping along. They finished their runs and formated on the damaged aircraft, nursing it across the North Sea. They were approaching the English coast just south of Cromer when the convoy escort opened up with ack-ack, without challenging. The two escorting aircraft fired off recognition colours to no avail. They were forced to take evasive action. The damaged aircraft tried to turn out to sea again, but did not have sufficient height and crashed into the sea and the crew was lost. The convoy was out of position. Next morning all crews were up on air test, their cargo – toilet rolls. These were distributed liberally, through the flare chute, over the convoy.

On the night of 8/9 March the squadron took a load of incendiaries to Essen as part of a force of 211 aircraft. Gee was used to navigate to the target but results were disappointing. The incendiaries caused large quantities of smoke, which made the results difficult to pinpoint. One load of incendiaries landed just to the south-west of the Krupps factory causing a red fire, which increased in intensity very rapidly and was visible 70 miles away. Four of the Stirlings were damaged by flak and four others failed to attack the target. P/O M.R. Green's, W7466:MG-B, was hit by flak in the mid-upper turret and the port inner engine. S/Ldr Leigh-Smith in R9300:MG-L was forced to turn back when Sgt Norvell became sick through lack of oxygen and F/O G.T. Heard, flying N3705:MG-R, had flak hits to the cockpit and the controls to the starboard outer carburettor severed. P/O N.L. Taylor DFC in W7471:MG-J failed to attack due to the failure of his undercarriage to retract. Gee failure caused Sgt W. Runciman in N3708:MG-E to return early and P/O J.D. Hart flying R9305 had to jettison his bombs when he suffered a starboard inner engine failure. P/O S.G. Matkin did not even get off the ground as his Stirling, N3679, was unserviceable.

Cologne was attacked by 135 aircraft on 13/14 March. The squadron provided eight. Five reached the primary target, dropping bombs and incendiaries. Many fires were seen starting and in progress in the town. Two aircraft returned early due to equipment failure and one with engine trouble. P/O Hart in R9305 suffered an oil-pressure drop in the port outer engine only 50 miles from the target and was forced to jettison his bombs in open fields. S/Ldr Lay DFC, flying W7501, had an escape hatch blow off on the way to the target. He pressed home his attack but the bombs failed to release and he had to bring them home. P/O Green in N3679 turned back with an unserviceable Gee set and an unreliable D/F loop. P/O Taylor DFC, flying W7471, was also forced to turn back near Ostend with an unserviceable Gee set. One of the new crews bombed an airfield south-east of Dunkirk. Sgt Tomkin in N6073 bogged his aircraft down on the airfield. F/Sgt Street in BK592:MG-F failed to return, the only crew survivor being Sgt Sharp.

Two nights later operations were cancelled and the weather kept the bombers on the ground till the 25th. The crew of N6074, flown by S/Ldr H.L. Leigh-Smith, were forced to ditch off Barmouth in North Wales on 25/26 March after running out of fuel returning from a 254 aircraft raid on Essen. The crew got lost on the return and had planned to bale out, abandoning the aircraft, but one member pulled his ripcord too soon and it filled the fuselage with parachute silk. Unable to bale out now the pilot put the Stirling down in the sea after four of the crew had jumped. The ditching was successful and furnished some very useful information on the behaviour of

Stirlings whilst ditching. Eleven aircraft took part in the raid and a large number of incendiaries were dropped. S/Ldr Leigh-Smith and two other new crews bombed St Nazaire, the former having failed to reach the primary target. This raid was Bob Pointer's first and he recalls his trepidation.

My first sortie was to the Ruhr, 8 March 1942. Take-off was at 1955 hrs, quite scary. Tony weaved through a searchlight and flak belt, very calmly. The light flak weaved slowly at the start of its climb, then as it got closer it quickened up and went by at terrific speed; the searchlights coned a luckless bomber to one side of us. Tony weaved past it and went on to bomb the target, which was under slightly hazy cover. Our bomb load was twenty-one small bomb containers (SBC) full of 4 pound incendiary bombs, which certainly made a long white splash in the target area. We took a photograph and set course for home. There was a single searchlight above Oakington, a very welcoming sight. Our flight lasted five hours, five minutes. We were met at dispersal by a crew bus and taken to be interrogated, hot coffee with rum, lots of questions, then back to the sergeants' mess for bacon and eggs, and so to bed.

My first op was over. I only did seventeen ops with Tony Hart, as the crew had done half a tour before I joined. We changed flight engineers a few times, one of them being a Canadian serving in the RAF, a very nice chap, Sgt W.G. (Nick) Carter. He flew in another crew and was shot down. Only three of them, including Carter, baled out and became POWs.

The following day saw the loss of yet another of the squadron aircraft when N3709:MG-K, captained by F/O E.T. Heard, was tragically lost on the Essen raid. The CO, W/Cdr Chapman was flying as second pilot. They were observed being shot down by a No. 311 Sqn Wellington over the target. The Stirling crashed at Gendringen in Holland. All of the crew was killed. Two aircraft took part in this raid, the other being flown by WO Nicholls, who returned with flak damage, and another bombed Le Havre.

During March the squadron was honoured by a visit from the 'Father of the RAF' Lord Trenchard and then were able to relax and enjoy themselves for a brief period when they were invited to lunch in London by Short Brothers, manufacturers of the Stirling.

Stirling Mk I, W7501:MG-Z was lost returning from Lubeck on the 28th/29th, crashing into the sea north of Terschelling, Holland. Ten aircraft had been sent to this target, but despite good bombing results, it was a bad night for the squadron, which lost three aircraft: P/O R.L. Hayes, flying R9305:MG-V, F/Lt J.H. Edwards, flying W7501:MG-Z, and P/O Green in W7466:MG-B. Hayes crashed near Hamburg and Edwards and his crew came down in the North Sea north of Terschelling. P/O Green and his crew were all killed. Nothing was heard from any of them after take-off.

Over Heligoland F/O Taylor was attacked by a Ju88 and during the engagement Taylor's gunners shot it down in flames. Having seen the night fighter crash Taylor dropped his bombs across the town of Heligoland, causing fires. This was the last operation of the month due to adverse weather. P/O N.E. Winch in N3679 saw the town clearly and the fires started by his own bombs. Fifty miles short of the target his port inner engine lost power, but he pressed on to attack the target and returned safely to base. *En route* to the target Sgt Davies flying R9300, had trouble with his

Stirling W7466:MG-B, shot down on the night of 28/29 March 1942 on a raid to Lubeck. 7 Sqn

exactor controls and turned for home. However, the fault was rectified and he turned about again and bombed the target.

On the last day of March W/Cdr Graham became Station Commander and S/Ldr D.J.H. Lay DFC took over as CO. The weather gave the squadron a break from operations until 5 April, when seven aircraft went to Cologne. Two hundred and sixty-three bombers took part in this raid, which was a new record for a force sent to a single target. The aiming point was the Humboldt works in the Deutz district of the city. Bombs were scattered all over the city, but bombing photographs showed the nearest to the target being 5 miles away. Six of the squadron's Stirlings dropped incendiaries and F/O H.G. Pilling, flying N3706, was hit from above by incendiaries dropped by another aircraft. He jettisoned his bombs north-east of the Hohenzollern Bridge. Sgt Tompkins in N6073 returned early due to exactor trouble. P/O Tayler in W7471:MG-J was hit by flak and Sgt Davies, flying N3708:MG-E, had his starboard inner propeller shot off by flak and his starboard outer propeller damaged. He continued to the target and returned to base on two and a half engines. P/O W.R. Butterfield went to Le Havre the same night but failed to identify the target and returned with his bombs.

Essen was the target on the night of 6/7 April. One hundred and fifty-seven aircraft, five of them from 7 Sqn, set off in appalling weather. Only forty-nine claimed to have reached the target and five were lost. All of the squadron aircraft turned back, fighting their way through continuous heavy rain, thunderstorms and squalls. S/Ldr Lay managed to reach the Dutch coast before turning back.

On 8/9 April the squadron sent aircraft to Hamburg and on 'Gardening' sorties. Some 272 aircraft raided Hamburg, once again encountering icing and electrical storms. P/O Sanderson, one of the 'gardeners' was unable to pinpoint his minelaying position and returned with his mines. P/O Butterfield successfully laid his. The accurate positioning of the mines was vital in order to deny the enemy safe passage and knowledge of their exact positions safeguarded Allied ships and submarines. Three of the nine Stirlings dispatched by the squadron abandoned the raid on Hamburg due to severe icing and another due to excessive oil temperatures. Only F/O H.G. Pilling and Sgt Davies reached the target. Pilling saw six bursts and some fires started in the target area. P/O J.D. Hart in W7500:MG-B returned with his rear turret unserviceable. P/O Winch in N3679:MG-D was unable to climb above the icing cloud and bombed Terschelling instead.

On 10 April W/Cdr B.D. Sellick DFC took over command of the squadron from S/Ldr Lay. That night Essen was raided and several new crews were sent to Le Havre.

Of the five crews sent to Essen P/O N.L. Taylor returned early due to his rear gunner, Sgt Arnold DFM, becoming ill. S/Ldr Lay DFC, flying W7517, was attacked by a night fighter but managed to escape, making a good landing back at base despite having a punctured tyre. P/O J.D. Hart in N3710 had his aircraft hit by flak and his engineer's oxygen system failed. The crews reported some good fires started by the incendiaries dropped on the town. F/O Pilling in W7468 returned with damage caused either by flak or from being bombed from above. F/O Winch belly landed Stirling N3679:MG-D at Newmarket after his undercarriage failed to lower. Sgt C.R. Hague in N6075 went minelaying but could not identify the target and, with an unserviceable intercom, returned to base.

On 12/13 April the squadron struck at Essen again. Eight aircraft were detailed to attack in a force of 251 bombers. Bombing was scattered all over the Ruhr area and crews reported that there were so many fires that the bombing results were difficult to observe. Fires were visible 100 miles away. Stirling N3679:MG-D was belly-landed at Newmarket by F/Lt N.E. Winch due to undercarriage trouble on returning from the raid. WO Nicholls brought his Stirling, N6075, back early with an unserviceable front turret. Sgt Tomkins had an engine failure, which almost caused his Stirling to overturn. Three aircraft, flown by S/Ldr Leigh Smith, P/O Sanderson and Sgt Hague, raided Le Havre. The first two successfully bombed the docks, P/O Sanderson's aircraft, R9308, being holed in the starboard wing, but Sgt Hague experienced trouble with his compass and returned to base.

Dortmund came under attack by 208 bombers on the night of 14/15 April. This force was several times greater than any previously sent to this city and included five aircraft from the squadron. Just over half the force claimed to have bombed the target and photographs showed bomb damage all over the Ruhr. Nine aircraft failed to return. Industrial haze made bombing difficult and four of the five squadron crews dropped their bombs but were unable to observe the results. P/O Winch had a battle with a Ju88. His aircraft was damaged in the fight but the Junkers was shot down by his gunners and was seen to crash. Once again crews went minelaying and S/Ldr Leigh-Smith and Sgt Hague were ordered off. Leigh-Smith was successful, but for a second night Hague had to bring his bombs back, unable to pinpoint the exact dropping position.

Dortmund was raided again the next night, the squadron dispatching four aircraft. Thick cloud and icing were encountered by the

Stirling N3706:MG-S banks away from another squadron Stirling. G. Pitchfork

Oakington in April 1942 with construction of three new runways underway.

crews. F/O W.R. Butterfield jettisoned his bombs due to the icing and returned to base. S/Ldr Lay, F/Lt Pilling and Sgt Runciman (W7468) all dropped bombs on the target but were unable to observe the results. Runciman had both turrets hit by flak. S/Ldr Leigh-Smith and Sgt Hague were out minelaying again, but once again Hague experienced problems. His mines would not drop separately and he was forced to jettison them in one group.

In the days prior to the famous raid on Augsburg by Lancasters of 44 and 97 Squadrons on 17 April, crews from the squadron were taken off operations and given intensive low flying practice. A squadron member recalls this period.

A number of crews were formed, from other crews, and given low-flying practice for a couple of weeks. One crew left its bomb sight on Bedford Bridge and many came back with branches sticking out all over the place. Suddenly the low-flying order was cancelled and the aircrew reverted to their own crews. A few days later we heard of Nettleton's raid on Augsburg.

The same Squadron member recalls the high spirits and the rivalries which could develop between crews. Sometimes this competition could have a deadly outcome.

A fine shot of 7 Sqn Stirlings lined up at Oakington in 1942. G. Pitchfork

A deadly rivalry developed between two crews in 1942. One crew was skippered by a short roly-poly Scot, the other by a tall, rangy American from Gary Cooper's hometown in Montana. The game was train busting. Returning from a raid both pilots would drop to deck level and shoot up any trains that were travelling by night. A funny incident, which caused some light-hearted acrimony, was the night the Scot came up behind a train and was about to open fire when it went into a tunnel. By the time it came out the Scot was well on his way, but who should come along to catch it but the American. The game ceased when the Scot's crew were reported missing.

On the night following the Augsburg raid the squadron sent seven Stirlings to Hamburg as part of a force of 173 Wellingtons, Stirlings, Halifaxes and Manchesters. One hundred and seven crews claimed to have bombed the target but the German estimate was that only fifty had done so. One load of bombs landed on a warehouse containing 60,000 bottles of alcohol, which were lost when the heat of the fires popped the bottle corks!

Four of the seven aircraft dispatched bombed the target area. P/O Tayler, flying N6073, returned early with engine trouble and WO Taylor was unable to identify the target. S/Ldr Leigh-Smith in W7520 landed at Feltwell on returning. P/O Winch, flying W7522, had his port inner engine fail on the run-up to the target but still dropped his bombs in the target area. Sgt Lewis was sent to Le Havre but failed to find the target, returning with his bombs.

On the night of 22/23 April Bomber Command send sixty-three aircraft out on minelaying sorties. No. 7 Sqn provided nine. Each Stirling was loaded with four mines and four 500 pound bombs. Twenty of the mines were dropped successfully and the remainder were brought back to base.

The *Altstadt* in the centre of Rostock, on the Baltic, was the target for 173 bombers on the night of 23/24 April. The squadron dispatched ten Stirlings. Sgt Runciman was attacked by two night fighters near the target and forced to jettison his bomb load. He turned for home and once over England he ordered his crew to bale out, fearful that the undercarriage was damaged. Four baled out and Runciman and the others made a safe landing at Newmarket. Having baled out, one crewmember knocked on the door of a nearby farmhouse and asked to use the telephone to call base. The farmer was not keen to allow this but eventually relented with a demand for 2d for the call. The airman gave the farmer 2s! S/Ldr Lay, F/O Winch and WO Nicholls dropped 2,000 pound bombs, the other aircraft dropping incendiaries. This was a most successful operation as far as the squadron was concerned, with several good photographs being obtained. The fires were visible for 100 miles on the return journey.

Two nights later the Stirlings went back to Rostock. One hundred and twenty-eight aircraft took part and the town was heavily bombed. Crews reported that the flak defences had been strengthened. P/O Winch, WO Nicholls and Sgt Tomkins dropped 2,000 pound bombs on the town and five others dropped incendiaries into the already blazing buildings. The fires were visible from 120 miles away. F/O Tayler in W7471:MG-J had to abandon his attack due to compass trouble. Two aircraft, flown by F/Lt B.M. Denny and Sgt Lewis, bombed the docks at Dunkirk on the same night, returning safely.

Mining sorties were among the most dangerous carried out by the aircraft of Bomber Command and the squadron lost Stirling N3727;MG-G, piloted by F/Lt B.M. Denny, on one to Heligoland in mining area Rosemary on 27/28 April. As Denny went missing over Heligoland nine Stirlings were bombing Cologne as part of a force of ninety-seven aircraft. F/O Winch, flying N3750:MG-D, was forced to abandon his sortie after an engine caught fire. Seven others bombed with good results and Sgt Davies in N3716:MG-A, who had trouble maintaining height, dropped his bombs north of Le Cateau. F/O Butterfield in W7522:MG-K returned with flak damage.

The last operation of the month for the squadron was to Kiel on the night of 28/29 April. S/Ldr Leigh-Smith dropped his bombs on Foar Island during a running battle with a Bf110 and F/Lt Pilling in W7517:MG-Z dropped his bombs in the sea off Sylt when he had trouble with both inboard engines and was forced to return. Sgt Hague in N3750 had to drop his bombs just west of Selentersee after he had to take violent evasive action to escape searchlights. The remainder of the crews dropped their bombs on target, though F/Sgt Lewis had his Stirling, W7470, damaged by flak. F/Lt Denny in N3727:MG-G failed to return from a mining sortie in the Rosemary area off Heligoland.

During April the squadron set several records. A hundred sorties were topped for the first time and out of 105, only one aircraft was lost. Throughout the months of spring improvements to the runways had been carried out and the main runway 05/23 was extended in length at the 23 end to 2,000 yards. Runway 01/19 was also lengthened to 1,526 yards at the 01 end resulting in the closure of the B1050 road. Extension to the perimeter track to reach the new runway ends meant the loss of some hardstandings, with only twenty-eight pan hardstandings, which were supplemented by eight loop stands. Later a B1 hangar would be added and the accommodation increased to house 1,591 officers and airmen and 350 WAAFs.

After two days of bad weather the squadron raided Hamburg on the night of 3/4 May. Ten aircraft were dispatched to a target obscured by cloud. Seven dropped their incendiaries on ETA, with only occasional glimpses of the river below to assist in pinpointing the target. Fires were seen indistinctly through the cloud. P/O Hart brought his bombs back and Sgt Davies in N3716:MG-A had trouble with his port outer engine and jettisoned his bombs in the Wash. F/O Butterfield, flying W7522: MG-K, did not reach the target. F/Sgt Lewis in N3710:MG-M failed to take off when his tail wheels collapsed.

May 1942 was another outstanding example of courage and determination, which resulted in the award of the BEM to Sgt Pierre Cecil Bion. The citation for the award tells his story.

> *One night in May 1942, Sergeant Bion was the air gunner of an aircraft which was recalled through bad weather. The pilot attempted to land but collided with some high trees on a hillside. The aircraft immediately caught fire. Sgt Bion managed to extricate himself from the aircraft and assisted the wireless operator, who, whilst in a very dazed condition, was endeavouring to get free. Having taken him to safety, Sgt Bion returned to the burning aircraft and with the assistance of the navigator extricated another member of the crew, who had been trapped in the second pilot's seat. Leaving the navigator to attend this member, Sgt Bion returned to the aircraft and, unaided, extricated the pilot, who was suffering from a compound fracture of the left leg and was unable to move, and carried him to a place of safety. Unfortunately the pilot died a few hours later. Sgt Bion, who had sustained lacerations, abrasions and an injury to his left knee, displayed presence of mind and complete disregard for his own safety whilst performing his gallant rescue work.*

Sgt Bion was later commissioned.

Stirling N3710:MG-M failed to return from Stuttgart on 5/6 May. Seventy-seven bombers went to the target. N3710, flown by F/Sgt Lewis was the only Stirling loss from eleven dispatched; there were no survivors. Visibility in the target area was very poor and eight aircraft dropped a large number of incendiaries in the vicinity of the target. P/O Hart returned with his pilot's escape hatch blown off.

On the night of 7/8 May eight Stirlings were dispatched on minelaying sorties in Kiel Bay. All of them were carrying two 500 pound bombs in addition to their load of mines. S/Ldr Leigh-Smith dropped his bombs on the northern end of Sylt. WO Black made his first trip to St Nazaire but failed to identify the target and brought his bombs back.

Warnemunde was attacked by 193 bombers on the night of 8/9 May, the squadron sending out eight crews to this target. The attack on this town to the north of Rostock was moderately successful, the Heinkel engine works and airfield being the primary targets. Visibility was moderate but was further degraded by the smoke and search-lights. S/Ldr Leigh-Smith in W7471:MG-J was hit by flak. All of the crews bombed successfully with the exception of Sgt Tomkins, who arrived late over the target and bombed the airfield at Waal. For the next week bad weather grounded the bombers

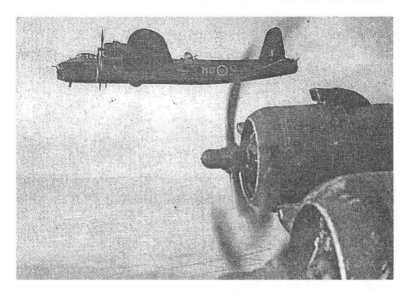

Short Stirling W7520:MG-S in flight. 7 Sqn Association

and the next sorties were carried out by two 'freshman' crews to Boulogne on the night of 17/18 May. Only one of the two aircraft bombed the docks.

On 19/20 May the squadron was hit hard when three Stirlings, N3716:MG-A, N6073:MG-Y and W7520:MG-S, flown by Sgt Hague, Sgt Tomkins and F/Lt Pilling respectively, were lost on a sortie to Mannheim. All of Hague's crew survived to be taken prisoner. The only member of the Tomkins crew to be lost was the captain, the rest becoming prisoners. F/Lt Pilling's crew were all lost. WO Nicholls in W7470: MG-U returned with an unserviceable engine and P/O Hart in W7517:MG-X returned early with trouble with both port engines. F/O Butterfield in W7522:MG-K was attacked by a night fighter and holed by cannon fire, which rendered the rear turret unserviceable. The bombing was scattered and little damage was done to the target, but a high price was paid by the squadron. Twelve aircraft had been dispatched and after bombing crews reported seeing large fires from a distance of 100 miles. P/O Hart and WO Nicholls returned early with engine trouble.

On the night of the 21st five other aircraft were out minelaying and on return were diverted, three of them, S/Ldr Leigh-Smith in N3750:MG-D, F/O Taylor in W7471: MG-J and P/O Hart flying W7571:MG-Z, who lost an engine in the circuit, landing at St Eval in Cornwall and two, P/O Sanderson in W7500:MG-B and WO Nicholls in W7470:MG-U at Marham. There were no further operations until the last night of the month due to poor weather.

On the night of 30/31 May 1942 nineteen Stirlings from the squadron took part in the first 'Thousand Bomber' raid on Cologne. The Stirlings bombed from between 12,000 and 15,000 feet. Some of those taking part came from No. 101 Conversion Flt. One Stirling did not reach the target. N3706:MG-S, flown by F/O Hart was forced to jettison its bombs in the Wash, due to exactor trouble, and return to base. A second crew, F/Sgt Templeman's in R9324:MG-X, jettisoned their bombs north-east of Antwerp after a night fighter attack. W/Cdr Sellick, the CO, had trouble with both starboard engines and also jettisoned his bombs off Orfordness, as did F/Lt Crebbin.

P/O Colwell, flying W7472:MG-C, was hit in the mainplane by flak and F/Sgt Winwood in R9301:MG-Q had his port inner exactor fail. Damage to the city was extensive and casualties were the highest for a single raid thus far with 469 killed, 5,027 injured and 45,132 bombed out. On return from the raid the crews were met by the King and Queen, who saw the target photographs showing the devastation of the city.

On the night of the first 'Thousand Bomber' raid many of the personnel at Oakington, realizing something very special was afoot, contrived to take part. A squadron member of the period recalls the event.

On the night of the first 1000 Bomber Raid on Cologne there were very few members of the ground staff, of commissioned or non-commissioned rank, left at RAF Oakington. MOs, Chaplains, Engineering Officers, dentists, Met men, and Signals officers, together with Sgt Fitters, armourers, and clerks – you name it, all hitched rides to Cologne and back. The RC Chaplain, a great rugby player, was always hitching rides and eventually 'went for a Burton' on an air test.

On 1/2 June the target for the squadron was Essen. This was the second 'Thousand Bomber' raid. The squadron sent out eighteen crews this time and Stirling N3750, flown by F/Lt N.E. Winch and carrying G/Capt Massey as co-pilot, failed to return, crashing in the North Sea off the coast of Holland. All of the crew were taken prisoner. F/Lt Winch was the last to leave the aircraft. His parachute opened and he swung twice before hitting the ground and breaking a leg. The newly commissioned P/O Runciman was hit by flak on this raid but returned safely.

It was Essen again the next night. Bombing was widely scattered and again the squadron lost an aircraft. W7500:MG-B, flown by P/O G.F. Sanderson RCAF, crashing into the sea off Holland, probably shot down by a night fighter. The squadron went to Emden on the 6th/7th, losing W7471:MG-J, which crashed near Blija in Holland. F/O Taylor and his crew all became POWs. Bill Goodman was a member of this crew and recalls his disappointment at being shot down and missing the Thursday night dance at Oakington because of it.

A recent intake had included an extraordinarily attractive young WAAF driver. She appeared to be of good breeding and was one of the few who looked really good viewed from behind when wearing battledress. Naturally, all the squadron Lotharios were soon trying to date her, but with no success. I still don't know what made me ask her if she would be my guest at the forthcoming dance, but she accepted my invitation. All my friends were amazed – I had actually dated a WAAF and moreover the apparition had accepted. It was beyond their (and my own) comprehension.

The dance was held on a Thursday, just five days after we took off late on the Saturday evening on what should have been the final operation of my first tour.

It was during the small hours of Sunday 7th June that Ludwig Becker spotted us as he was returning to his base at Leeuwarden to rearm and refuel after having shot down another bomber (a Wellington I think) and was flying lower than we were. We had the midnight summer sun lightening the sky to our north and a full moon to the south, nicely silhouetting us to Becker, who was beneath our defined horizon. He attacked from below and our starboard wing was immediately ablaze. If I remember correctly, we had that terrible phosphorus in our wing bomb bays. In addition, throttle control had been lost, as had the ailerons. There was no way we could have flown any sort of a course and the order was given to abandon aircraft.

Aircrews sometimes had premonitions of impending doom and would not survive that particular trip they were about to make and left last letters to mothers, wives and sweethearts on the table in their rooms, to be posted in the event of their death or non-return. I also had a premonition, but mine was that I would survive the war, no matter what was thrown at me. As I waited my turn to bale out I was quite unafraid. After all I had my premonition of survival, trust in God and the wonderful girls of the Parachute Section who looked after our parachutes for us. Then it hit me! How was I going to get back to Oakington in time for next Thursday? I was frightened that I might not manage it. I was frightened that that handsome womanizing friend of mine should try to step into my shoes. I was frightened that I would be unable to prevent him from trying to have his evil way with her.

I was the unwilling guest of the Luftwaffe *for just under three years, putting my feet back on English soil during the early hours of VE Day. I cannot remember the name of that delectable WAAF, but will never forget anything else about her!*

Bob Pointer flew his last trip with Tony Hart, to Essen, on 8/9 June 1942. One hundred and seventy aircraft took part in the raid. The bombing was scattered and nineteen aircraft were lost. The crew almost failed to get back. 'My last trip with Tony Hart was to Essen in W7539:K. When he became ill Bill Green, our navigator, by now a pilot officer, helped him fly the plane back to base and was awarded the DFC.'

On the 16th/17th R9324:MG-X, captained by F/Sgt Thomas Templeman, was shot down on a sortie to Essen. Three of his crew, Sgts Cooper, Duckworth and J.E. Thomas became prisoners. Once again the bombing was widely scattered, causing little damage, and Bomber Command called off its offensive on this target, which would not be raided in strength for another three months. Templeman was attacked by night fighters and shot down, winning a DFM in the process. The citation for the award was brief and only told part of the amazing story.

The airman was captain of an aircraft which attacked an objective in the Rhineland one night in June, 1942. On the return flight his aircraft was attacked by two Junkers 88s and severely damaged. In most hazardous circumstances, which followed, this airman displayed great fortitude and determination in keeping with the highest traditions of the Royal Air Force. Throughout, Flight Sergeant Templeman has proved himself to be an outstanding captain, who has set an exceptionally high standard by his courageous example and extreme devotion to duty.

The words of the citation do not come close to describing the epic of courage and determination that is Templeman's story. On the return trip two Ju88s attacked his Stirling and set it on fire. Templeman struggled to keep the blazing aircraft under control while his crew baled out, and only left the controls when he was certain that they were all safely out of the aircraft. Parachuting from the stricken bomber, he landed heavily and broke his ankle. Stunned for a few moments he then gathered his

Date	Hour	Aircraft Type and No.	Pilot	Duty	REMARKS (including results of bombing, gunnery, exercises, etc.)	Flying Times	
					Time carried forward:— 187·13		107·50
						Day	Night
5·6·42	23·35	STIRLING W7472	P/o COLWELL P/o BAKER	REAR GUNNER	RAID ON ESSEN		4·20
6·6·42	23·15	STIRLING W7472	P/o COLWELL P/o BAKER	REAR GUNNER	RAID ON EMDEN		4·15
8·6·42	2340	STIRLING W7472	P/o COLWELL P/o BAKER	REAR GUNNER	RAID ON ESSEN, RETURNED INTER.COM. U/S		1·30
10·6·42	10·00	STIRLING W7472	P/o COLWELL	REAR GUNNER	COMPASS SWING	1·35	
15·6·42	10·00	STIRLING W7472	P/o COLWELL	REAR GUNNER	BASE MILDENHALL BASE	·40	
16·6·42	2300	STIRLING W7472	P/o COLWELL	REAR GUNNER	RAID ON ESSEN	¼	4·35
24·6·42	10·00	STIRLING N3765	P/o COLWELL	REAR GUNNER	HEIGHT TEST & COMPASS SWING	2·10	
					TOTAL TIME ... 191·40		122·30

An extract from the log-book of Sgt T.L. Taylor for the period 6–24 June 1942.

wits and made a quick escape from his landing area. Stopping to bind his broken ankle with wire from a fence wrapped around his flying boot, he continued on his way.

Templeman walked for four days, reaching France, but here his luck ran out and he was captured. Seeing a chance he managed to escape from captivity and continued on into Vichy France and eventually reached the Pyrenees. From escaping to reaching the mountains had taken six weeks, all on foot, except for a short 18 mile train journey, in extreme pain from his broken ankle. His escape was made more difficult by a lack of food and assistance. He could not seek medical aid for his ankle, was forced to sleep rough and only ate when he could manage to beg or steal food, going without for a week at one stage.

By the time he reached the Pyrenees the wire wrapped around his boot had worn through the leather and cut into his ankle. Cutting the boot and wire away, he made a crude splint before making an attempt to cross the border into Spain. During the attempt, carried out at night, his ankle support gave way and losing his balance he fell 20 feet into a ravine, breaking his back in the fall. With a broken back and ankle most men would have given up – not Thomas Templeman. Though in agony from the injuries he crawled to a village and gave himself up. The Spanish authorities, whom one might have expected to provide immediate medical aid, threw him into a prison camp for several days before providing any treatment. He was repatriated in October 1942 to undergo major medical treatment of his spine and ankle spending many months in a plaster cast. In October he was recommended for the DCM but this was not approved and he was awarded the DFM instead.

Air Gunner Fred Mills joined the squadron in May 1942. He had previously served on a night-fighter squadron and was now crewed up with a group of airmen from Australia, Canada, New Zealand and the British Isles. After a few training sorties they were allocated Stirling 'M for Mother', serial number BF316. The crew's first operation was to Essen. Fred Mills recalls this sortie.

We didn't have time to think what it would be like, we just had to get all the equipment checked before briefing. Owing to the size of the aircraft, it was necessary for the pilot to have assistance for take-off. Every crew member checked the equipment that they were dealing with. The ground crew had done all their checks and bombs were loaded during the day. We were taken to the dispersal point with our flying gear and entered the aircraft.

Checks were carried out, the engines started and run at high revs. We moved to the start of take-off and orders from control were given to go. We roared down the runway and used most of it before take-off, undercarriage up, circled and set course to the target.

Everyone in position, the rear and mid-upper gunner tested their turrets and the elevation and depression of their guns. The bomb aimer and front gunner carried out their routine checks; the wireless operator and engineer carried out their procedures while the navigator gave alterations of course.

The turrets were cramped, with the controls between the legs, and the only thing one could wear with any degree of comfort was the heated suit, which was plugged in. If the electrical system became damaged one could freeze to death.

Now over the Channel, the rear gunner reported a boat on the port side of the aircraft; it was probably a fishing boat. Orders were given to test guns by two short bursts and all positions reported in order. Short bursts were made in case our position was given away to the enemy, who might have a spotter plane in the area. Essen was our first operational trip and it was quite an experience to see all the flares dropped by aircraft on the target before us and to see the bombs going off like stars on the ground. Searchlights lit up a bomber, which could be in trouble if it didn't get away before the guns were trained on it. The ack-ack was accurate and it was necessary to get away from the searchlights trained on the aircraft, either by diving or rolling over.

Our course was corrected by the navigator for the run in to the target. The bomb aimer was in position, bomb bays were opened and instructions to the pilot were given – left, left, etc. – bombs away, close bomb bays and head for home. A photograph is taken when the bombs are released.

I was looking around to check if any fighters were in the area and saw a shadow about 2,000 feet below, which was probably another bomber over the target area. This was reported to the skipper and the fact that a large concentration of the target area was on fire.

We returned to base at 3 a.m., reported to the intelligence officer as a crew and gave all the details that we could see over the target and on the way home. We had coffee and returned to our room for bed.

The squadron's Stirlings returned to Emden again on the 20th/21st losing W7472:MG-C, which came down in the North Sea off Bergen, Holland. P/O Calvert and all of his crew were killed. N3754:MG-O was lost on 26 June, failing to return from Bremen on the third of the 'Thousand Bomber' raids. Pilot, Sgt E.E. Green and

Sgts Morris and Mason survived to become prisoners; the remainder of the crew was killed. The results were not as good as the first raid to Cologne but better than those at Essen. Bomber Command conducted only minor operations on 28/29 June and W7539:MG-K went down in the North Sea on an attack on the French port of St Nazaire. Sgt K.J.C. Richards captained the aircraft, which took off at 2332 hrs, bombing on Gee before turning for home. It was thought to have been shot down or collided with a Messerschmitt Bf110. At 0454 hrs the Stirling crashed in the Bay of Biscay near Piriac. Sgts Tait, Woollard, Green and Harrison were killed. Richards and Sgts Collins and Jones became POWs.

The last day of June saw the loss of N3706:MG-S. The Stirling is believed to have ditched 50 miles off Cromer on the return leg of a raid on Bremen. An SOS was received at 0207 hrs and the signal continued for over an hour before fading out. The pilot, F/Sgt Bailey and Sgts Peachey and Keatley survived and became POWs.

The crew of W7563:MG-M had little luck on 2 July. Taking off for Bremen a tyre burst and the Stirling swung of the runway, crashed and burst into flames. This was Bob Pointer's fourth operation with a new crew led by S/Ldr Cook.

Taking off for Bremen our starboard tyre burst on take-off. Suddenly 'M-Mother' lurched to one side. We tilted over and caught fire. We had a full load of 30 pound incendiaries and full petrol tanks on board. The starboard wing touched the runway and came off and the port wing was sticking up at a crazy angle. It turned out that we had run over a live round and it burst our starboard tyre. Luckily we all scrambled out with no serious injuries. I had been standing between the two pilots, holding on to their seats for take-off. I was wearing a gold signet ring under my three pairs of gloves, but the pressure pulled the skin on my finger up. All the emergency services came into play, crash tender and the duty officer from the watch tower with a WAAF driver. The fire tender covered the aircraft with foam, as a fire had started. With all the fuel aboard for our long trip, plus our incendiary load, we made a dash from the plane.

A WAAF came up to me, took me to her van and gave me a cigarette. It was a fair-headed MT driver I had met at the YMCA a previous evening. We got on well from then on, went everywhere together and were married on 14 September.

With an operation completed the work of the squadron was not finished. The following day the cycle continued in preparation for the next raid. Ground crews would prepare the aircraft, servicing and bombing up. Crews would check equipment, carry out air tests and attend lectures and other training. Some crews would be lucky enough to be stood down from the coming operation and grab a night of entertainment in a local pub or the mess. Fred Mills recalls the daily routine of preparation and training.

The next day we had to check our parachutes and had a clothing parade and lectures on aircraft identification. That evening we were off duty and after a meal we went by taxi into Cambridge. The officers' and sergeants' messes had different meal times and therefore we met up at an agreed place. Mostly during our off-duty evenings we went to the Eagle public house and after closing time we went for either a Chinese or Indian meal before returning to the station.

Two views of the remains of Stirling Mk I W7563:MG-M, which crashed on take-off on 2 July 1942. R.C. Pointer

All air and ground crews were very busy during this year and did not have much spare time. Aircraft had to be made serviceable for operations, all the equipment checked to make sure it was in good working order.

Our skipper made every member of the crew familiar with everyone else's job in order that if a crewman was injured somebody could take over. The skipper was a tough Australian who gave orders in a decisive manner and was respected by his air and ground crews.

The ground crew would not be told the target, but would have a good idea by the amount of fuel required – 1,485 gallons for the Ruhr, 1,895 for Nuremberg.

When an operation was called off owing to bad weather conditions or for other reasons such as the aircraft being u/s at the last minute, the air and ground

Bob Pointer flew his first operation in Stirling R9305:MG-V pictured here with his crew. L to R: Sgt Precious (flt eng, killed in action 2 June 1942), Sgt Bob Pointer (W/Op/AG), Sgt Les Young (rear gunner), Sgt Jack Davies DFM (2nd pilot, killed in action 21 December 1942), Sgt Fred Pool (Mid-upper gunner). R9305 failed to return from Lubeck on 28 March 1942. R.C. Pointer

crews used to get on their bicycles and race to the aircraft to get the food packs stored in the various crew member positions. They contained concentrated food, cigarettes and chocolates as rations consumed on the way back from an operation or needed if the aircraft was shot down in enemy territory.

On one occasion I raced out to the aircraft after an operation was called off owing to adverse weather conditions. I jumped off my bicycle as somebody came up behind me. I lifted myself up into the bomb aimer's compartment, but I hit my head on the armour plating, nearly knocking myself out. The ground crew got all the packages and just left me, saying 'You'll be OK after a quiet lay down!'

As the strength of the forces Bomber Command sent out each night increased the Germans countered with more advance control of the night fighters, searchlights and anti-aircraft guns. Systems of night-fighter control boxes were introduced, master searchlights – radar controlled – were used to guide the other searchlights on to the bombers, and radar-predicted flak was used to deadly effect. These advances made it increasingly difficult for the crews to complete their sorties and return safely. Fred Mills remembers the gradual increase in defences.

While on operations we noticed as we progressed to various targets that the anti-aircraft fire was getting very close and accurate. Our skipper decided that the enemy had some type of radar equipment, which could beam on to our aircraft through 10/10 cloud. This being increasingly noticeable near the target, it was decided to jink, i.e. dive 30 degrees and climb up to 60 degrees, in order to make

Fred Mills with his crew and the ground crew of 'M for Mother'. F. Mills

it difficult to get a fix on our aircraft. It also meant that the fighters couldn't get into a straight firing position. These tactics were carried out all the way to the target and on the return journey. By the time we got back the skipper was nearly all in with the exertion, but it did pay off.

When over the target area, searchlights were sweeping the sky. If a master searchlight, with twice the power, picked up an aircraft other searchlights would beam in and form a cone. Any aircraft unable to get out of this cone within seconds would be shelled out of the sky.

On 13 July the squadron lost an unidentified Stirling on a training sortie. It came down near Leek in Staffordshire, killing the pilot, Sgt Morrison, and his crew. Two passengers, Sgt Atkins attached from No. 101 Sqn and Sgt Dolphin, were also killed.

The pilot of R9331:MG-Y landed too fast at Waterbeach returning from Duisburg on 14 July and overshot the end of the runway crashing the aircraft. On the 16th a large force of Stirlings was sent to

Wireless Operator/Air Gunner William J. Anderson.
D. Milne

bomb U-boat construction yards at Herrenwyk, near Lubeck but the results were poor and two of the twenty-one Stirlings dispatched were lost. A member of one of the crew recalls the operation.

The raid necessitated crossing Denmark at 50 feet and crossing to Lubeck to bomb at 7,000 feet. A humorous, though pathetic, story told by one crew was of a poor old Danish woman ploughing a field with two oxen, with the reins around her neck. The aircraft frightened the oxen, which bolted and the last they saw of her was a welter of petticoats flying through a hedge. The raid was made at teatime and one crew scored a direct hit on the Naval Academy, whose parade ground was on an enormous flat roof. They got the fright of their lives when this giant slab of concrete seemed to be rushing up to meet them. On the way home the squadron had to fight its way, for every inch of airspace fighters were taking off and attacking, then landing on another field, refuelling and rearming to attack again.

AN AIRMAN'S DIARY – JULY/AUGUST 1942

New Zealander William James Anderson worked as a welder and cutter before applying for aircrew training in February 1940. Trained as an air gunner in Canada he was posted to the UK and after further training at No. 11 OTU at Bassingbourn joined No. 7 Conversion Flight in July 1942 and was posted to 7 Sqn on 29 August. During this period he kept a diary. The entries are brief, as one would expect from

William Anderson's log-book entry for the period 24 July–14 August 1942, whilst with No. 7 Conversion Flight at Oakington. D. Milne

Date	Hour	Aircraft Type and No.	Pilot	Duty	REMARKS (Including results of bombing, gunnery, exercices, etc.)	Day	Night
					Time carried forward:—	98·55	54·50
24·7·42	1000	NO. 7. CON. FLIGHT. STIRLING RQ297	P/o RUNCIMAN.	OAKINGTON CIRCUITS.	WOP/AG.	1·00	
24·7·42	1450	RQ297	R/o NICHOLLS	"	" "	·55	
25·7·42	1040	RQ300	P/o RUNCIMAN.	"	" "	1·20	
25·7·42	1550	RQ300	P/o RUNCIMAN	"	" "	·50	
27·7·42	1050	RQ301	P/o RUNCIMAN	"		·45	
28·7·42	1135	W7470	W/o NICHOLLS	"	AIR SWING. LOOPS	1·00	
				MONTH O/6.7.CON. FLIGHT	DAY FLYING 5·50 HOURS. TOTAL = 5·50 NOURS.		
5/8·42	1035	J N3764	P/o HEYWARD		BIRCHAM NEWTON	0·30	
5·8·42	1330	N3764	P/o HEYWARD		RETURN TO BASE	·30	
6·8·42	1115	" P	P/o HEYWARD		COMPASS SWING.	1·10	
10·8·42	1440	R9297	P/o RUNCIMAN		AIR FIRING 200 RNDS.	1·20	
11·8·42	0950	"	P/o RUNCIMAN		CIRCUITS.	1·45	
13·8·42	1000	RQ297	P/o RUNCIMAN.		"	·15	
13·8·42	1015	RQ297	P/o DALLENGER		"	1·35	
14·8·42	1040	RQ301	P/o RUNCIMAN		FLT. MAHADIE	·20	
14·8·42	1050	RQ301	FLT MAHADIE			·30	
					TOTAL TIME....		

many of the young men of the squadron who had many other things on their minds. It gives little information on his training with the conversion flight or on joining the squadron, but shows quite clearly that a young man's main interests on an operational squadron revolved around sleep, food and entertainment. In addition to his diaries a few letters also survive.

21 July 1942 – Up at 9 – breakfast, packed, over to Club. Went for mail – none. Shopping all morning, dined. Train at 2.25. Hitch and walked to new drome [Oakington].

22nd – Up at 7.30 – Breakfast. Over to flights and fixed accounts and papers. Sorted kit. Listened to Don's records. Bed.

23rd – Up at 8 – Dined on fair meal, briefing at 9. Flew in Stirling for 50 minutes. Maiden trip for crew – enormous machine. Another 50 minute trip after lunch. Tea, had sleep, went for walk, bed.

24th – Up at 8 – breakfast. Flew for 1 hour. Lunch, Crew Room, Flew 1 hour circuits. Tea, very tired. Sent two cards – Dad and Aunt Teen. Parcel to Harry, one to Mrs Coup.

25th – Up at 8 – breakfast. Flew for 1 hr 20 mins. Lunch, Crew Room. Three letters from Mrs Coupe. One letter Kumara in reply to letter sent in appreciation of parcel. Letter from mother. Reading 'Gen' all afternoon. Over to gym for 1½ hours. Shower, supper, bed.

26th – Up at 8 – breakfast. Over to flights. Went for trip on air test. Flew for miles at about ten feet – great fun. Testing gear all afternoon. Wrote to mother, went for a run, supper, bed.

27th – Up at 8 – breakfast. Crew room, raining heavily, did daily inspection. Trouser ?? changed. Had ??. Wrote to Roy Max. Cricket practice and gym. Supper and bed.

28th – Up at 8 – breakfast very poor. Crew room. Air test and compass swing. Dinner. Messed around all afternoon. Diner and letter to M. Gym, supper, bed. 10.00 p.m. raid. Telegram home.

29th – Up at 8 – Crew Room. Daily inspection, then lunch. Went to Cambridge to do shopping – couldn't get a thing I wanted. Went to pictures, poor show, home and bed.

30th – Up at 8 – Daily inspections all morning. Dinner, letter. Gym all afternoon and then messing about. Bed. About 2 a.m. Ju88 shot up the barracks – it got shot down!

31st – Up at 8 – over to crew room. Daily inspections. Tried to get to see Ju88 crash – no chance. Four killed. Target firing all afternoon, tea, loafed around all evening.

1st August 1942 – Up at 8 – Daily inspections all morning. Cable from Laurie [son] very pleased. Collected cycle from repair shop. Wrote letters to Capt. Hart, Mrs Parkinson, M. Murray. Bed after supper.

2nd – *Up at 8 – Bacon & egg breakfast. Raining. Daily inspection. Burge in London playing cricket. Letter to Harry G. letter to Joyce Milne. Supper and bed.*

3rd – *Up at 8 – over to crew room. CO lecture – seems good sort. Daily inspection all morning. Gym all afternoon. Tea, went to pictures in camp armoury. Supper and bed.*

4th – *Up at 8 – over to crew room. Gen on wave motion. Morse. Letter to M. Murray. Burge in hospital – pleurisy. Tea, over to gym. Supper and messed about. Bed after shower.*

5th – *Up at 8 – Briefing. Down to 'J' to clean guns and turret. Air test half hour. Briefed to go on trip. Cancelled at 8 p.m. Over to gym, supper, shower and bed.*

6th – *Up at 8 – Crew room. Down to kite. Checked turret. 1½ hour air test. Dinner. Cleaned guns ready for trip. Another chap got in my place. Gym, supper, bed.*

7th – *Up at 8 – Daily inspection. On w/t and mid turret. Cup of tea. Pay parade – five pounds eighteen shillings. Sent Graham's dressing gown. Went to gym, supper, shower and bed. Snaps in album.*

8th – *Up at 8 – Over to crew room. Daily inspection. Wet all day. Lecture on crew drill. Went to picture 'Sea Hawk' good show. Supper. Wrote to Deryck. Bed.*

From a letter home 8th August – *We had a Jerry over the station recently, rather annoying when at 2 in the morning one is awakened by bombs. Then guns of ground defence belting away, zowie! The cheeky devil. While lying in bed on second floor of barracks block we could see him flying past, then wow! His rear gunner decided to let a ground crew have it and bullets whizzed past and hit the walls. That shook one up a bit. There is only a brick wall to stop the bullets coming into the room but luck was our way, and Jerry well a second later the whole place felt as though hit by a bomb. It was a faithful old Lewis gun which caused all the noise – and four youthful lads died for their own cause.*

9th – *Up at 8 – Egg for breakfast. Crew room. Daily inspection all morning. Dinner. New Skipper. Bit of writing home. Gym and bed after supper.*

10th – *Up at 8 – Daily inspection. Burgess's bike pinched. A bit of flying. At 5 missed wallet. Wallet found in WC cistern in morning – minus twelve pounds Blow! Gym, bed.*

11th – *Up at 8 – Crew room. Daily inspection. Circuits with new pilot Ben Dallenger. Met new mid upper gunner Jeff Warner. Circuits all afternoon. Moped around, gym, bed.*

12th – *Up at 8 – Daily inspection. Messed around all morning. Letters from Mother, Dad, Capt. Hart, M. very pleased. Supper and a bit of reading, bed.*

13th – *Up at 8 – Crew room. Daily inspection. Circuits and landings – 2 hours. Dinner. Gen all afternoon, tea. Went to musical concert – great show, supper and bed.*

14th – *Up at 8 – Crew room. Daily inspection. Circuits for 1 hour with Flt Lt Mahaddie. Dinner. Cake from Aunt Teen. Wrote to M. Jigsaw puzzle 5 hrs. Shifted to main mess, 2 in room, bed.*

15th – *Up at 8.30 – Crew room. Daily inspection. Sorted gear out – big job. Flying all afternoon. Tea. Went for a ride to village. Evening at British Legion, bed.*

16th – *Up at 8 – Did a compass swing – OK. Dinner. Nothing in flights. Bull then with Don & Ron. Meet P/O Smith and wife. Had a swim at Pike and Eel. Visited orchard, home.*

17th – *Up at 8 – Crew room. Compass swing, cross country till 6.16 p.m. Tea. Flying at 9 till 12. Supper, shower and bed.*

18th – *Up at 10 – Dinner. Flying in afternoon. Night flying scrubbed. Wrote to mother. Supper of spaghetti & toast. Shower and bed.*

19th – *Up at 8 – breakfast fair. Compass swing, cross country in afternoon. Circuits and landings at night.*

20th – *Flying in afternoon. Commando raid on Dieppe.*

21st – *DR trip in afternoon.*

23rd – *Asked to volunteer to Pathfinder and somehow found we were in before we knew it.*

25th – *Up at 8.30 – Crew room, did some WO practice, messed around, game of snooker. After dinner dinghy drill, tea. Went to Manston to ferry crew, back at tea, billiards, bed.*

26th – *Up at 10.30 – Did some sewing of buttons, dinner. Astro shots in afternoon. No flying. Played billiards after tea, bed at eleven after bath.*

27th – *Up at 8 – Breakfast of eggs. Crew room, did some morse practice. Posted to Squadron. Got own plane 'D' for Donald. X country flight 4 hours (night and not in D for Donald). Bed.*

28th – *Up at 11 – Dinner, crew room fixing up about posting papers to the Squadron. Went to Pike & Eel for a swim – water warm as toast, cycled home, bed.*

29th – *Up at 8 – Breakfast, 2 eggs we had given to us. Went down to our plane and checked on it. Dinner. Tested machine for height. Tea. Went to pictures, bed. Pain in forehead – got electric shock off intercom.*

30th – *Up at 8 – Egg for breakfast. Daily inspection in forenoon, lunch. Lecture in afternoon on navigation. Tea and had a sleep. Head still very sore. Had supper, bed early after two aspirin.*

31st – *Up at 8 – Daily inspection. First flight in our own machine 'D' for Donald. Perfect order. Dinner, wrote home. Worked on plane, tea, sleep. Briefing – op cancelled – bath and bed.*

1st September – *Up at 8 – Daily inspection on plane all morning. After dinner worked at electrical system, fixing lights in 'D'. tea, had a nap, game of snooker. Ops at 12 – Good trip – a weird experience our first trip in enemy country. Good job made of it (Saarbrucken). Note – they missed, got next town! Wrote to M.*

2nd – *Up at 1 – Down to crew room. Not on ops. Collected kit from 'D'. Game of snooker, slept till tea, game of billiards, supper and bed.*

3rd – **Anniversary of 3rd year of war**. *Let it be the last. Up at 8, crew room, daily inspection. Photographs of crew by plane. Dinner, went to Cambridge – pictures. Home & bed. One of our a/c missing – good show (Karlsruhe).*

4th – *Up at 8.30 – Daily inspection. Airtest. Off colour a bit today. Dinner, worked on a/c till four. Tea, sleep, supper. Briefing 00.18 left for Bremen – heavy flak, searchlights.*

5th – *Back at 6. Interrogation till 8. Breakfast, bed. Up at 1.30, dinner, briefing, daily inspection. No ops tonight. Tea. Two letter from home – just one month. Tidied up room.*

6th – *Up at 8 – Breakfast, checking over aircraft all morning. Lunch, briefing, working all afternoon. Left for Duisburg at 1.30.*

7th – *Back at 5. Interrogation, breakfast, bed at 7.30. Up at 1.30, dined, briefing, worked on aircraft. Going to Stettin – in plane at 8.30, op cancelled, bed.*

8th – *Up at 8 – On leave for six days. Chasing around all morning on passes , pay etc. Left Cambridge at 2.30. Had dinner with Mrs Lamb – had our usual round table discussion.*

9th – *Up at 10.30 – Went to club for lunch. Went to show 'Get a load of this' by Vic Oliver – great show. Went to Soho to see club life – very unnatural.*

14th – *Up at 8.30 – Daily inspection on new machine. Dinner and working on gun til tea. 8.00 ops to Wilhelmshaven. Hit by flak – just one hole through wing.*

15th – *Up at 11.30 – Dinner. [Last entry].*

Stirling Mk I, R9328:MG-A went down on the Hamburg raid of 26/27 July. Nothing was heard after take-off but the captain, F/Lt J.N. Harris, and Sgts Stewart-Moore, Caldwell and Blythe became POWs. Four hundred and three bombers were dispatched in a maximum effort with the bomber crews battling through cloud and icing to reach the target, where clear weather was found. Good results were claimed and Hamburg reported severe damage, mostly in residential and commercial districts. Two days later the target was Hamburg again, the squadron losing W7533:MG-G and W7565:MG-B. W7565 took off at 2229 hrs from Oakington, captained by F/Lt D.W. Whiteman, who lost the starboard inner engine to flak and was then attacked and shot down by night fighters, crashing at Aschmoehor. Whiteman and Sgts J. Boyle, A.H.C. Bates and F.L. McIntyre were killed. The rest of the crew escaped to become POWs. P/O Sidwell and WO Carter both ended up in Colditz.

MG-G, captained by WO Black, had only one survivor, Sgt Thoms. Two hundred and fifty-six aircraft took part in this raid. The planned force was much larger but bad weather at the bases of 1, 4 and 5 Groups prevented their aircraft taking off. The

Date	Hour	Aircraft Type and No.	Pilot	Duty	REMARKS (Including results of bombing, gunnery, exercises, etc.)	Day	Night
					Time carried forward:-	1/2·35	54·50
15·8·42	1445	W7470	P/O DALLENGER		T.R. TRAINING. W/OP	1·45	
16·8·42	1000	W7617	P/O DALLENGER		COMPASS SWING "	1·20	"
16·8·42	1015	R9297	"	"	" "	1·30	
17·8·42	1535	W7470	"	"	X COUNTRY "	3·50	
18·8·42	1430	W7529			X "	3·55	
18·8·42	2100	R9300	P/O RUNCIMAN		CIRCUITS + LANDINGS...	3·00	3·00
19·8·42	1445	W7470	P/O DALLENGER		BEAM APPROACH + T.R.	1·25	
11·8·42	1440	R9301	P/O RUNCIMAN		CIRCUITS	·35	
11·8·42	1515	"	P/O DALLENGER		"	·30	
20·8·42	2015	9297	S/LDR CREBBIN		CIRCUITS W/OP	1·	1·10
" - "	2225	"	P/O DALLENGER		"		·50
21·8·42	1450	7470	P/O DALLENGER		T.R. "	1·35	
23·8·42	1540	9297	P/O DALLENGER		DAY BOMBING - HEIGHT 20.000	2·30	
24·8·42	2125	9297	P/O DALLENGER		NIGHT X. COUNTRY		3·00
25·8·42	1820	9297	P/O DALLENGER		MANSTON R·GUN + W/OP	1·05	
27·8·42	2000	7470	P/O DALLENGER		X - COUNTRY W/OP		4·10
						27·55	12·10
		7 CON. FLIGHT.	MONTH TOTAL.		DAY 27·55 HOURS.		
					NIGHT 12·10		
		" - "	TOTAL FLYING		DAY 33·45 HRS.		
				NIGHT	12·10 HRS		
		S/LDR 7. CONVERSION FLT.			TOTAL TIME....	132·45	67·00

William Anderson's log book entries for the period 15–27 August 1942 whilst serving with No. 7 Conversion Flight. D. Milne

weather worsened *en route* to the target and many aircraft were recalled or turned back. The Stirling squadrons suffered heavy losses that night, with nine from 3 Group being lost. Fred Mills went to Hamburg and recalls the flak and the night fighters.

We got caught in a searchlight cone over Hamburg, but managed to dive to 10,000 feet before levelling off. Then light ack-ack picked us up and set the inside of the aircraft on fire, which we managed to put out by extinguishers and blankets. We left the target area at low level over the sea with a Messerschmitt 109 on our starboard side. The hydraulics to the turrets were shot away and they could only be rotated manually. With one engine out of action we were an easy target. We could not understand why the fighter didn't attack us as it was with us for what seemed a long time, and then suddenly it turned back to the land.

We managed to limp to our base, making a belly landing as the undercarriage had been shot away. The aircraft was in a bad state, with holes and torn sections along the fuselage.

During July 1942 Bomber Command carried out a large number of Gardening minelaying sorties. The Stirlings carried out several operations during the month and Fred Mills, who now classed his crew as experienced, took part in them.

These operations were easy trips for experienced crews such as us. We were at low level over the sea with everything very quiet, except for the noise of our engines and with no lights anywhere. During these trips the moon was in

Some of the crew of Stirling W7569:MG-D at Oakington. L to R: Don Lamb, G. Burgess, Ron Crabtree, Harry Goddard and Bill Anderson. D. Milne

evidence and sometimes we flew over a fishing boat. We knew that fighters were waiting above us, but while we were over the water it would be difficult for them to catch us.

We had an area and line where to drop the mines. On these operations the navigator had to be on target for the run-in. If we overshot the target area it would mean another turn, which could prove disastrous as sparks from the engines during turning could give our position away.

August 1942 saw several changes. The Pathfinder Force (PFF) was formed and the squadron was transferred into it, tasked with a marker role, flying ahead of the main force and dropping flares to illuminate the aiming points and the target area. At the same time it began to re-equip with the Stirling Mk III. Gordon Paterson, a Canadian bomb aimer, was one of the first squadron Pathfinders and recalls the early sorties for this new force.

I was a bomb aimer, flying 'W for Willy' with F/O Jim Watt from Argentina. We had a great crew and were called the 'League of Nations' crew. Our flight engineer was a South African, W/Op Jock Ross from the north of Scotland, tailgunner from the French Foreign Legion. Jack Brain, mid upper gunner from Wales and Buzz King, a Canadian, our navigator for a short while. He was severely injured on one of our trips to Dusseldorf and never flew again. Tommy Tomkins took over from him. Tommy was English. We were one of the original crews selected to participate on the first Pathfinder operation. We continued on Pathfinders throughout our tour.

W/Op/AG Bill Anderson in the crew door of Stirling W7569:MG-D. D. Milne

Duisburg felt the weight of a Bomber Command attack on 6/7 August, the squadron losing Stirling R9154:MG-F, piloted by Sgt C.G. Pullen, which crashed at Huthum Emmerich; there were no survivors. This target was proving to be a difficult one to destroy and on this, the fifth attack in three weeks, the results were disappointing, most of the bombs falling into open country west of the target.

Bomber Command placed a high priority on minelaying. Stirling Mk I MG-Y, captained by Sgt H.M. Clark, was lost on such a sortie to Kiel Bay on 13/14 August. The sole survivor from the crew was Sgt V.H. Sharp, who landed in shallow water and was arrested. The Stirling crashed off Nymindegab, near Norre Nebel in Denmark. The mining areas in Kiel Bay were codenamed Radishes, Wallflowers and Forget-Me-Nots.

On 16 August the squadron had the dubious honour of presenting the *Luftwaffe* with a serviceable Stirling. N3705:MG-F had been on a mining sortie off Borkum when the pilot, Joe Orrell, had to crash land at Loevenstein Castle, near Gorichem in Holland. Approaching the mining area the Stirling was hit by fire from a flak ship. It yawed violently with the loss of both port engines, and dived towards the sea. Orrell managed to recover it at a very low altitude and the flight engineer managed to restart one of the failed engines. With the compass failed and unable to obtain a fix due to their low level and with the additional problem of low fuel, they elected to crash land. The aircraft came to rest against a mud bank with little more than a damaged nose. The crew immediately went through the procedures for destroying secret equipment and the aircraft, but attempts to set it on fire using incendiary devices were unsuccessful. The crew then set off in a bid to escape, but were subsequently betrayed by a collaborator and captured. The *Luftwaffe* repaired the damaged aircraft and sent it to the test unit at Rechlin.

The strain on the aircrews during this period was tremendous. Losses were high and in an effort to relieve some of the pressure they would have huge parties in the messes and blow off steam, sometimes, in unusual ways. The ground crews were under a different pressure, working in all weather, day and night, to repair and

Repairs being carried out to the nose of captured Stirling N3705:MG-F of 7 Sqn. 7 Sqn

Stirling N3705:MG-F in flight with Luftwaffe *marking and a temporary nose repair.* 7 Sqn

prepare the huge Stirlings for each night's operations. Life could be hard, brutal and short. Fred Mills remembers these days in 1942.

Our skipper had a Labrador dog, which was told to wait at dispersal point until our return from operations. Even in winter, when it was cold, the dog was always there on our return. The ground crews used to bring out the bombs on long trailers and wind them up into the bomb bays, fill the ammunition boxes for the guns, check the engines and fill the petrol tanks. When the tanks were full the petrol used to run over the wings to make sure they were completely full.

Life in the mess was extraordinary during that time. We played cards and sang around the piano and I remember one evening before an operation twenty of us were having a great time singing and next day only five returned.

We used to wear unconventional clothes during operations, such as jerseys and running shoes. We had a compass and escape equipment sewn into our clothes.

Luftwaffe *personnel examining captured Stirling N3705:MG-F.* 7 Sqn

Another view of captured N3705:MG-F in flight. 7 Sqn

During the onslaught of July and August 1942 we used to do two or three operations on consecutive nights. We were given tablets to keep us alert, but when they wore off it was the reverse.

If you missed a clothing parade there would not be another one for a month. I was attending one after a night's operation and I was in line waiting for my turn when I fell to the ground asleep. Somebody picked me up and got my clothes for me and took me to my room. As I didn't close and lock my door while asleep, somebody entered my room and took the clothes I had just received, together with my shoes, which I did not get back.

During that time we had many losses of airmen and aircraft and new faces were arriving all the time. We were losing thirty airmen every operation, which was nearly every night. We had numerous airmen from Australia and Canada

Stirling MG-E (possibly BF335) at Oakington. D. Milne

sent to our station and the mess was turned into a gambling den similar to Las Vegas. The billiard table was used for crap games and other rooms turned into card schools and for backgammon, with money changing hands quickly.

The mess was full of airmen singing 'This Old Shirt of Mine' and some without a stitch on. Mess WAAFs went about their usual jobs pretending not to notice what was going on. Often the officers were invited to come into the sergeants' mess and enjoyed themselves.

The WAAFs on the station were so busy that they didn't have much time for relaxation. They got married to aircrew members and were soon widows. They were often called 'chop girls' and the crews did not mix with them because they were superstitious. Our lives during that time were very precarious and before a raid we used to give instructions who to tell and what to say if we did not return. We got rid of our money and gave things away to friends because the chances of survival were slim.

We had no time to sit and talk for any length as we were needed to do some training or to go somewhere, which was a good thing as it took our minds off operations. Some airmen used to get into a very nervous state and were taken off operations because of 'lack of moral fibre'. They were sent to Uxbridge and stripped of their rank.

Bob Pointer flew his first op with his new captain on 27/28 August. It was a leaflet-dropping sortie to a French target.

We went on our first trip with our new skipper, S/Ldr T.G. Mahaddie. Our first trip was a paper round on 27/28 August, 'Nickels' [leaflets] to Roubaix, plus six 500 pound bombs in case we saw an enemy airfield in use. We dropped our 'Nickels' on target, but brought the bombs back. No airfields lit up. I thought with a bit of luck we might not get another trip before my wedding, but that was not to be.

On the 28/29 August the squadron took part in a raid on Nuremberg, marking the target with great accuracy. Unfortunately the main force crews following up, though reporting good bombing, actually spread their loads over a wide area. The pilot of R9158, F/Sgt Rawdon Hume Middleton, made for Manston, short of fuel, on his return. Unfortunately he overshot the landing and crashed. He would later win the VC, but his crew's performance on this raid left something to be desired. Middleton had briefly been with the squadron in January 1942 but left after a month to join 149 Sqn, returning on 25 August. Due to navigational errors on the raid, he found himself over Munich. Descending to a few hundred feet to strafe the streets, they had insufficient fuel to reach Oakington and made for Manston, where the engines cut due to lack of fuel and he crashed through a group of parked Spitfires, scattering the station medical officers, fire crew and others before coming to rest, minus wings, near the station armoury after bouncing off a Bellman hangar. The aircraft also hit a wooden hut occupied by fifteen sleeping airmen; the Stirling's wheels went between the beds and no one was hurt! The following day the damage was surveyed and an Albacore was found crushed beneath the Stirling, which had also flattened a Spitfire with one of its wheels. Hamish Mahaddie collected them from Manston and gave Middleton the choice of changing his navigator or leaving the squadron. Middleton refused to split the crew and returned to 149 Sqn.

Fuel shortage also caused the loss of BF316:MG-M, which was crash-landed at Boscombe Down by its pilot, F/O Boylson RAAF. Fred Mills was a gunner on this crew.

I assisted the skipper for take-off and took over the front gun position for the purpose of map reading, which I knew something about being a trainee civil engineer previously. We were only at about 12,000 feet crossing the French coast when ack-ack caught us and shells were bursting all around, the smoke filling the front position. We managed to get to the target and lined up for our bombing run when we were caught in a searchlight cone. We managed to manoeuvre out of it and had to do another bombing run over the target area. We were over the target for some time before returning home.

We were short of fuel over the North Sea during our return and had to be diverted to Boscombe Down. There the engines cut out and we dropped down. We bounced six times and then the aircraft caught fire. We got all the crew out, some with injuries, and we hid behind a wall because the aircraft's ammunition was exploding.

The fire engines and ambulance did not arrive for half an hour and after reporting to the control, the duty officer informed group headquarters that he didn't think there would be any survivors. The next day four of us were taken straight back to our station and put on operations the following day, as there was a shortage of crews.

On the night of 1/2 September F/Lt Bennett in MG-J and F/O Malcolm in MG-O took part in a 231 aircraft raid on Saarbrucken. Bombing in clear conditions they dropped a large number of flares, incendiaries and bombs. Unfortunately the target had been misidentified and they actually bombed Saarlouis 13 miles to the north-west. The small town was heavily damaged. F/Lt Bennett took MG-J out again the next night, dropping twenty-three 250 pound incendiaries and a bundle of flares on Karlsruhe. Two hundred aircraft took part in the raid, which was successfully

Oakington MT Section in 1942. via 7 Squadron Association

New Zealand aircrew of 7 Sqn outside a favourite haunt, the Three Tuns Hotel. L to R: Sgt Harry Goddard, Sgt Ron Crabtree, Sgt Don Lamb, Sgt G. Burgess. D. Milne

marked by the Pathfinders. Two hundred fires were estimated to be burning in the city and much damage was caused.

On the night of 4/5 September the target was Bremen. This time 251 aircraft took part and the Pathfinders used several new techniques, splitting their aircraft into three forces. The first of these were the 'illuminators', lighting up the target with white flares, followed by 'visual markers' dropping coloured flares and then 'backers-up' dropping incendiaries onto the coloured flares. P/O Dallinger, flying MG-D, was one of the crews taking part and his bomb aimer, Sgt Crabtree identified the target by the river and docks in the light of flares and fires already started, dropping four 1,900 pound and one 1,000 pound bomb on the city before turning for home. The Pathfinder plan worked well and the target was heavily bombed, causing widespread damage.

Duisburg was raided on 6/7 September and the squadron lost Mk I, W7629:MG-Z captained by F/Lt Bennett. Cloud and haze over the target caused scattered bombing, but Duisburg reported this as its heaviest raid to date with the loss of 114 buildings, another 316 seriously damaged and eighty-six people killed. P/O Watt identified the target by the confluence of the Rhine and Ruhr rivers and dropped his bomb load from 14,000 feet. Twenty minutes later at 0302 hrs P/O Dallenger in MG-D dropped his five 1,900 pounds bombs onto the markers and ten minutes later P/O Kennedy flying MG-M dropped his five 1,900 pounds bombs onto the city through 7/10ths cloud cover onto the already burning fires.

The aircrew of Stirling W7569 of 7 Sqn taken on 3 September 1942. This view shows to good effect the Stirling's huge undecarriage. L to R: ?, Bill Anderson, Ben Dallenger, Ron Crabtree, Don Lamb, Harry Goddard. Don Lamb

Another photo of the crew of Stirling W7569. The rear row is the ground crew who worked all hours maintaining the aircraft. Front row L to R: ?, Bill Anderson, Ben Dallenger, Ron Crabtree, Don Lamb, Harry Goddard. Don Lamb

Pictured by the crew door of Stirling W7569 are L to R: Ron Crabtree, Harry Goddard, Ben Dallenger, Don Lamb, Bill Anderson, ?. Don Lamb

In the weeks before his wedding Bob Pointer had been hoping to avoid any more ops, but on the night of 8/9 September he was sent to Frankfurt. Two hundred and forty-nine aircraft took part in the raid, but the Pathfinders had difficulty in locating the target and most of the bombs fell on the town of Russelsheim, 15 miles away:

We took four 1,900 pound and one 1,000 pound bombs and were flying in BF339:C. We took off at 2040 hrs and went over France to the south of our target, turned port and came into Germany below our target. Turning north towards Frankfurt, there was plenty of activity ahead of us, lots of fires and bombs exploding. Tommy, our navigator, said, 'Hold on. I think some of those fires are fake, carry on a bit further.' This we did and as we dropped our bombs all hell let loose. We had about a dozen shells explode around us, all of them rattling on the fuselage. Searchlights everywhere. Our port engine was hit and feathered over the target and I must admit I sent up a prayer. I didn't think we would get home.

We set course for home and Jock, on testing the fuel gauges, said we had lost some fuel and wouldn't have enough to reach base. The skipper said we would have to land at Manston and when we arrived in their circuit and the skipper called up and asked for a priority landing, flying on three engines and short of fuel, another plane said he was on two engines and got preference. Much to our amazement we saw a Wellington land. We went in after that and another engine cut as we landed. We then did a ground loop and the tail of the plane swung round and went through the fence around the MT yard and wrote off the Manston CO's new car, a camouflaged Humber saloon.

We had to leave BF339 there and came back the next day by train, via London, carrying all our kit. We did stop off at a pub in Oxford Street for a quick half. I think it was called Mooney's. Then on to King's Cross station for a train back to Cambridge, where we were met by transport and were taken back to camp for debriefing.

Between 2300 hrs and midnight the 7 squadron crews arrived over the target. F/Sgt Bishop, on his last operational sortie, in MG-D bombed from 12,000 feet dropping his bombs and bundles of flares onto the target despite an unserviceable intercom system. Bishop, a Canadian from New Mines, Nova Scotia, and by then a P/O, would be awarded the DFC on 2 November. The recommendation for the award reads.

During the time Flight Sergeant Bishop has been captain of an aircraft he has carried out 17 operational sorties against Bremen, Hamburg, Duisburg, Dusseldorf and other heavily defended industrial targets in Germany. Six of these sorties were as a marker in the Pathfinder Force and although he has not volunteered to continue with these duties, on these occasions he made every effort to mark the target as he has previously done to bomb it.

Flight Sergeant Bishop has in all done 31 sorties, comprising 157 hours, thus completing an exceptionally successful operational tour.

The citation echoed the recommendation.

P/O Watt in MG-W bombed a few minutes later, his flares and incendiaries landing in a built-up area near the river. He encountered flak on the way out of the target. W/Cdr Sellick was the captain of MG-Y, bombing at 11,300 feet. He dropped his

Don Lamb, a member of P/O Ben Dallenger's crew, photographed in an Anson during training in Canada. No. 7 Sqn also operated Ansons during 1939. Don Lamb

flares and incendiaries in the light of earlier flares over the bridges crossing the river. Two minutes later F/Lt Barr in MG-M arrived over the target at 11,000 feet and his bomb aimer, P/O Runnicles, dropped his flares and incendiaries to the east of the River Main. Just before midnight F/O Trench arrived over the target in MG-T at 14,000 feet. His bomb aimer, Sgt Thorpe, dropped the Stirling's load of twelve 250 pound incendiaries and twelve bundles of flares onto fires close to the River Main. All of the crews taking part returned safely.

The captain of Stirling W7564, F/O J.P. Trench, pulled off a miraculous landing on the night of 10/11 September. The Stirling had been hit by flak over Maastricht and severely damaged. The port inner engine was out of order and the port outer had been blown completely off the wing. Struggling home on two engines on the starboard side they had almost reached the English coast when the starboard inner engine cut out. Now on only one engine the Stirling was going down and the pilot made a crash landing near Weeley in Essex. Knocked out in the crash, Trench and the wireless operator were pulled clear by the navigator, P/O C.L. Selman. Three of the crew were sitting on top of the cockpit when fire broke out and they jumped down and ran clear. Unknown to them the rear gunner, flight engineer and bomb aimer had gone back into the aircraft to recover the gunner. The Stirling blew up, throwing the rear gunner clear of the aircraft, though he was badly burned. The rear gunner, P/O W.N. Gledding was then pulled clear of the burning wreckage by the mid-upper gunner, F/Sgt Jenner. The two crew members lost in the incident were Sgt Thorpe and Sgt Hallott. Trench was subsequently awarded the DSO, Selman the DFC and Sgt Edwards, the wireless operator, the DFM. Jenner was awarded the George Medal and his citation tells the full story of that dreadful night.

One night in September 1942, Flight Sergeant Jenner was a member of a crew of an aircraft detailed to attack a target at Dusseldorf. The target was bombed successfully, but whilst still over the objective, the aircraft was repeatedly hit by anti-aircraft fire. The port inner propeller came off and shortly afterwards the port outer engine fell out. The petrol tanks were holed in many places during the return journey. The crew displayed coolness and skill, doing all they could to keep the crippled bomber in the air. Shortly after crossing the English coast the aircraft crashed in a field and immediately caught fire. All the crew, with the exception of the rear gunner, managed to extricate themselves. The whole aircraft was soon blazing fiercely. Knowing that the fuel tanks might explode any moment, two sergeants re-entered the aircraft in an attempt to rescue the rear gunner. They went right forward

P/O Ben Dallenger as a leading aircraftman during flying training. D. Milne *to reach the place where they thought he would have been thrown, but a petrol tank exploded and both were killed. Flight Sergeant Jenner, who had seen his two comrades killed and knew that a further petrol tank might explode, then re-entered the burning fuselage. He found the rear gunner who was severely burned and succeeded in removing him to safety. Throughout, this airman displayed extreme courage, fortitude and devotion to duty in keeping with the highest traditions of the Royal Air Force.*

F/Sgt Raoul De Fontenay Jenner was subsequently commissioned and served until 1956.

That same night W7630:MG-M failed to return from Dusseldorf, crashing at Echt in Holland. F/Lt Barr and his crew were killed, with the exception of P/O Cook, who became a prisoner. The navigator on this aircraft was F/O Philip Freberg from Vancouver. Freberg successfully parachuted from the stricken Stirling landing in Holland and evaded capture. He would be awarded a posthumous DFC having been shot down again in January 1943, the citation reading: 'This officer, as navigator, has participated in a number of operational sorties during which he has displayed great determination and a high standard of courage and tenacity.'

P/O William King, from Alton, Ontario, was navigator to P/O Watt in another Stirling on this raid and would be awarded the DFC for his actions.

One night in September 1942, Pilot Officers Watt and King were captain and navigator respectively of an aircraft detailed to attack Dusseldorf. When nearing the target area the aircraft was held by a concentration of searchlights and hit by anti-aircraft fire. The intercommunication was rendered unserviceable and Pilot Officer King was wounded in the leg and stomach. Despite this he bravely continued his duties. His subsequent navigation was of the greatest assistance to Pilot Officer Watt, who succeeded in flying his damaged aircraft back to this country. These officers, both of whom have completed many operational sorties, displayed outstanding devotion to duty in difficult circumstances.

S/Ldr Gilmour in MG-Y also took part, arriving over the target at 2215 hrs and dropping his flares and bombs in a shallow dive from just under 15,000 feet. Fifty minutes later it was the turn of S/Ldr Hamish Mahaddie in MG-O. Loaded up with 8,600 pounds of bombs his bomb aimer let them go over an area of flares and fires. Bob Pointer was in this aircraft, leaving behind his very worried fiancée.

The wife to be was getting a bit worried now. On 10/11 September we were sent out again. Our aircraft being u/s we had to borrow W7581: O-Orange, F/O Malcolm's aircraft. We took the same bomb load as last time. Visibility was good. There was intense searchlights and flak, but nothing untoward happened and we all arrived back safely. The wedding went ahead as planned on 14 September.

A few minutes later P/O Nicholls arrived over Dusseldorf with his bomb load in MG-U, dropping them in a very large concentrated fire. All returned safely.

Four hundred and forty-six aircraft raided Bremen on the night of 13/14 September. This was a heavy raid, which caused damage to the Lloyd dynamo works and the Focke Wulf factory. S/Ldr Gilmour arrived over the target at 0116 hrs and his bomb aimer, Sgt Gough, dropped the load of six 1,000 pound bombs and fourteen bundles of flares through heavy haze onto the target. Almost two hours later P/O

Nicholls was over Bremen at 9,000 feet to drop almost 8,000 pounds of bombs. Bremen would not be attacked again by Bomber Command for another five months.

The following night the port of Wilhelmshaven was attacked by the squadron in a force of 202 bombers. The Pathfinders did a good job of marking the target and P/O Dallenger, flying MG-D, had no trouble identifying the target as he ran in at 13,500 feet to drop 6,000 pounds of bombs. Ten minutes later and slightly higher S/Ldr Gilmour in MG-Y homed in on the flares over the docks and dropped his bombs. Wilhelmshaven reported this as its worst raid to date.

Essen was on the target list again on 16/17 September and the squadron lost W7569, which crashed in the Ijsselmeer in Holland. P/O Dallenger, who had had so little trouble in finding the target the previous night, went down with all his crew. Despite the loss this had been the most successful raid on Essen to date. Though the bombing was scattered, much damage was done to the city and the Krupps works received several hits and damage caused by a crashing bomber loaded with incendiaries. S/Ldr Gilmour was out again in MG-Y over Essen and dropped his load of flares to illuminate the target from 14,000 feet in a shallow dive. He observed that they lit up the bend in the River Ruhr to the south of the city.

W/Cdr C.R. Donaldson DSO DFC took over the squadron on 2 October and that night the crews went to Krefeld, but there was dense haze over the target and the Pathfinders marked late. Bombing was widely dispersed and caused little damage. Some crews had a difficult time finding the target and P/O Barron in MG-C reported that he believed he had dropped his bombs on Krefeld using flares, Gee and the built-up area to identify it. Likewise, F/Lt Smith in MG-S reported that the target was not recognized but he still dropped his bombs. F/O Stickell had the same difficulties and his flares and incendiaries were dropped on the target believed to be Krefeld. In

Ground crew working on Stirling W7569:MG-D. D. Milne

Stirling W7569:MG-D being loaded with bombs for an operation. D. Milne

November Stickell would be awarded the BEM. The recommendation, written in September when he was a P/O reads:

> *Pilot Officer Stickell has done 25 major operational sorties, 23 of which have been as captain of Stirling aircraft. In all these attacks against Cologne, Essen, Hamburg, Bremen and other heavily defended targets in Germany, his captaincy and determination have been of the highest order.*
>
> *Pilot Officer Stickell has recently joined the Pathfinder Force and has carried out seven attacks as a marker and the fact that he has on many occasions brought back photographs of the target has enabled him to qualify as a marker. This officer's personal example has been an inspiration to the rest of the crew.*

Air Cdre Bennett, Air Officer Commanding (AOC) 8 Group, added his comments:

> *This officer was the first member of Bomber Command to be awarded the Pathfinder Force Badge – on the conclusive evidence of his results and after an exacting test. His determination in attack and his skill are proved by the results he obtains. I recommend him most strongly for the non-immediate award of the DFC.*

The award would be promulgated in November 1942.

Fred Mills went on this operation with the squadron commander and carried out air-to-sea firing and practice bombing during the following week. After returning from an operation, when he was fast asleep in bed, he had a rude awakening on the day the Duke of Kent came to inspect the squadron.

A bomb being loaded into the bomb bay of Stirling W7569:MG-D. D. Milne

Someone shook me to say, 'Get dressed in all operational flying gear and report to Hangar No. 1 for inspection by the Duke of Kent.' We knew an important person was due at the station some time because airmen were all day trying to obliterate a slogan written in large letters over the officers' mess – 'Russia starves as Britain bullshits.' Everything was spick and span on the station – roads swept, paper collected, grass cut and all the food prepared ready to be heated in the cookhouse.

In the hangar nearly everyone was on parade waiting for His Royal Highness and he eventually arrived. He walked down the lines of airmen and occasionally

The ground crew complete the servicing of Stirling W7569:MG-D whilst the crew waits.
D. Milne

stopped to talk to some who were previously picked out. Before dispersing the Station Commander said a few words and we all had tasks to perform before off duty.

There was a raid on Aachen on 5th/6th October and then Osnabruck on the 6th/7th. This raid turned out to be more successful. The Pathfinders found and marked the Dummersee, a large lake to the north-east of the target, which was used as the run-in point for the bombers. Osnabruck was then marked accurately and the bombing was concentrated, falling mostly in the central and southern areas of the town. Damage was heavy. Target illuminators would arrive at intervals over the target to keep it lit up for the Main Force crews. One of these was P/O Barron in MG-G. He ran in from the Dummersee in a shallow dive from 14,000 feet down to 10,000 feet in 9/10ths cloud cover to drop his flares on ETA. F/Lt Smith in MG-S arrived over the target a few minutes later dropping his bombs onto red fires seen in the area on ETA. F/O Brady's bomb aimer, P/O Winder, dropped their load of bombs from Stirling MG-L from 14,000 feet onto a target they believed to be Osnabruck, and the recently promoted W/Cdr Gilmour arrived a short while later in MG-Y to drop his flares north of the Workum district. The crews all returned safely.

Among the first aircraft over Cologne on the night of 15/16 October was that flown by F/Lt Wicketts. His bomb aimer, Sgt Jarvis, thought he had dropped the flares from MG-U onto the southern end of the city close to the river. In fact, he had dropped them on Bonn. Ten minutes later Sgt Ness, bomb aimer in MG-K, dropped his load of flares also over Bonn. Many of the Pathfinders were decoyed by a dummy target using a large decoy fire site in the Bonn area. F/Lt Malcolm, another Pathfinder, was over the target in MG-S five minutes later, just one minute after the flares began to drop and he dropped his flares on ETA, having arrived over what he though was Cologne, by dead reckoning. In quick succession F/Lt Trench in MG-T, S/Ldr Mahaddie in MG-C, W/Cdr Donaldson in MG-Y and F/Lt Christie all dropped flares followed by two Pathfinders under training, Sgt Terry in MG-M and P/O Brady in MG-A, both dropping bombs onto the target. The decoy site received most of the bombs and Cologne was only slightly damaged. A squadron member recalls the raid.

Aircraft B-Baker, with a new crew except for the W/Op, found itself the only aircraft over Cologne – the target. The rest of Bomber Command was over Bonn. There had been wind changes, which apparently had gone unnoticed, except by the navigator of B-Baker. The aircraft was not carrying a bomb aimer as he had gone sick just before take-off, so the navigator did the bomb aiming and despite the fact that the aircraft was boxed by flak carried on with his run until hit in the face. The bombs were jettisoned live and by this time the Stirling had lost three engines. The aircraft limped home, steering on bearings received by the W/Op. It reached the English coast and was directed to Wattisham after a 'Darkie' broadcast received by Martlesham Heath. The crew received a group citation. The navigator did not fly again.

The bombers were not just at risk from enemy flak and fighters, as was proved on the 21st when the crew of BF390:MG-A was returning from mining the Nectarines area off the Friesians. Coasting in 30 miles south of their intended track they failed to identify themselves with the correct colours of the day and were fired upon by anti-aircraft batteries at Great Yarmouth and shot down. F/O N.S. Brady and his crew were all killed.

Italy felt the weight of a Bomber Command attack on the night of 22/23 October when 112 Lancasters of No. 5 Group attacked Genoa, led by the Pathfinders. No. 7 Sqn dispatched stirlings loaded with incendiaries to mark the target for the force. The marking was described as prompt and accurate and Genoa suffered heavy damage, including the loss of several museums, churches and the Palazzo Ducale. The attack had a severe effect on the morale of the population. The raid had been in support of the Eighth Army offensive at El Alamein and the next night the Stirlings were back again, leading 111 other bombers. Eleven were sent out but only six reached the target, three others attacking Turin and one Savona. In fact due to total cloud cover the weight of the raid fell on Savona, 30 miles along the coast.

The first person from the squadron to bomb Genoa was F/Lt Smith in MG-S, arriving over the target at 2205 hrs. His bomb aimer, Sgt Fee, dropped the load of 1,080 incendiaries onto the built-up area. Twenty minutes later F/Lt Trench in MG-T arrived over the target at 8,000 feet to drop his load of flares and bombs. Minutes after his bombs hit the target the next of the squadron's Stirlings, MG-L flown by F/Sgt Trottman arrived and, finding a gap in the cloud cover over the harbour, dropped its incendiaries, which landed east of the inner harbour. Last over Genoa was F/O Donaldson in MG-Y. He dropped a mix of flares and bombs onto the north-western area of the city. F/Lt Stickell in MG-K failed to reach Genoa and bombed Savona instead, and F/Lt Watt took his load of bombs to Turin.

On the night of 24/25 October it was the turn of Milan. The Stirlings battled through low cloud and heavy icing to cross the Alps and reach the target. The storms *en route* scattered the force and some wandered into Swiss airspace, where they had warning shots fired at them by the anti-aircraft guns. Bombing at Milan was widely scattered and only thirty-nine aircraft out of a force of seventy-one claim to have bombed the target. Among those bombing was F/Lt Barron, who dropped his bombs through a gap in the clouds from Stirling MG-C.

Gordon Paterson took part in several of the Italian raids during this period.

We did seven or eight trips to Italy – Turin, Genoa and Milan. Very interesting! We could go low level or high level. We decided to go low level. At the briefing they said anything moving was legitimate. However, by the time we reached our target the first time both gunners had used up all their ammunition. So it was quite a dicey trip home. It was also damned cold trying to get over the Alps – no heat, no height. We had to go through between the peaks. We got quite a surprise when an Italian biplane attacked us, made a few holes, then disappeared.

Another squadron member also recalls the operations to Turin and Milan during this period.

The raids to Turin and Milan were really a doddle, except for the crossing of France and the length of the trip. These trips were made so that the moon was up when you reached the target. The usual formula was to sneak through the Swiss Alps, Mont Blanc looking very lovely with its mantle of snow, the neutral Swiss firing a few warning shots miles away from you and then to Turin or Milan, where the flak was so spasmodic we swore that the Italians were sitting in air raid shelters, with a large piece of string attached to their guns. Then one brave lad would dash out and push a round up the spout, dash back again and the string would be pulled. The night fighters were the same. We saw many biplanes buzzing around, but not one ever attacked any aircraft in sight. We used to bet they were giving fantastic commentaries to their controllers.

Stirling W7620:MG-L set out to mine the waters off the Friesian islands on 6/7 November and did not return. The bombers on these missions were sent out in small numbers, often alone, and the requirement to lay the mines accurately, as specified by the Admiralty, meant that the aircraft often had to remain in the target area for a long time. Consequently they were at greater risk of being shot down by flak or intercepted by night fighters. F/Sgt D.J. Trottman and his crew died on this mission.

Fred Mills's crew was reunited in November after being treated for the wounds received on the Nuremberg raid. On the night of 7/8 November they went to Genoa. Once again Fred Mills manned his guns. 'We bombed the centre of the target, the city. The searchlights and flak were inaccurate and most Italians left their posts and went to the hills. On the way back along the French coast the German flak was heavy and accurate.'

The first crew from the squadron over Genoa that night was that captained by F/Lt Barron, in MG-G. In excellent visibility they bombed the docks and the railway station. Twenty minutes later it was the turn of S/Ldr Mahaddie to deliver a load of flares and bombs from MG-C followed by F/Lt Heywood in MG-J, dropping 4,500 pounds of bombs onto the city. P/O Boylson in MG-B dropped 4,500 pounds a few minutes later and the last two over the target, F/Lt Nicholls in MG-U and Sgt Young in MG-N both dropped their bombs at 2152 hrs in clear conditions before turning for home.

On 9/10 November 1942 three Stirling's, N3764:MG-J, R9169:MG-Y and BF387:MG-U, were lost during a raid on Hamburg. Two hundred and thirteen aircraft set out but the crews encountered cloud and icing and stronger than forecast winds, which caused widespread bombing of a poorly marked target. MG-Y was flown by Sgt H.A. Harris. F/Lt W. Nicholls and his crew were all lost in MG-U. Bob Pointer recalls the loss of his friend Jimmy Raven in MG-J.

My pal Jimmy Raven flew with his own crew, skippered by F/Lt Peter Heywood DFC, a very experienced crew, well liked by everyone on the station. My last skipper, Hamish Mahaddie, did his first three ops with them as second pilot when he first came to the squadron. On 9 November 1942 we all set out for a raid on Hamburg at 1710 hrs, with a full load of marker flares. It was 10/10ths cloud over the target; heavy flak and the searchlights lit up the clouds beneath us making us very visible from above.

We carried out our duty and came home. Unfortunately we lost three aircraft that night; U, Y and J, the last being the aircraft of Peter Heywood – they were all killed. We never found out how but it looked like they collided over the target. It was very lonely in room 35 of the sergeants' mess after that. I sent his personal items to his parents with my condolences. It was never quite the same after that.

Gordon Paterson's crew went to Hamburg several times.

On one of our trips to Hamburg we were attacked by a Bf110. I was able to bomb and instructed Jock Ross to release our photoflash – but no reply! I finally went back and found Jock, photo flash still in, out cold. He had been hit by a round in the head from our attacker. We sure dumped the photoflash in a hurry. It was more of a flesh wound in the head. Jock came to and there was a lot of blood, however we made it back to base OK.

Bomber Command made several forays into Italian territory during November 1942. Bob Pointer recalls raiding Genoa on the night of the 13th/14th.

Over the Alps with the squadron CO, W/Cdr Donaldson, as pilot, with a mixed load of bombs and marker flares. The weather was kind and we bombed the aiming point. Two nights later we went to the same target, this time with Hamish as skipper. Once again with a mixed bomb load, once again the weather was kind and the target was blitzed. Both trips took around nine hours each. Then the bad weather set in and we had two weeks stand down. Things seemed too quiet – a trip to Cambridge was called for.

So we all set out for town, air and ground crews. We finished up at the Eagle public house. A good time was had by all, Hamish tucked two of his S/Ldr's rings up his sleeve so he looked like a flying officer.

In the meantime the weather closed in on us, a real pea-souper. Hamish got on the phone to Oakington because the local buses had been withdrawn and, lo and behold, a Dodge crew bus arrived on the scene. We all piled in and set off for camp, a very slow job, it meant someone having to get out and walk in front of the bus for most of the way, which they all did in turn. Most of the 'Bods' were the worse for wear. As we passed the officer's mess Hamish, Tommy, Archie and Len got off the bus and Hamish said to me, 'Get a couple of shillings each off

The crew and ground crew of Stirling N3764:MG-J with a scoreboard showing twenty-one operations. 7 Sqn

them to pay the driver for fetching us back.' I said, 'OK, Skipper', but as the bus stopped by the H blocks they all made a dash for it, so I got nothing from them, but I heard no more about it.

Nine Stirlings went to Genoa again on the night of 15/16 November. The bombing was accurate and no aircraft were lost.

Turin was the target on 20/21 November. Three of the squadron's Stirlings were damaged on this sortie. S/Ldr Crebbin's aircraft, MG-S, was damaged by flak hits to the bomb bay, F/O Duro in MG-G had his starboard elevator almost shot off and his escape hatch blown in by flak and P/O Boylson had the constant speed unit of his starboard outer engine blown off.

On the 28th/29th the squadron went back to Turin, this time with thirteen Stirlings. Two hundred and twenty-eight aircraft took part, some of them bombing before the Pathfinders. It was on this raid that F/Sgt R.H. Middleton of 149 Sqn won his VC. Hamish Mahaddie and Bob Pointer took part.

Our next trip was supposed to be to Stettin on 27/28 November but the met forecast was very bad. We were recalled to base, so after we had jettisoned our bombs in the sea, we landed OK. The next night our target was Turin. All went well, we bombed our target and got back OK – Stirling BF358:C was certainly a lucky aircraft for us.

The next night the squadron went back a third time to Turin to strike at the Fiat works. Once again bad weather and heavy icing were encountered and only eighteen aircraft are known to have definitely crossed the Alps to bomb the target. Stirling R9150:MG-O failed to return. Nothing was heard after take-off from F/Lt R.M. Smith's crew and the only survivors were Sgt M.G. Low and Sgt R.E. Fee.

Fred Mills's crew went to Turin several times.

The next trip was to Turin and there was no cloud cover over the target area, just a slight haze. There were no searchlights but considerable light flak and tracer. We were hoping to hit the Fiat works, but did not do so. On the return we sighted a fighter above us over the Alps but it turned away.

Further trips to Turin showed that the defences had been increased and were certainly more accurate, because the ack-ack guns and searchlights had been taken over by the Germans. We were still able to pinpoint our targets and cause considerable damage to the city and Fiat works. Unfortunately the cathedral was also damaged.

Returning from Italy over the Alps did not cause any problems as the aircraft was lighter, having released the bombs and thus able to get height. Going over the Alps to the target was much more difficult as Mont Blanc was higher than we could reach and therefore we had to pass between mountains. If there was any trouble with the engines we were very vulnerable.

Fred Mills went on to complete two tours with the squadron and ended up as an air gunnery leader, commissioned as a flight lieutenant with the DFM. After the war he went into the airfield construction industry.

Bob Pointer went to Frankfurt along with 111 other bombers on the night of 2/3 December. The target was covered in thick haze and the Pathfinders could not find the city. Most of the bombs fell in open country to the south west of the city.

This was my forty-second operation – three more to go before I was finished. We took off for Frankfurt at 0135 hrs with a load of twenty-three 250 pound incendiary bombs. The reception here was different to Italy, intense searchlights, very heavy flak and visibility was bad. Much damage was done to the fuselage, wings and tailplane, caused by approximately twelve shell bursts that really rattled us. Got back to base safely. It took us six hours, twenty-five minutes flying time. BF358:C had to go in for repairs. (It was lost with another crew on 12 December on a trip to Munich.)

December saw the loss of Stirling R9259:MG-J, piloted by F/Lt W.H. Arnott, on a raid on cloud-covered Mannheim on the 6th/7th. Nothing was heard from this crew after take-off. It was later discovered that three men, P/O H.F. Perrott, Sgt H.G. Wilson and Sgt J. Simmons, had been killed. They were the victims of a night fighter flown by Ofw Fritz Shellwat of 5/NJG 1, who shot them down at Saunveniere in Belgium. The rear gunner, Sgt W. McLean, completed a report on their fate.

The Stirling took off from Oakington at 1730 hrs to attack Mannheim. The aircraft was lost approximately 40 miles east of Gembloux, Belgium. The inner port engine was hit and the aircraft was on fire. Pilot was F/Lt Arnott.

The target area was reached without incident, but as they went in to drop their bombs at 10,000 feet, the aircraft was hit by flak. The rear turret was rendered u/s and the rear gunner believed that the electrical connections must have been damaged. He, however, took all necessary steps to render the turret manually serviceable so that it could be hand rotated and the guns elevated or depressed. At the same time he requested the mid-upper gunner to keep a sharp lookout on the beams. As it turned out he had no occasion to use his guns.

The bombs were dropped at approximately 2000 hrs from between 8,000 and 10,000 feet and the aircraft turned for home, regaining height up to 10,000 feet. After flying for about three-quarters of an hour there was a sudden explosion underneath the front portion of the aircraft and the rear gunner believes that they were attacked by a night fighter from below, although he did not actually see the same.

The port inner engine was hit and caught fire and the pilot went into a dive in order to make the very best use of the fire extinguisher. However, almost immediately there was an explosion and the Captain ordered the crew to abandon the aircraft. The rear gunner got out of his turret into the after part of the fuselage with the aid of a torch, which he fortunately carried, was able to clip on his parachute quickly, pull the handle on the jettisonable door and baled out. This he states took him less than thirty seconds and he thought that the rest of the crew did not have much chance as the aircraft immediately went into a steep dive and crashed about a mile away.

He himself was only about halfway down when he saw the aircraft explode on the ground and start to burn fiercely. Sgt McLean came down safely in a ploughed field. He used his compass and started to bury his parachute harness, Mae West, and Irvine trousers at intervals of 150 yards in an easterly direction. As soon as he had done this he turned west and got away as quickly as possible.

The Stirlings went to Italy again on the 12th; attacking Turin for the third time in four nights. BF379:MG-D, piloted by F/Lt W.T. Christie failed to return from this raid. Six of the eight-man crew became prisoners.

On the 22nd R9262:MG-A, W7632:MG-N and BF358:MG-C all failed to return from Munich. MG-A was flown by F/O H. Duro and all the crew were killed except Sgt P.G.E. Ross, who survived to become a POW. The captain of MG-N, P/O J. Davies and all of the crew died, as did F/Sgt J.K.P. Rumboll and his crew in MG-C. This raid was a costly failure for the squadron, as almost all of the bombs dropped by the bomber force fell in open countryside, possibly due to a decoy.

By December twelve of the squadron aircraft had been equipped with H2S bombing radar, which was cleared for use over occupied territory in January 1943. Despite the continuing improvements reaching the squadron – Stirling Mk IIIs, Oboe and H2S – it had been a difficult year, particularly the winter months, with high losses, struggling against the flak, the fighters and the weather. (Oboe was a blind bombing aid, which could guide one aircraft at a time to accurately mark the target for the rest of the bomber force. It had a range of 300 miles and was first used on the night of 20/21 December 1942 by Mosquitoes of 109 Sqn.) The difficulties would persist into the early months of 1943 but a new aircraft was on the horizon and better days were on the way.

T.J. 'Jock' Elliot was an air gunner in Colin Hughes's crew and recalls the Pathfinder training they received on joining the squadron from No. 15 Sqn and also the raid on Munich on 21/22 December 1942.

Whilst I was on a ground-to-air training exercise the tail of the Stirling we were flying vibrated so violently that I became convinced the plane was not safe and

Prime Minister Winston Churchill watches early Stirling Mk I N3641:MG-D (note lack of mid-upper turret) take off. This was air gunner 'Jock' Elliot's aircraft. MG-D was later passed to No. 26 Sqn Conversion Flight. T.J. Elliot

Rear Gunner T.J. 'Jock' Elliot's crew at Oakington. L to R: Alec Perkins (flight engineer), ?, Tom Cox (mid-upper gunner), Colin Hughes (pilot), Gerry Boreham (navigator), Jock Elliot (rear gunner), Peter Brown (bomb aimer). P. Brown via T.J. Elliot

on returning to base refused to fly in it. The following day the plane was fully checked out and nothing found amiss. A test flight was then undertaken with the engineer officer, airframe riggers, the sergeant in charge of ground crew with our pilot, Wally Hood RNZAF, at the controls. This Stirling was last seen coming out of cloud at 4,000 feet diving vertically into the ground. This left our experienced crew without a pilot.

We were then posted to No. 1657 Con Flt, where we crewed up with Colin Hughes DFC and Gerry Boreham DFC on 28 November 1942. Colin flew solo after one and a half hours. Night-flying tests followed, cross-country flights and some circuits and bumps at night until 20 December 1942. Pre-ops night-flying test was 21 December. It was Colin who suggested we apply for posting to Pathfinder Force. We all agreed. On acceptance we were posted to 7 Squadron stationed at Oakington.

At the time no specific training was given but we had two very experienced navigators in our crew – Gerry Boreham and Peter Brown – and I had been operational on night fighters. After NFTs etc. we were given Stirling R9623/G, equipped with H2S. We then did various day and night altitude flights to iron out bugs and to give the navigators training and experience with H2S under different conditions.

Our first operational trip was to Munich on 21/22 December 1942. We used strings of standard 4 inch parachute flares to illuminate the target and got a successful photo of our aiming point – a rose garden. I shot down two fighter Me109s and an Me110 that night on the way home.

CHAPTER FOUR
JANUARY–DECEMBER 1943

Flight engineer Fred Fray and his captain, Clarence Ince, joined the squadron from No. 1651 HCU on 2 January. Apart from Ince, who had been injured during their tour with No. 214 Sqn, the rest of the crew had been instructors on the HCU. Now joining the Pathfinders they went through a settling in period learning the Pathfinder techniques before commencing operations. Fred Fray's first operation was one of two raids carried out against the French port of Lorient in the middle of January. The first was on 14/15 January and was carried out by 122 aircraft. It was the first raid by the newly operational Canadian No. 6 Group. Although the marking was accurate the bombing by the Main Force was described as 'wild'. The following night Fray was back over Lorient and this time the bombing was better. Fray's crew had to wait until early February for its next operation.

On 30/31 January 148 aircraft attacked Hamburg in the first H2S attack of the war. H2S was not a success on this night, though it would prove its worth later in the war. The bombing was scattered and five Lancasters were shot down. Bob Pointer flew on this raid in a new aircraft, replacing the one damaged on the 2/3 December raid on Frankfurt.

We changed our aircraft after this for special training. Our new plane was R9273/G:C [The G after the serial indicated that the plane was to be guarded at all times – this was due to the still secret H2S installation]. The skipper was awarded his firs 'gong', the AFC. We put in nearly a month of special training, both day and night flying, then on 30/31 January, with the skipper now sporting a DSO and DFC, plus the Czech MC, we set out at 0035 hrs to have a go at Hamburg with the new H2S set. The equipment went u/s over the Zuider Zee and we returned to base. Other aircraft from the squadron had also returned for the same reason.

Ernest Davenport was a bomb aimer newly arrived at Oakington and was allocated to the crew of F/Lt Ince. He recalls his arrival and his first impressions of Oakington.

I joined 7 Sqn at Oakington on 1 February 1943, having been delivered to the end of the runway with my kitbag from the Wellington aircraft, which ferried me over from Marham where I had attended a training course attached to No. 1483 Bombing and Gunnery Flight. I picked up my bag, walked to the perimeter track and hitched a ride with a kindly WAAF who was going by in a 15 hundredweight van, to squadron HQ.

I found the adjutant, who took me in to meet my flight commander to be, W/Cdr T.G. Mahaddie DFC, DSO, AFC. The Wingco greeted me with, I thought, a certain reserve, told me that in being posted to 7 Sqn and to his flight I was being accorded a privilege not bestowed on many and that if I did not measure up I would be on my way back from whence I came very quickly. He also said that he would do his best to get me on an 'op' as soon as he possibly could, as if this was a favour I was desperate for.

Oakington was a permanent RAF station built in peacetime and suitably equipped for its purpose. The Commanding Officer of the station at that time was G/Capt Fresson. Oakington was shared with a meteorological flight consisting of three or four unarmed Mosquitoes, which went out several times a day to bring back the latest weather information from enemy territory but was otherwise 'owned' by 7 Sqn. The Commanding Officer of 7 Sqn when I joined was W/Cdr C.R. Donaldson DSO, DFC and he was succeeded in May 1943 by W/Cdr Burnell.

The living quarters at Oakington were mostly brick structures and they were well planned and comfortable. I was allocated a room shared with one other in the sergeants' mess and when I compared my lot with that of some of my RAF friends who had trained with me and who were now living in corrugated iron Nissen huts on muddy temporary wartime airfields in the bitterly cold winter weather, I thought myself fortunate. I am sure that morale was adversely affected by the conditions in which some personnel had to live. One incongruity was that I shared a room in the mess with a sergeant who was ground staff and he was not issued with sheets for his bed. Sheets were for aircrew only. I found it most embarrassing that I had sheets put on my bed and he did not. Also, on the tables in the dining room there were halibut oil capsules for aircrew only. Of course, pre-operations meals, of 'luxury' foods like bacon and eggs were for aircrew only and this was perhaps understandable in the severe rationing situation of the time.

Soon after my arrival I was introduced to my captain of my crew, F/Lt C.D. Ince DFC and crew members F/O Winfield, F/Sgt Fray, Sgt Stokes, P/O Collings and Sgt Alcock. F/Lt Ince and F/Sgt Fray had done a tour of ops together with 218 Sqn but we were otherwise not known to each other. After a briefing where we were told that the Oakington radio callsign was 'Judgement' and that we were 'Baxter' aircraft, we were given a temporary allocation of a Stirling Mk I, issued with bikes to get us to the dispersal, such was the state of transport facilities (these were ladies' bikes and, I found later, had been taken away from the WAAFs who had originally been issued with them, to their resentment) and on 3 February took off on our first flight together as part of our familiarization and training on the then secret H2S radar blind bombing device (and also for some of us our first flight in a Stirling). The secret of the existence of H2S was then so carefully guarded that only pilot, navigator and bomb aimer in the crew were told about it and should an H2S-equipped aircraft land away from its home base the aircraft captain was authorized to demand that an armed guard be placed outside the aircraft with orders to permit nobody to approach. The H2S equipment was fitted with explosive charges and a switch to electrically detonate the explosives if the aircraft was likely to fall into enemy hands.

The bombers went to Cologne on 2/3 February. One hundred and sixty-one aircraft took part and five were lost. The markers were dropped by Oboe-equipped Mosquitoes and H2S-equipped heavy bombers, but the bombing was scattered. Hamish Mahaddie's crew was lucky to return, as Bob Pointer recalls.

We did an air test on 1 February and on the 2nd we took off on what was to be a very eventful trip. This was my forty-fifth operation, after which aircrew members on a Pathfinder squadron were rested. It was therefore with a little

Stirling Mk I R9237/G:MG-C. This Stirling became known a 'C for Colander' and the photo shows the damage inflicted on the starboard side by flak and an Me110 on the bombing run over Cologne on the night of 2 February 1943. R.C. Pointer

trepidation that I approached this evening's trip. For reasons best known to themselves, the powers that be decided that, because of the lack of height attained by the Stirling over the target, all armour plating, except that shielding the pilot and the flare chute, should be removed. This included the rather large piece behind the wireless operator, which protected him and the radio equipment, but also the small piece that formed the seat of the mid-upper turret, which was replaced by a canvas sling.

It was a cold but dry February afternoon with some cloud as we trooped into the Ops Room for the briefing. The Station Commander welcomed us as usual and gave us the news that tonight's target was Cologne. There on the large map behind him was the black tape with its doglegs to the target and back. The Met officer with his usual – 'Some cloud cover en route, but clearing over the target', then the instructions from the various leaders.

We gathered our flying rations, which contained a can of orange juice, a small bar of chocolate, a small packet of plain biscuits and a few barley sugar sweets, then the NCOs amongst us made our way to the YMCA hut, where the people in charge always filled our flasks. It tasted better than the coffee they dished up in the sergeants' mess!

From there we went to the crew room in the hangar to get kitted up in electrically wired inner suit and the leather outer suit, Mae West and parachute harness, picked up our parachutes and boarded the crew bus to take us to Stirling

A view of the damage to the H2S radome and the starboard fuselage. The ground crew found 174 shell holes. R9237/G was sent to Cambridge for repairs and was transferred to a conversion flight, where it swung on landing at Stradishall, its port wing hitting a hut on 9 May 1944. It was then written off. R.C. Pointer

C-Charlie, standing in line on the perimeter track at the south-western end of the main runway.

They were certainly a magnificent sight: a dozen large aircraft in a curve around the edge of the airfield. A small knot of men clustered about each giant Stirling, quite subdued talk coming from them as they completed their various tasks. We climbed aboard and stowed our chutes and rations in their respective places. Next we checked our own equipment, in my case cocking my guns a couple of times to make sure they worked smoothly. The rear gunner fired a short burst into the ground at the rear of the aircraft.

With everything looking OK we left the aircraft for a last stretch and, if necessary, relieved our bladders under the tailplane, as was our usual practice. I gave my pack of biscuits to the flight mechanic (superstition) and we then got back on board. One by one the Hercules engines roared into life, the aircraft now belonged to the skipper and the engineer. The rest of us tended to our own duties, for my part the testing of the turret and the gun-release mechanism, with the guns on safe. The skipper called each position over the intercom in turn and we were ready to take our place on the end of the runway. It was our turn next. A green light from the Aldis lamp and we were away. Bags of chat between the skipper and Jock, the engineer – rich mixture, flaps, full power. The undercarriage up, course setting from the navigator, we were off – time 1915 hrs.

This was only our second trip with H2S equipment on board, the first being two nights earlier on a raid on Hamburg. The equipment went u/s over the Zuider Zee and the mission was aborted. This time, however, all appeared OK. As we climbed over the English countryside I kept thinking – this is my last trip.

Some of the cannon shells from the Me110 attack went right through the aircraft just missing bomb aimer P/O 'Jock' Luton, who was at his station waiting for the aiming point photograph to be taken. R.C. Pointer

Damage to the port side of R9273/G on return from Cologne on the night of 2 February 1943.
R.C. Pointer

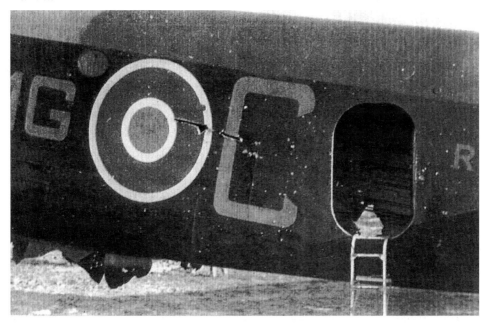

I hoped everything was going to be OK. My mind went back to the other crews I had flown with since joining the squadron in October 1941, some of whom had completed their tour of ops and more who had not made it. Half of me was sorry to be leaving this close-knit crew of ours and the other half glad I was nearly there. I was asked many years later, 'Did you ever carry a luck charm?' My first reaction was to say no, but I suddenly remembered the rabbit's foot I wouldn't fly without. My mother had sent it to me. That went on every trip.

We were over the North Sea by then. Eyes were accustomed to the darkness and from Alec, the rear gunner, a request to test the guns. On the affirmative we both gave a short burst, we were on the alert from then on. More thoughts as we flew out over the sea. I wondered how Joan, my wife, was this evening. She was five months pregnant and living with my parents in north Buckinghamshire. Maybe I'd get some leave after this op to see her.

Enemy coast ahead, there were a few searchlights sweeping the night sky and the occasional flak burst. As we were among the first aircraft in the bomber stream there was not a lot of opposition at first, but it got heavier as we crossed the coast. A new heading from the navigator. The skipper turned to the new course and started a gentle weave, there was a certain amount of cloud cover, for which we were thankful. We had dodged the searchlights so far; others were not so lucky and were having a hectic time. The navigator gave the final course correction to take us into the target. As we approached, some of the early birds were already there, the flak and searchlights had increased and the cloud cover decreased, proving the met officer correct. The skipper increased his weaving and the bomb aimer, Len, left his front turret ready to drop our marker flares and bombs. In the mid-upper turret I had now to cover the front of the aircraft as well, doing a 360-degree search for enemy night fighters.

The bomb aimer now gave his instructions to the skipper and we were flying straight and level with the target coming up in the bombsight. Bomb doors open – with a left, left, steady, right, steady – bombs gone.

Our wireless operator, Archie Bywater, wasn't flying with us that evening. We had F/O I.J. 'Eddy' Edwards DFM flying with us instead. We had come out of cloud and were approaching the target on a straight and level run. It was one minute to nine o'clock. Eddy was tuning in to the BBC to get the news. We had just dropped our load of target markers, and then there was an almighty explosion as a flak shell burst on our starboard side, which blew two holes in our side. At the same time a Bf110 came in from astern and gave us a long burst of cannon fire. There was the sound of cannon shells ripping through the fuselage and the smell of burnt cordite filled the plane. This put both our turrets out of action. The hydraulic pipes giving me power had been shot through. I tried to speak over the intercom but this was dead also. I felt a sharp pain in my right buttock, as if a knife had been stuck in me. My first thought was – this is it. So much for the canvas seat.

Alec, the rear gunner, managed to fire a single gun manually and claimed he could have hit the enemy. In any case it turned away, putting on green and white wing tip lights. Going into the wireless cabin I found that Eddy, our wireless op for the night, had been injured. A cannon shell had ripped open the sleeve of his flying jacket and it took off Eddy's two middle fingers from his right hand and blew our radio set up. There was a first-aid pad on by then and I gave him a shot of morphine and put a tourniquet on it. By then another member of the crew came back and relieved me. It also knocked out our intercom and severely damaged the aileron controls amidships. We were flying at 18,000 feet at the time. The aircraft went into a dive and my first reaction was to get out and we lost 9,000 feet before the skipper gained control by juggling the engine throttles. The inside of the aircraft glowed like a Christmas tree, there were green spots everywhere. I presumed them to be some sort of phosphorus. As the aircraft had come to a more even keel I went towards the rear turret to see if Alec was OK, he appeared to be moving his turret by hand, so I assumed he wasn't injured.

Looking forward I could see several large holes in the starboard side, then I noticed a torch being flashed amidships. Making my way towards this light I found the engineer at work repairing the aileron controls with pieces of wire he had conjured up from somewhere. The flight engineer managed to join the controls together and without a word of command the navigator and the skipper got us back to base. Besides the damage already done the special equipment was all smashed and the rear wheels were punctured. I then went back to my turret and kept watch, trying to work my guns manually, which proved to be next to impossible. Luckily we were not attacked again. Meanwhile the skipper was fighting the aircraft. Having the aileron controls badly mangled by the cannon shells he could only fly the aircraft by varying power of the engines. Jock, our engineer, clambering in the wing root with his pieces of wire, the skipper managed to regain partial control on C-Charlie and set course for home.

With all special equipment u/s, Tommy, our navigator, guided us with the astro-compass and did such good work that we broke cloud over Waterbeach, just 5 miles from base, on our home circuit. Never was I so pleased to see the homing searchlight that invariably shone over Oakington. By word of mouth we received orders to take up crash positions and a red distress cartridge was fired. Alec Clift and I sat with our backs to the bulkhead, facing aft and just before touchdown put our hands behind our heads. My hands felt wet and sticky, having banged my head a few times during the return flight. I wondered what on earth had happened.

The skipper made a very good landing and the emergency crews raced to us as we taxied to a halt. Alec shone his torch on my hands and head. The sticky liquid, although red in colour, turned out to be tomato juice. It had dripped from the dinghy pack stowed above my head, which had been punctured by the shrapnel.

As soon as we had rolled to a stop and climbed down, the first thing I did was to kiss the ground. The forty-fifth op was over. The injured W/Op was taken away in an ambulance, the rest of us were taken for debriefing. When I reported the sharp pain in my rear the Medical Officer had my trousers down. I was given an injection and shipped off to Ely hospital for X-rays. It was found that a small piece of shrapnel was imbedded in my right buttock, but it was left there and I was told it would work itself out; to this day it has never done so.

In the cold light of day the aircraft looked a sorry mess. The H2S cupola and scanning gear had been shot away and the ground crew told the skipper that there were 174 cannon shell hits on the fuselage and wings. One of the rear wheels was punctured and there were one or two large holes from a flak burst. I still have in my possession a 20 mm cannon shell that buried itself in the skipper's *seat parachute – Hamish was a very lucky man that night, as indeed we all were. It was not my last trip, however. On 8 February the original crew flew in Stirling BK610:V-Victor to drop incendiaries on Lorient.*

We had some survivors' leave after that. My mother embroidered KOLN round the hole in my underpants, made by a small piece of shrapnel that had entered my right buttock.

The *Luftwaffe* was gifted with yet another item of great intelligence value when Stirling R9264:MG-L, flown by S/Ldr W.A. Smith, was lost on a sortie to Cologne on 2/3 February. The aircraft was shot down by a Bf110 night fighter flown by Hauptmann Reinhold Knakke, a night fighter ace of 1/NJG1, crashing at Hendrik Ido Ambacht in Holland. The Germans managed to recover the badly damaged H2S set from the wreckage and the Telefunken laboratories re-assembled it, providing the enemy with their first example of this equipment. This eventually led to the development of Naxos equipment, which allowed the German night fighters to home in on bombers using H2S. Two of the crew, Sgt R.G. Newman and F/Sgt G.P. Bragg, survived the crash.

On 3 February F/Lt Garbutt, a Canadian bomb aimer with the squadron, was awarded the DFC. He had been recommended for the award in December 1942 by W/Cdr Donaldson when he had flown twenty-nine sorties. The recommendation read:

This officer has completed 29 operational sorties as a Wireless Operator/Air Gunner and Air Bomber. During 17 of these he has been engaged on Pathfinder

G/Capt Mahaddie with his crew and ground crew and the replacement for R9237 'C for Colander', R9257, also coded 'C'. Rear L to R: F/Sgt Bob Pointer DFM, F/Lt Tommy Thompson DFC*, G/Capt Hamish Mahaddie DSO DFC, F/Sgt Alec Clift DFM, F/O Archie Bywater DFC, F/Sgt Jock Stewart DFM, P/O Len Luton DFC, F/Sgt Robbie Urwin, AC Les Elvidge, AC Ampstead and Sgt Wood. Front L to R: AC Beard, AC Biggins, AC Sutton, AC White, AC Olney, Cpl Miles and AC ?. R.C. Pointer

duties. He has always carried out his duties in a most exemplary manner. He has consistently guided his pilot over the target and has taken great care to bomb the exact aiming point even in the face of heavy opposition. His coolness and courage in action have been most outstanding and an inspiration to other crews.

G/Capt Bennett added:

This officer has throughout his operational career displayed those qualities most essential for an Air Bomber. By his determination, resource and courage, he has, whenever possible, been largely responsible for pressing home the attack to a successful conclusion. In recognition of the excellent services he has rendered and is still rendering, I have no hesitation in recommending him for the non-immediate award of the Distinguished Flying Cross.

On the night of 4/5 February F/Lt Ince and his crew took their Stirling, loaded with four 1,000 pound bombs, to Turin together with another 187 bombers. One hundred and fifty-six reached the target, causing serious and widespread damage. Ince lost his starboard inner engine over the target and Fred Fray, the flight engineer, struggled for the next four hours to manage the fuel to keep the three remaining engines going on the return to Oakington. Ernest Davenport, the bomb aimer, recalls this first mission with F/Lt Ince, though with no comment on the loss of an engine.

On 4 February we went on our first op together to Turin. As so often happened on Italian targets the very tidy cone of searchlights was extinguished and the guns stopped firing as soon as we arrived. We dropped our load of four 1,000 pound bombs and turned for home. A quite uneventful trip, the only difficulty being gaining enough altitude to clear the Alps (typical for the Bristol Hercules engines).

Having completed this operation Ince's crew continued with H2S training and Ernest Davenport recalls some of the problems encountered.

The next ten days were spent in training on the H2S and we carried out dummy blind bombing runs on York, Darlington, Oxford, Plymouth, Newcastle, Carlisle, Bradford, Northampton and Norwich. The H2S plan position indicator [PPI] gave a blurry, fuzzy green 'picture' of the shape of the target on the face of a 150 mm diameter cathode ray tube and the controls required constant attention to keep the image in tune and readable. Positive identification of a target was easier if there was a river or any body of water of known shape in the area as water gave a black image, but in tidal situations exposed mud banks could be misleading. As the subject was so 'cloak and dagger' and 'hush-hush' it was difficult to find just who one could talk to about the operational problems, and they were many. If the equipment didn't work one reported this on landing and a technician would arrive from 'special signals' and work his magic. By 9 February we had been given our permanent aircraft R9278, J Johnny, and we were able to feel less spare 'bods' and more part of the squadron.

Bob Pointer flew his last mission with the squadron on the night of 7/8 February. Some 323 aircraft, led by the Pathfinders, attacked Lorient for the loss of seven bombers. The Pathfinder marking was successful and the Main Force, attacking in two waves, produced devastating results. 'After leave we flew one more mission in a new aircraft, BK610:V, to Lorient. Lit the place well up and the op was a great success. We spotted a Ju88 near the target, but there was no attack. This was my last operational flight with 7 Sqn.'

After this trip Bob Pointer was posted to Eastbourne on an aircraft recognition course then, after leave, to No. 26 OTU at Wing. His skipper, Hamish Mahaddie, went to PFF headquarters as 'chief poacher' for AVM Don Bennett, selecting Pathfinder crews.

On the night of 11/12 February the bombers made their way to Wilhelmshaven. Finding the target completely cloud-covered the force employed sky-marking with parachute flares dropped by H2S. This was the bombing force's least reliable technique for target marking, but on this occasion it was highly accurate and crews reported a huge explosion through the cloud with the glow lasting for over ten minutes. The ammunition depot at Mariensiel had been blown up and the devastation covered almost 120 acres. Both the town and the dockyard were heavily damaged. Jock recalls this raid: 'I remember doing the first blind target marking with skymarkers – target Wilhelmshaven. Memory says the Germans were astounded as there was 10/10ths cloud. Considerable damage and very large explosions were later noted.'

Target marking was carried out using several methods by the crews of the Pathfinder Force. They would fly ahead of the main bomber stream dropping target indicators (TI) onto the aiming point. A TI contained sixty pyrotechnic candles, and a barometric fuse set to operate at an altitude of 3,000 feet would blow the canister open spreading the candles over the target area, igniting as they fell. From above the TI would give off an intense pool of light and would burn for about three minutes. Due to the short burn period they would need to be replenished regularly, hence the back-up aircraft, which followed the markers. The TIs were produced in several colours so that decoy fires lit by the Germans could be countered.

Sky marking was more complicated and involved dropping parachute flares of various colours by Oboe – or H2S-equipped aircraft. Sky marking was only ordered when the target was cloud-covered. In addition to marking the target the Pathfinders would also mark turning points along the route to assist the Main Force to stay on track.

Pilot Clarence Ince and flight engineer Fred Fray took their Stirling, R9278, to Cologne on the night of 14/15 February. Two hundred and forty-three bombers took part and nine were lost. The Pathfinders used H2S and sky markers but with only limited success. Ince and his crew almost did not return from this raid. Over the Dutch coast they were attacked by a Bf110 night fighter. The port wing and tailplane were damaged and the fuel tanks in the port wing were holed. In addition the fuel cock control cables and the electrical system were also damaged. Ince managed to evade the fighter and, after assessing the damage, pressed on to the target. Fred Fray had his work cut out managing and balancing the fuel in the damaged tanks and Ince managed to fly the damaged bomber back to Oakington for an emergency landing. Three weeks later he was awarded a Bar to the DFC. Ernest Davenport, the bomb aimer, provides a detailed description of the events of the sortie.

We took off on an operation to Cologne with orders to back up the sky marking target indicators dropped by the blind marker aircraft. At about fifteen minutes from the target we were attacked by a night fighter, but by sheer good fortune we had just commenced a turn to starboard prior to the run-up to the aiming point. Most of the enemy projectiles hit the port wing rather than the fuselage and the gunners' return fire seemingly deterred any further attack. The gunners reported that the fighter was an Me110. We were now in a precarious situation. The electricity generator was wiped out and petrol was running in a steady trickle from the main spar of the port wing onto the floor of the fuselage. After a quick assessment of the state of things, as nobody was injured and the engines continued to run, we pressed on to Cologne, did our backing up with green flares and turned for home. The rubberized floor covering dissolved in the petrol, which made things a bit slippery, but by keeping oxygen masks on the fumes were not too bad (we were careful not to strike matches) and F/Sgt Fray, our flight engineer, thought that we might have enough petrol to get back if we headed for RAF Manston, the emergency landing field close to the coast. With about half an hour to go F/Sgt Fray, Sgt Stokes and myself started to manually wind down the undercarriage. It required 700 turns with a crank handle to wind down each leg and by the time the undercarriage was down and locked we were so hot that we were stripped to the waist on a very cold February night. On landing the slight impact further damaged the main spar and the port wing sagged towards the ground. We left R9278, our J Johnny, at Manston. It was later repaired and rejoined the squadron and was allocated to another crew, but they failed to return on 15 April on a raid to Stuttgart. In recognition of our efforts on Cologne F/Lt Ince and F/Sgt Fray, the senior members of our crew, were decorated with a Bar to the DFC and a DFM respectively.

The next operation for Ince and his crew was to Bremen on the night of 21/22 February as part of a force of 130 Lancasters, seven Stirlings and six Halifaxes. Ernest Davenport recalls: 'We did our first operation in a blind marking capacity (using H2S to aim the markers) on 21/22 February to Bremen using Stirling R9255. We marked the target with four red target indicators (250 pound incendiaries) through 10/10ths cloud. The aircraft was damaged by several close anti-aircraft shells.'

The Ince crew received a new Stirling, a Mk I R9266:MG-J, but their first operation to Nuremburg on the night of 25/26 February was not a success, as Ernest Davenport relates. 'We took off for Nuremburg and after about half an hour, when we were over northern France, the flight engineer reported that the starboard inner engine was unserviceable and F/Lt Ince decided that we should return to base. Our bomb load was jettisoned "safe" in the English Channel.'

An extract from Ernest Davenport's log-book for the Cologne operation on 14/15 February 1943. E. Davenport

14/2/43		Stirling Rg278. F/o Ince	Air Bomber	Air Test. Levelled MK III B.S. at 52000 lbs.	35	
14/2/43	1835	Stirling Rg278. F/o Ince	Air Bomber	Operation COLOGNE. D.C.O. 2 x Green Flares. 2 x Green Flares with red signs. 2 x 1000 lb g.p. H.E. Attacked by Messerschmitt 110 Night Fighter. Damage to Port Mainplane and Tailplane.		4·20

The new 'J for Johnny' continued its inauspicious start with the crew after repairs, as Ernest Davenport recalls.

On 27 February, after repair work had been carried out on the starboard inner engine of our aircraft, R9266, we took it on an air test, but the starboard inner engine caught fire on take-off. Fortunately the fire extinguisher worked and we landed safely. R9266 went back to the workshops for further repairs, we air tested it on the morning of 1 March and all seemed well. We took off for Berlin in the evening.

Ince and his crew were part of a force of 302 bombers sent out that night. The Pathfinders had great difficulty in providing concentrated marking of the huge city of Berlin and the attack was spread over a 100 mile area. One good thing to come out of the raid was that the Telefunken factory was hit and the H2S set taken from the 7 Sqn Stirling shot down near Rotterdam was completely destroyed. Ernest Davenport recalls:

On the way home we strayed over the Bremen defences in heavy cloud and the aircraft was damaged by anti-aircraft fire. Sgt Alcock, our rear gunner, was injured in the foot by a shell splinter. He had to hobble about with a stick for some time. We had marked the turning points with yellow indicators and the target with red indicators, using H2S, as well as dropping explosive and incendiary bombs. No. 7 Sqn was one of the first to remove the rear gunner's perspex panel in order to improve visibility and help him to spot an incoming night fighter, possibly a split second earlier. This, of course, meant that he was

Sgt Ernest Davenport, bomb aimer, at Oakington in 1943.
E. Davenport

sitting 'in the open air' in temperatures of about –30°C. The electrically heated flying suits that the gunners had were essential equipment, but when our electricity generator failed, as on our trip to Cologne, the gunners had a bad time.

S/Ldr W.A. Smith DFC took Stirling R9264:MG-R to Cologne with a load of flares and target indicators on the night of 2/3 March and was shot down by Oblt Reinhold

Ernest Davenport's log-book entry for the Berlin raid of 1/2 March 1943. E. Davenport

1·3·43	11·05	Stirling Rq266	F/O Ince	Air Bomber	Air Test.	·40
1·3·43	1820	Stirling Rq266	F/O Ince	Air Bomber	Ops BERLIN . D.C.O. Successful Photo obtained. 3½ miles WSW aiming pt. A/c damaged by flak over BREMEN. R/Gunner Slightly injured . 1× yellow T.I. 1 bndle red flares. 4× red T.Is. 1×2000 lb. HC. N8BC. Incend.	8·15

Knacke near Rotterdam. F/Sgt P. Bragg and Sgt R.G. Newman were the only survivors. The Germans managed to recover their first intact example of an H2S set from this aircraft.

During the winter of 1942/43 losses were high and crews came and went with monotonous regularity. Experience might save a crew, but not always. The first few trips for an inexperienced crew were the most difficult and many did not return. Gordon Paterson recalls the loss of a newly designated squadron commander.

I had taken our new CO on his first trip. He came from Training Command. His name was W/Cdr Shewell. No ops experience. He had a crew with no ops experience and he panicked running in on the target. Wouldn't listen and jettisoned the complete bomb load and turned back to base. On my return I discussed the problem and we decided to keep an eye on these characters. However, they took off on their next trip and didn't return. We heard they baled out over Holland, but it was never confirmed.

The next operation for F/Lt Ince and his crew was on the night of 3/4 March when 417 bombers attacked Hamburg. The H2S plot was confused by the mud banks of the Elbe and most of the bombs landed 13 miles downstream at the small town of Wedel. Not all of the crews were fooled, though, as Ernest Davenport relates.

This attack was spoiled by being inaccurately marked by some of the earlier arrivals who, it appears, were confused by the shape of the Elbe estuary as portrayed on the H2S screen. We were able to see on our approach to the target that some markers had been misplaced and went on to drop our five red target indicators in the target area.

On 8/9 March the squadron went to Nuremberg, the Stirlings bombing with H2S. There was no moon and clear skies but haze over the target prevented accurate bombing, with the result that both the marking and bombing was widely scattered over more than 10 miles on the line of attack. R9270:MG-Q, captained by F/Lt J.P. Trench DSO, failed to return. BK610:MG-V, flown by F/Lt Selman, was also lost, the crew baling out. Over France and fearing he would not make it back with fuel running low the captain ordered the crew to abandon the aircraft. The mid-upper gunner, Sgt Spanton, did not hear the order and stayed with the pilot, coming down on a sandbank off Dungeness. The rest of the crew parachuted into the Channel. Ernest Davenport also took part in this raid with F/Lt Ince. 'We set off again for Nuremburg and this time successfully marked the target with five red target indicators. We were damaged by flak over the target.'

Munich was the objective on 9/10 March and Stirling R9149:MG-B, piloted by P/O F.M. Tomlinson, a Canadian, failed to return from this attack, being shot down by a night fighter. There were six survivors from the crew. Sgts Davies, Fox and Jennings became POWs, while Sgt L. Marsh, Sgt D.M. Cox and Sgt G.R. Howard managed to evade capture. Fox, a Canadian, was killed later in the war, marching in a POW column which was attacked by Allied aircraft. Two hundred and sixty-four bombers attacked the target, forty-one of them Stirlings. Strong winds caused the bombing to be concentrated on the western half of the city, rather than the centre; nevertheless, damage was severe. Ernest Davenport's crew took part and on this occasion they took along a 'second dicky', a new pilot to the squadron, who was to fly many operations with the squadron.

We took off for Munich with F/O Baker as second pilot. Our H2S failed after about an hour's flying and as our orders were to blind mark the target using H2S there was no point in continuing. We returned our load of indicators to base. F/O Baker continued with 7 Sqn until the end of the war and completed in excess of 100 operations.

Two days later it was the turn of Stuttgart to feel the weight of a bomber raid. W7617:MG-A failed to return; S/Ldr M.E. Thwaites DFC and his crew were killed. It was brought down by flak and crashed into a small lake near Miracourt; the Germans kept the local villagers away from the wreckage. The Pathfinders marked the target accurately but the Main Force arrived late and the raid was not a success. This raid saw the first use of dummy TIs by the Germans in an attempt to decoy the bombers away from the real aiming point. The bomb aimer on S/Ldr Thwaites's crew was P/O L.R.S. 'Len' Luton ,who had previously flown with Hamish Mahaddie's crew (as had all of the crew). On the day of the raid he was awarded the DFC, the citation reading:

Throughout his operational career, this officer has completed his duties conscientiously and efficiently. Whatever difficulty or opposition might be encountered, he has always endeavoured to secure accurate and precise bomb aiming. Many successful photographs bear witness to the effectiveness of his work. Throughout, Pilot Officer Luton has displayed high courage and disregard of danger.

The first aircraft over the target was from 7 Sqn as Ernest Davenport recalls. 'We were the first aircraft on the target and marked with five red target indicators. Obtained a good photo of the aiming point.'

Following this raid Ince's crew were given leave, and Ernest Davenport gives a good account of a typical leave period.

In the period 16–25 March we took seven days' leave. Operational aircrew were allowed seven days' leave every six weeks. This might seem generous, but regrettably not many people stayed on a unit long enough to take advantage of it.

Regarding recreation, it might seem that we had adequate free time, but operating at night, trying to sleep in the day, doing air tests, training flights and many routine tasks we never seemed to have time for anything. Far from living a riotous life, which is the impression the media have managed to convey, the average aircrew member would, after the evening meal, possibly write letters, play cards, chat in the mess over a beer or, on occasions, walk over to the local pub for a drink and play darts. We were always tired and frequently had an early night. We did, of course, go into Cambridge for the occasional night out and had adopted the Angel as the squadron pub. The last time I was in Cambridge in 1964 a lot of our names were still on the ceiling of the bar in candle smoke varnished over.

On the 13th BK592:MG-F failed to return from Essen. F/Sgt D.E. Street and his crew were lost without trace. This raid was marked by Oboe-equipped aircraft and 457 bombers dropped their loads right across the huge Krupp factory to the west of the city centre.

Stirling Mk I, R9255:MG-G, flown by F/O S. Baker, who had gone to Munich on 9/10 March with the Ince crew, was hit by flak in the port outer engine over

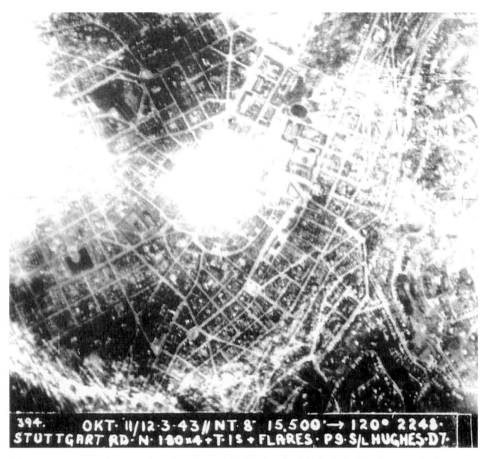

394.   OKT. 11/12·3·43 // NT· 8˙ 15.500' → 120° 2248.
STUTTGART RD· N· 180×4 + T·1S + FLARES· P9· S/L HUGHES·D7.

The aiming point photograph taken from 15,500 feet by S/Ldr C.A. Hughes on the Stuttgart raid of 11/12 March 1943. The original photograph is marked on the rear with 'That's it – spot on!' T.J. Elliot

Berlin on 27/28 March and swung on landing at Oakington, causing the under-carriage to collapse. It was written off. BF317:MG-D, captained by P/O M. Lord, a New Zealander, was also lost on this raid. Hit by flak the Stirling came down at Melchiorshausen near Bremen. The Pathfinders marked two separate areas of the city but unfortunately they fell well short of the intended areas and no bombing photographs were plotted within 5 miles of the aiming point in the city centre. Most bombs fell between 7 and 17 miles short.

The following night the squadron returned to Berlin in a 329 bomber force. The weather conditions were appalling and the bombers had to struggle through icing and inaccurately forecast winds to the German capital. Most of the bombs fell in open country to the south-east of the city. F/Lt Ince in R9266:MG-J returned to Oakington with fifty-two holes in his aircraft from predicted flak. Ernest Davenport makes only a brief comment on this sortie and nothing at all about the fifty-two holes. 'We took off for Berlin and marked the target with red target indicators as well as marking the turning points *en route* with yellow indicators. A good photo was obtained.'

Berlin was attacked several times in March 1943 and Jock Elliot gives a good account of what it was like to fight through the flak and night fighters to this distant target.

One memorable trip to Berlin – course via the Baltic – turn in near Stettin. By this time we were appointed first aircraft to mark and as we had struck a jetstream airflow barely even recognized we were fifteen minutes early and ahead of all the other aircraft and had to kill time before marking. Consequently the German defence had us well in their sights. When we dropped out target indicators they opened up on us – we believed with the claimed 4,000 flak guns and searchlights. They shot down their own Ju88 prior to its attack on us. We were flying at 16,000 feet – flak pretty deadly – we got through with very violent evasive action on Colin's part, losing 7,000 feet. Colin, who seldom swore, came through the intercom – 'By Christ this is f— hard work.' He and I were the only ones with intercom on all the time and I could hear him puffing and blowing. We got back without further trouble until we got to the Channel when it was a case of ditching stations. Used up a lot of petrol taking evasive action. The flight engineer was busy draining tanks (seven in each wing) until all except Nos 3 and 4 on either side were dry – (these tanks needed for landing). We approached Coltishall (a fighter base) on the Norfolk coast – as we touched down one engine cut out and by the time we reached the end of the runway all engines had stopped. Stayed the remainder of the night – put petrol in and returned to base.

Berlin was the target again on the night of 29/30 March when 329 aircraft took part. Weather conditions were difficult with inaccurate wind forecasts and icing to contend with. Marking was concentrated but too far south of the aiming point and the Main Force arrived late on target. Most of the bombs fell in open countryside. Ernest Davenport recalls this difficult sortie.

This operation was a fiasco. It was originally to be a 1900 hrs take-off, but after going out to the aircraft we were recalled because of the very unfavourable weather and returned to squadron HQ. The operation was then rescheduled for a later take-off and we eventually took off at 2045 hrs. Due to a disastrous error somewhere in the Bomber Command organization most of the aircraft originally scheduled did not get the new orders and as a result a very small number of aircraft eventually took off. The effect of this was that the enemy defences were not subjected to the usual degree of saturation and losses would have been very high if the very bad weather had not curtailed enemy night-fighter operations. Our aircraft was severely damaged by the anti-aircraft defences. We marked the

Ernest Davenport's log-book entry for the Berlin raid of 29/30 March 1943. E. Davenport

29·3·43	11·30 Stirling Eq266	F/L INCE	BOMB AIMER	AIR TEST	35
29·3·43	2045 Stirling Eq266	F/L INCE	BOMB AIMER	OPS. BERLIN. D.C.O. 6 T.I. ·8 White flares. 1-Gr R✗. Photoflash failure. A/C Damaged by heavy flak over BREMEN	8·30

target through 10/10ths cloud with red target indicators, but due to photoflash failure did not get a photo.

Eleven Lancasters, seven Halifaxes and three Stirlings were lost that night.

Ernest Davenport and the other members of the crew became fully fledged Pathfinders shortly after this operation.

At about this time our crew members all received a letter from the AOC 8 Group, Air Cdre D.C.T. Bennett DSO, granting us permission to wear the Pathfinder Force badge. We were also told that we must not wear the badge on operations in case we fell into enemy hands. The AOC frequently visited the squadron, he was a very amiable man and took a great interest in all our activities.

We had other visitors from time to time. Lt Mars RN, who was a submarine commander, addressed us on one occasion. He politely declined an invitation to accompany one of our crews on an operation, saying it did not appeal. We said that we felt the same way about submarines. Our crew took a Royal Artillery officer with us on one operation. His duty was to observe the enemy anti-aircraft defences. We got the impression he did not enjoy the trip and did not want to repeat it.

On the night of 4/5 April the squadron sent out fourteen Stirlings as Pathfinders and a further two on minelaying sorties. The target was Kiel and 577 bombers took part in what was the largest raid of the war so far (discounting the 'Thousand Bomber' raids). The Stirlings encountered strong winds and thick cloud over the target, making marking difficult, and decoy fires were used to draw off the bombers, so only a few bombs actually fell in the town. Ernest Davenport recorded it thus:

We blind marked Kiel with red target indicators through 10/10ths cloud and got a photo of 10/10ths cloud. We also marked the turning points en route *with yellow indicators. This was the only occasion when we fired the enemy 'colours of the day' from the signal pistol to get ourselves out of a critical situation when we were isolated and 'coned' by searchlights over the Kiel Canal. To our gratification and astonishment the ruse worked. The fact that we had the enemy codes was, of course, extremely secret at the time and the enemy colours were only to be used in dire emergency.*

On 8/9 April the squadron went to Duisburg and R9199:MG-T failed to return. Nothing was heard after take-off and all of F/O L.J. Stewart's crew were lost. Once again thick cloud thwarted the target markers and bombing was scattered. Two days later R9275:MG-Y and BK760:MG-X failed to return from Frankfurt. F/O F.A. Terry was the captain of MG-Y, and this was the only Bomber Command crew to lose their lives in the Grand Duchy of Luxembourg in 1943. Only two members of S/Ldr W.A. Chesterman's crew survived. Shot down by a night fighter of II/NJG1 flown by Hptm Walter Ehle, Sgts S.J. Moore and D. Ferguson managed to escape and returned to England. Chesterman had served in the RAF in the 1920s and had been recalled for war service. His Stirling was the first Mk III lost by the squadron. The squadron sent sixteen Stirlings to this target and a further four on minelaying sorties. The bombers returned with bombing photographs showing nothing but thick cloud, and they had no idea where their bombs had fallen. Frankfurt reported only a few bombs south of the River Main.

The losses continued to mount throughout April and the squadron was hit particularly hard when Stirlings R9278:MG-E, BK709:MG-P and BK769:MG-G were lost attacking Stuttgart on the 14th/15th. Four of the crew of MG-E – the captain P/O J.T.R. Taylor, S/Ldr R.H. Lunney, Sgt A.H. Smith and WO D. Ness were taken prisoner. The remaining three all evaded capture. Sgt N. Morley escaped to neutral territory and F/Sgt F.G.H. Weight and F/Sgt D.K. Nolan both reached Gibraltar. The Stirling had been on the homeward journey when it was shot down by a night fighter. P/O J. Mank, a Canadian, and the crew of MG-P were killed. Like Taylor's crew they were attacked and shot down by a night fighter, coming down at Biblis near Worms. S/Ldr R.W. McCarthy's crew in MG-G were all lost. The Stirling crashed at Lembach, near Homberg. The Pathfinder crews marked the target accurately but the attack developed to the north-east and the bombing began to creep back.

Sgt Donald Smith was flight engineer of this aircraft and recalls the events of the raid, his nineteenth sortie, and its aftermath.

On 20 April 1943 crew were assigned to mark target at Stettin. On first run we were hit by ack-ack which knocked out port inner engine. Mission had to be abandoned on second run as H2S and bombsight would not function. On way north the bomb aimer dropped bombs visually on an aerodrome near Peenemunde, hitting hangars and other buildings. When crossing Denmark we were shot down by Unteroffizier Berg of 7/NJG53, who was stationed at Kastrup.

After being shot down I headed in a north-easterly direction towards Copenhagen. After three days I managed to get some civilian clothes from a Mr G. Rasmussen. Had dinner on Easter Friday with Mr and Mrs Sorensen, who

F/Lt Parish and crew. D. Smith

lived near Tastrup. My next helper was a Mr Petersen, who put me in touch with a schoolteacher who spoke English, Mr Marborg. He took me by train to Helsingor. He had to leave but after two days I was befriended by another couple named Dalsborg who had some contact with the Resistance. For the next couple of days I stayed with Mr and Mrs Baumgarten in Copenhagen. After a tour of Copenhagen I was taken to a police station to be given instructions and to meet an officer cadet, Lars Troen, who would be going with me. That night we were taken up the coast to Skodsberg. The kayak they had assembled had a hole in it so the trip was postponed. That night I slept at the home of Ejner and Sylvia Tjorn; Sylvia was an active member of the Resistance. The following night we went up the coast again. The two-seat kayak was ready and at 11 p.m. we set out for Sweden. Arrived at 0300 on 1 May.

Donald Smith was awarded the DFM in June 1943. The remainder of the crew – Parish (flying on this trip as second pilot for experience), Blake, Vance, Krulicki, Marshall, Farley and Lees – all died in the crash and are buried in Svino Churchyard.

F/Lt Ince took his Stirling, R9266:MG-J on this raid. Only recently repaired after the Berlin raid at the end of March the bomber was damaged again by light flak over Denmark. Losing fuel, flight engineer Fred Fray had to use all his skill to get the aircraft home. He would be awarded the DFM in May. Ernest Davenport recalls this operation.

On a very bright night we took off for a raid on the Baltic port of Stettin. Our orders were to mark from high altitude but to then descend and return at low level across the Baltic Sea, the idea being that in the bright moonlight we would be less subject to night-fighter interception. We also carried yellow indicators to mark the turning points en route. After marking the target with red target indicators and getting a good photo we decided to delay our descent until almost at the Danish coast, where we must mark a turning point, as we could see a large amount of shipping on our H2S screen and surmised that these might be enemy 'flak ships'. Sadly, we were right and we observed a large number of aircraft below us destroyed by enemy action over the sea.

Twenty-one of the 339 aircraft despatched to Stettin were lost.

On 30April/1 May the squadron sent aircraft to Bocholt on H2S training attacks and R9263:MG-D failed to return – the only loss. The Stirling, captained by Sgt E.C. Hallding, who had come from Canada to fight with the squadron, was attacked and shot down by a night fighter flown by Lt Heinz Grimm of NJG1 and crashed at Akkerwoude in Holland. The only survivor was Sgt F.A. Painter.

The Ijsselmeer became the watery grave of BK773:MG-T when it was shot down by a night fighter flown by the ace Helmut Lent of IV/NJG1 raiding Dortmund on the 4th/5th. P/O W. Holden and crew went down with the Stirling. This was the first major attack on Dortmund and 596 aircraft took part. The initial marking was accurate but a combination of a short backing up and a decoy fire attracted many bombs to the wrong targets. Nevertheless, severe damage was inflicted on the city. The raid caused the highest number of German casualties yet recorded; unfortunately 200 POWs were among the dead.

A new CO arrived for the squadron in the person of W/Cdr H.H. Burnell on 3 May and the month also saw the beginning of the end for the Stirling on the squadron when,

ROYAL AIR FORCE

PATH FINDER FORCE

Award of
Path Finder Force Badge

This is to certify that

1182428 *Flight Sergeant R.C. Pointer D.F.M.*
R.A.F.V.R.

having qualified for the award of the Path Finder Force Badge, and

having now completed satisfactorily the requisite conditions of

operational duty in the Path Finder Force, is hereby

Permanently awarded the Path Finder Force Badge

Issued this 11th *day of* April *in the year* 1943 *A.D.*

No. 8 (P.F.F.) Group Bomber Command

The certificate awarding the Pathfinder Force Badge to F/Sgt Bob Pointer DFM on 11 April 1943. R.C. Pointer

on the 11th the first Lancaster Mk IIIs were delivered. The Stirling would remain in service a while longer, however, whilst the crews worked up on the new bomber.

After a nine-day break in major operations Bomber Command sent 826 aircraft to bomb Dortmund on the night of 23/24 May. Among them were twenty crews from

Stirling R9261:MG-M lost on the raid to Stettin on 20/21 April 1943. G. Pitchfork

7 Sqn. The clear weather and accurate marking saw widespread destruction of the city centre and in areas to the north and east of the centre. This was the heaviest raid carried out in the Battle of the Ruhr, and the bombing tonnage exceeded 100,000 tons on a single target for the first time. Seventeen Stirlings from the squadron attacked Dusseldorf on the 25th/26th as part of a force of 759 bombers. The raid was a failure due to heavy cloud layers over the target, coupled with poor marking and several decoy fires and markers in the target area. The squadron lost EF361:MG-B and P/O J.E.G.F. Berthiaume RCAF and his crew. This crew were unfortunate to be caught in the blast of an exploding 77 Sqn Halifax and crashed near Julich. There were no survivors.

Ernest Davenport recorded the reason for the break in operations and his crew's return to the fight after a period of leave.

At this time of year the nights were shorter and long-distance destinations out of reach for night bombers. The Battle of the Ruhr was in progress and marking of the targets was within range of Oboe-equipped Mosquitoes, a more accurate

Donald Smith and Lars Troen point towards Sweden and freedom. D. Smith

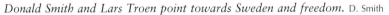

and economic method of marking. The heavy bomber markers were temporarily out of work until it was decided that they should be used as 'backers-up' on the Ruhr targets rather than stay at home and do little but air tests.

After some leave in the middle of the month our next operation was to Dortmund on 23/24 May and required us to back up the red target indicators dropped by Oboe Mosquitoes with green target indicators placed at the mean point of impact of the red indicators. We also dropped three 2,000 pound bombs.

On the night of 25/26 May we went to Dusseldorf as backer-up. We took F/Sgt Negus, RAAF, who had newly joined the squadron, as second pilot. Visibility was very bad. We dropped our three 2,000 pound bomb but returned the green target indicators as there was no clearly defined mean point of impact of red indicators to place them on and we did not wish to add to the confusion.

Nineteen Stirlings were dispatched to Wuppertal on 29/30 May. The attack was centred on the Barmen district of the town and was an outstanding success, with accurate marking and bombing. The devastation was widespread and the development of a 'firestorm' caused much of it. Dennis Routen and his all SNCO crew took part in this, their first sortie with the squadron. Having previously served with 90 Sqn, they transferred at the end of April and spent the next five weeks learning the Pathfinder trade. The Stirlings were equipped with H2S and the bomb

Sgt Donald Smith in relaxed pose. D. Smith

aimer, Leonard Noll, had to learn new skills in order to operate the equipment. Navigation was now shared between Noll and the navigator, Cyril Wolstenholme.

Following several navigation exercises and a high-level bombing run using H2S, the crew set off in Stirling EF363 for Wuppertal in a force of 719 bombers. At this stage they were still under training and carried a normal bomb load. The target was marked by Mosquitoes and accurate backing up allowed the Main Force to deliver a devastating attack. Noll dropped the load of bombs and incendiaries over the target and Routen turned for home on the course given by Wolstenholme. After clearing the target area, Sgt Geoffrey Woodcock, the rear gunner, spotted a Bf110 closing on them at a range of 500 yards. Woodcock ordered Routen to corkscrew to port just as the night fighter opened fire. Woodcock and the mid-upper gunner, Sgt James Kanelakos, returned fire as it dived away. The Bf110 was not gone, however, and it closed on the bomber again from below and to starboard. The gunners opened fire again and the Bf110 broke off at 300 yards with its port engine on fire. It was last seen

Fred Fray (centre) during his ground crew service. Fray was the flight engineer on F/Lt Ince's crew.

G. Pitchfork

disappearing into the glare of the fires below and consequently could only be claimed as probably destroyed.

F/Lt Ince also took his crew to Wuppertal that night as Ernest Davenport recalls. 'We took off for Wuppertal with orders to back-up the red target indicators with green indicators as well as marking the two turning points *en route* with yellow indicators. We also dropped one 500 pound bomb.'

Navigator S/Ldr Harry Shapiro was awarded a Bar to his DFC on 3 June 1943, the citation reading:

A conscientious and reliable navigator, this officer has always executed his task in a very commendable manner while his untiring efforts have played no small part in the successes achieved. By his cheerful courage, determination and devotion to duty, Squadron Leader Shapiro has set a splendid example to the other members of his squadron.

On the same day WO William Senger, an American serving with the RCAF on 7 Sqn, was awarded the DFC. The citation read:

A most able operational captain of aircraft, Warrant Officer Senger has many successful sorties to his credit. With cool courage he has taken part in attacks against targets in Germany and Italy, resolutely pressing home his attacks despite the heaviest opposition. At all times showing a fine fighting spirit, this airman has, by his untiring efforts and conscientious attention to detail, raised the efficiency of his crew to a very high level.

F/Lt Stickell, who had been awarded both the BEM and the DFC in 1942 received the DSO in June 1943. The citation in the *London Gazette* for 11 June read:

During a most successful tour of operational duty in heavy bomber aircraft, this officer has proved himself to be a most valuable member of his squadron. He is an outstanding operational captain and has invariably made the utmost efforts to complete his duties, regardless of opposition and other difficulties. His courage, determination and devotion to duty have been most outstanding over a long period. Since the award of the DFC in November 1942, Flight Lieutenant Stickell has completed numerous sorties, all of them against heavily defended targets in enemy territory.

The North Sea claimed another victim when Stirling R9286:MG-C, flown by F/O De Ville, ditched returning from Munster on 11/12 June. The marking for this raid was very good and the crews observed many fires. W/Cdr Burnell carried out a search for the missing crew the next day off East Anglia, but without success. The raid on

Munster was a diversion for another raid on Dusseldorf and was flown as a mass trial of H2S as a bombing radar. The Station Commander at Oakington, G/Capt Fresson, flew on this raid with F/Lt Ince and his crew. Ernest Davenport recalls:

> G/Capt Fresson came with us as second pilot. This attack was carried out entirely by 8 Group aircraft, while the Main Force bombed the Ruhr, and was very successful with damage concentrated in the port and industrial area to the south-east of the town. We marked with yellow indicators and also dropped one 2,000 pound and two 500 pound bombs.

This raid was the first carried out by P/O Wilson and crew. They flew in Stirling MG-M and the bomb aimer, F/Lt Porteous recorded in his log-book that they had bombed wide of the target by 1 mile.

Not all of the squadron's losses were due to enemy action. Stirling Mk I R9267: MG-S was lost on a training flight, crashing at Hatley St George, Cambs, on 14 June after engine failure.

During this period the squadron was beginning to convert to the Lancaster and the crews began a training period on the new type. This did not halt operations, however, the Stirlings continued to fly.

Two targets, Le Creusot and Montchanin, were attacked on the night of 19/20 June. Twenty-two crews went to Le Creusot and ten continued on to attack Montchanin as well. Both targets were successfully attacked and for good measure F/Sgt Routen also blew up a goods train near Orleans. This was the Routen crew's first sortie as a fully fledged Pathfinder crew, and they dropped flares for the Main Force. They were the second crew over the target and obtained a perfect aiming point photograph, on which they were congratulated on landing by the AOC and each given a copy. On the return from the raid they dropped to low level and carried out an attack on a goods train near Orleans, blowing it up with machine gun fire. This was an approved method of returning to base after a raid on a moonlit night.

F/Lt Ince and his crew were converting to the Lancaster but flew a Stirling on this operation, as Ernest Davenport relates.

> We now had a brief training period on Lancaster aircraft as the squadron was in the process of converting from Stirlings. We took delivery of our new Lancaster EE119 and flew it on two air tests on 15 and 16 of June. On 19 June we went to Le Creusot and Montchanin in occupied France and because our Lancaster was not yet ready for operations and our Stirling R9266:J Johnny was having some repairs done we took Stirling EF387. This operation was a precision attack on the Schneider armaments plant at Le Creusot followed by an attack on an electricity transformer station at Montchanin.

Bomber Command attacked Krefeld on 21/22 June and the squadron lost R9272: MG-W, captained by F/Lt J.S. Watt DSO DFC, which crashed at Gilze, Holland. P/O J.H. Ross and P/O M.P. Ellis survived. The Stirling was brought down by a night fighter of NJG3 flown by Hptm Walter Millius. Watt had travelled from Argentina to fight in the RAF. Gordon Paterson, who was not with his crew that night, recalls the loss of Watt and R9272.

> Having done an extra trip I was stood down from our last trip. We were all going up to Scotland for Jock Ross's wedding. The boys flew me up – I was to be best

Stirling MG-W being serviced at Oakington. G. Pitchfork

man. *That night the boys took off and were shot down over Germany. Jock was the only one to get out of the aircraft and spent a few years in a POW camp. The rest of the crew was all killed. Jock Ross eventually married his sweetheart after the war.*

The aiming point photograph of Denis Routen's attack on Le Creusot. G. Pitchfork

F/Lt James Stanley Watt DSO DFC was listed as missing on the Runnymede memorial alongside the thousands of other lost aircrew. His DSO was promulgated after his death, the official citation reading:

This officer has taken part in many missions since the award of the DFC. He has completed bombing attacks on many of the most strongly defended European targets, such as Kiel, Berlin, Frankfurt and Hamburg. Undeterred by the most adverse weather or the stiffest opposition, he has invariably displayed commendable determination and courage. F/Lt Watt has raised the efficiency of his crew to a high level and the standard of their work would be hard to equal.

EF387:MG-D, piloted by S/Ldr C. A. Hughes, also crashed in Holland. Hughes was OC 'A' Flight and a very experienced bomber pilot. EF387 was attacked and shot down by Major Werner Streib of I/NJG1. The Stirling crashed at 0130 hrs on the 'defence canal' between St Anthonis and Oploo, south-west of Boxmeer. Sgt Samuel Cox, the mid-upper gunner was killed in the crash; the others survived to become POWs. By April 1943 they were one of the senior crews of the squadron. Their last operation is recalled by Jock Elliot.

S/Ldr Bas Bastion, the squadron Gunnery Leader and an ex-RFC pilot from World War I, decided he would come for a last trip as he was posted to Training Command and it was to be an easy trip. As usual we were first in to mark using our 250 pound marker flares. An uneventful trip until two or three minutes from the target when a head-on attack by a night fighter set the starboard outer on fire. He rounded to attack from astern. I recognized the type of plane as one with an extended tail, which opened out to act as an airbrake. I got a burst in and set him alight. He didn't fire again. By now the starboard outer engine was burning well and our target indicators were burning and dropping candles. Engineer Alec wanted to jettison but Pete Brown refused as we were too close to the aiming

point so turned 180 degrees and headed away. Our crew were always concerned to mark the target accurately and made a practice, unless under pressure, of circling the target area after we had marked and dropped our bombs.

The light from the fires lit up the fuselage and I could see the mid-upper gunner had left his turret and was clipping on his parachute. My intercom was out – another Me210 made a direct astern attack – no doubt to finish us off. I had to operate the turret and guns manually – he too went down. I was shooting at about 300 yards. I had had no communication with the rest of the crew since the first attack so I decided I

S/Ldr C.A. Hughes, OC 'A' Flight, in the cockpit of his Stirling. T.J. Elliot

must get out. Shots from the fighter had cut the hydraulics and jammed the turret doors and I had a hard job getting the turret centralized and the doors open. When I managed to release the doors and I got into the aircraft, I clipped on my chute, pushed out the hatch and looked inside and didn't like it. Flames still pouring from the wing and fuselage so I decided to leave. Some twenty or thirty seconds later – maybe less – the plane exploded and collapsed my chute.

After the roar of the engines and flames, peace and quiet whilst floating down. I was thirty-six hours adrift in Holland – Limberg area – before being picked up by a German soldier attached to a flak battery. I learned later that three of the crew were picked up immediately. Three got help from friendly Dutch families and were adrift for three months. We were told that Tom [Samuel] Cox had not survived.

F/Lt Ince in R9266:MG-J was shot down just after midnight over the target by flak. Ince held a DFC and Bar and had travelled from Barbados to join the RAF. He ordered his crew to bale out and they all left the aircraft successfully, except Ince himself, who remained at the controls, dying in the crash. Having given his life to his crew, he has no known grave. Ernest Davenport, the bomb aimer, recalls this final operation.

Our final operation was carried out on 21/22 June to Krefeld with Stirling R9266: J for Johnny restored to us. This was midsummer's night and was fine with a bright, full moon. On this occasion our wireless operator, Sgt Stokes, did not accompany us as he was away doing an interview for a pilot's course which

The crew and ground crew of Stirling EF387:MG-D. Rear row: The ground crew. Front row: Sgt i/c ground crew, Sgt W. Hansen (W/Op/AG), Sgt Alec Perkins (flight engineer), Tom Cox (mid-upper gunner), F/Lt G. Boreham (navigator), P/O T.J. Elliot (rear gunner), S/Ldr C.A. Hughes (pilot). T.J. Elliot

he had applied for, and his place was taken by F/Lt Roche the squadron Signals Leader. Shortly after leaving the target, having carried out our orders, F/Sgt Fray, the flight engineer, reported a fire between the engines in the port wing. F/Lt Ince put the aircraft into a steep dive in an attempt to snuff out the fire, but this was unsuccessful and as the fire grew worse F/Lt Ince ordered us to abandon the aircraft. After destroying the secret equipment F/Lt Winfield, F/Sgt Fray, F/Lt Roche, P/O Collings, Sgt Alcock and myself abandoned the aircraft by parachute. To our great sorrow we discovered later that F/Lt Ince DFC and Bar was reported by the enemy to have been killed when the aircraft crashed. Our crew was to go on leave on 22 June.

Warrant Officer Ernest Davenport, bomb aimer, photographed in 1945 after release from POW camp. He was shot down on the night of 21/22 June 1943. E. Davenport

EF366:MG-L, captained by F/O R.B. Meiklejohn, an Australian from Wagga-Wagga, was also lost on this raid. Five of Meiklejohn's crew, Sgts L.E. Ellingham, F.W. Cole, F. Hugo and J. Kilfoyle and F/Sgt E.A. Brown, survived to fall into the hands of the Germans after being shot down by Hptm Siegfried Wandam of I/NJG5. Wandam and his radio operator, Feldwebel Schoepke, would themselves be shot down and killed a few weeks later on 4 July. EF366's navigator was F/O Charles Redwood from Woodville, New Zealand. He had joined the squadron in April 1943 after completing seven operations with No. 218 Sqn at Downham Market. The sortie to Krefeld was his seventh and final operation with the squadron; like Meiklejohn he did not escape from the doomed Stirling.

Bill Cole, the flight engineer and one of the survivors recalls the events of that night and the days that followed.

I remember clearly the moments from the start of the combat with the German night fighter until after I evacuated the aircraft from the bomb aimer's

The last entry in Ernest Davenport's log-book. E. Davenport

		STIRLING						
21. 6.43.	14.35	R9266	F/L INCE.	BOMB AIMER.	AIR TEST.		1.15	
21. 6.43	23.45	STIRLING R9266	F/L INCE.	BOMB AIMER.	OPS - KREFELD -			2.05
					- AIRCRAFT FAILED TO RETURN -			
					TOTAL HOURS FLOWN		329.20	156.06

L. R. Butterfield s/L.

O.C. 'A' FLT. 7 SQDN.

An aerial view of Oakington in June 1943.

Sgt Jack Kilfoyle, one of the survivors from the shooting down of Stirling EF366. J.P. Sleurs

hatch in the nose. Before that both of our gunners had reported the sighting of the Luftwaffe plane, our mid-upper gunner reported having seen two. This might have been an impression made in the confusion of the fight. The official German report refers to only one fighter being involved and I think that might be correct. I don't know how long the combat lasted, but from the first exchange, I had time to leave my position at the engineer's panel, to join the Skipper and sit with him in the second pilot's seat. Both of our gunners were repeatedly in action and the fighter made repeated attacks without causing us serious damage. Our altitude was just under 12,000 feet when I joined the pilot.

F/O R.B. Meiklejohn, pilot of EF366. J.P. Sleurs

Shortly after we were attacked from the rear and the Stirling went out of control. There was no fire but we lost both rudder and tailplane control and the aircraft went into an almost vertical nosedive and the Skipper gave the order to bale out. I had time in pitch darkness to make my way back to the engineer's panel, where my parachute was stowed. I clipped it on and passed the navigator's table, down the steps to the bomb aimer position and exited the aircraft, the bomb aimer having already left. Although I cannot be positive I am sure the navigator had been injured or killed during one of the exchanges. He would certainly have got out before me if he had been able.

I made an uneventful descent, the parachute working as it should and came to earth within a kilometre or two to the west of the village of Neerpelt. I landed at the side of a small river, or perhaps it was a canal. Above me at the top of a fairly steep slope there was a wooded area. Some big trees and a good amount of ground-covering small bushes. I hid my parachute and harness there and rested for a while trying to calm my bewildered thoughts. The night was quiet, I didn't

The final entry in F/O RB Meiklejohn's log-book. J.P. Sleurs

YEAR 1943 Month Date	AIRCRAFT Type	No.	Pilot, or 1st Pilot	2nd Pilot, Pupil or Passenger	DUTY (Including Results and Remarks)
					Totals Brought Forward
JUNE. 21.	STIRLING	EF366.	SELF.	CREW.	BOMBING RUNS – AIR TEST.
" 21.	STIRLING	W.7529.	F/O. LEITCH. SELF.	CREW.	AIR - TEST.
JUNE 21	STIRLING	EF366	SELF	P/O REDWOOD F/S. BROWN S. HUGO S KILFOYLE. S ELLINGHAM. S COLE.	OPERATIONS – KREFELD.

hear any sound of the aeroplane crashing, nor of the bombs exploding; which is surprising considering the short distance from my landing site to the site of the crash at Achel. After some time there I decided to try to find out where I was: I didn't know for sure where I was. It could have been Belgium or Holland or I thought perhaps we had crossed the German border and I was among the enemy. Anyway I decided to leave the sanctuary of the wood and try to find some habitation and perhaps help.

By pure chance I walked in an easterly direction. I don't know for how long or how far, but after passing some houses in complete darkness I heard someone or something approaching me from the opposite direction. I hid in the hedge at the side of the road while the somebody was Frank Hugo. After some joyful greeting we decided to return to the woods where I had been earlier to be at least out of sight for a while.

Early next morning, looking down from our vantage point up the slope we saw two men walking along the waterside. They were the Spelter brothers from Neerpelt, who suggested we laid down for the rest of the day and they would return that evening. This they did with some food and the offer that they would help us get away from the area where we knew the Germans would be searching for us. From Neerpelt we went to Hasselt, from Hasselt to Liege, from Liege to various safe places en route to Brussels. Brussels to Paris, where we were caught by the Gestapo. An unpleasant stay in the prison Fresnes not far from Paris and eventually being declared prisoners of war and taken to Germany to spend the rest of the war at Stalag IVB and returning home in the early summer of 1945.

Frank Hugo, the bomb aimer, had already left the aircraft and was to have many adventures before finally being betrayed and captured whilst attempting to escape.

On the night of June 20/21 1943 my aircraft was detailed with two others to mark a turning point south-east of Eindhoven, for the guidance of the Main Force bombers who were attacking Krefeld. The Stirling bomber was not well suited to this task because in the summer months it could only gain about 12,000 feet and the markers ignited barometrically at 10,000 feet, thus silhouetting us as we flew over them, enabling German fighters to attack.

We were set on by three Ju88 fighters, which damaged us on each run until my pilot ordered us to abandon the aircraft. The escape hatch was badly damaged and I had great trouble in opening it and, when I did jump out, found that my parachute was not

Hauptmann Siegfried Wandam, the night fighter pilot who shot down Stirling EF366. J.P. Sleurs

properly fixed. However, it did eventually open but I swung and spun on the end of a solitary strap until I hit the ground.

After burying my chute near an irrigation ditch, I followed a dirt road, being frightened by cows and horses, which I imagined to be Germans, until I heard voices – one of which had a Birmingham accent. I had found the flight engineer, Bill Cole. He had hurt himself on his parachute harness and could not walk well. He had been found by some Dutch people, but they seemed rather frightened and there were young children about, so we decided to move away southwards.

EF366 was one of the leading bombers in the stream and had been tasked with marking a turning point south-east of Eindhoven on the way to Krefeld. Wireless operator, Les Ellingham was the last to escape from the doomed Stirling.

I was the last one to leave the aircraft as I had not heard the order to bale out because I was 'jamming' radio stations. We were quite low and my flying boots were ripped off in the slipstream. I landed in soft, marshy ground without injury, except for a bloodied forehead and a slight knee injury. There were people about but I could not see anyone, but could hear

F/Sgt Frank Hugo. B. Hugo

shouts. Our orders were if shot down to move as fast as possible, though I had no footwear. I set off. I don't know how far or how long I walked, but it was getting light. I came to a farm and decided to watch and decide what to do. Men came and left, but no military, so I took a chance and knocked a door. It was opened and shut again very quickly. I had been cut and must have, at first glance, looked ghastly. Anyway the door opened again and I was beckoned in – shortly afterwards a lady arrived. What a relief – my position was accepted. I slept. Later that day I was taken to a small farm. I only saw the farmer and his daughter, who was churning butter and only stayed a couple of days. The next period is very vague, moving from house to house until I arrived in Lanklaar, where I stayed for about seven days, staying hidden in the hay loft during the day and coming down at night. I have a vague recollection of heading towards Denmark for a ship journey, then Brussels, Hasselt, Liege and finally catching up with Bill Cole and Frank Hugo in Fresnes jail.

Jack Kilfoyle was arrested by the enemy, having been injured on landing. Years later he said, 'Duke, I hit one of those fighters.' He said that the German pilot visited him in hospital.

Local priest Adriaan Claassen witnessed the final moments of EF366 as it plunged earthwards.

A night, as usual filled with the roaring of aircraft and occasionally with the rattle of heavy machine gun fire. I stepped out of my front door and on the

The crash site of Stirling EF366. J.P. Sleurs

north-eastern horizon I saw a vague silhouette of a large aircraft. The silhouette
was on fire.

It then went very fast. In a sea of flames and with a deafening scream
the large black cross plunged straight down towards the centre of Achel. At
about 40 degrees the burning cross suddenly swerved off to the west, as if
the pilot was trying to avoid the village centre. I stood on my toes to see where
the aircraft would crash. I was immediately pushed to the ground by the
enormous pressure wave. Doors from houses and stables flew open. The parish
church had no glass left in the leaded windows and the heavy door had flown
open. The Herringstraat looked heavily shelled. Most houses were roofless. Some
roofs had been ripped off in one piece. Luckily, no one from Achel was heavily
injured.

The aircraft bored into the ground by the pond in the hamlet Het Ven. Almost
at the same time I noticed that a German night fighter was going down in the
area of the monastery De Achelse Kluis. Early in the morning the interested
crowd was chased away by Wehrmacht soldiers. They angrily slashed bicycle
tyres with bayonets.

Many of the inhabitants of the village of Achel observed the destruction of EF366,
as recounted by Jos Van Werde.

Many people from Achel saw the burning aircraft losing height. Then there was
an enormous explosion and a huge pressure wave lifted the tiles from the roofs
and glass windows were smashed up to hundreds of metres away from the crash
site. Everyone was immediately awake. The crash site was in marshland close to
the pond known locally as Papeweierke.

The farmhouse used by Les Ellingham as a hideout whilst trying to evade the Germans. J.P. Sleurs

At this time word came that the crew managed to escape with the help of parachutes and had got stuck in the marshland (Sijskesbroek). The occupying forces were very alert in situations like these and could count on the help of collaborators. Every second was valuable to start off the evacuation. Farmer Van Hertum helped dig out one of the men who was stuck, having smashed up to his waist in the marshland.

The prison identity card issued to Les Ellingham following his capture. L. Ellingham

In the meantime many curious onlookers had arrived, some of which tried to give assistance, like Dr Louis De Bont, resistance member Francois van Meensel, Piet Lauwers and others. When the Germans and collaborators arrived on the scene and tried to locate the missing crew the situation changed and many onlookers left the area. They were well aware that contact with these people could get them into trouble.

When the morning approached, the Germans secured transport for one of the crewmen from farmer Schurmans and his son Jef on an open horse cart normally used to transport bricks. The guarding of the cart was entrusted to the collaborators.

The sad procession then set off through Haringstraat, where the locals unmistakably showed their sympathy with the wounded crewman. Some went in ostentatious manner to the injured man, possibly unaware that it made them look suspect in the eyes of the collaborators.

The procession stopped near the house of Willem van Werde, where the guards allowed drinks to be offered. The daughters of Thijs van Werde gave the man a blanket to cover him in his wet uniform. Rene van Werde spoke a few words of French to his best ability and the man replied in equal brevity. He could have been Canadian, other people said he was a New Zealander.

The prisoner of war was taken to Achel-Statie, where there was a permanent German watch-post, which was well known to once arrested occasional smugglers who had to stay there temporarily. Thereafter he was moved to the military camp at Leopoldsburg.

The crew of Stirling EF366:MG-L. J.P. Sleurs

Jack Winters, another Achel resident, remembers the sudden arrival of Stirling EF366.

Due to the deafening noise from the aircraft, I went outside that night. I saw a burning aircraft that was flying very low. The howling of the engines was terrifying. I ran quickly inside to call my brother-in-law, Gradje Van Otterdijk. At that moment an enormous explosion took place. The lodger, Frans Vandeweyer, who slept upstairs, was terribly frightened. The explosion had blown off a piece of the roof and he was looking directly outside. At first he thought that the house was on fire, but actually he was looking out into the great fireball from the crashed aeroplane.

The farmhouse of the Cox family was also badly damaged by the explosion as Paul Cox recalls.

I remember the night of 23 June as if it were yesterday. My parents' house was at Het Bien. It was a farm. That particular night my parents and me were in bed. We were awoken by an enormous explosion. The roof of our farmhouse was totally ruined. We had no idea what had happened. My father told me to lie down next to the sink, where it would be safer. After waiting a while, we went outside.

The first thing we heard was the sound of whistles. We had no idea what that meant. In the meantime the neighbours, Schuurmans, had also gone outside. Together we headed in the direction of the whistles. It was in Het Sijskesbroek, the marshland area not far from where the aircraft had crashed. During our search we came across a rubber boat, which I later used to make a coat, but was not wearable because it made you sweat enormously.

There was a marshy area that was behind the thickly overgrown Sijskesbroek. It was there that we saw a large white sheet. After a closer look, it turned out to be a parachute. Nearby we found a wounded soldier, who had sunk up to his waist into the ground. This had happened because his parachute had not opened completely, which caused him to smash into the ground with great force.

The wounded man reached out with both hands and asked for help. We attempted to lift him, but it was impossible. He had a tankard on him. In this I collected some water from a nearby brook, called De Vliet. He emptied it at one draught. I rummaged in the wounded man's pockets to find out his identity. I found a number of documents that indicated he was from New Zealand. We saw that the man was annoyed at our rummaging around in his personal documents. Therefore I immediately put his wallet back in his jacket.

After a while, Jan from Beret van Hertum and Jef Schuurmans came towards us. We decided to dig the man out and went back to get a spade. We were only 50 metres away from the man, when two Germans appeared, pointing their guns at us. They in turn searched the New Zealander's pockets and found a paternoster. Sarcastically one of the German soldiers said; 'Ah, Sir is a Catholic, but this does not keep him from murdering women and children in Germany.'

Jef Schuurmans was ordered by the Germans to collect a horse and a wagon. Meanwhile we started digging out the wounded New Zealander. Once he was out we saw his crushed feet. The man was in a lot of pain. His chin was also injured. Once it started to get light the journey with the horse and wagon to Achel-Statie began. There the wounded soldier was taken away to be treated. When the wagon passed in front of the house of Jef Schuurmans, Francois Van Meensel jumped on the wagon and spoke to the soldier in English. Francois stayed on the wagon until it arrived at Achel-Statie.

The wounded soldier was in fact F/Sgt E.A. Brown, the rear gunner. He had been fortunate to land in the marsh and thus survive the bale-out at low height. Doctor Louis De Bont recalled the wagon carrying the wounded airman pass his house on the way to Achel-Statie.

I can still remember very well that Toon Vissers took an injured crew member on an open wagon to Achel-Statie. When they came past my house I went down to the wagon to take a look. In the Station House at Achel-Statie the wounded soldier had put all his belongings on a table. I came to the conclusion that he had to be a Catholic, because he had a paternoster in his pockets.

Such losses hit the squadron hard. Forty-four bombers were lost on this raid, nine of them Stirlings. Most of the losses were thought to be from night fighters. F/Sgt Dennis Routen flying as a 'backer-up' on this raid observed that there were plenty of fighters around.

Whilst the crews nightly flew their operations the ground crews worked all hours to keep the aircraft in the air. Their work is often unmentioned and undervalued, but without them no operation would ever have taken place. Jock Elliot recalls his ground crew.

The aircraftsman armourer who was responsible for the functioning of our turrets was shifted to another aircraft but the afternoon before we went on ops he always came back and checked my turret. The sergeant in charge of ground crew on our aircraft and some others were always at dispersal when we returned to base to ask how it all went.

On 22/23 June the target was Mulheim. Some 557 aircraft took part, bombing through a thin layer of stratus cloud, including five crews from the squadron, who reported a successful raid with a huge area of fire, still visible on reaching the Dutch coast. One bomb load caused a terrific explosion in the target area and the local authorities reported widespread damage and a breakdown in communications. F/Lt Plaistow did not reach the target, turning back early with compass trouble.

Two nights later three squadron aircraft failed to return. Mk I R9281:MG-V flown by F/O A.J. Davis, who had come from Lancala Bay in the Fiji Islands to fight, crashed into the North Sea off the coast of Holland returning from Elberfeld. EF392:MG-N2 shared the same watery grave coming down off Zeeland. S/Ldr J.R. Savage, OC 'C' Flight went down in MG-N2. Savage was an Australian and a very experienced bomber pilot. He was on his second tour of operations and his crew included Sgt Arthur Caley as wireless operator. Caley was also on his second tour, having previously served with 90 Sqn. Savage and his crew are thought to have crashed into the North Sea off the Dutch coast with no survivors. W/Cdr Barrell DSO DFC and Bar, OC 'B' Flight, in Lancaster ED595:MG-Q also failed to return from this raid. It was his sixtieth mission and the last before he would have become tour expired on his second tour of operations. He was killed when his parachute failed to open. Most of his crew would have become tour expired also. There were four survivors, P/O S.G. Keatley, F/Lt J.A. Emery and WO J.A. Pearson, who became POWs, and P/O H.J. Hudson DFM, who managed to evade capture. ED595 was the first Lancaster lost by the squadron. The raid itself was well concentrated, with good fires and a huge, high column of smoke coming up.

On the night of 28/29 June the target was Cologne. Six hundred and eight aircraft set out in poor weather to attack the target using sky-marking techniques. The squadron dispatched eight crews, four aircraft loaded with 1,560 gallons of fuel and three 2,000 pound bombs, the others with twenty-two incendiaries each. Six of the eight crews attempted to bomb through the 10/10th overcast. Stenhouse, the pilot of R9260:MG-O, had to return with his bombs after the bomb doors failed to open and Forbes, flying in BF345:MG-H returned early after being shot up by a night fighter at the Dutch coast. Despite the weather the raid was most successful, causing severe damage for the loss of thirty aircraft.

The squadron's first Lancaster attack was on Turin on the night of 11/12 July when four aircraft took part. The first, EE200:MG-A took off at 0223 hrs followed by JA678:MG-S, EE129:MG-Y and EE119:XU-G. All four returned safely. By this time the squadron was also using the code XU in addition to MG, due to the number of aircraft now being operated. The raid caused the highest number of casualties during the ten raids carried out on Turin by Bomber Command during the war.

F/Sgt Dennis Routen, who had joined the squadron in April, was recommended for the DFM on 15 July, the citation referring to '... cool courage in pressing home his attacks in spite of fierce opposition having displayed a keen, aggressive spirit which has reflected in his crew.' The Station Commander commented, 'This NCO's determination and offensive spirit is an inspiration to his crew and an outstandingly good example to other captains.' Routen and his crew were awarded their Pathfinder Badges on 25 July and around the same time began converting to the Lancaster alongside the other members of the squadron.

On 22 July the squadron establishment was changed from sixteen Stirlings and eight Lancasters to twenty-four Lancasters. The Lancasters were all equipped with H2S, vital to their Pathfinder target-marking role. They were a marked improvement on the Stirlings, both in load-carrying capability and in ceiling. Speed and range were also better.

On the night of 24/25 July 'Bomber' Harris launched the Battle of Hamburg, sending 791 aircraft to this city. Nine Stirlings and eight Lancasters from the squadron took part in the raid which saw the first use of Window (metallic strips dropped to confuse the radar). Both the H2S and visual marking was a little scattered but a concentrated raid quickly developed and severe damage and heavy casualties were caused. Stirling EF369:MG-Z aborted the sortie with the port inner engine unserviceable and returned to base, as did Lancaster JA693:MG-W with a failed intercom. P/O Wilson flew on this sortie as a backer-up carrying two yellow and four green TIs, and five 500 pound MC [Medium Case] bombs. During the flight the propeller of the starboard inner engine fell off and, as if this was not bad enough, the port inner also had to be feathered. Wilson managed to get back to Oakington on only the two port engines.

Eight Stirlings and one Lancaster bombed Essen on the night of 25/26 July in a raid in which the Krupps works suffered its greatest damage of the war.

Luck ran out for the crew of EF369:MG-Z on 27/28 July. Returning from Hamburg, having contributed to the firestorm that devastated the city, they were on

F/O Tony Davies and crew emblazoned their Lancaster EE129:MG-Y with a symbol of delivery 'The Stork' at Oakington in the autumn of 1943. The 'pilot' is one of the many dogs 'owned' by the squadron during the war! 7 Sqn

The crew of Lancaster 'A for Apple' at Oakington in 1942. via 7 Squadron Association

the approach to Oakington when suddenly the Stirling lost power and sank rapidly. The huge bomber hit an obstruction and crashed. P/O G.R. Wood and his crew all escaped with injuries. Hamburg was attacked again in July, the squadron losing EF364:MG-X on the 29th/30th. Nothing was heard after take-off from Canadian P/O A.G. Forbes and his crew. Lancaster JA718:MG-T returned with both starboard engines giving trouble.

F/Sgt Routen and his crew flew one of the few remaining Stirlings, R9829, on this raid. The bombers encountered very large thunderstorms and severe icing on the way to the target and many were forced to turn back. Routen pressed on. Finding cloud up to 15,000 feet over the target he dropped down to a lower lever and Cyril Wolstenholme guided him back over the target for a second run. This also failed and Routen turned the Stirling round for yet another run, this time at 5,000 feet. Leonard Noll, the bomb aimer, managed to place the load of green TIs, flares and 500 pound bombs 3 miles from the aiming point. Routen's was one of only two crews to get this close to the target. He was commissioned as a P/O in August.

The undercarriage of the Stirling proved to be its Achilles heel and once again it caused the crash a Squadron aircraft when R9260:MG-O returned to Oakington. It had encountered an engine problem shortly after take-off for a raid on Hamburg on 2/3 August, the port outer backfiring. On landing the aircraft swung and the undercarriage collapsed. This aircraft, flown by P/O W.E. Stenhouse, was the last Stirling lost by the squadron. Stirling EF363:MG-G aborted due to icing, as did EF368:MG-A, which landed at Bourn with a leaking port inner engine. Lancaster JA713:MG-V also returned early due to icing.

On the 10th/11th Lancaster JA931:MG-X failed to make it back to base from Nuremberg, running out of fuel 10 miles north-east of Canterbury and crashing. F/O A.J. Belsey and his crew escaped without injury.

The Italians were on the receiving end of the squadron's bombs on 12/13 August, when Milan was attacked. Lancaster JA682:MG-D, captained by S/Ldr W.R. Butterfield, OC 'A' Flt, failed to return from this otherwise successful raid. S/Ldr C.J. Myers, F/Lt E.S. Baker and WO H.E. Croney escaped the stricken bomber to become POWs. Edward Baker, a Canadian, had been awarded the DFC on 6 August. The citation for the award read: 'This officer has taken part in a large number of operational sorties during which his ability as a navigator has been outstanding. A most dependable member of aircrew, his skill and perseverance have been invaluable in the training of junior navigators.' Butterfield, Sgt P. Fairweather, F/Lt M.C. Bridges and WO R.W. Graham all evaded capture. The only casualty was F/Sgt E.G. Sheil. Lancaster JA917:MG-P returned early after it was discovered to have petrol leaking from the starboard fuel tanks.

Two days later the squadron went to Milan again and lost JA850:MG-M, captained by F/Lt S.G. Matkin DFC, the only loss of the night. The bomber crashed at Sassenay, near Chalon in France. Matkin was on his forty-fourth sortie. P/O Wilson took JA911:MG-Q to Milan as a backer-up carrying four green TIs one 4000 pound HC 'cookie' and three 500 pound MC bombs. His bomb aimer, F/Sgt Porteous, dropped the bombs 1,500 yards south-east of the aiming point.

The next night Milan was the target once more and this time Wilson and crew took four red TIs, three 500 pound MC bombs and a 'cookie'. They returned with the TIs unused.

On the night of 17/18 August the squadron took part in the raid against Peenemunde by 596 aircraft. The objective was the destruction of the V-2 rocket experimental site and it saw the use of a master bomber to control the raid for the first time. Seventeen Lancasters from the squadron took part, carrying 4,000 pound 'cookies' for the first time. F/Sgt Whittlestone was the first to drop one on his thirty-nineth sortie. Among those taking part was S/Ldr Charles Lofthouse, who was on his second tour and had joined the squadron in June 1943. Prior to the Peenemunde raid he had taken part in five raids on Hamburg. For Peenemunde he acted as deputy master bomber to G/Capt John Searby of 83 Squadron.

Ten Lancasters were dispatched to Leverkusen on the night of 22/23 August, although three aborted: JA713:MG-V with the guns in the rear turret unable to depress below the horizontal; JA911:MG-Q with the wireless operator's oxygen mask unserviceable; and JA964:MG-D with an unserviceable mid-upper turret and navigational aids. The remaining aircraft bombed the primary target along with over 400 others. The IG Farben factory was the aiming point but thick cloud and a partial failure of the Oboe system caused the raid to fail.

On 23/24 August the squadron attacked Berlin, losing Lancaster JA678:MG-S from a force of nineteen dispatched in a raid which saw much of the bombing fall outside the city. S/Ldr Charles Lofthouse was shot down by a nightfighter. He was flying a blind marker aircraft and had the station commander, G/Capt A.H. Willetts as second pilot. JA678 was probably the first Lancaster shot down over Berlin that night. Charles Lofthouse recalled the mission, as quoted by Martin Middlebrook in *The Berlin Raids*.

The H2S set started playing up soon after crossing the Dutch coast and Cayford, the navigator, had been trying hard to rectify it. In retrospect, if we had not had the Station Commander on board, I would have decided halfway to the target that we were not going to be able to mark and would have dropped back then, but I decided to press on and do everything possible to become a valid marker. We actually reached the target about seven minutes early and were flying straight and level, trying to get an astro fix, when we were heavily coned. I couldn't lose them. This was all before the raid started. I shot off the colours of the day, as advised by Intelligence, but it had no effect.

Then, I saw a great, bright 'whoosh' of tracer come past the cockpit on the port side. I don't suppose anyone saw the attacking plane; the gunners must have been blinded by the searchlights. This coloured tracer just rushed by us and all the damage was on the port side. The wings and engines were badly hit.

The engineer tried to put the fire out in the engine; I felt that I wasn't getting proper response from the ailerons and we were losing height. Then Denis Cayford came up on the intercom, asking if he should get out and put the fires out on the wing, presumably by going out through the astrodome and crawling along the wing like the VC chap had done on a Wellington once. But we weren't on a Wellington and he had no chance at all; I said 'No.'

At some stage I told the bomb aimer to jettison the bombs, but not the markers, and soon after this I ordered 'Abandon'. G/Capt Willets left the aircraft like a rat out of a trap when I said, 'I think it's time we got out.' I had welcomed him aboard with a jaunty, 'Don't forget to bring your sandwiches for the trip home, Sir.' The flames were very fierce by now, stretching back from each engine, and there was a large hole in the wing between the two nacelles, with flames coming out of it, being beaten back by the airflow.

The crew started going. The flight engineer put my parachute ready beside me. The wireless op came forward and gave me a thumbs-up to indicate that the boys at the back had gone. Cayford came back at that stage, went back into his 'office' and then went forward and out. He told me later that he had come back for a

Two views showing the remains of Lancaster JA850:MG-M flown by F/Lt J.G. Matkin DFC at Sassenay. 7 Sqn

A 7 Sqn Lancaster crew in 1943. L to R: F/O Ed Edson, Ralph Stutt, P/O Sam Weller, Mickey McGuire, Sgt Johnny Fisher, P/O Robbie Roberts, Bill Mayne, WO Bob Notley. 7 Squadron Association

gold signet ring from his girlfriend, which he always took off when flying because it got so cold. That horrified me because I was fighting the controls hard by then, but I managed to get out.

Charles Lofthouse came down in a tree with a broken arm and was hanging from his parachute outside the window of a building used by a concentration camp working party. He was quickly taken prisoner. All of the crew survived.

Four Lancasters aborted the mission: JA935:MG-O with an unserviceable rear turret; EE119:XU-G, also with an unserviceable rear turret and intercom; JA962:XU-W with its starboard outer engine leaking oil; and JA971:XU-J due to navigational trouble.

On the night of 26/27 August the crew set out for Nuremburg. P/O Wilson carried a mixed load of TIs, a 'cookie' and two 1000 pound bombs acting as a visual marker. In the event they did not bomb Nuremburg, but a secondary target at Heilbronn, bringing back the TIs. The bomb aimer, William Porteous recorded in his logbook that the bombing was a 'scattered raid all around'.

On 27/28 August twenty of the squadron Lancasters bombed Nuremberg. A force of 674 aircraft set out for this target, which was marked with H2S. Much of the bombing was wasted on this very dark night as many crews were short of the target, despite the efforts of the master bomber. Only one of the crews aborted, that flying JA971:XU-J, which returned with an unserviceable intercom.

Twelve Lancasters went to Munchengladbach on the night of 30/31 August. With good visibility and accurate Oboe marking by the Pathfinders over half the city was destroyed. This was a double attack with the Pathfinders first marking Munchengladbach and a few minutes later shifting their attention to Rheydt. Bombing was concentrated and both towns suffered heavy damage. The squadron lost three Lancasters: JA710:MG-N, JA936:MG-J, flown by S/Ldr C. Anekstein, and

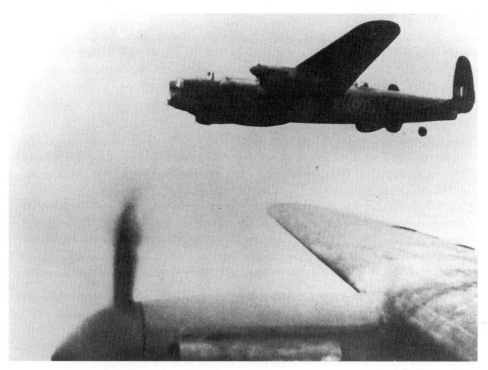

Lancaster JA678:MG-S flown by S/Ldr Charles Lofthouse. It had an unusual depiction of the code letter 'S', which appeared to be a reversed 'Z'. 7 Sqn

Ground crew, with one of the squadron dogs, photographed in front of Lancaster MG-H. This may have been F/Sgt J Sutherst's JA937 lost during a raid on Munchengladbach on 31 August 1943. (It is also possible that the Lancaster is JA968.)

JA937:MG-H, flown by F/Sgt J. Sutherst. Sgt J.W.C. Genney and F/Lt G.A. Atkinson were the only survivors from S/Ldr Anekstein's crew. The remaining bombers returned safely. JA710 was piloted by F/O M.O.J. Wells, who survived with all of his crew after being shot down by a night fighter which had approached unseen from below on the port quarter.

Oliver Wells recalls the raid:

My career with the squadron was swiftly terminated by a BF110 on 30 August near Munchengladbach. I joined in early July 1943 when the squadron was just converting to Lancaster IIIs from Stirlings and operated from then until the end of August, including the very successful and important raid on Peenemunde. We achieved a photo aiming point on that occasion.

I am glad to say my crew all got out with parachutes, but I was less lucky as the aircraft went out of control due to a tail explosion adding to the burning port fuel tanks and I became wedged in the front escape hatch. I must have been thrown clear with only a broken collarbone and spent the next week walking out of Germany into Holland and Belgium, where the Comet Line looked after me until I was caught on a train between Brussels and Paris.

The night of 31 August/1 September saw a heavy raid on Berlin with the squadron providing seventeen of the 622 aircraft which took part. Two aborted: JA978:MG-S with an unserviceable starboard outer engine and JA917:MG-P with a faulty coolant temperature gauge for the starboard outer engine and the starboard aileron out of order. The remainder all bombed the city in an unsuccessful raid hampered by cloud cover and problems with H2S. F/O Wilson flew as a blind marker on this raid and his bomb aimer, F/Sgt Porteous dropped their bombs and markers 3,000 yards south-east

Two 7 Sqn pilots, named Ralph and Ernie, at Oakington in 1943. 7 Squadron Association

of the aiming point. The fact that they achieved the best aiming point photograph in Bomber Command that night says a lot about the difficult conditions encountered.

In the summer of 1943 Roy Claridge was lecturing in the Signals Office at the OTU at Desborough. He had completed a tour of thirty-six operations with No. 104 Sqn in the Middle East and was on a rest from operations. He recalls how he was recruited into Pathfinders and the very different world he discovered.

One morning I was walking to the signals office when one of our staff, a flying officer, came up to me. He had had a lot to drink in the mess that evening and had volunteered to return to ops with a pilot who was recruiting a crew for his return to 7 Sqn on Pathfinder Force. He told me he did not want to return to flying with an operational squadron. Did I want to take his place? I agreed at once and by that time F/Lt G.B. Frow had met up with us. We introduced ourselves and Brian Frow and I got along from the very first. We were the same age, married and older than most aircrew. I did not know at that time that 7 Sqn was having many losses and needed crews in a hurry.

I cleared Desborough and the same day we were on our way to the Pathfinder Training Unit, where we had three weeks converting onto Lancasters and meeting the rest of our new crew: Brian Frow, captain; F/Lt Wharton, who had been the station gunnery officer; and Taff Erasmus who completed his second tour of ops while with us on his sixteenth birthday! He was mid-upper gunner. Navigators and bomb aimers seemed to come and go, as for some reason they proved to be unfit, especially when we became a master bomber crew.

When we arrived at 7 Sqn it seemed to be another world. We seemed to make our own rules, we were all equal. The first thing that happened was we were all promoted one rank and we were allowed to wear the Pathfinder badge, which was thought of as our highest award. It was made plain that it would only become permanent after the crew had obtained at least ten aiming points. I think we realized that this was almost impossible, especially as the losses on the squadron were so high.

Nobody was worried about rank or bullshit. I remember the only time I wore a proper uniform was when we went into Cambridge. I mainly flew in civilian clothes to make it easier if we were shot down and had to go on the run. During the first month on the squadron we lost two wing commanders, W/Cdr Rampling and W/Cdr Barron. I had known W/Cdr Rampling at Chipping Warden. He was much older than the usual run of senior officers. A number of air attachés had returned from their posts all over the world, having volunteered to go back on flying duties. These men were mostly in their late thirties and really too old for wartime flying. I had been the radio instructor for a group of about ten men. Some of the old-time RAF thought it funny to be instructed by a flight sergeant and it was W/Cdr Rampling who, one day, brought these senior officers to attention and told them that while they were under instruction they had no rank! They were very good after this telling off. Rampling asked me to go back on ops with him in the crew he was forming. I refused because I thought he was too old for operations and I was right. He had been made CO on the squadron when we joined and he was killed just a month after our arrival. A great shame, as he was a delightful man.

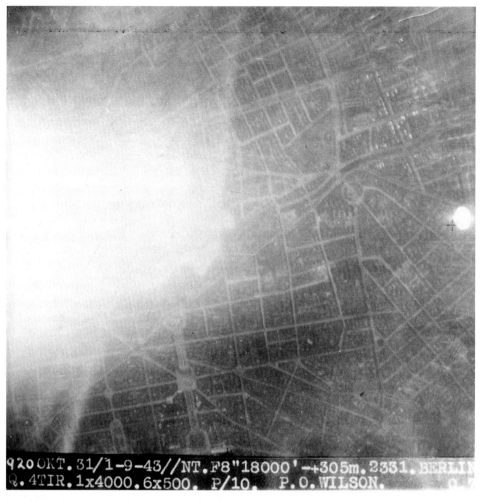

920OKT.31/1-9-43//NT.F8"18000'-+305m.2331.BERLIN
Q.4TIR.1x4000.6x500. P/10. P.O.WILSON.

The 'best photo in Bomber Command'. The aiming point photograph from P/O Wilson's Lancaster on the Berlin operation of 31August/1 September 1943. Mildred Watson Scales

The next CO to go missing was W/Cdr Fraser Barron. I was lucky, as I had volunteered to take the place of his sick radio operator the operation before the whole crew was lost.

The domestic side of Oakington was an interesting experiment. First of all rank was ignored, the station was like a good club. We had no duties apart from an air test in the morning, reading the latest intelligence and drinking very large mugs of Horlicks, which I can remember to this day. Our food was very good. On Pathfinder Force we had two 'last meals' before we flew, one served when we went on an op and one when we returned. These consisted of bacon, eggs and very good sausages, toast and plenty of butter. We had waitresses. I always felt my worst time was not on the actual op, but to be served by young girls, many of whom were crying, especially as on a lot of occasions we were the only crew in the mess – the rest would be missing. Many had lost lovers, boyfriends and in one case the girl's husband. I think a lot of these WAAF's had a harder time than us.

A typical day consisted of calling in at the crew room to find out from the skipper if we were on ops that night or day. We did daylights and night flights and often to carry out an air test. Sometimes we went low flying, which we all loved, especially over the fens. One day we came back with a tree branch lodged in the air intake!

If there was a stand-down we either picked up our girlfriends, most of us had our own cars, or the whole crew drove into Cambridge, where we would drink large quantities of 'near beer'. I remember one such night. For some reason we went into Cambridge in the skipper's Austin Ten. We left it in the empty market square and retired to the Bun Shop, a famous Cambridge pub. We all got well and truly oiled and returned to the square got into Brian's car and he started the engine and put the car into gear. The engine roared but nothing happened. Brian tried again – the same thing happened. We got out to find we had no wheels – they had been replaced by fish boxes! It was now late at night and we had no transport. I had noticed, when we arrived, there was a Jeep parked at one end of the square – some American visiting his girlfriend? In those days Jeeps did not have keys, so I stole it and drove the crew back to Oakington.

We had had a lot to drink and I really had forgotten the incident. Brian said there was a strange Jeep outside the officers' mess and the CO had thought there were some visiting Americans! The next day the same Jeep was outside the sergeants' mess, and so it went on. Eventually the CO got in touch with the Americans, who told him all their Jeeps were accounted for. For a time we used it to run about the station, but as we were going to have two important visits I thought it would be diplomatic to take it back to where I had stolen it. I left it on the corner of Cambridge Market, where it remained, it seems, until after the war!

We had absolute confidence in our ground crews, who worked all hours and never complained. The Lancasters were large and, for their time, very complex aeroplanes and took a lot of maintenance. The only time our ground crew got upset was when we returned with nasty little holes in their aeroplane! Now I understand what their trouble was. It was not the holes they could see, but the ones hidden away, which they may have missed, endangering our lives at a later date.

I cannot remember seeing much security around the station. Our hardstanding was practically in Oakington village and most of the schoolchildren would watch our bomb load going on to the aeroplane. In fact, they could tell us where we were going before we had been briefed and they were usually right! From our hardstanding we could see the village pub and it was a great temptation not to take a short cut. We knew the perimeter wire was sensitive and the alarm would go off if anyone broke into the station. What the powers that be did not realize was that it also went off if anyone broke out. For months we fixed it to enable us to take a short cut to the pub and on the way back before the guards could be mobilized. For a long time security was in a panic every night we were not on ops. I think we were found out later, but there was not much they could do with us, only stop us operating!

On 3 September the squadron was presented with its Standard to mark twenty-five years of service and that night sent fifteen Lancasters to Berlin again. Only one, JA685:MG-Z, aborted, but the squadron lost four: JA713:MG-V, piloted by F/O

A. Crockford, shot down by a night fighter when homeward bound crashing into the sea of the Danish island of Tuno; JA854:MG-X, captained by F/Lt R.O. French, from which F/Sgt G.F. Thighe escaped to become a POW; EE119:MG-J, which was shot down by an Me410 and JA929:MG-N, flown by WO T.H. Hatchard, a New Zealander. Because of a high casualty rate on recent raids among the Stirlings and Halifaxes, this was an all-Lancaster raid and 316 of them made the attack. Most of the bombs fell short of the intended target but still caused serious damage. P/O Dennis Routen carried a load of red TIs, a 4,000 pound HC [Heavy Case] bomb and several 1,000 pound GP bombs. Just as bomb aimer, Leonard Noll, was about to drop the bombs the Lancaster was coned by about forty searchlights. As soon as the bombs were released Routen threw the bomber into a series of violent manoeuvres to avoid the flak being directed at it, pulling out of a dive at 2,000 feet. Their troubles were by no means over, however, as the rear gunner, Geoffrey Woodcock, spotted an Me210 closing in. The night fighter opened fire at 300 yards and Routen turned the bomber hard to starboard as Woodcock and Kanelakos, the mid-upper gunner opened fire, hitting the fighter. It passed astern in flames hitting the ground shortly afterwards. Following this sortie the navigator, Cyril Wolstenholme, was commissioned.

The next raid was on the night of 5/6 September, when the squadron sent fifteen crews out to Mannheim in a force of 605 aircraft. The Pathfinder markers were placed on the east side of the city with the intention that, as the bombers crept back with crews releasing their loads early, it would continue into Ludwigshafen. This plan worked and much damage was done to both towns. All of the squadron crews returned. P/O Dennis Routen's crew commented that it 'looked like the best blind marking seen yet'. After this raid Routen's navigator, Cyril Wolstenholme was awarded the DFM. The award covered the period prior to his commissioning and the citation read: 'His fine accuracy maintained throughout the flights allowing him to direct his captain with such precision that very successful bombing runs resulted. The courageous execution of the NCO's work has in large measure contributed to the success of his crew.'

The following night it was the turn of Munich and thirteen crews set out, with only one aborting: JB115:MG-G. The target was cloud-covered and the marking was not very effective, most crews bombing on a timed run in from the Ammersee. F/O Wilson, acting as a blind marker in Lancaster MG-Y, arrived over the target with his H2S out of order and descended below cloud to 10,000 feet before bombing visually.

Lancaster JA978:MG-S was lost at Waterbeach on the 12th, when P/O Woodward overshot on landing and hit a tree. During a training trip he had an engine fail and decided to land. While making the approach to land he realized he was too high and opened up the throttles to go around again. As he did so he hit the trees and crash-landed on the airfield.

Thirteen crews set out for Montlucon on the night of 15/16 September, in a force of 369 aircraft, including some American B-17s. One Lancaster, JA685:MG-Z, aborted. The target was the Dunlop rubber factory, which was bombed in bright moonlight. The accurate marking by the Pathfinders and the good work of the master bomber combined to make this a very successful attack. F/Sgt Porteous recorded in his log-book that he had bombed from 5,500 feet and that it had been a 'good raid'.

The next night five Lancasters set out for Modane. JA685:MG-Z again aborted, this time with intercom trouble. The target marking was inaccurate and the bombing was not successful.

On 20 September W/Cdr Burnell was replaced by a new CO, G/Capt K.R. Rampling DSO DFC, the only group captain to command the squadron.

Attacks on Hanover were becoming a feature of the autumn months of 1943 and the squadron went there again on 22/23 September, losing Lancaster JB184:MG-V, flown by P/O W.E. Stenhouse, from a force of fifteen dispatched. Sgt G.N. Breedon survived the crash at Geeste-Munde on the east bank of the Weser. One Lancaster, JA932:MG-M, returned early with an unserviceable rear turret. Mannheim was on the target list for the night of 23/24 September and the squadron again sent fifteen crews. JB185:MG-X aborted and JA718:MG-T returned early with a sick navigator, but the rest took part in a raid which caused widespread damage to Mannheim and neighbouring Ludwigshafen.

Hanover was struck on 27/28 September by nineteen crews and Lancaster JA849:MG-F, flown by P/O Dennis Routen, was lost. This was their thirty-sixth operational sortie and nothing was heard from them after take-off. The Pathfinders bombed on faulty winds and though the bombing was concentrated it fell 5 miles to the south and south-east of the intended target. Routen's Lancaster was at the head of the Pathfinder attack and close to the target. Canadian F/Sgt James Kanelakos was the rear gunner. Near Hanover they were attacked on the beam by a night fighter equipped with *Schrage Musik*, two upward-firing cannons, which allowed it to attack from the blind spot under a bomber, who virtually chopped off Kanelakos's rear turret and set the Lancaster on fire. Wounded in the leg and stomach Kanelakos

A remarkable photograph of a 7 Sqn Lancaster going down over a target in 1943, photographed from an aircraft of No. 156 Sqn. 7 Sqn

F/Sgt James Kanelakos with his ground crew. G. Pitchfork

was trapped in the jammed turret. The night fighter made a second attack, wounding him again. The Lancaster fell apart, the wreckage landing near the town of Quackenbruck, and Kanelakos was thrown clear. His parachute was only partially attached and cut him on opening. Landing unconscious in a field he was captured by

The crew of JA849:MG-F. L to R: R.J. Frewer, J. Kanelakos, G. Woodcock, C. Wolstenholme, D. Routen, L. Noll. G. Pitchfork

Lancaster JA849. G. Pitchfork

the Germans and taken to a *Luftwaffe* hospital, where he was visited by the pilot who had shot the Lancaster down. Eventually transferred to POW camp at Sagan he had a long recovery from his wounds. Towards the end of the war the POWs were marched from Sagan to Luchenwald, 30 miles from Berlin, in dreadful conditions. Kanelakos was finally liberated by the Russians whom he described as 'wild and woolly, but they're great guys'. In April 1945 he would be awarded the DFM effective from the day before he was shot down. The citation read:

> *This airman has completed a large number of operational sorties. Both in the air and on the ground he has displayed great keenness and devotion to duty. On a recent operation Flight Sergeant Kanelakos shared with the rear gunner in the destruction of an enemy night fighter whilst over the target area. An excellent air gunner with a fine fighting spirit, he has spared no effort to improve his technique.*

Geoffrey Woodcock would never know about the award of his DFM; the six other members of the crew were all killed.

This was a tough raid for the squadron, F/O Wilson, flying Lancaster MG-Q was coned over the target for twenty minutes, during which the second pilot along for the trip, the flight engineer Sgt Joseph Kofoed and the rear gunner F/Sgt Lawrence were all injured by flak. Bomb aimer William Porteous noted in his log-book that they had 'navigated home by guess and by God'.

In November 1943 F/O Wilson (who already held the DFC and DFM) was awarded the DSO for this

F/Lt William Porteous, bomb aimer to F/O Wilson, S/Ldr Dennis and W/Cdr Fraser Barron. He died with S/Ldr Dennis and the rest of the crew on the same raid as W/Cdr Barron. It is suspected that they collided with W/Cdr Barron, though other sources claim to have seen both aircraft shot down. Mildred Watson Scales

sortie and F/Sgt Mulholland and F/Sgt Porteous were both awarded the DFM. The citation in the *London Gazette* gave the details:

> *This officer and airmen were pilot, mid-upper gunner and air bomber respectively of an aircraft detailed to attack Hanover one night in September 1943. On the run up to the target the bomber was hit by anti-aircraft fire. Four members of the crew were wounded and much essential equipment was rendered unserviceable. In spite of this, Flying Officer Wilson resolutely held to his course, enabling Flight Sergeant Porteous to execute a successful bombing attack. On leaving the target, the bomber was intercepted by a fighter which attacked with great persistence. Nevertheless, Flying Officer Wilson succeeded in evading the fighter, being greatly assisted by Flight Sergeant Mulholland who kept his captain fully informed of the attacker's movements. On the return flight, Flight Sergeant Porteous assumed the duties of navigator and executed his task with skill. These members of the aircraft crew displayed great courage, skill and tenacity in the most trying circumstances.*

On 29 September Lancaster JB225:MG-V was lost after an engine cut and the undercarriage collapsed in a forced landing at Swanton Morley. F/Lt J.L. Spiller had returned early from a raid on Bochum due to engine failure. The crew escaped the crash landing unhurt. Eight Lancasters went to Bochum that night and took part in a concentrated raid, which was marked accurately by Oboe by the Pathfinders. The *Altstadt* was particularly hard hit.

On the 1/2 October only four crews were sent to Hagen by the squadron. Perfect Oboe sky marking resulted in complete success for this mission and the destruction of an important factory producing accumulator batteries slowed down U-boat production considerably. The following night it was the turn of Munich to feel the weight of Bomber Command's destructive force when 294 aircraft attacked the city. No. 7 Sqn provided nineteen of the bombers in a scattered attack. The crew of Lancaster JA971:XU-J abandoned their attempt to reach the target after they were attacked by an unidentified aircraft, which set fire to the tailplane, causing ammunition to explode and damage to the fuel tanks, resulting in a loss of fuel. Kassel was attacked on 3/4 October by sixteen Lancasters, with only one abort, JA968:MG-H with the oxygen supply to the mid-upper and rear turrets unserviceable. The visual markers failed to correct a serious overshoot of the aiming point by the initial H2S markers and the main attack fell upon the suburbs of the city. Large fires were started at both the Henschel and Fieseler aircraft factories and a large ammunition dump at Ihringshausen was hit by a stray bomb load, which attracted other aircraft, resulting in its destruction.

Six crews set out for Frankfurt the following night, though two aborted: JA905:MG-K with a sick navigator and JA706:MG-C with complete electrical failure. The remaining four bombed the primary target in clear weather. Good Pathfinder marking resulted in the most successful attack on this city so far, with crews describing the target as a sea of flames. Tragically an orphanage was hit, killing many young children during the raid.

The bombers did not go out again until the night of 7/8 October when thirteen Lancasters were ordered off for Stuttgart. Two aborted: JB303:MG-F with an unserviceable rear turret and JA718:MG-T unable to maintain height. The night-fighter force was successfully diverted away and the force bombed successfully on two Pathfinder-marked areas.

The squadron returned to Hanover with twelve crews on 8/9 October, losing two Lancasters: JA706:MG-C, captained by WO P. Hartstein, which crashed on the Wormstal Estate at Altenhagen, Sgts F.E. Bryant, R.J. Reeves and R.A. Woodward surviving to become POWs; and JB181:MG-V, which was flown by F/O B.E.C. McPhearson, which crashed north-west of Assen in Holland. Sgt E.A. Brinton was a member of this crew and at only seventeen was the youngest airman killed on operations in Bomber Command. On this night the German fighter controller correctly guessed that the target was Hanover and scrambled many night fighters. Twenty-seven aircraft, fourteen of them Lancasters were lost.

The squadron took part in a raid on Hanover on 18/19 October after a break of ten nights and lost two Lancasters: JA917:MG-P, flown by Sgt H.R. Boness, who was killed along with Sgt Dick, although the rest of his crew escaped to be made prisoners; and JB347:MG-V, flown by WO A.M. Marshall, which came down at Rehburg to the west of Hanover. F/Sgts J.R. Penny, and J.G. Kernaghan and Sgt F.E.B. Lyle were captured.

On 19 October F/Lt William Senger, who had previously been awarded the DFC as a warrant officer, was awarded the DSO. The citation read:

This officer has completed a very large number of sorties involving attacks on a wide range of enemy targets. He has displayed skill of a high order while his unfailing determination to inflict loss on the enemy has been a noteworthy feature of his work. Flight Lieutenant Senger is a model of efficiency and his gallant example has proved a rare source of encouragement.

Leipzig was hit again on the 20th/21st and Lancasters JA907:MG-U, captained by F/O J.W. Leitch, and JB175:MG-A, flown by F/Sgt D.M. Watson, failed to return. Leitch was Australian and held the DFC. His Lancaster was shot down by a night fighter, bursting into flames at low level. Sgt F.W. Lashford was the only survivor. Watson was the victim of Oblt Heinz-Wolfgang Schnaufer of IV/NJG1, crashing at Gieten, near Assen in Holland. This raid was carried out in appalling weather conditions and the bombing was widely scattered. Sixteen Lancasters were lost, 4.5 per cent of the force dispatched.

Lancaster JA717:MG-C, piloted by F/O J.W. Payne, was lost raiding Frankfurt on the 22nd/23rd. Payne and rear gunner Sgt B.D.S. Lovell were killed, but the rest of the crew escaped and were captured. Lovell had been seen to leave the Lancaster from the rear turret uninjured by Sgt Farrag, who was himself exiting from the rear entrance door. This was a diversionary raid by eight Mosquitoes and twenty-eight Lancasters for a much larger Main Force raid on Kassel. JA717 was the only loss, falling close to Bad Homburg. Two crews aborted: JA698:MG-H with the oxygen supply to the rear turret unserviceable; and JA693:MG-W with a port engine out due to icing.

Eleven crews went to Dusseldorf and Cologne on the night of 3/4 November, three to the former the remainder to the latter. Extensive damage was caused to Dusseldorf and the raid on Cologne was extremely accurate, with many bomb loads landing in the centre of the city, some damaging the cathedral.

There was a break of a week before the crews were put on operations again. This time the target was Modane. Six crews took part in a raid by 313 Lancasters on the

Lancaster MG-H with ground crew. The nose shows sixty-eight operations successfully flown. This may be JA968. 7 Sqn

railway yards on the main line to Italy. Two hundred dropped their bombs within 1 mile of the target and seriously damaged the rail system. There was a further week's break until the night of 17/18 November, when fourteen crews went to Mannheim again. An accurate attack on the IG Farben factory was carried out.

The Battle of Berlin commenced on the night of 18/19 November and such was the strength of Bomber Command now that Harris was able to send two forces out that night. Four hundred and forty bombers went to Berlin whilst Mannheim was the target for 395 aircraft, including three and seventeen respectively from 7 Sqn. Berlin was cloud-covered and the bombing widely scattered, but the Daimler Benz factory was among the targets damaged and a 90 per cent loss in production was suffered after the raid. Two Lancasters aborted: JB398:MG-C, with the rear gunner's oxygen supply and guns out of order, as well as the navigation aids; and JB185:MG-X, with an engine failure. Lancaster JA970:MG-N failed to return from Mannheim, which received scattered bombing, and F/Lt A.C. Harding and his crew were lost. Andrew Harding, a Canadian, had enlisted in May 1941 and was commissioned in 1942. He was awarded the DFC in October 1943 as a pilot officer. The recommendation read: 'This officer has captained bomber aircraft on sorties against many targets in Germany and Italy, obtaining some excellent photographs. He has consistently shown courage and determination in bringing his missions to a successful completion.' His crew was to have been screened from operations after this sortie.

The same Lancaster, MG-H, showing sixty-eight operations, this time with the aircrew proudly posing in front. 7 Sqn

JB115:MG-G went down on a Berlin raid on 22/23 November, crashing near Hanover with the loss of S/Ldr E.H.M. Nesbitt and his crew. Nesbitt had completed at least thirty-seven operational sorties. This raid saw the largest number of aircraft sent to Berlin so far and also marked the last Stirling raids on Germany. Two Lancasters, JB468:MG-A and JA971:MG-J2, aborted with a sick flight engineer, and a boost and rev surge on all engines respectively. Lancaster EE119:MG-N was also lost, with WO S.G. Dorrell and his crew all being killed.

On a very bad night for the squadron Lancasters JA932:MG-M, captained by F/Sgt G.W. Tindle, JB480:MG-N, flown by F/Sgt F.R. Page and JB538 went missing on a raid to Berlin on 23/24 November. Hit by flak, M-Mother came down between Oudeschild and Brakenstein on the island of Texel. All of the crew were killed. N-Nuts and its crew were lost without trace. JA971:MG-J2 almost made it home but the crew, captained by F/O P.K.B. Williams had to abandon her near Oakington. The Lancaster had its elevators shot away by flak over the target and on return to base five of the crew baled out successfully. Williams and the navigator remained in the aircraft but eventually baled out 20 miles north of Oakington. JA718:MG-T turned back with the rear turret intercom unserviceable and the pilot's escape hatch blown off. JA905:MG-K turned back when the pilot found the airspeed dropping off and the aircraft becoming sluggish to control.

An aircrew group photographed with Lancaster JB175, which went down on the Leipzig raid of 20/21 October. 7 Sqn

Another aircrew group photographed in front of a Lancaster coded MG-A in 1943. This may also have been JB175. 7 Sqn

Berlin featured again on the 26th/27th when JB303:MG-F, flown by F/O G.H. Beaumont, went down. The Lancaster crashed north of Frankfurt with the loss of the whole crew except the rear gunner and the observer, Ted Ansfield. Ted later recalled his ordeal.

We were attacked by Oblt Albert Walter of NJG 6, flying Bf110 G-4 720187 at 2012 hrs on the night of 26/27 November 1943. He was subsequently killed in action along with his radio operator Uffz Otto Meyer on the night of 24/25 February 1944. His gunner baled out and landed safely. His attack on us was a copybook one. He took the engines and fuel tanks out and sent us down in flames.

The order to 'bale out' was given and a few seconds later there was a blinding flash and I knew no more until I woke up in a forest almost one and a half hours later, numb with cold. My parachute lay open beside me. It must have either been blasted open or I had subconsciously pulled the ripcord whilst falling. Apart from a severe head pain I appeared to be in one piece. I hid my parachute and Mae West and struck off in a south-westerly direction.

After a few hours I collapsed and revived at 0600 hrs stiff with cold. The ground was frozen. When I got up and looked around I was surprised to see a parachute draped over a bush about 100 yards away. I went to investigate and found the body of my engineer. I covered him with his parachute and after checking my escape map continued walking. I had turned my electrically heated waistcoat inside out so that it appeared to be more like a civilian jacket.

Two photographs of Ted Ansfield as a POW following his capture in November 1943. E. Ansfield

Towards nightfall it started to rain which turned into a continuous downpour. I had to lay up under bushes, as it was impossible to make any progress in the extreme dark and now boggy conditions. The following day was no better; it just continued to rain and prevented me making any progress. I found that I was having difficulty orientating myself; unbeknown to me I had sustained a fractured skull.

For a while I laid up in an abandoned quarry hoping the rain would abate, but it didn't. Later in the day I made a further attempt at cross-country walking but the fields were now flooded. I had a narrow escape when a Fieseler Storch passed overhead at treetop height apparently searching for escaping airmen. From the cover of bushes I could see someone scanning the countryside through binoculars. I eventually reached a river, presumably the Lann. It was in full flood and the only available bridge was carrying an unhealthy volume of traffic so I hid up until darkness fell.

I remained on the roadway, which helped speed up my progress. By the fourth day I had almost worn through my flying boots, which was making walking even more difficult. The rain never ceased and I was suffering from severe head pains. As it grew darker I came across a wooded slope. I had climbed about halfway up when the ground gave way beneath me and I slid down into an abandoned quarry some 20–30 feet deep. Shaken by the fall I decided to stay there until daylight. I awoke some hours later to a strange warmth. The rain had turned to snow and I was almost buried. I was now beginning to feel weak and ill and realised that the snow had further reduced my chances of evasion.

I had hopes of getting to Paris where I had contacts with persons connected with the Resistance, who would give me every assistance. I pressed on and eventually came to a railway, which appeared to be going in the right direction. I followed the tracks for about a mile when I came to a railway station. Avoiding railway workers I hid up and awaited a train going in the right direction. After a while I was rewarded, a freight train was approaching and slowing down. I crossed the tracks and as it got to me I stood up and leaped at one of the wagons. I found a handhold, was dragged off my feet, but before I could haul myself on board my strength gave out and I almost fell under the wheels. My best chance had gone.

Through the falling snow I followed the tracks for a few miles and collapsed beside them, not waking until dawn. I left the tracks and picked up a road running parallel. It took me to a small town. In all of my six days as a fugitive I had never dared to come into close contact with people. I now became incautious, wrapped my scarf around my head to cover my growth of beard and entered the little town. In the main street I noticed a policeman talking to a man in a long leather coat and felt hat. I watched their reflections in a shop window and noticed that one was pointing in my direction. I casually sauntered down the street and out of the corner of my eye I could see that I was being followed.

I came to what appeared to be a small cinema, the doors were open so I quickly darted inside, ran down the aisle between the seats and out of the rear exit and back into the countryside. On a hillside above the town I again collapsed. I was exhausted and terribly weak. I could only be a few miles from the Rhine. A burly farmer driving a horse and cart spotted me and challenged me. He jumped down from the cart and helped me to my feet. This was the end;

it was 2 December 1943. He took me back to his home where his wife gave me a cup of ersatz coffee and a piece of bread. The police arrived and I was force-marched to the police station where I was thrown into a stinking dungeon.

I lay down on a filthy bunk and fell fast asleep only to be wakened after a very short time. I was dragged from this filthy hole into the police station where a female interpreter commenced to question me in the presence of the police chief and my escort. I would only give my name, rank and service number. My escort threw me to the floor and said in a strong broken American accent, 'Smart guy eh, vot vud you say if ve hang you?' I burst out laughing and told him, politely, that under those circumstances I could say a damned sight less. He realized his error and just as he was about to put his rifle butt into my ribs in walked a Luftwaffe officer who stepped smartly between us and floored the guard. He helped me to my feet and apologized. For me this part of the war was over. My escort to captivity had arrived.

W/Cdr F.W. Hilton and his crew were also lost in JB358:MG-G, though all survived to become POWs except P/O A.M. Leonard. They were attacked by a night fighter and set on fire. Sgt Naylor tried to fight the fire with an extinguisher, sustaining severe burns in the process, before being forced to bale out with the remainder of the crew.

The 443 Berlin raiders and a diversionary force attacking Stuttgart flew a common route almost to Frankfurt before splitting. The Germans, thinking Frankfurt was the target, sent many night fighters to this area and several bombers were shot down. The weather was clear over the target but the Pathfinders marked an area to the north-west of the city centre. Due to the size of the city most of the bombs fell in the target area. German casualties were high and included many of the animals in the Berlin Zoo. Two crews turned back early: JB468:MG-A had its tail badly damaged over the target in a collision with another Lancaster and JA968:MG-H had a defective compass.

On 3/4 December the bombers went to Leipzig and the squadron lost Lancaster JA685:MG-Z, flown by Sgt C.H. Phillips. It was shot down by a night fighter and witnesses on the ground reported that it came down in flames in great circles before crashing near De Krim. The following day the wreck was found, with some of the crew lying nearby. There were several craters and some bombs, including a 'cookie', lying a distance from the plane. The captain, Sgt C.H. Phillips and Sgts B. Cooper and W.R.J. Craze managed to escape.

Lancasters JA853:MG-L, JB543:MG-J, JB552:MG-K and JB656:MG-D went down on the Berlin raid on 16/17 December. MG-D, flown by F/O F.W. Rush, crashed east of Alkmaar, Holland; Sgt J.S. Ogg, the sole survivor, successfully evaded capture. WO W.A. Watson, an Australian, took off from Oakington at 1624 hrs and was brought down in JA853:MG-L near Follega, Holland by a night fighter flown by Major Heinz Schnaufer. Prior to joining 7 Sqn Watson's crew had flown with No. 460 Sqn from Binbrook, completing five operations there. Berlin was their fourth and last operation with 7 Sqn.

A flurry of combats started as soon as the Dutch coast was crossed, and at least fourteen bombers were shot down on that section of the route. An account of the loss of Watson's Lancaster comes from *Unteroffizier* Fritz Rumpelhardt, who was the radar operator in *Oberleutnant* Heinz-Wolfgang Schnaufer's crew of IV/NJG 1,

The remains of a Merlin engine from JA853:MG-L recovered fifty years after the crash in Holland. D. Robinson

quoted by Martin Middlebrook in *The Berlin Raids*. Rumpelhardt picked up his first contact at a range of 4,000 metres. The aircraft was fitted with the *Schrage Musik*. That first contact was swiftly shot down. It was the 7 Sqn Lancaster of WO W.A. Watson; there were no survivors. Fritz Rumpelhardt wrote of the combats that night:

> *For many days there had been bad weather over Holland and the whole occupied territory. At night, therefore, it was impossible, because of the thick fog, to get the night fighters into the air against the British bomber squadrons who were targeting Berlin.*
>
> *So, on the night of 16 December 1943 the crews of IV Gruppe, night fighter squadron, sat in their*

19-year-old Sgt James Hurst, mid-upper gunner of Lancaster JA853:MG-L, killed on the Berlin raid of 16/17 December 1943. D. Robinson

The five Australian crew members of WO W.A. Watson's crew of JA853:MG-L lost on 16/17 December 1943. Rear L to R: WO W. Waterman, WO W.A. Watson and F/Sgt C.L. Robinson. Front L to R: F/Sgt J. Butterworth and F/Sgt R.D. McWha. D. Robinson

readiness room waiting – in vain, they thought – for action. The enemy had sent up two strong bomber formations from the British Isles. However, there was no one in command ready to take responsibility for sending the night fighters up in such terrible weather conditions.

The commander of IV Gruppe, Heinz-Wolfgang Schnaufer, couldn't bear to keep his crew waiting. He asked the command post to get in touch by telephone with Fighter HQ to get permission to oppose the bombers – even if it was for him alone. On his personal insistence, this was granted.

So Hauptmann Schnaufer took off with his crew, Leutnant Fritz Rumpelhardt as radio operator and Oberfeldwebel Wilhelm Gaensler as gunner – the sole night fighter against the approaching formation of bombers. The members of the crew did not ask themselves whether this was a risk worth taking.

The cloud level was 35 metres and, under that, the flight-path lights could only just be made out in the mist. In seconds, the Me110 was lost in thick cloud. The motors were running on full tanks. Schnaufer knew full well that he had to fly through a very difficult time, with great danger of icing. (This both changed the profile of the wings and increased the weight of the machine.)

Despite reduced response from the controls, he succeeded in getting through the very dangerous zone and, after seemingly endless climbing and with a mixture of fear and hope, the cloud ceiling was reached at about 5,000 metres above sea level. A brilliant, starry sky quickly led to all anxiety being forgotten.

157

Radio contact with the ground station in Area 'Polar Bear' was excellent and very soon came the order to fly in the direction of 360 degrees. In fact, this came just in time as the bombers had already reached the north-west border of the combat zone.

Pilot and gunner stared spellbound into the night while the radio operator kept his eyes on the radar screen. Soon he had fixed on an enemy target about 4,000 metres away.

After various course corrections, which Rumpelhardt passed to Schnaufer over the intercom, Gaensler could discern the bomber they were chasing – just as a weak shadow to start with. In the approved manner, the pilot positioned himself under the still unsuspecting Lancaster. After a short manoeuvre to improve his position still further, came the attack with the Ragged Music of almost vertically firing weapons – the two Mk 108 cannon, which were built into the rear portion of the fuselage.

Whenever possible, Schnaufer preferred to shoot at the fuel tanks, which were slung under the wings between the two motors. On the one hand, the most telling effect was achieved (explosion of the tanks); on the other, the crew had the earliest possible chance of saving themselves through parachute jumps.

Soon, after a short fire, a colossal sheet of flame shot out of the fuselage. The night turned to day. Schnaufer turned the Me110 on its head so that he could come out of the area of fire and wreckage right side up.

With an eerie movement and trailing a long streak of fire behind it, the mortally wounded bird plunged downwards, and, before the cloud enveloped it,

P/O Tyler and crew, lost in Lancaster MG-J on the Berlin raid of 16/17 December 1943.
D. Cheetham

it tipped over. It crashed at Follega on the Friesian Canal at 1801 hrs. As it later turned out the plane was JA853 of 7 Squadron RAF.

P/O G. Tyler went down in MG-J with only F/Sgt A. Smillie and Sgt D. Woolford surviving. They were shot down by *Hptm* Heinrich Prinz zu Sayn-Wittgenstein crashing at Wilsum near the Dutch border. F/Lt J.R. Petrie was the captain of MG-K, which went down with the loss of the whole crew near Werte. Such losses, the worst in a single night, were a heavy burden to the squadron.

The bomber route was directly to Berlin across Holland and northern Germany, and the fighter controllers plotted the course with great accuracy, guiding night fighters into the stream from the Dutch coast. More fighters were waiting over Berlin and there were many combats. Twenty-five Lancasters were lost in combat and twenty-nine Lancasters and a Stirling on returning to England, where they encountered very low cloud covering their airfields.

Lancaster JB652:MG-A went down east of Halesworth in Suffolk on the 21st, when the crew baled out after it was attacked and damaged by a German night fighter. Tragically WO R.B. Smith DFC, the rear gunner, hit the tail as he baled out and was killed. Christmas Eve saw the loss of JB735 in a take-off crash at Oakington. P/O H.C. Williams, a New Zealander, and all of his crew were injured in the crash.

P.K. Patrick, who completed his first tour on Stirlings with 149 Sqn at Lakenheath, served on the squadron from November 1943 to March 1944, when his flight was transferred to Little Staughton to form No. 582 Sqn. He recalls the winter of 1943/44.

Lancaster MG-L with air and ground crew. The nose shows twenty-one operations flown.
Seven Lancasters, JA853, JB661, ND365, ND443, ND445, PB474 and PB623 were coded 'L'.
7 Sqn

No. 7 Sqn pose with a Lancaster at Oakington in December 1943. F. Stephenson via D. Cheetham

One scene which will always remain in my mind during the 'Berlin Winter' of 1943/44 was when the Station Commander, G/Capt Coombe and the Squadron Commander, G/Capt Rampling used to stand by the caravan at the end of the runway and salute each aircraft as it commenced its run. For my part, as my right hand was on the throttles I could not return the salute in the usual way, so I gave an 'eyes left' salute as we began to take-off. I thought that it was a thoughtful and typical gesture by the two commanders, sometimes in miserable weather.

The crew member who was vital to survival of the crew on those long trips was the rear gunner. No matter how experienced or capable were the pilot and other crew members, the ability of the rear gunner, in the most uncomfortable location in the aircraft, to spot a fighter aircraft approaching from below was vital. To swing his turret and crouch forward for hours on end demanded both stamina and concentration. I know from my own experience the importance of a good rear gunner.

F/O Don Field DFC and crew with Lancaster JB652:MG-A. D. Cheetham

CHAPTER FIVE
JANUARY–DECEMBER 1944

The hard work of many aircrew when not flying was not forgotten when it came to honours and awards. On 1 January 1944 Sgt Gordon MacAdam received a Mention in Despatches, the citation recording:

This non-commissioned officer as a flight engineer has displayed constant devotion to duty requiring many hours of overtime work. He is responsible for the submission of many ideas which have resulted in the improvement of the working conditions for the squadron crews while on patrol. His unceasing efforts have been devoted to the maintenance of a high standard of efficiency in his flight.

The same day F/O Eld Martin, a navigator, was also awarded a Mention in Despatches for his work:

Flying Officer Martin is a skilled navigator who has performed difficult tasks with accuracy and reliability. Hi keen interest in navigation has resulted in the development of a crew trainer which is of inestimable value to his unit. In addition he has at all times displayed energy and initiative of a high standard.

The New Year was only two days old when Lancaster Mk III EE129:MG-V was lost on a raid to Berlin. F/Lt K.C. Kingsbury and his crew all survived to become prisoners. JB 682:MG-A, captained by S/Ldr H.R. Jaggard, also failed to return from this raid. This Lancaster was shot down on the outbound journey by a night fighter, coming down at Ramsel. None of the crew survived. The German controller was not fooled by a spoof raid by Mosquitoes on Hamburg and night fighters were active in the target area. The following day JB677:MG-U flown by F/Lt I.M. Pearson DFC failed to return from Berlin. Pearson was a veteran bomber pilot with at least forty-eight operational sorties to his credit. F/Sgt M. Davis was the sole survivor. The night fighters were vectored to the wrong area by the German controller and missed the bomber stream. This did not prevent the loss of twenty-seven Lancasters, ten of them from the Pathfinders.

The crews who had flown the first trip of the year to Berlin were shocked to hear that they would be going back again that night as W/Cdr Philip Patrick, a flight commander on the squadron recalled (quoted by Martin Middlebrook in *The Berlin Raids*):

That was the nearest thing I ever saw to a mutiny in the RAF, when the guys walked in and saw the map showing Berlin again. There was a rumble of what I might call amazement, or horror, or disbelief. The Station Commander quietened the chaps down and there was no trouble, but you can imagine what it was like to be dead tired and then having to go again. Fatigue was the main problem; I always think it was worst for the gunners, having to stay awake and keep look-out for seven or eight hours at a time.

The bombers went to the Baltic port of Stettin on the 5th/6th and Lancaster JB651:MG-K, flown by WO J. McGinlay, failed to return. The crew was lost without

Gerald South's crew at Oakington in January 1944. L to R: F/O G.J. South, F/Sgt W. Gould, P/O G. Inverarity, F/Sgt N. Kaye, F/Sgt C. Welch, F/Sgt A.R.G. Fonseca and F/Sgt J.G. Miles.
G.J. South

trace and are commemorated on the Runnymede Memorial. A Mosquito diversion to Berlin had kept most of the night fighters away from the Stettin force but sixteen bombers still went down.

Braunschweig was raided on the 14th/15th and the squadron lost Lancasters JA905:MG-V, flown by F/Lt J.N. Newton, JA935:MG-O flown by F/Lt D.L.C. Thomas DFC, an experienced Pathfinder pilot with forty-four operational sorties to his credit, and JB398:MG-C, flown by F/O R.J. Croxford. Croxford was shot down by a night fighter, his Lancaster crashing at Torfhaus. P/O W.H. Bacon and Sgt L.W. Clarke from Croxford's crew became POWs. These were among eleven Pathfinders lost to flak and fighters that night. JA935 took off from Oakington at 1659 hrs carrying as a crew member rear gunner Lawrence C Hartman, who had joined the RAF from Essex Constabulary. He was lost with all of the crew over Germany, aged thirty-one. Gerald South joined the squadron on 15 January, having previously served on another Pathfinder unit, No. 405 Sqn RCAF at Gransden Lodge.

> *I was to take over the crew of a flight commander who had finished his second or third tour, leaving the rest with a number to complete. I didn't know what to expect, but they proved to be very good. We had a reasonably uneventful time despite the four or five trips to the 'Big City' as Berlin was always known and the disastrous trip to Nuremberg on 30/31 March.*

On 20/21 January Berlin was attacked again. The small diversionary raids did not fool the German controller and the night fighters scored steadily ND368:MG-U going down. S/Ldr Maurice Baird-Smith DFC was the pilot. He had served with 37 Sqn before joining 7 Sqn after a lecture tour of the USA. 'Bomber' Harris asked him what he wanted to do next and he recalls: '"Go back on operations, Sir", a rather stupid reaction I suppose!' Considering what happened to him, and his crew, on the night of 20/21 January, one might agree.

> *I suppose that sitting in the middle of a city street is, at the best of times, a rather eccentric pastime, so you can imagine how foolish I felt when I regained*

consciousness and found myself in the centre of Berlin with bombs falling all around me, guns barking – oh, all hell being stirred up. It was about 1900 hrs on a drizzly winter's night when it all started.

At 1850, I had been sitting at the controls of a Pathfinder Lancaster at 20,000 feet with six other men – my crew. The job had been done – the bombs and markers gone – and we were headed for home. Now I was down here and what had happened to Ray, Andy, Waddy —oh, all of my crew? I remembered a little, then a little bit more but everything in reverse.

The bump when I hit the ground must have knocked me out – the 5,000 feet of clouds I had floated through – Yes, I remember now – when the parachute trailed, the harness caught round my throat and it seems that, having escaped from the explosion, I would die this way. Yes, the explosion – that gave me another lead but I couldn't quite orientate my mind. But this wasn't the time to start working out what had happened or how. The fact was that I seemed to be close to the aiming point of a near 1,000-bomber raid on Berlin and there were about 999 Lancasters and Halifaxes bent on killing me into the bargain! That seemed ironical because, being a Pathfinder, we had been responsible for marking the very target that we were now part of. All I hoped was that my crew had been as lucky as me – or was that wishing them a worse fate – to be hit by one's own bombs?

Luckily, the street where I had landed was deserted – the Germans were down in their shelters. If they had seen the Terrorflieger *– the name Goebbels had given us – goodness knows what they would have done. We were briefed that we should go to ground as soon as possible. As it happened, my bombardier, Sgt Bartholomew, was discovered and beaten up – he died as a result. I knew I had about thirty minutes to get clear of the area as they were bound to find my parachute. I hid it as best I could in a doorway. But standing up proved a problem because, every time I got to my feet, another violent explosion would knock me down – or, if it didn't, I would throw myself flat on my face. It was an automatic reaction learnt from the Blitz in London when only drunks and fools stood up to have a look.*

The RAF raids were a thousand times worse than the London Blitz. It sounded as though all the pilots had decided to commit suicide and dive their Lancasters straight onto the target. Bu this falling down business wasn't getting me anywhere. A quarter of an hour had gone by and the raid only lasted about half an hour. So, I was determined to move off. It was only then that I realized I had sprained both ankles and my boots had come off. I suppose it was a question of whether my feet would have come off in the explosion but, as it happened, my boots were too big and stayed behind instead. However, walking around in bare feet in the middle of winter was no joke. It almost decided me to give up after a night or two of trudging along cobbled streets.

Baird-Smith and F/O D.F.M. Waddington survived to be taken prisoner. Sgt E.F. Bartholomew also survived the shooting down but died six days later of his injuries. Another crew member was F/Lt R.N. Ridley, who was well over the normal aircrew age at 40.

William Porteous flew in Lancaster MG-J on this raid with WO Aslett, rather than his usual crew. Over the target they encountered and shot down an Me110.

JB408:MG-A, captained by F/Lt I.J. Robertson, an Australian, also failed to return from Magdeburg on the 21st/22nd. 8.8 per cent of the force dispatched was lost, a large number of them to night fighters. Fifty-seven aircraft was a heavy price to pay for the poor results obtained on this raid. Some of the Main Force arrived before the Pathfinders and bombed early, causing other bombers to drop on the fires they had started rather than the target markers.

Yet another Lancaster was lost when JB308:MG-B, flown by Canadian F/Lt C.R. Power overshot on landing from a training sortie at Oakington on the 24th. On the 28th/29th the squadron went to Berlin again, part of a 677-strong force, losing Lancasters JA718:MG-T and JB717:MG-V. WO N.J. Clifford flying MG-T and one other crew member, F/Sgt S. Jarvis, survived the loss of the bomber, which crashed at Zuhlen. MG-V was flown by W/Cdr R.E. Young DSO DFC, who survived along with F/Sgts A.G. Ryder and Ivan T. Taylor to become POWs. Young had served in the Royal Engineers before transferring to the RAF in 1940, flying fighters prior to converting to bombers and joining the Pathfinder Force. S/Ldr Curtiss, flying JB455:MG-P, had four combats with enemy night fighters but managed to return to base. Ivan Taylor, an Australian, was the bomb aimer of his crew, detailed as blind markers. He recalled being shot down (quoted by Martin Middlebrook in *The Berlin Raids*):

The first of our markers cascaded right below us and caused everything possible to be thrown at us. The gunners shouted that there were three Messerschmitt 110s approaching from behind and I spotted a fighter approaching from the front, firing tracer. There was then a terrific jolt and the port wing became a mass of flames. The skipper gave the order to bale out. I remember putting on my parachute; then I must have become temporarily unconscious, as the next thing I remember was a dead silence and seeing my knees in front of me and my chute handle. Then I must have blacked out again, because I cannot remember pulling that handle, but I did of course, as the next thing I remember was hearing

W/Cdr R.E. Young DSO DFC and crew. Young was shot down in Lancaster JB717:MG-V over Berlin on the night of 28/29 January 1944. D. Cheetham

ammunition exploding and seeing myself still strapped in my chute harness which was hanging from a tree. Not many yards away was what was left of the burning aircraft, hence the exploding ammunition.

Berlin was on the target list again in February 1944, the squadron suffered heavily raiding this target on the 15th/16th losing JB224:MG-W, which went down with the loss of F/Lt R.L. Barnes DFC and his crew. JB414:MG-Y, captained by S/Ldr J.A. Hegman DSO DFC also went down with the loss of all of the crew except Sgt F.I. Cook, who became a POW. S/Ldr Hegman was older than the average at 40 and hailed from New Zealand. F/Sgt Nicholls of his crew was also 40.

It appears that age was no barrier to forming a successful Pathfinder crew. ND365: MG-L and ND445:MG-D were also lost. MG-L was captained by F/Lt P.K.B. Williams DFC, who survived to become a prisoner along with F/Sgt G.S. Staniforth. The remainder of the crew, including P/O J.H. Alexander, who held the CGM, were killed. The Lancaster was attacked by a night fighter and blew up over the Baltic, throwing the two survivors clear. F/Sgt Staniforth was later repatriated in February 1945 due to the serious leg fractures he had sustained in the explosion.

WO1 Walter Hawkins was the wireless operator. The previous day he had been awarded the DFC. Buried in Denmark, his recommendation for the award reads:

Warrant Officer Hawkins has completed 37 operational sorties with the Pathfinder Force, 35 of which have been as a Marker. This Warrant Officer has taken part in all the recent bombing operations against many of the heavily defended targets in Germany. His devotion to duty and ability have proved a valuable

S/Ldr John Hegman DSO DFC RNZAF and crew, killed in action on the night of 15/16 February 1944. They are pictured with their Lancaster JB414:MG-Y and German Shepherd 'Kim'. D. Cheetham

Lancaster MG-B photographed with air and ground crew. Several aircraft operated with the squadron coded 'B' throughout 1943–44. Note the censored artwork on the nose. 7. Sqn

asset to the squadron. His co-operation and coolness have contributed in large measure to the success of the many operational flights carried out by his crew. Warrant Officer Hawkins has at all times displayed the most commendable courage and devotion to duty.

The citation for the award mirrored the recommendation.

MG-D was captained by S/Ldr R.D. Campling DSO DFC. Between them his crew, who were all lost, held a total of one DSO, five DFCs and two DFMs. This Lancaster came down near Linde. The squadron could not afford to lose such highly experienced crews.

The Main Force had not been out in strength for two weeks and Harris dispatched 891 aircraft on this raid. Berlin was cloud-covered and most of the bombs fell on the central and south-western districts, causing extensive damage. This raid was the penultimate attack of the Battle of Berlin.

On the 19th/20th JB468 and ND470 failed to return from Leipzig. S/Ldr Kenneth Davis flew JB468. Five of the crew survived to become POWs: the navigator, F/O R.F. Powell, the flight engineer, Sgt J. Woolston, F/Lt F. Stephenson, F/Sgt A. Grange and Sgt R. Child. Taking off from Oakington at 2359 hrs they were flying at 18.000 feet over Wittenburg when a night fighter attacked them from below. F/O Marriott, the W/Op, was injured and Davis attempted a forced landing. Both died in the crash. ND470 was piloted by S/Ldr F.B. Curtis. Taking off at 0002 hrs they were attacked by a night fighter and the Lancaster exploded. S/Ldr Curtis and the second pilot, F/Sgt R. Jordan were thrown clear and became POWs. Forty-four Lancasters and thirty-four Halifaxes were lost and it was after this raid that the Halifax Mk IIs and Vs were

Oakington, December 1943. L to R: S/Ldr K. Davies (pilot), F/O R.F.B. Powell (navigator), F/O K. Marriott DFM (W/Op), F/L F. Stephenson (bomb aimer), Sgt R. Maugham (engineer), Sgt R. Child (air gunner), W/O A. Grange DFM (air gunner). via 7 Squadron Association

withdrawn from operations over Germany. Forecast winds were inaccurate and many bombers arrived early and were forced to circle awaiting the Pathfinders. This caused the loss of four aircraft in collisions and another twenty went down to flak.

Some 734 aircraft were dispatched to Schweinfurt on 24/25 February. The raid was in two parts, with a two-hour split between them. Both phases suffered from creep-back and the raid was not a successful as had been hoped. F/O Williams's Lancaster was hit from above by falling bombs, but he managed to get it back to Woodbridge for a forced landing. S/Ldr South also had his aircraft hit by bombs from above but also got away with it. On 25/26 February two members of a crew, WO H.J. Smith and F/O J.L. Brown, baled out after being attacked by a night fighter whilst raiding Augsburg. Both were made prisoner.

By March the squadron could regularly muster over twenty aircraft for raids, but it was to see its strength reduced during the month, with one flight being sent to Little Staughton to become No. 582 Sqn on the 24th.

On the night of 15/16 March the bombers raided Stuttgart. Altogether 863 aircraft took part. No. 7 Sqn lost ND557:MG-F flown by P/O D.C. Carter, an Australian. Strong winds delayed the opening of the attack and much of the marking fell short of the target, causing some of the early bombing to fall in open countryside. The night fighters had also arrived just before the bombers reached the target and thirty-seven Lancasters and Halifaxes went down.

F/Lt Frank Stephenson, bomb aimer in S/Ldr Davies's crew, shot down on the Leipzig raid of 19/20 February 1944. F. Stephenson via D. Cheetham

F/O R.F.B. 'Dick' Powell, navigator, who also survived the loss of Lancaster JB468 on the Leipzig raid.
F. Stephenson via D. Cheetham

On 22/23 March the bombers went to Frankfurt once again and this time the squadron lost Lancasters JA964:MG-P, piloted by F/O K. Hinde and ND523. Hinde, an Australian, F/Sgt H.S. McMaster and Sgt I.A. Love survived the loss of JA964. The CO, G/Capt Rampling DSO DFC, flying ND523, was lost, though three of the crew, F/Lt Ferguson, F/Sgt W.C. Birch and F/Sgt F.C. Marshall, survived. Rampling's Lancaster was attacked by a night fighter whilst approaching the aiming point at 17,600 feet. It caught fire and Rampling managed to clear the target area and ordered the crew to bale out. Seconds later the bomber fell into a spin then exploded. F/Sgt E. Haslam had been helped into his parachute after being seriously wounded, but failed to leave the crippled bomber. Marking was accurate and bombing heavy, causing severe and widespread damage to the city.

The squadron suffered losses again over Berlin on 24/25 March when ND457:MG-O and ND581:MG-M went down. MG-O was flown by P/O T.E.R. Kyle, an Australian, and crashed at Warder. Two of the crew, Sgt R.A. Hyde and F/Sgt C. Hughes, from New Zealand, survived to become POWs. MG-M, flown by F/O J.M. Mee, a New Zealander, crashed north-east of Berlin, the victim of a night fighter. F/O Leonard Berrigan, a Canadian from Dunedin, Prince Edward Island, was the mid-upper gunner with this crew. The previous month he had been recommended for the DFC. The recommendation read as follows:

> *Flying Officer Berrigan has completed thirty-five operational sorties, fifteen with the Pathfinder Force, ten of which have been as a Marker.*
>
> *This officer, as mid-upper gunner, has taken part in most of the recent raids on the heavily defended targets in enemy territory. Recently, his aircraft suffered severe damage over the target when attacking Berlin. In the ensuing combat, the rear turret was placed unserviceable. However, this officer, through his decisive and clear-cut instructions, proved invaluable and enabled his skipper to avoid further action and returned safely to base.*
>
> *Flying Officer Berrigan has at all times displayed a high sense of duty and conscientiousness in all his work.*

He is remembered on the Runnymede memorial.

That night became known in Bomber Command as the 'Night of the Strong Winds'. The bombers were blown south of the route at every stage and became very scattered. On the return leg many were lost to radar-predicted flak; it is believed that fifty of the seventy-two casualties were lost in this way. The remainder fell to night fighters; Berlin reported fourteen shot down by fighters over the city. This was the last raid in the 'Battle for Berlin'.

Flight engineer Tommy Marchant took part in seventeen of the Berlin raids and recalls the feeling at the time (quoted by Martin Middlebrook in *The Berlin Raids*):

Being a mere lad of nineteen, with little emotional or imaginative maturity, I probably did not notice the signs of people cracking up. So far as I recall, none of our crew exhibited any signs of the stress etc. so beloved of dramatic filmmakers. I did sometimes wonder if I would survive but it certainly wasn't a recurring or dominant thought. I was more concerned as to whether the local pub would run out of beer and if a certain WAAF would be there.

I am sure that morale was high on the squadrons with which I served. I personally look back on those days as a happy and exiting adventure – the old 'Biggles' book of my youth come true for me – and a feeling that you really were contributing to the war effort. But then I didn't get shot down or injured.

The following day the squadron received another new CO. This time it was W/Cdr W.G .Lockhart DSO DFC.

Nuremberg felt the crushing weight of bombs again on 30/31 March. This would normally have been a stand down period for Bomber Command due to the moon phase but a raid was laid on on the basis of a forecast of high cloud on the outward route and clear skies over the target. Some 795 bombers were sent and Bomber Command had its most serious losses of the war: ninety-five bombers were lost in all. No. 7 Sqn dispatched twenty Lancasters, of which sixteen bombed the target. It lost JB722:MG-Q and ND443:MG-L. F/Lt S. Evans, flying the former, crashed at Kunreuth, north of Nuremberg, the victim to a night fighter just before reaching the aiming point. MG-L, piloted by S/Ldr C.H. Wilson DFC, came down at Obermoos, south-west of Fulda, also the victim of a night fighter. At thirty-eight, Wilson was another of an apparently large number of experienced Pathfinder crew members well over the age normally expected of bomber crews.

Gerald South also took his crew to Nuremberg. 'On that trip we were primary blind markers, on target early, and that may have been our salvation. The squadron lost two aircraft plus one crashed and burnt out at Feltwell, with no casualties.'

Sgt H. Maxwell, a flight engineer in one of the 7 Sqn Lancaster's described the scene over the target just before Zero Hour (quoted by Martin Middlebrook in *The Nuremberg Raid*).

There was usually a certain grandeur about the scene with the markers, the flak, the searchlights and the night fighters, even though there was always the death and destruction – it was a spectacle. But on that Nuremberg do it was eerie. It was as though we had no right to be there. I suppose we hadn't really.

ND350:MG-Z was also lost, crashing when trying to land at Feltwell. Canadian F/Lt A.H. MacGillivray had been diverted, almost out of fuel on return to Oakington, and on reaching Feltwell the crew found the conditions there little better. The navigator, F/Lt F. Bell used Gee to find the aerodrome and the pilot took them straight in from out of the cloud base, touching down halfway along the runway. Reaching the end of the runway he tried to swing the aircraft round to avoid overshooting but a tyre burst and the Lancaster came to rest after hitting a concrete pillbox. The crew made their escape from the wrecked bomber as it burst into flames, the fire being assisted by four TIs that were still aboard. Bell described the scene (quoted by Martin Middlebrook in *The Nuremberg Raid*).

We stood well back watching the blaze; ammunition and TIs were burning and exploding merrily when, from a house just over the perimeter, came two elderly ladies with a small child between them. They had their nighties well tucked into red flannel drawers and went across the field as if the very devil was after them. The poor kid's feet never touched the ground. This incident relaxed the tension.

Sgt C.A. Thompson, who flew on the Nuremberg raid, had this to say about the strange contrast between operations and the 'normality' of life when not flying after the raid, in another quote from *The Nuremberg Raid*: 'Anyway it never really happened. How could you fight a war and be able to walk through the Backs at Cambridge the next day?'

William Porteous flew his fifty-fourth operation on the Nuremburg raid, acting as a 'Y' operator [The 'Y' operator attempted to jam the radio receivers of the German 'Y' or Listening Service] for W/Cdr Fraser Barron, who was flying as a visual marker. They returned without having dropped their TIs. This time they were lucky, but fate was to take a hand for both of these men a few months later.

Fred Phillips and his crew joined the squadron from No. 622 Sqn at Mildenhall; they were to become known as the 'Lucky Crew'. In all they flew sixty-four operations, fifty-three of them with 7 Sqn. Like many crews, they found that the weather could be just as dangerous as any night fighter or flak, as Phillips's flight engineer, Tom Jones, recalled of a sortie in 1944. 'We were forced down by ice from 19,000 feet to 8,000 feet. Waiting for the order to abandon aircraft I remember clearly saying "Don't cry Mom when you get the telegram." Luckily we ran out of the icing area at 8,500 feet and managed to get back to base.'

On 9/10 April the squadron went to Lille. Two hundred and thirty-nine Lancasters, Halifaxes, Stirlings and Mosquitoes took part for the loss of one Lancaster. The target was the Lille-Delivrance goods station, and the raid was highly successful. Unfortunately 456 French people were killed by the bombing.

Aachen was the target on the night of 11/12 April with 341 Lancasters and eleven Mosquitoes causing widespread damage to the centre, for the loss of nine Lancasters. Tom Jones noted in his log-book that 1,928.4 tons of bombs had been dropped on the target.

Tom Jones flew his fourteenth operation with W/Cdr Lockhart, rather than with his normal crew, on a sortie to Tergnier to bomb the rail yards. A hundred and seventy-one aircraft took part, blocking fifty railway lines for the loss of six Halifaxes.

On the night of 20/21 April the bombers went to Cologne. On the outbound leg F/Lt A.H. MacGillivray, flying Lancaster JA973:MG-A, was cruising at 18,000 feet when an Fw190 was spotted at 800 yards range on the starboard quarter. The fighter closed to 500 yards but did not open fire. The rear gunner, Sgt R.E. Smith, opened fire and the fighter broke away, diving vertically through the cloud below. Smith claimed it as damaged. Throughout the fight the captain kept up evasive action by corkscrewing.

WO H.W. Thompson piloted Lancaster ND496:MG-T on the same raid. They were on the way home when the rear gunner, F/Sgt S. Muir, spotted a twin-engined enemy aircraft 700 yards away, approaching from the starboard quarter. Thompson corkscrewed to starboard and Muir and the mid-upper gunner, Sgt J.E. Watts, opened fire on the fighter, which broke away to starboard. Two minutes later it reappeared, again on the starboard quarter. Once again Thompson corkscrewed to starboard as the gunners opened fire. The fighter broke away again, but the German crew was determined and reappeared a third time, again to starboard at a range of 600 yards.

Thompson was still corkscrewing and the gunners opened fire again. This time the fighter broke off, probably discouraged by the alertness of the gunners, and was not seen again. In all, the gunners fired 900 rounds at the night fighter.

P/O A.R. Speirs, flying ND744:MG-F, was engaged in a combat over the target. The mid-upper gunner, Sgt E. Feather, spotted a Bf110 at a range of 300 yards on the port beam, which was being attacked by three other Lancasters. Feather fired a four-second burst at it but did not observe the results. The night fighter, coming under such concentrated fire, broke away and was not seen again. Three minutes later, however, the rear gunner, F/Sgt J. Clift, sighted a twin-engined night fighter, believed to be an Me410 500 yards away on the starboard quarter. It was on a curve of pursuit and Speirs corkscrewed to starboard as his gunners opened fire. Hits were observed on the fighter, which broke away with flames coming from the port engine. It was not seen again and the gunners, who had fired 360 rounds, claimed it as damaged.

On 21 April 1944 the *London Gazette* carried the award of a Bar to the DFC held by F/Lt Peter Wilby. He had been awarded the DFC, whilst a flying officer, on 6 November 1943. The award citation stated that he had 'completed many successful operations against the enemy in which [he] displayed high skill, fortitude and devotion to duty.' The citation for the Bar read: 'Since the award of the Distinguished Flying Cross this officer has continued to operate with unremitting zeal and enthusiasm. He has taken part in recent attacks on Berlin, Mannheim and Cologne, frequently making three or four runs over the target to make sure of the aiming point in the face of the fiercest opposition.'

F/Lt Peter Wilby DFC* and crew with Lancaster JA853:MG-L. The Lancaster was lost on the night of 16/17 December 1943. D. Cheetham

Dusseldorf was attacked on 22/23 April and Lancaster Mk III ND353:MG-N failed to return. Four of the crew – pilot F/Lt A.H. MacGillivray, WO L.S. Weir, F/Lt F. Bell and Sgt T. Durbin – survived to become prisoners. German fighters penetrated the bomber stream and twenty-nine out of 596 bombers were lost. The same night ND592MG-J, captained by P/O Percy Ronald Aslett, went down on a raid to a pre-invasion target at Laon. The Lancaster was shot down by a night fighter at Maizy, north-west of Reims and crashed with a full bomb load, killing the crew. A force of 181 aircraft was sent to this target, attacking the railway yards in two waves. Heavy damage was caused for the loss of nine aircraft.

F/Lt Gerald South and his crew managed to escape the attentions of a night fighter on this raid. He was homeward bound in Lancaster ND588:MG-Q when a fighter attacked from the starboard quarter. The rear gunner, WO J.G. Miles, did not open fire immediately, but waited till the fighter had closed to 600 yards and then told South to corkscrew to starboard. He then opened fire and hits were observed on the fighter, which was seen to stall and fall into a dive. Miles fired another burst and scored further hits. Another fighter appeared and once again Miles opened fire. This

An aiming point photo from the Laon operation on the night of 23/24 April. Mildred Watson Scales

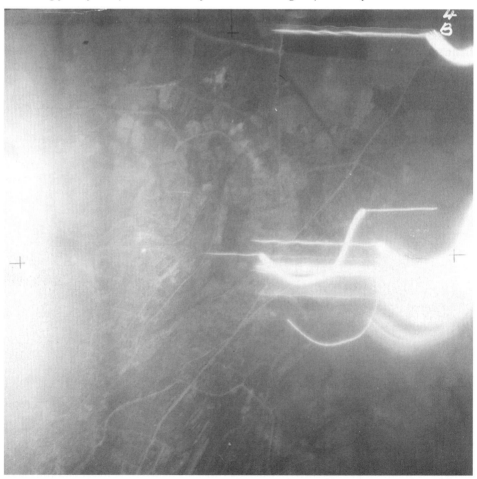

fighter broke away at 250 yards with its starboard engine on fire, fell into a dive and hit the ground.

Karlsruhe was bombed on 24/25 April and the squadron lost Lancaster Mk III JB719:MG-B. Captained by P/O J.M. Napier, it was shot down by a night fighter near Plittersdorf, to the south-east of the target, with no survivors. Fred Phillips took his crew to Karlsruhe and flight engineer Tom Jones later wrote of the operation:

> *Leaving Karlsruhe we were attacked by night fighters and during the twisting and turning of evasive action the navigator lost our precise position. After flying on a rough course for some time he found out where we were when we flew, alone, over Strasbourg and into a heavy barrage of predicted flak. The next morning we went out to the aircraft and, starting at the tail, counted eighty-seven holes between the rear and the mid-upper turret before we decided to stop counting. The rest of the aircraft and wings were equally peppered with jagged holes; we had used up a little more luck out of our reserve.*

He noted in his log-book for the Karlsruhe raid: '637 aircraft, 19 lost. ASI frozen up. Flak over Strasbourg. Port inner oil cooler holed.'

The sixteenth operation for F/Lt Phillips crew was to Essen on the night of 26/27 April in the company of 492 other crews. The Pathfinder marking was accurate and followed up by an equally accurate Main Force bombing. Seven aircraft were lost. S/Ldr A.H.C. Roberts was guiding his Lancaster, JB653:MG-R, towards the target when an enemy aircraft was sighted at the same level about 400 yards away. The rear gunner, P/O G.A.A. Hope, gave instructions to dive to port. The fighter turned into a curve of pursuit and Hope instructed Roberts to roll and corkscrew. Whilst giving these instructions he fired four two-second bursts, but no hits were observed. The

Fred Phillips and crew in front of a Lancaster at Oakington in 1944. The three crew members on the left are L to R: Fred Phillips, Dave Goodwin and Stan Williamson. Second from right is Tom Jones. The others (order not identified) are Clive 'Thirsty' Thurston, Ron Wynne, John Naylor and J.W. Taylor. P. Jones

P/O Napier and crew, killed in action on the Karlsruhe raid of 24/25 April 1944. L to R: P/O J. Napier (pilot), P/O Harry Wallis (navigator), P/O Leo Brenton (bomb aimer), F/Sgt Arthur Derby (W/Op), F/Sgt Hubert Martin (mid-upper gunner), F/Sgt Cyril Spencer (flight engineer), P/O David Wynne-Evans (rear gunner). D. Cheetham

German pilot was determined and could not be shaken off, so Hope gave instructions to orbit to starboard and the night fighter was lost. The German had not opened fire during the combat. The mid-upper gunner, Sgt N.L. Humphries, had to sit and watch, unable to open fire, as his turret had a burst pressure line.

Unfortunately of poor quality, this photograph shows P/O Napier and crew with ground crew in front of Lancaster JB718:MG-B. This Lancaster and crew were lost on the night of 24/25 April 1944. D. Cheetham

The bombers went all the way to Friedrichshafen on 27/28 April; JB676:MG-K failed to return. Captained by W/Cdr W.G. Lockhart, the CO, this bomber fell at Reichenbach. Lockhart would be replaced by W/Cdr J.F. Barron DSO DFC DFM. The Air Ministry had insisted on a raid on this small town because of the important factories making gearboxes and engines for tanks. It was a very long flight in moonlight to the target but the many diversionary raids confused the German controllers and the night fighters arrived too late to thwart the main raid. Nevertheless they still shot down eighteen Lancasters. F/Lt A.O. Price, piloting Lancaster ND849:MG-M, was involved in a combat with a night fighter on the homeward journey. Flying at 18,000 feet the mid-upper gunner, F/Sgt C.W. Buffham, observed an Fw190 at 800 yards on the starboard quarter. The fighter was on a curve of pursuit and Price immediately corkscrewed to starboard as the rear gunner, F/Sgt S.N. Etridge, fired a one-second burst at the fighter at a range of 600 yards. No hits were seen but the fighter broke off without opening fire, and was not seen again. The reactions of the two gunners and the corkscrew had undoubtedly saved them from being shot down.

The night fighters were very active on this night and P/O A.R. Speirs, who had evaded a night fighter on the night of 20/21 April, was also attacked in Lancaster ND590:MG-G. Speirs was on the way to the target when the W/Op received an indication on the 'Fishpond' [Tail Warning Radar] of an unseen aircraft approaching

Fred Phillips and crew. This crew had a lucky escape after straying into heavy predicted flak over Strasbourg returning from Karlsruhe on the night of 24/25 April 1944. P. Jones

dead astern at a range of 2 miles. The Fishpond indications ceased at 800 yards and the aircraft was still unsighted. Speirs commenced corkscrewing. The first indication of the night fighter was a burst of cannon fire from a range of 600 yards, which damaged the starboard inner engine and shot away the hydraulic gear. The rear gunner, Sgt J. Clift, fired a four-second burst and the mid-upper gunner, Sgt E. Feather, joined in with a two-second burst aimed at the source of the tracer. The gunners claimed hits on the nose of the enemy fighter, which ceased firing and broke away. The gunners had fired 400 rounds between them.

Frank Clear joined the squadron from No. 149 Sqn on 25 April 1944 and has many memories of his tour at Oakington as a Pathfinder.

The blue master beam of searchlights were somewhat tricky to be caught in, especially when the other beams joined in. Luckily our skipper, Jim Berry, managed to dive out of the situation.

From my mid-upper position I had a ringside seat for all the colourful action and towards the end of our op flights something odd happened. I suddenly saw a shape that wasn't a fighter, but I asked for a corkscrew anyway. The 'shape' reappeared after we got back to level flight. It all happened within a few seconds, but there were no props visible and it made no attempt to attack in any way. In retrospect I suppose I should have fired off a round or three. I suppose I was bemused and even wondered if it was an illusion or trick of light or tired eyes. Anyway, the navigator logged it and it was reported at debriefing without comment. Long after the war we thought it was one of the German jets on a test flight without guns, and its limited fuel supply made it depart fairly pronto.

On the ground at Oakington – a couple of memories – the WAAF batwoman who quietly opened the bedroom door to see if we had made it back each time. The WAAF in flying control stacking up the Lancs above the drome, only to find that her boyfriend pilot and his crew were not amongst the arrivals. Probably happened dozens of times throughout the war, but heartbreaking to the girl, who had to repeat her duties time after time, by sheer willpower.

In the mess on a dining-in night I shrank from my 5 feet 4½ inches. Reason – while at the dining table as a brand new P/O and my first appearance amongst all the silver and general glitter I had a call of nature that needed almost immediate attention. My immediate neighbour muttered that I would need permission to leave the table. Red faced, I rose from my seat and 'marched' – tottered down and around the horseshoe table arrangement to the top table. The CO obviously knew my position and waved me gently away without a word. I retired and wondered if I could make it out of the room before further disgracing myself, and found it somewhat of a problem to 'march' with semi-clenched knees!

After the departure of the CO and his wife and the few WAAF officers, to the singing of 'Goodnight Ladies' after the dining-in night ... the rugby scrums led by Tubby Baker and the quiet reappearance of some of the WAAFs to join in the frolics! Their mothers wouldn't have believed the antics.

I suppose utter tiredness, especially after two trips on the trot is memorable: and going to breakfast to see the upturned plates of those who didn't get back.

Communications targets were the order of the day in May, preparatory to the invasion of the Continent. Chambly was attacked on the 1st/2nd with the intention of destroying the railway and stores depot there. ND901, one of only three Lancasters and two Stirlings lost, did not return. P/O A.R. Spiers survived the loss of his aircraft and managed to return to the UK. The rest of his crew was killed. Lancaster JA693:MG-A, piloted by F/O I.G. Bennington, was *en route* to the target when the rear gunner, F/Sgt K. Spencer, who had completed his gunnery training in Karachi, India, spotted a single-engined enemy fighter approaching from the port quarter at about 900 yards' range. Bennington commenced a corkscrew to port and as the fighter closed to 600 yards it was seen to be a Bf110. Spencer opened fire with a three-second burst, without observing the results; however, the fighter broke away to starboard and was not seen again. The 200 rounds fired by the gunner had saved the crew. Another crew, captained by F/Lt Phillips, in Lancaster MG-O achieved a good aiming point photograph.

By the end of April F/Lt William Porteous was flying as Navigator II to S/Ldr Dennis and they took part in this raid, with S/Ldr Dennis acting as master bomber. Porteous recorded the operation as an 'excellent effort'. He would fly twice more with Dennis. S/Ldr Dennis was awarded the DSO for this operation. The citation relates his part.

> *One night in May 1944, this officer captained one of a formation of aircraft detailed to attack the railway junction at Chambly. In the operation Squadron Leader Dennis displayed notable skill and, regardless of the enemy's defences, pressed home his attack with great accuracy. His brilliant work was a prominent factor in the great success achieved. This officer has taken part in a very large number of sorties and has set a rare example of skill, courage and devotion to duty.*

Lancaster ND906:MG-A, flown by New Zealander F/O I.C. Bennington, was lost on the 5th when it flew out of cloud on a training sortie and crashed at the Ashby & Ledger works near Church Lawford, killing all of the crew. Gerald South recalls the sorties during this period.

> *It was a comparatively pleasant change when, immediately after Nuremberg, the bomber force was employed on softening up communications in northern France in preparation for the invasion. I could not say that morale was low in early 1944, but there was certainly concern about the high loss rate. Things were not improved by the loss of three squadron commanders within some three months: G/Capt Ken Rampling in February, W/Cdr Guy Lockhart in April and W/Cdr Fraser Barron in May. This last was on a French target and also resulted in the loss of my flight commander, S/Ldr Johnny Dennis, possibly in a mid-air collision between the two, but it will never be known for certain [see below]. The rot was stopped by the arrival of W/Cdr Reggie Cox, an ex-Halton apprentice, who had been an original member of the squadron when first equipped with Stirlings in 1941 and who took part in some of the early Stirling operations.*
>
> *So it will be seen that French targets were not all 'a piece of cake' as some had hoped. After D-Day there was much emphasis on attacking flying bomb (V-1) sites, when these could be located, interspersed with the more familiar German industrial targets.*

On the night of 7/8 May 3 and 8 Groups sent ninety-three Lancasters and six Mosquitoes to bomb the airfield at Nantes. The bombing was accurate and only one

Lancaster was lost. W/Cdr Barron played an important part in this operation, receiving a Bar to his DSO. The citation relates the part he and his crew played.

> *One night in May 1944, this officer participated in an attack on the airfield at Nantes. By his appreciation of the responsibilities entrusted to him and the skill and precision with which he executed his attack, Wing Commander Barron contributed in large measure to the success achieved. Since being awarded the Distinguished Service Order this officer has taken part in many attacks on dangerous and difficult targets. He is an outstanding captain whose example of skill, bravery and determination has impressed all.*

On the night of 11/12 May Bomber Command dispatched 725 sorties to communications targets in France as part of the pre-invasion softening up. One of those who almost did not make it back was P/O A.P. Hookway, piloting Lancaster JA677:MG-U. On the way back to base he suddenly saw tracer fire from an aircraft on the port bow, which had crept up unobserved. He quickly put the Lancaster through some violent evasive action and lost the attacker – a lucky escape.

The squadron's Lancasters went to railway yards at Le Mans and a radar station at Mont Couple on the 19th/20th JB653:MG-R and ND845 failed to return from the former and ND736:MG-G from the latter target. ND845:MG-C took off at 2222 from Oakington, piloted by squadron CO W/Cdr James Fraser Barron DSO* DFC DFM, as the master bomber's aircraft. He was last heard stating his intention to descend below cloud to join the deputy master bomber, S/Ldr J.M. Dennis in JB653, also of 7 Sqn. It is thought that the two collided, though it is possible that Barron collided with HK547 of 115 Sqn, which came down in the same area, whereas JB653 came down several kilometres away. There were no survivors from any of the three aircraft.

A New Zealander, Barron joined the RNZAF in July 1940 qualifying as a sergeant pilot. After leaving the OTU at Lossiemouth he completed a tour on No. 15 Sqn. Rested from operations he became an instructor at No. 1651 HCU and whilst there was awarded the DFM for his service with No. 15 Sqn.

Joining No. 7 Sqn in September 1942 he flew a further sixteen sorties before ending his tour in February 1943. During this period he was commissioned as a flight lieutenant and awarded the DFC and DSO. Once again he was posted to a training unit, No. 20 OTU at Westcott, but managed to persuade Hamish Mahaddie to approve his return to operations with No. 7 Sqn. Now flying Lancasters he returned to operations in December 1943 and was promoted to wing commander in February 1944. On 28 April he was appointed CO of No. 7 Sqn. At the time he was lost, he was just twenty-three years old.

The wireless operator on ND845 was F/O Jack William Walters, another New Zealander, who was on his second operational tour. The squadron had lost a highly experienced crew, who between them held four DSOs two DFCs and three DFMs.

S/Ldr Dennis's wireless operator was an ex-Essex policeman named Reginald Hunt. It is not widely known that a large number of policemen became aircrew with the RAF. This was due to the fact that it was a reserved occupation and the only way a policeman could join the armed services was to volunteer for aircrew duties. Hunt was just twenty-four when he died with the rest of his crew.

The third loss of the night, ND736:MG-D was captained by S/Ldr I.D. Oliver DFC. His target was the radar station at Cap Gris Nez. The Lancaster was hit by flak and exploded in mid-air, crashing at Landrethun-le-Nord, north-east of Marquise. Oliver was thrown clear as the bomber blew up and survived, injured, to become a POW. The rest of the crew were killed. Frank Clear was on his first tour with No. 115 Sqn, prior to joining 7 Sqn and took part in the same raid. He believes he witnessed the demise of the master bomber and the deputy master bomber.

It was our practice for me to memorize the course out of the target and then to douse my navigating light and to come out from behind my curtain to stand between the pilot and the engineer and help to look out for fighters.

It has always been said that W/Cdr Barron collided with his deputy master bomber, resulting in the total loss of both crews. I have never accepted that explanation. As we ran up to the target I came out from behind my curtain and almost the first thing that I saw was a combat slightly ahead and above us out on our starboard side. First there were the large, and few, white balls of a German night fighter's cannon and then the thin red lines of .303 tracer from a rear gunner in reply. Very soon there were sparks as the cannon shells started to hit. At the same time the master bomber had just started his broadcast. His callsign that night was 'Little John', and I heard 'Little John to Main Force, bomb the centre . . .' and at this time his transmission cut out. I then saw an awesome sight, which I will never ever forget. The Lancaster started to burn from nose to tail and from wingtip to wingtip, with short flames as if the plane was a spectre. It rose up and the port wing dropped and it passed above and ahead of us before spiralling down on our port side. I saw no parachutes.

Quickly there came over the R/T 'Little John 2 to Little John' (pause) 'Little John 2 to Little John' as the deputy master bomber tried to contact W/Cdr Barron. Then came 'Little John 2 to Main Force taking over. Bomb . . .' And then he, too, cut out. Just at that moment in the same direction as the previous combat I saw German cannon fire firing up at an acute angle and immediately the cannon shells hit. In the dim light of a fire starting I thought I saw an Fw190 standing almost on its tail as it hosepiped the belly of the Lancaster. Did I see two combats in which first the master bomber and then his deputy perished? I have always thought so.

The highly experienced W/Cdr Barron was replaced by W/Cdr R.W. Cox DFC AFC, who would command the squadron for less than five months.

Duisburg was the target on 21/22 May and the squadron lost ND588:MG-Q, flown by P/O A.F. Hookway, who had escaped being shot down by a night fighter only a few days previously. This time his luck ran out as the Lancaster and crew were lost without trace. This was the first large raid on this target for over a year. The Oboe sky marking was accurate and much damage was caused to the southern part of the city.

The following night the squadron went to Dortmund and P/O K. Perry's crew had a combat with a Bf110. Lancaster JB661:MG-L was homeward bound when the mid-upper gunner, Sgt B. Loosely, spotted the enemy low down on the port beam. The Messerschmitt positioned for an attack but Loosely anticipated this and ordered Perry to dive to port. They lost sight of the night fighter but it reappeared below them a short while later. It made another attack and Perry continued to take evasive action. Suddenly another Bf110 attacked from above on the starboard quarter and

Sgt Loosely opened fire. This fighter broke away, as did the first. No damage was sustained during the battle, which saw several hundred rounds fired by the mid-upper gunner.

F/Lt Daniel Row, a Canadian W/Op with the squadron was awarded the DFC on 24 May. He had commenced operations on 24 June 1943 with a sortie to Elberfeld and had completed thirty-eight by the time of the award. Six of his last seven operations had been to Berlin. The recommendation read:

> Flight Lieutenant Row has completed 38 operational sorties with the Pathfinder Force, 29 of which have been as Marker. Flight Lieutenant Row has been Wireless Operator to a crew, which has carried out many successful sorties against all the recent targets in Germany. His cheerful confidence and ability are most praiseworthy and have set a fine example to the more junior Wireless Operators in the squadron, to whose training he has devoted much time and interest. This officer has at all times displayed an exceptionally fine spirit and resourcefulness in the completion of his operational duties.

On the same day WO Allan Fonseca, a fellow Canadian and air gunner on the squadron, was also awarded the DFC. With thirty-nine operational sorties behind him by the time of his recommendation he was a highly experienced airman. His recommendation for the award read:

> Warrant Officer Fonseca has completed 39 operational sorties with the Pathfinder Force, 38 of which have been as a Marker. Warrant Officer Fonseca has been mid-upper gunner to two captains in this squadron, both of whom have found his coolness and reliability in the face of the fiercest opposition to be of a high order. His fine aggressive spirit has set a splendid example to the more junior air gunners in the squadron and his keenness to operate is most praiseworthy. Warrant Officer Fonseca has at all times displayed a very high sense of devotion to duty.

The border city of Aachen was the target for the bombers on 24/25 May. The squadron lost Lancaster JB313:MG-H, flown by F/Lt G.C. Crew DFC. A highly experienced crew with thirty Pathfinder sorties to their credit when they were lost, they were captained by a pilot who is believed to have joined the RAF in the 1920s! The railway yards were the aiming point and they were hit hard, disrupting movement from Germany to France.

The W/Op on P/O A.C.W. Grant's crew was monitoring the Fishpond when an indication of an aircraft moving in from the starboard was seen. He warned Grant and the rear gunner, Sgt Newton took up the search spotting a Bf110 coming in to attack. Newton ordered Grant to corkscrew the Lancaster, ND496:MG-T, to starboard and opened fire. The night fighter broke away without opening fire and was not seen again.

P/O Perry, who had had a lucky escape the previous night, was involved in another fight on this raid, flying NE129:MG-G. At 17,000 feet and homeward bound the mid-upper gunner, Sgt B. Loosely, spotted an Fw190 600 yards away, turning to attack another Lancaster. He opened fire and it broke away without attacking the other bomber. Loosely had undoubtedly saved the other crew from being shot down.

F/Lt F.A. Phillips was the captain of ND744:MG-F on this night and was on the way home at 15,000 feet when his mid-upper gunner, Sgt R. Wynne, saw tracer coming from the port quarter. The rear gunner, Sgt J.W. Taylor, also saw it and ordered Phillips to corkscrew to port. Nothing further was seen until seven minutes later a Ju88 approached them from high on the port quarter. Taylor ordered a corkscrew to port and both gunners opened fire. The Ju88 broke away to starboard and came in for another attack. Phillips put the Lancaster into a corkscrew to starboard and lost the night fighter.

Gerald South, who flew with the squadron throughout this period, recalls life at Oakington.

I found life in general at Oakington very pleasant; the possibility that one might not have very long to enjoy it was very much at the back of my mind, though this did not necessarily apply to all. However, I can only recall one case of 'LMF' ['lack of moral fibre'], a flight lieutenant pilot who was quietly removed soon after he joined us.

As operational aircrew were given a small petrol allowance, I acquired a battered Ford 8. Several of us had cars and shared them for visits to Cambridge, some 6 miles away, pubs and village dances. There were a number of romances, mostly involving local girls and WAAF. Though in flying training and no doubt other non-operational commands fraternization between officers and airwomen was severely discouraged, this did not seem to apply in Bomber Command, and there were a number of marriages, apart from casual affairs. Often boyfriends didn't return from ops, causing obvious distress, yet the WAAF got on with their jobs. I have the greatest admiration for all the ground troops, not just the women, though it was a remarkable sight to see a frail girl handling an unwieldy crew coach or tractor towing bomb loads (no power steering!).

As I recall, relations with the local community were very good, though their lives must have been disturbed by aircraft noise (and there were many airfields in the vicinity, such as Waterbeach), not to mention their daughters being pursued by lusty aircrews! Especially I remember Mr and Mrs Hartnell, who kept the Bailey Cow at Histon and always seemed to produce sandwiches when needed; food was short and we always seemed to be hungry, even though we were well fed at Oakington and had extra rations such as bacon and eggs when ordered on ops. Garage proprietors were often generous (2 gallons for one coupon, for example); I recall Rudd's Garage on the Huntingdon road, the daughter of the family being a WAAF in the MT Section at Oakington. A favourite Cambridge pub was the curiously named Bun Shop, also the Eagle and Baron of Beef. Nearer home were the Crown at Girton and King William IV on the Huntingdon road.

As so many aircrew were NCOs it was accepted that officers, by invitation, could visit the sergeants' mess (though not vice versa) if there was a special celebration and I went there several times as my gunners and radar operator were NCOs or warrant officers (several were commissioned later).

As May drew to a close the concentration on pre-invasion softening up continued and the squadron crews made their way to Rennes airfield on the night of 27th/28th. Only seventy-eight Lancasters and five Mosquitoes took part in this raid, in which accurate marking resulted in much damage to the airfield. One hundred and fifteen

bombers, including those of 7 Sqn, went to Mont Couple on the night of 31 May/
1 June, completely destroying a radio jamming station.

The first days of June 1944, leading up to the invasion, were filled with numerous
raids by Bomber Command on ports, gun batteries, signals and radar stations along
the French coast. Many of the targets were outside the planned invasion area in
Normandy to maintain the deception that the assault would come in the Pas de Calais
area. On 3/4 June the squadron sent nine Lancasters to attack the heavy coastal
battery at Calais. Visibility was good and the crews accurately dropped their red and
green TIs. Two explosions in the target area were observed and an orange fire could be
seen for some time after leaving the target. The next night three Lancasters returned to
the same target bombing on Gee and H2S through the overcast. The glow of the TIs
could be seen through the cloud and the Germans put up a weak flak defence.

On the night of 5/6 June the squadron was out in force. Firstly, five aircraft
attacked the light coastal battery at Merville-Franceville. One of the crews was that
of F/Lt Phillips in Lancaster MG-O, completing their twenty-fourth operation.
The target was cloud-covered and the crews bombed using Gee and H2S. Both
visual backers-up and two of the emergency markers did not drop their TIs due
to the conditions, but many bomb bursts were observed on leaving the target as the
Main Force did its deadly work. The second target for the night was another

coastal battery at Longues, which was attacked
three and a half hours later by eleven of the
squadron's Lancasters. Again the target was
cloud-covered and the crews bombed through
it. On the return flight several crews saw
the first intimation that the invasion of the
Continent was underway.

G/Capt R.W. Cox had completed a tour
with the squadron early in the war and then
went on to command an HCU before returning to take command of the squadron. He
recalls the D-Day period.

*After my first tour I set up No. 1657
HCU at Stradishall. Knowing that one
was expected to complete two tours of
operations, after about fifteen months
I was offered command of 7 Sqn on
Lancasters in 8 Group (PFF). I was
honoured to accept.*

*After completing a tour of 60 ops on
PFF and becoming a day and night master
bomber I was promoted acting G/Capt
and given command of RAF Downham
Market.*

*Members of Fred Phillips's crew in high spirits at
Oakington in June 1944.* P. Jones

On 5 June 1944 I flew Lancaster G-George on a blind marking operation as part of the invasion. We had H2S Mk III and a small display tube taken off this for smaller detail, named Fishpond.

As we were crossing the French coast on return my nav/radar asked me if I could come back and have a look at Fishpond. I handed over to my second pilot and went back and saw a well-organized pattern of white blobs on the screen, which we assumed were ships. We reported this at debriefing. We thought it was to do with the invasion but the intelligence officer was non-committal. However it soon transpired that our 'softening up' op was on D-Day

During June 1944 Bomber Command was actively supporting the invasion troops in their advance through France. On the 7th/8th F/Lt Phillips and his crew went to the Foret De Cerisy along with 111 other Lancaster and ten Mosquito crews to bomb a fuel dump and a concentration of Panzer units. The raid was highly successful with the loss of only two Lancasters. The following night the bombers struck the railway, including the squadron's target, Fougeres. On the 9th/10th the bomber force returned to airfield targets and 7 Sqn once again struck at Rennes. All of the attacks were successful and only two Halifaxes were lost.

The squadron struck at Dreux railway yard on the 10th/11th, losing NE129: MG-G, captained by P/O H.J. Bonnett, following this with raids on Tours on the 11th/12th, communications targets at Amiens on the 12th/13th and Lens, attacking the Valenciennes marshalling yard, on the 15th/16th, where they lost JB455:MG-N, flown by P/O Thomson. The Lancaster came down at Anzegem, Belgium. Thomson

The log-book of Tom Jones, flight engineer of F/Lt Phillips's crew, recording the operations on the night of D-Day and the days beyond. P. Jones

7 SQUADRON OAKINGTON PFF								Time carried forward :—	110·40	155·10
Date	Hour	Aircraft Type and No.	Pilot	Duty		REMARKS (including results of bombing, gunnery, exercises, etc.)			Flying Times Day	Night
JUNE		LANCASTER.								
2	10·35	A	F/LT PHILLIPS	ENGINEER.		F/A. & BOMBING			02·20	
2	22·45	D	"	"		"Y" EX. & BOMBING.				02·15
6	02·40	O	"	"		24 OPS. FRANCEVILLE (COASTAL GUNS) 122 A/C 2 LOST				03·30
7	23·36	B	"	"		25 OPS. FORET DE CERISY. FUEL DUMP & PANZER UNITS 113 A/C 4 LOST				03·00
8	21·55	O	"	"		26 OPS. FOUGERES. RAILWAY JUNCTION 401 A/C 2 LOST				04·20
9	00·10	G.	"	"		27 OPS. RENNES. AIRFIELD. 329 A/C 4 LOST				04·40
11	21·40	O	"	"		28 OPS. TOURS. RAILWAY YARDS. 671 A/C 23 LOST				06·30
12	23·50	O	"	"		29 OPS. AMIENS. COMMUNICATIONS				02·55
15	10·25	C	"	"		A/F & BOMBING.			01·25	
15	23·05	G	"	"		30 OPS. VALENCIENNES. RAILWAY YARDS. 224 A/C 11 LOST				02·50
16	23·55	G	"	"		31 OPS. RENESCURE. FLYING BOMB SITE 405 A/C				01·55
18	09·55	O	"	"		A/F & BOMBING. 721 A/C 3 LOST			01·55	
27	23·55	W	"	"		32 OPS. OISEMONT. FLYING BOMB SITE				03·05
29	11·15	O	"	"		F/A & BOMBING.			01·55	
30	14·00	K.	"	"		F/A & BOMBING.			01·35	
						OPS. HRS. 32·40				
	TOTAL FLYING TIMES FOR JUNE 1944									
	DAY	09·10								
	NIGHT	34·55								
	TOTAL	44·05								
						TOTAL TIME ...			119·50	190·05

evaded capture and eventually made his way back to the UK. ND744:MG-F, flown by P/O A.C.W. Grant, was also lost over this target, crashing near the station at Arras. F/Sgts S.C. Masters, S. Nathanson and R.H. Neills survived.

The main effort during this period was aimed at the railway network and flying-bomb launching sites. One such site at Renescure was attacked by squadron Lancasters on 16 June. Roy Claridge recalls how he discovered the existence of the flying-bomb sites and the urgency with which they were attacked.

It was 20 June and I had only been in the mess about five minutes when I had a call from Brian Frow. He told me that he had an urgent call from the Air Ministry and he had to report the next morning, would I like to make the trip with him as he was taking his car? We lived near each other and our parents were available on the phone. He picked me up about seven in the morning and drove to the nearest tube station, where I got out and agreed to meet up after Brian had finished at the Air Ministry. He would give me a ring at my parents' home. We had expected to have a couple of days off. I had only been home about four hours when I received a call from Brian. He said we must get back to Oakington as soon as possible, there was a great flap on! Brian met me with his car at the entrance to Northolt tube station. On the way back to Oakington he told me there was one of the biggest flaps on since the beginning of the war. The next three weeks were crucial to us winning or losing the war!

The Germans had developed their secret weapons and were launching them today. At first there would by flying bombs – these would be launched at London twenty-four hours a day – we really had no defence! Later this would be followed by large rockets, which could wipe out whole streets of houses, which of course they did. British Intelligence had belatedly discovered dozens of launch sites in the Pas de Calais area.

We tore back to base at about 50 miles an hour, the pre-war Austin flat out. On base by five that afternoon we were airborne and looking for these bases. These were very well camouflaged and we only found the first one by seeing one of these bombs being launched against London. We destroyed the site.

On that day, 21 June, 322 aircraft attacked three sites. Two of the raids were called off after only seventeen aircraft had attacked due to cloud obscuring the targets. The third site, at St Martin l'Hortier, was bombed through a solid overcast. No aircraft were lost. Claridge was out again the next day looking for more sites. The bombers struck at Mimoyecques and Siracourt. 'The following day we knew what to look for and were successful in destroying a number of these sites. The only problem was the sites were now being protected by German fighters. On this day we shot down one and damaged two.'

On the night of 23/24 June 412 bombers of 3, 4, 6 and 8 Groups bombed flying bomb sites including L'Hey, which was targeted by 7 Sqn. The crew of JB911:MG-A, captained by S/Ldr Brian G. Frow, a flight commander, was homeward bound when it came under attack on three separate occasions. They were at 7,000 feet when the pilot spotted a Ju88 positioning for an attack on another Lancaster, slightly below on the port beam. He ordered the front gunner, F/Lt Cutchey and the mid-upper gunner, WO O.G. Erasmus, to open fire. Both did so as the Ju88 fired a burst at the other Lancaster. It immediately broke away and was not seen again. The unidentified Lancaster's starboard outer engine caught fire, but the crew lost sight of it and it was not seen again. Five minutes later the rear gunner, F/O Ernest Wharton, sighted a pale amber light on the port quarter, slightly below the Lancaster and steadily closing in. He called for avoiding action and for Erasmus, the mid-upper gunner to search to starboard. Identifying it as twin-engined, Wharton gave the enemy fighter a short burst at a range of 550 yards. After a second burst the fighter's starboard engine burst into flames and it dived steeply through the cloud and a large explosion was seen through the cloud.

Five minutes later, WO Erasmus, spotted a night fighter on the starboard quarter, 300 yards away. Due to a faulty intercom he was unable to warn the pilot and attempted to use the indicator lights in the cockpit. Unfortunately, the pilot did not see the lights flash and the next indication to the crew that they were under attack was a burst of cannon fire, which hit the starboard tailplane and fin and the starboard mainplane. Erasmus opened fire on the night fighter, an Me210, whilst F/O Wharton quickly turned his turret to starboard and opened fire. Wharton's intercom was also unserviceable in the starboard position and on opening fire he found that his guns were jammed with belt and link stoppages. Rotating his turret back to port restored the intercom and he informed the pilot to dive to starboard, working desperately to clear the stoppages. Swinging the turret back to starboard he fired a short burst, joining Erasmus in the fight. The Me210 closed the range again and Wharton ordered the aircraft to corkscrew port beam down, and the gunners opened fire. The fighter broke away after strikes were observed on its fuselage and was not seen again.

On assessing the damage to the Lancaster it was found that most of the main systems were not functioning correctly, the undercarriage had to be lowered manually and the brakes had failed. The bomber was leaking like a sieve and the engines were in a poor state. Frow assessed that a controlled landing could be made but that there was a high risk of a fire due to the leaking fuel. He made an approach to Woodbridge and landed successfully – 'A for Apple' returned home victorious. However, it was a write off, with over 100 cannon and bullet holes.

Frow had completed tours with 144 and 408 (RCAF) Sqns before extending his tour with 61 Sqn and joining 7 Sqn in early 1944. His crew is believed to have flown with a dog as a mascot on operations. Five Lancasters from the force were lost.

ND590:MG-B flown by F/Lt W.A. Irwin DFC and ND766:MG-P, captained by F/Lt M.G. Wakefield, were lost over another invasion area target, Coubronne, on the 24th.

The crews went to Oisemont, yet another flying-bomb launching site, on 27 June. Siracourt was struck again on the 29th, when ND897:MG-C, flown by F/Lt S.E.C. Clarke, acting as master bomber, failed to return. Two members of the crew, Sgt C.A. Farrington and F/O D. Mortimer, survived to become POWs. At 1358 hrs, approaching the target and flying into heavy flak, the aircraft took a mortal blow. The skipper ordered the crew to abandon. The aircraft was already corkscrewing when Farrington jumped. Convinced that he was going to be hit by the inner props, he was amazed to be free-falling, counting and then feeling his canopy breaking open above him. He saw only one other parachute, that of the bomb aimer, F/Lt D. Mortimer, and then the aircraft exploded in mid-air.

Upon landing in a cornfield, Farrington scrambled into the nearest bomb crater and endured the rest of the force making their bomb runs. With the raid over, the Germans were soon out looking for bodies and did not take long to find him. Having gone through a number of potentially deadly situations – the target marking, the flak, the escape, the landing and the rest of the bombing – he faced one more major worry when he found himself staring down the barrel of a German rifle. Eventually he was taken to a POW camp near Krakow in Poland and then marched back to within 15 miles of Berlin. After being abandoned by the German army he was able to search through German filing cabinets prior to the Soviets arriving and managed to secure his POW papers. He was finally 'liberated' by the Red Army.

On 2 July there was another raid on Oisemont, followed by another daylight raid, this time to St Martin L'Hortier three days later. By now F/Lt Phillips's crew had gathered sufficient experience to be named as master bomber for a daylight raid, their thirty-fourth sortie. The crew had also carried out this duty on the raid on the flying-bomb launching site at the end of June. On the 6th the squadron went to Wizernes and Foret-De-Croc, targeting the flying bombs.

Between 7 and 18 July they were kept busy giving close support to the ground troops in their break-out from the Normandy beachheads. Operations included Liuzeux on the 8th/9th and Thiverny on the 12th/13th. On the night of the 15th/16th the squadron went to Chalons-sur-Marne to drop flares for a force of 229 aircraft attacking the railway yards. The raid was successful.

The squadron attacked cagney in daylight on the 18th and followed this up with attacks on the night of the 18th/19th on the railway junctions at Aulnoye and Revigny were the targets for the Lancasters and Mosquitoes of 1, 3, 5 and 8 Groups. Just two Lancasters were lost raiding Aulnoye but the Revigny force was hit hard by the night fighters and lost twenty-four Lancasters, almost 22 per cent of the force dispatched. Luckily, 7 Sqn went to Aulnoye.

Sgt C.A. Farrington, third from right, with a Lancaster crew. (This was not the crew he flew operations with.) Tony Farrington

ND912:P was orbiting to the starboard of the target when the rear gunner observed an aircraft on the starboard quarter showing red and green navigation lights and turning to attack from dead astern. The rear gunner, F/Lt G.A. Howe, held his fire until the twin-engined night fighter was at 650 yards and gave it a short burst, instructing the pilot to dive to starboard. The night fighter immediately went into a steep dive to port and was not seen again.

Ten minutes later, at 0101 hrs, PB124:H was attacked. Leaving the target at 12,000 feet the W/Op reported a Fishpond indication of an aircraft closing rapidly from low on the port quarter. The rear gunner, F/O H.F. Brundle, immediately began to search the area. A fighter flare was observed close to starboard and shortly after an unidentified aircraft was seen on the port side, flying slightly above. The aircraft switched on two red lights and then switched them off again. Brundle ordered a corkscrew to port as the enemy aircraft opened fire. Luckily the tracer passed below the Lancaster. Brundle returned fire and the night fighter was lost using the corkscrew manoeuvre.

The crew of NE126:W was just leaving the target when they were attacked from above on the port quarter by an unseen fighter. Four streams of tracer flashed past. The rear gunner ordered a corkscrew to port and the mid-upper gunner, S/Ldr H.C. Hill, quickly swung his turret round from the starboard, where he had been searching, and opened fire. The rear gunner also joined in and the fighter was lost during the corkscrew. The Lancaster went on its way.

On the night of 20/21 July 147 Lancasters and eleven Mosquitoes attacked the oil plant at Homburg. Severe damage was caused but the force suffered high losses, with twenty Lancasters going down. The night fighters were particularly active and two of the squadron's crews fought running battles with several of them. PA964:K was proceeding at 16,000 feet when the rear gunner, F/Lt Ernest Wharton, sighted an Me210 on the port side, flying slightly above and 400 yards away. He informed his pilot to stand by to dive to port and the mid-upper gunner to keep a lookout to starboard. He opened fire with a two-second burst just as the night fighter did the same. Hits were observed and the Me210 burst into flames and dived to the ground, where it exploded. Its destruction was confirmed by F/Lt Phillips, who was nearby in Lancaster ND387:O.

A few minutes later Wharton spotted another night fighter attacking a Lancaster flying slightly above on the port side. Warning the pilot to stand by to dive to port, and the mid-upper gunner and W/Op to keep a lookout to starboard, he opened fire. The twin-engined night fighter immediately broke away and dived to starboard. The crew did not observe whether it was damaged, as almost immediately the mid-upper gunner sighted another Me210 slightly above then on the starboard quarter. It was closing in a turn to bring it dead astern and level with the Lancaster. The bomber was committed to the bombing run at this point and the rear gunner was unable to give the pilot avoiding action. Wharton opened fire with a long burst just as the fighter replied and once again he scored hits. The Me210 broke away to starboard. On completion of the bombing run Wharton ordered the pilot to begin weaving, as there were several fighter flares in the area. The Me210 was claimed as probably destroyed.

Whilst Wharton was fighting his running battles with the night fighters another crew was also fighting for their lives. The W/Op of JB661:L reported a Fishpond indication a mile away on the starboard beam and closing rapidly. Both gunners searched the area and the rear gunner, WO W. Aspey, sighted a twin-engined fighter at a range of 600 yards. Aspey ordered the pilot to standby to corkscrew to starboard and at 450 yards Aspey and the night fighter simultaneously opened fire. The mid-upper gunner ordered the pilot to corkscrew on seeing the fighter's tracer. The night fighter broke away at 400 yards and Aspey followed it round, keeping up a steady stream of fire. The mid-upper gunner lost the fighter behind the tailplane and could not join in, but Aspey observed strikes.

Five minutes later he sighted a Ju88 astern at a range of 500 yards, which immediately opened fire. It could be clearly identified in the glare of fighter flares and Aspey and the mid-upper gunner, F/O G. Horsburgh, opened fire together. Horsburgh shouted to the pilot to corkscrew and he threw the aircraft to port. The gunners saw several strikes on the Ju88, which broke away. Aspey continued to fire at the crippled night fighter, which appeared to be out of control. 300 yards from the Lancaster it burst into flames and the port wing and engine were enveloped. Aspey only stopped firing as it dived out of control towards the ground.

The battle was not over for the crew of JB661:L, however. Almost immediately the W/Op picked up another Fishpond indication, this time on the port quarter and closing rapidly. Horsburgh and Aspey took up the search and Aspey spotted the twin-engined night fighter at a range of 400 yards. It opened fire, which Aspey returned immediately, shouting to the pilot to corkscrew to port. The corkscrew was successful and they lost the fighter. Only two minutes later Horsburgh saw tracer coming from the starboard quarter. He returned fire at a twin-engined aircraft and gave the pilot instructions to corkscrew to starboard. The pilot manoeuvred violently and once again they escaped. JB661:L and its crew had earned their pay this night.

Kiel was visited by a force of 629 bombers on the night of 23/24 July. The force consisted of 519 Lancasters, 100 Halifaxes and ten Mosquitoes in the first raid on this target in two months. A successful RCM [Radio Counter Measures] operation and deception plan resulted in a very successful raid and the loss of only four Lancasters. The squadron did not get away without a fight however. JB661:L was on the way to the target, flying at 18,000 feet, when the rear gunner, F/Sgt S. Starling sighted a Ju88 attacking another Lancaster. The combat was taking place about 1,000 yards away and Starling ordered the pilot to turn to starboard to put the enemy fighter into the lightest part of the sky. It was still attacking the other bomber as JB661 closed in, and at 400 yards Starling opened fire. The Ju88 broke away to the port side of the other Lancaster and was not seen again.

Just over half an hour later on the homeward leg Starling and the mid-upper gunner, F/Sgt H.H. Bell, both spotted an Fw190 on the port quarter. The fighter was only 200 yards away and both gunners opened fire, calling for a corkscrew to starboard. They saw their fire hit the enemy, which had also opened fire before diving away out of control. The gunners claimed it as probably destroyed.

The following night the target was Stuttgart in the first of three heavy raids. Four hundred and sixty-one Lancasters and 153 Halifaxes attacked for the loss of seventeen and four respectively. Over the target the rear gunner of PB124:H suddenly saw cannon tracer coming towards him from low on the port quarter. The enemy fighter, an Fw190, was about 400 yards away and closing rapidly. By the time both gunners opened fire the Fw190 fighter was at 250 yards and the rear gunner ordered the pilot to corkscrew to port. Several strikes were observed on the fighter, which caught fire, but the German pilot was determined and continued to close on the Lancaster, firing until he reached a range of 150 yards. The gunners were equally

One of the crews to fly JB661:MG-L was captained by F/O Vic Brammur, seen here in the cockpit with the crew on the port inner engine. This was one of the 'above average' crews to join PFF direct from training in autumn 1944. They would complete their tour. 7 Sqn

determined and continued firing until the fighter broke away enveloped in flames and went into a steep dive into the clouds, followed shortly afterwards by an explosion. The gunners of H-Harry were able to claim it as destroyed.

On 25 July F/Lt Phillips took his crew to Ferfay as deputy master bomber in Lancaster MG-O. His was one of only two Lancasters in the force of 112 aircraft. The master bomber halted the attack on the flying-bomb site after only seventy-three of the force had bombed. Only one Halifax was lost.

The squadron crews went to Stuttgart again on the night of 28/29 July and many of them had combats with night fighters. The danger did not always come from the enemy, though. Lancaster NE126:R was *en route* to the target at 0120 hrs, flying at 18,000 feet, when the pilot observed another Lancaster on the starboard side, slightly above and about 600 yards away. After maintaining the same position for two or three minutes it turned steeply to port and lost height levelling off at the same altitude as NE126:R. Suddenly its rear gunner opened fire, scoring hits on NE126:R, damaging the starboard mainplane and starboard outer engine. The pilot took evasive action by climbing steeply, narrowly avoiding a collision, and managed to lose the aggressive Lancaster – a lucky escape from friendly fire!

Whilst the crew of NE126 were busy avoiding this gun battle the gunners of Lancaster JA677:U were having their own problems. Over the target the rear gunner, S/Ldr R. Dixon, and the mid-upper gunner, F/O J.R.H. Morrison, observed a twin-engined night fighter, which they identified as a Ju88, 400 yards away on the starboard quarter. Dixon ordered the pilot to dive to starboard and corkscrew just as the Ju88 fired a burst of green and yellow tracer, which flew past just 15 yards astern of the Lancaster. Dixon and Morrison immediately returned fire and Dixon saw his fire hit the fighter in the port engine. Morrison missed with his first burst but, quickly correcting his aim, fired again and hit the Ju88 in the starboard engine. It continued in to 200 yards but both of its engines burst into flames, still being fired upon by the gunners. Dixon and Morrison watched the night fighter as it fell away and saw it explode on the ground.

The Lancaster gunners were very twitchy on that night and the crew of ND912:P came under friendly fire a few minutes later. On the way to the target at 18,500 feet the pilot saw another Lancaster dead ahead. A few seconds later a double stream of yellow machine gun tracer passed very close overhead. The pilot quickly took evasive action by diving and escaped undamaged. Another close shave on a night with heavy losses.

Lancaster Mk III, PB212, captained by H.K. Perry crash landed at the USAAF base at Bungay that night after being damaged by flak on the raid to Stuttgart. Sgt Robert Stanley Roberts was the wireless operator on this aircraft. He was on his firty-first sortie and his actions during the flight would earn him an immediate DFM. The recommendation for the award tells his story:

After leaving the target, the aircraft was hit by anti-aircraft fire and burst into flames. The Captain gave orders to abandon, but this NCO was unable to move from his position owing to fires and consequently became severely burnt in the face, hands and legs. The Captain subsequently was able to get the aircraft under control and, although all members of the crew, including this NCO, were injured, managed to bring this aircraft back to this country.

Throughout the return flight, this NCO showed courage and fortitude of the highest order. Disregarding his own physical suffering through burns, he managed to put out the fires in the vicinity of his position and send an SOS message before his equipment became totally unserviceable. Realizing that the bomb aimer had received severe burns and was very ill, this NCO administered First Aid and morphia and spent the whole of the return journey attending to his safety. Not until the aircraft had returned to this country and crash landed did this NCO make any mention of his own injuries and his action throughout the flight was instrumental in relieving the badly injured bomb aimer of the serious effects of his burns. This NCO has proved himself to be an outstanding member of a gallant crew and his conduct throughout the action, without consideration for his own personal safety, is worthy of the highest praise.

The rear gunner of this Lancaster, Sgt F.W.J. Shane, baled out at some stage during the crew's ordeal and landed in enemy territory; sadly he did not survive.

German fighters intercepted the bomber stream *en route* to the target and thirty-nine Lancasters were lost. No. 7 Sqn Lancaster Mk III, NE122:MG-V was one of those engaged by night fighters. Attacked on the return leg at 0153 hrs the pilot wrote later in his combat report:

Rear gunner observed a twin-engined aircraft flying on tops of illuminated cloud approx. 5,000 feet below, and identified it as an Me210 or 410. Enemy approached from starboard quarter making a climbing attack, and opened fire at

600 yards. Rear gunner opened fire and instructed pilot to corkscrew starboard. Mid-upper gunner joined in the combat at 350 yards. Both gunners observed strikes on the enemy, and at 100 yards the port engine exploded, and the aircraft turned over and spun towards the ground into the cloud, with port wing on fire and pieces of burning debris falling away. Enemy scored hits on starboard inner engine, which caught fire. Other damage – No. 1 fuel tank holed, main hydraulics shot away, hydraulics to both turrets unserviceable. Whilst still ablaze from the first attack, rear gunner observed green cannon tracer coming from port quarter level. He turned turret from engaging earlier aircraft to engage second aircraft, identified as another Me210 at 300 yards, and fired a short burst, when turret went unserviceable owing to damage sustained from first attack. Pilot dived starboard whilst enemy was at 250 yards, lost 4,000 feet in the diving turn, and did not observe enemy again. Owing to Lancaster being on fire strikes from second aircraft not observed. Pilot ordered crew to abandon aircraft, as he had lost control. Engineer extinguished the fire in the dive, and the pilot regained control. Crew had experienced difficulty in trying to abandon the aircraft, consequently they were still aboard when control was regained.

V for Victor returned safely to Oakington and eventually after many more operations was transferred to No. 1669 CU [Conversion Unit] where it served out its life training new Lancaster crews.

Richard H. Smith, a member of this crew recalls three sorties during July 1944.

The crew were R.P. Todd, pilot; R.H. Smith, navigator; R. Martin, flight engineer; Stanton, wireless operator; Drinkwater and Tracy, gunners; Grant, bomb aimer and Talbot, radar operator.

On the 24, 25 and 28 July 1944 Bomber Command attacked the city of Stuttgart. R.P. Todd's crew took part in all three attacks. Their duty was to drop marker flares to guide the main force of bombers to the target. The 24th operation took seven hours, thirty minutes, the one on the 25th eight hours, ten minutes; the extra time was due to engine trouble. The aircraft they flew was NE122:V. For the 28th operation they were again allocated NE122:V. They air tested it for an hour in the afternoon after the engineers had checked it, and took off for Stuttgart at 2240 hrs carrying one 4,000 pound bomb and four 1,000 pound target indicators.

The Luftwaffe was well prepared to oppose the attacking force, having been warned by the previous two attacks. It was a moonlit night and the German fighters were very active. It was later estimated that about 200 fighters were employed. Sixty-two of the bomber force were lost (which was the third heaviest loss of the war). During the run to the target many air combats and ground fires were seen.

The crew of NE122 were briefed to drop their markers visually and to facilitate this they were to locate the small town of Pforzheim which gave a good return on the H2S radar, and there set up a piece of equipment called a ground position indicator [GPI]. This threw a spot of light on a target chart. The spot moved along giving the aircraft's position. The distance to fly was about 15 miles; about four minutes time. During this action the aircraft had to be held straight and level. What happened during this run-in is described in the official combat report prepared after the crew was debriefed after the operation was completed and they had returned to Oakington [See pilots report above].

What follows is a first-hand account compiled from the memories of the pilot, the flight engineer and the navigator, Richard Smith.

After setting up the GPI over Pforzheim I was giving the pilot direction instructions. The bomb aimer was lying prone over his bombsight and also pushing out handfuls of window – strips of metal foil to confuse the enemy radar. Window was carried in small packets and stacked by the bomb aimer's position over the lower escape hatch. Suddenly there was an explosion on the starboard side. Also a tremendous racket as the gunners fired their eight Browning machine-guns causing empty .303 cartridges to cascade from the mid-upper turret and rattle against the inside of the fuselage. Also there was a lot of noise over the intercom as the gunners called for evasive action. The aircraft dived violently to starboard and I watched the navigator's altimeter record a loss of 4,000 feet.

The aircraft filled with smoke and the captain gave the order to abandon. My immediate reaction was to grab and fix my parachute and make for the lower escape hatch ready to leave the aircraft as soon as the bomb aimer opened the hatch. We learned later that the hatch could not be opened because the parcels of window were lying across it. The bomb aimer was desperately flinging the parcels out of the way and they were bursting open as he flung them. Suddenly the hatch came open and a blast of freezing air blew through the opening carrying with it masses of strips of tin foil. I was standing in a direct line with the blast and was covered with the stuff. While this was happening the pilot had regained control. The engineer had operated the starboard inner engine fire extinguisher and the captain had cancelled the abandon order. All the crew was still aboard, which fact was probably due to the delay caused by the blocked escape hatch.

The Lancaster was settled in straight and level flight, the starboard inner propeller feathered to reduce drag and the crew gradually resumed their stations and regained some of their composure. The bomb load was still aboard and could not then be dropped because the bomb doors could not be opened.

We were now some distance away from the target and the position was not known with any accuracy. The important thing was to be heading in the right direction, so a course was set to the westward. The main compass system had gone u/s in the dive, so we were reduced to using the standby compass, which was not linked to the H2S radar, which was therefore useless. The aircraft was now flying steadily at about 10,000 feet and everyone was gradually recovering his wits and starting to think straight once more.

In the event of another fighter attack we had very little defence. The gun turrets could only be operated manually and any violent evasive action was not possible on three engines. The captain decided that we would stay with the aircraft as long as possible.

The westerly course was held for about two hours, when we saw searchlight activity ahead, which coincided with the estimated position of Paris. We altered course to pass this active area on the starboard. By this time we had begun to hope that we might reach the French coast. Shortly after this I was delighted to see signs of signals on the Gee navigation system and was able to get a position line which confirmed our DR [Dead Reckoning] position. From then on the Gee came in stronger and about three hours after the fighter attack we crossed the French coast near Le Havre.

The captain decided to try to get rid of the bomb load by dropping it fused safe into the English Channel. The bomb doors were opened manually and the load was jettisoned. I do not remember our height at this time but we were low enough for the bomb aimer to see that one of the bombs exploded. When the bombs were jettisoned the undercarriage came down and could not be retracted. The effect of this was to reduce the speed, but increasing the engine revs enabled us to maintain height at around 4,000 feet.

The Gee was now working well and we knew our position. We crossed the English coast somewhere near Brighton above and into cloud. The W/Op had informed Bomber Command Control of our plight and emergency services were alerted. We were in touch with the emergency landing ground at Manston in Kent, which was equipped with the FIDO blind landing system. They were giving us QDMs [direction steers] to help our approach.

Arriving over Manston the controller told us over the R/T that the cloud base was 300 feet but the weather was clearer to the north of the Thames estuary. Dawn was breaking and we could see we were above a sheet of unbroken cloud. I can remember the controller's words. 'All right lads. I will find you a home.' He then gave us a course and distance to steer. I plotted the course on the map and saw that it met the coast of Essex about 30 miles north-north-west of Manston. Turning on to this we headed out over the cloud sheet. The cloud began to break up and the north coast of the estuary came in sight. There ahead was an airfield and they were giving us a welcome green landing light.

I cannot remember whether we made a preliminary circuit of this airfield, or whether we went straight in, but the pilot made a rather heavy but safe landing. The screech of the tyres as we touched down was the most beautiful sound we had ever heard.

We all climbed thankfully out. The assembled ground crew told us that we were at Bradwell Bay. It was 0610 hrs, seven hours, thirty minutes since we had taken off from Oakington. For all of us the most memorable seven and a half hours of our lives, still vividly remembered over fifty years later.

We saw that the starboard engine was badly damaged. I tore off a small piece of jagged Duralumin sheet and wrote on it in pencil V, 28/7/44, Stuttgart. I have kept it amongst my various war souvenirs.

The Bradwell Bay airfield became the site of one of Britain's first atomic power stations, built during the 1950s and since closed down. Later in the day we were transported the 60 miles back to Oakington in an RAF 3-ton truck, where we were debriefed by the intelligence officers.

Paul Todd, the captain also recalls this operation.

After being hit over Stuttgart the undercarriage came down, which is why we could only maintain height at about 7,500 feet. I remember Stanton reporting there was several inches of petrol slopping around in the wireless operator's area, which did little to alleviate my concern. The landing at Bradwell Bay was, in fact, on one wheel as I knew that the starboard tyre had been shot to pieces.

Between July and September Todd's crew would fly another twenty-two operational sorties.

On the same raid F/O Keith Hadland Perry, flying PB212, was recommended for an immediate DSO by the CO, W/Cdr R.W. Cox. This was Perry's fortieth operation and his twenty-fifth since joining the squadron as a Pathfinder. The recommendation cited the details of his courage and fortitude.

Flying Officer Perry was captain of a Lancaster aircraft detailed to attack Hamburg on the night of 28/29 July, 1944. After successfully completing his bombing run and leaving the target area, his aircraft received direct hits from three anti-aircraft shells, one in the fuselage and the other two in the starboard main plane. The aircraft immediately caught fire, the flames spreading from the nose through the fuselage, almost to the tail of the aircraft. The Pilot's cockpit became a mass of flames. The Pilot was unable to see anything, and as the situation appeared very grave, Flying Officer Perry ordered his crew to abandon aircraft. The Rear Gunner was able to abandon, the Mid-Upper Gunner was unable to abandon, as the force of the explosion had blown him from his turret into the fuselage, and the last thing Flying Officer Perry remembers was the remaining members of his crew moving through the flames to the forward escape hatch to abandon. He was overcome by the smoke and the fumes, and when he eventually regained consciousness, he found the aircraft still on fire, diving steeply at about 350 knots and height 5,000 feet. Realizing that his crew had been unable to abandon, owing to their being overcome by fumes and the attitude of the aircraft, by superhuman efforts this Officer, although burnt on the face and hands, managed to pull his aircraft out of the dive at 500 feet. The fire on the underside of the fuselage had subsided, but fire still existed in the Pilot's cockpit and throughout the inside of the fuselage. Although the remainder of the crew had all received severe burns, this Officer, by displaying unsurpassed coolness and fearlessness in spite of his physical suffering, rallied his crew together, and after they had extinguished the fires, managed to fly his badly damaged aircraft back to this country. The long sea crossing was accomplished at a height of 3,000 feet, the Pilot only having two engines on the port side and one defective on the starboard side, the starboard outer having been feathered. The damage to the aircraft made it very hard to control but in the face of these very heavy odds, this Officer showed coolness and courage of the highest order and eventually managed to effect a crash landing on an aerodrome in this country without further injury to his crew.

Throughout this hazardous flight, this officer's conduct inspired a high standard of morale in his crew, all of which are now recovering from burns received.

Flying Officer Perry, throughout the whole course of his operational career, has shown a high degree of courage, skill and initiative, and this action is typical of the determination he has shown throughout.

Both the Station Commander and the AOC Pathfinder Force strongly recommended the award.

Another of the squadron's Lancaster's was attacked that night, but F/Lt McCarthy and his crew managed to escape the attentions of a night fighter in Lancaster JB661:MG-L. McCarthy wrote in his combat report:

At about 0150 hrs on the night of 28/29 July, while on the run in to Stuttgart, I heard the rear gunner say 'Port – Go.' Immediately after and just as I started my dive I observed four or five streams of tracer passing about 2 feet over the cockpit. I could hear our guns firing back at the enemy aircraft, which was a Ju88. I lost about 1,000 feet in my initial dive and then pulled up to starboard, banking steeply. During this time I observed no more fire from the enemy aircraft.

The enemy aircraft must have broken away to starboard, since we apparently followed him round at about 50 yards, during which time the two gunners reported a large amount of hits on the enemy aircraft, both on the fuselage and the port engine, which later caught fire. The gunners then reported that the enemy aircraft dived away very sharply into the cloud. Shortly after we saw the glow of an explosion through the cloud in the direction the enemy aircraft had taken. The whole combat lasted about half a minute, during which both gunners gave very clear and concise directions. There were no further incidents on the trip.

During July 1944 the King and Queen visited the station for an investiture and Gerald South was one of those on parade.

In July the King and Queen, accompanied by Princess Elizabeth, held an open air investiture on the tarmac; there were many recipients, including two or three DSOs. Our Squadron Commander, W/Cdr Cox, was given his AFC, earned as an instructor and flight commander at a Stirling HCU, and I received the DFC. We were all out-medalled, as it were, by the OC WAAF, Flt Off Daphne Pearson, who early in the war was given the George Cross as a medical corporal for rescuing the pilot from a crashed aircraft. She was on parade in charge of the WAAF flight.

The last operation in July was on the 30th, a daylight raid to the Normandy battle area by 692 bombers. The target was German positions in front of the American lines in support of their ground attack in the Villers Bocage-Caumont area. Cloud cover hampered the attack and only 377 aircraft managed to drop their bombs on the target markers dropped by Oboe-equipped aircraft. Only two of the six targets were effectively bombed.

By the last weeks of July German industrial cities were back on the target lists and losses mounted. Roy Claridge recalls his crew's rapid rise up the 'promotion list'.

We moved rapidly up the 'promotion list' from backers-up to markers to deputy master bomber and finally master bomber. So many previous master bomber crews had gone missing that we decided to agree a different approach in attacking the targets. Somehow we managed to get permission to ignore briefings and make our own way to the target. This worked, as we had noticed that most of the turning points which Main Force made on the way to the target were marked by the Germans before Main Force arrived. We made no fancy turns but flew straight to the target. We always made and marked the target on time, within two or three minutes. We had very good navigators. Over the target we would circle, but all the time we would lose height while directing the raid. We were at risk from light flak the lower we went, but the fighters must have thought we had been hit and were going down. This worked and often we spent half an hour instructing up to three waves of Main Force bombers. We returned to base using the fastest route possible. It was almost impossible to fly straight and level over Germany in those days but we had certain advantages over the enemy. When we became master bombers I was given a new piece of radar. It was called Fishpond, mainly because it had a circular screen, and when it picked up enemy fighters it showed them as dark blips on a green background. Fishpond could pick up fighters from a range of 15 miles, behind, to the side and in front, but not in certain positions beneath the aeroplane. It had three ranges and was useful in preparing the gunners for surprise attacks. It must have worked as our gunners shot down three enemy fighters.

One night we found ourselves flying alongside another Lancaster, flying straight and level. We were about 100 yards away when suddenly a Bf110 night fighter opened fire. No fire was returned so our gunners got permission to attack the fighter, who had not seen us. The gunners shot it down, but we had not realized there was another Bf110 who promptly opened fire on us. We were hit again and again, but we went into a power dive and the gunners managed to shoot this other fighter down. We managed to pull out of the power dive at about 5,000 feet. We limped home, but we were so badly damaged we had to make an emergency landing at Woodbridge in Suffolk. We found in the morning that we had 183 holes in the plane and it never flew again. We were all uninjured.

This episode was not remembered for being shot up but for what happened to me in a transport café on the main road back to Oakington. We pulled in in our RAF transport to have some tea. Inside the café was a fruit machine. All the crew had a go on the machine and as we were leaving I found a sixpence in the corner of my trouser pocket and had one more go. We all thought we were being attacked again by our German friends. The fruit machine went berserk, lights flashed, machine-gun-like noises began and the machine went mad, spewing out sixpencees - £25 in all. This confirmed we had someone watching over us. It certainly paid for a lot of beer.

Our gunners were awarded immediate DFCs. Brian Frow was promoted to squadron leader and awarded the DSO. Brian and I completed seventy-four operations.

Daylight raids were the order of the day in August, commencing with a sortie to Novelle en Chausse on the 1st. This raid was to numerous targets but was not a success, only seventy-nine of the 777 bombers despatched dropping their bombs due to poor weather.

On the 3rd the squadron returned to the flying-bomb sites of the Forêt de Neippe for a successful raid. On the 4th Bomber Command carried out daylight raids against flying-bomb storage sites, oils storage depots and the railway bridge at Etaples. No. 7 Sqn were sent to the oil storage depot at Pauillac. Accuracy was good and only three sticks of bombs dropped outside the target area. The refineries were hit hard and two tankers were set ablaze. Crews from the squadron also attacked flying-bomb sites in the Forêt d'Adam. Frank Leatherdale was a navigator on 'A' Flt and joined the squadron with his crew on that day.

My crew had just finished a tour of ops with No. 115 Sqn in 3 Group and we came almost complete, except that our flight engineer did not wish to do a second tour and so we picked up a new flight engineer at Oakington. Thus

Gerald South's crew and ground crew at Oakington in Summer 1944. Top left, F/Lt V.T. Fowler, RCAF (navigator); Second right, F/Lt G.J. South (captain); Extreme right, Cpl V. Denver (i/c ground crew). G.J. South

our crew was: pilot, Flt Lt D.S. McKechnie DFC, a Canadian; navigator, F/O F.R. Leatherdale; bomb aimer, Sgt K.T. Denly; wireless operator, Sgt B. Payne; flight engineer, F/Sgt S. Haralambedes; mid-upper gunner, P/O C.E. Wilkin, and rear gunner, Sgt J. Hayes.

We were soon made a primary visual marker crew and so were given an additional bomb aimer – F/Sgt Peter Greenaway. Ken Denly then came to join me in the 'nav' office to work the H2S.

After two weeks at the Pathfinder Force Training Unit at RAF Warboys we settled in to ops at Oakington. Initially we had to prove our mettle and so were designated as 'supporters'; as such we did not carry TIs nor incendiary bombs – just HE bombs which we dropped at the beginning of the raid to help suppress the defences and to take some of the heat off the real PFF marker crews.

During this time, like all PFF crews, we also flew several training flights – cross-country exercises, high-level bombing by day and night and fighter affiliation exercises. All these were carefully assessed to measure our competence.

On joining the PFF aircrew had to qualify before being accepted as a competent marker crew. Once qualified each member was awarded the coveted gold eagle to wear on the left breast pocket – except when flying on ops – which was authorized by a certificate signed by AVM Bennett; but this award was only valid for as long as you remained in the PFF.

We received our awards on 4 October 1944 and were consequently promoted to an acting rank one above our present ranks and we received a higher rate of pay. This was to induce aircrew to volunteer for the PFF. I was very proud of my PFF badge. I think we all were – it meant a great deal, because it was hard to win. On completion of our tour we were each awarded the permanent right to wear the PFF badge – this right was authorized by a more formal certificate signed by Bennett.

The pilot, F/Lt Donald McKechnie would be awarded the DFC in January 1945, retiring as a wing commander in 1977. The recommendation of 20 October 1944 noted that he had flown forty-eight sorties, seventeen of them as a Pathfinder.

Fred Phillips and his crew took part in several daylight operations during the period and flight engineer Tom Jones recalls a close call returning from one still carrying a full bomb load.

I recall on one occasion returning from a daylight op with a full bomb load and bouncing badly on landing. 'Round again,' shouted Fred Phillips and I opened the throttles to full power. We roared across the grass at an angle to the runway, directly toward the village church steeple. The pilot coaxed every inch of height from the aircraft as the steeple loomed closer every second and flashed beneath us with inches to spare. Looking down I saw the villagers scattering. A child standing in the lane staring up at us screaming with fright at the sudden appearance and deafening noise. A woman, wearing an apron, running to scoop up the child in her arms and racing to safety. Farm animals stampeding. It all registered on the mind in the second or two we were over the village. After landing the rear gunner said that if we had warned him he could have leaned out of his turret and removed the steeple weather vane for a souvenir.

Assistance to ground troops was still being provided in August and ND460:MG-W was lost over Normandy on the 7th/8th. The operation was codenamed Totalise. The force of 1,019 bombers attacked five aiming points, mainly German strongpoints and surrounding roads. MG-W, flown by F/O I. Kidd, an Australian, was taking part in the bombing of the fifth aiming point. None of the crew survived. Ten Lancasters were lost, seven of which were shot down by night fighters. On the 9th another daylight raid was flown, this time to a fuel-storage depot in the Forêt de Normal.

On 10 August the squadron received orders from 8 Group that it was to supply the master bomber and deputy, six illuminators and three backers-up for a raid on railway targets in France. The squadron would set course from Oakington to coast out at Sidmouth before routing to a turning point leading to the IP [Initial Point] for the target. Fifty miles from the target they were to begin dropping Window. Once at the IP, which was to be identified using the GPI [Ground Position Indicator], they

Fred Phillips and crew in front of a Lancaster at Oakington in late 1944. This crew had a close shave with the village church steeple returning from a daylight op with a full bomb load. P. Jones

would run in and release the first of the illuminating flares after a timed run followed by a salvo of the remaining flares. The marking was successful and the bombing caused much damage. Three Halifaxes were lost from the 124-strong force. Crews from the squadron, including F/Lt Phillips, acting as deputy master bomber in Lancaster MG-O, also attacked the oil depot at La Pallice.

On 12 August the squadron had a busy day, with two raids being flown. The first was in daylight to a fuel dump at Forêt de Montrichard, which was successfully plastered. F/Lt Phillips and his crew took part in Lancaster MG-O and returned to Oakington, where they were briefed for a sortie to Falaise along with 143 other crews in a night raid to stem the retreat of the German forces in the area. Phillips did not take his usual aircraft, O-Orange, but flew T-Tommy as deputy master bomber on this highly successful raid.

The Opel motor works at Russelsheim was bombed on the night of 12/13 August by a force of 297 aircraft. Most of the bombs fell in the open countryside and little damage was done to the works for the loss of thirteen Lancasters and seven Halifaxes. Two of 7 Sqn's crews had to make a fight of it. NE126:R was flying at 18,000 feet and the bomb aimer had just released the bombs when the mid-upper gunner sighted a twin-engined aircraft flying slightly above on the starboard quarter. It was a Bf110 and was clearly visible in the brightly lit sky over the target. The night fighter began to position for a stern attack from below and at a range of 750 yards the mid-upper gunner called for a corkscrew to starboard. WO A.D. Price, the rear gunner, fired two short bursts at the fighter before the pilot's evasive action plunged them back into the darkness and they lost it.

Just over an hour later, at 0123 hrs, it was the turn of Lancaster PB241:X. The crew was on their way home when the rear gunner, F/O C.J. Marchand, spotted a single-engined night fighter approaching from below and dead astern. It was 750 yards away and closing to 650 yards it opened fire. Marchand shouted to the pilot to corkscrew and opened fire. The green and yellow cannon and machine gun tracer from the night fighter went below the Lancaster, followed by another burst over the cockpit. Marchand saw his bullets hit the fighter and kept up his return fire until it broke away, diving to port. The mid-upper gunner, F/Sgt H. Stenhouse, joined in the fight at a range of 350 yards, getting in three bursts. The quick actions and keen eyesight of the gunners had saved the crew from being shot down.

On 14 August there was a carefully planned attack on seven targets in the Normandy battle area, marked by Oboe and visual marking. No. 7 Sqn provided two master bombers, two deputies, four backer-up crews and six bombing crews. The squadron attack was split into a master bomber, deputy and four backers-up along with four more from 35 Sqn on Target Six. Target Seven would have a master bomber and deputy from the squadron, with two backers-up from 35 Sqn and two more from 582 Sqn plus the six bombing crews from 7 Sqn. These would mark this target for sixty aircraft from No. 4 Group. The bombing aircraft from the squadron were armed with eighteen 500 pound instantaneously fused bombs each. Most of the bombing was accurate, but unfortunately some of the bombs fell not on the enemy but on elements of the 12th Canadian Field Regiment. The mistake may have been caused by the Canadians lighting yellow identification flares, which were mistaken for the yellow target markers being used. Despite the efforts of the master bombers to stop crews bombing the wrong target around seventy crews bombed the Canadian position, killing thirteen men and injuring fifty-three.

On 15 August the squadron provided two groups of Pathfinders for attacks on *Luftwaffe* night-fighter airfields. The attack, codenamed Operation Butterscotch, was in preparation for a return to attacks on targets in Germany. For one target a master bomber, a deputy and four backers-up were provided, for the other only a master bomber and a deputy. Some 1,009 bombers took part in these raids, each force being escorted by fighters of the 8th USAAF, which rendezvoused with them over the enemy coast. The crews bombed in perfect visibility and carried out a series of successful attacks.

On the night of 16/17 August the squadron went to Stettin, and in addition to much damage to the town the force sank five ships and badly damaged another eight in the harbour. F/Lt D.S. McKechnie's crew carried out their first PFF operation to this target as Frank Leatherdale recalls. 'After a week we made our first PFF operational flight taking three 2,000 pound, one 1,000 pound and one 500 pound HE bombs to Stettin. This was a typical bomb load for a supporter, although smaller than most due to the amount of fuel we needed to reach Stettin. Indeed we were airborne for eight hours, fifty-five minutes that night.'

Sterkrade was struck on the 18th/19th. PB148:MG-C, under the command of F/Lt PG McCarthy DFC, failed to return. She was the only Lancaster lost, going down with no survivors.

The Lancasters went to Russelsheim again on 25/26 August to bomb the Opel motor factory and ND582:MG-D did not return. F/Lt T.H. Strong DFC, from New Zealand and his crew survived with only one loss, fellow New Zealander P/O R.B. Ede DFC. Several other aircraft were attacked by night fighters. Marking was accurate and the whole raid, by 412 Lancasters, was over in ten minutes. Severe damage was caused to the forge and gearbox assembly plants, but production resumed only two days later.

The first of the squadron crews to come under fighter attack on this raid was that of PA964:MG-K. *En route* to the target, at a few minutes after midnight, the mid-upper gunner, S/Ldr H.C. Hill, saw a four-engined bomber being stalked by a Ju88 and an exchange of fire between them. As the fight moved from the starboard beam to the port quarter, above PA964, the Ju88 suddenly dived sharply towards them. S/Ldr Hill immediately ordered a corkscrew to port and F/O G.A. Hall, the rear gunner, opened fire. Hill could not bring his guns to bear and shortly afterwards the night fighter broke away and was not seen again. Moments later a single-engined fighter was sighted by Hall, but a corkscrew to port soon lost it. F/O Gavin Hall, a native of Minitonas, Manitoba, was commissioned in 1943 and in December 1944 he would be recommended for the DFC, which was subsequently awarded in March 1945. The recommendation for the award read:

On his second operational tour, this officer has now completed 59 sorties, 26 of which have been successfully concluded in the Pathfinder Force on this squadron. He has been a member of a Marker crew on fifteen occasions.

Flying Officer Hall has always displayed complete coolness in combat with the enemy. His fine handling of guns, his devotion to duty, and his all-round ability as an Air Gunner have, on more than one occasion, enabled his captain to avoid combat in the air, and has thereby contributed to the safety of the crew. His strong sense of discipline and devotion to duty are highly commendable.

Less than an hour later the crew of NE126:R had a lucky escape. Leaving the target area at 18,000 feet the pilot sighted an Fw190 dead ahead and flying on a reciprocal course. The pilot warned the rear gunner, F/O Beale, and as the Fw190 flew behind the Lancaster, oblivious to its presence, Beale gave it a short burst. The fighter climbed rapidly and was lost to view. A few minutes after this incident the crew of PB357:S got into a fight with a Ju88. The W/Op, who was searching from the astro-hatch at the rear of the cockpit, spotted the night fighter approaching from the port quarter and the pilot immediately dived to port. At the same moment the fighter opened fire and the gunners, WO A.D. Price and F/Sgt A. Scott, responded. The Ju88 broke off and dived to starboard and was not seen again. Its pilot probably thought he had bitten off more than he could chew as he had not only come under fire from Price and Scott but also from other Lancasters close by.

The crew of PA975:G was working its way back from the target, through intense searchlight activity and a scattering of heavy flak, and had just altered course at the first turning point from the target when the pilot, F/O McCollah, noticed another Lancaster corkscrewing violently on his port beam. The mid-upper gunner also saw and reported it. The pilot had been weaving at the time, but even so, the other Lancaster was coming dangerously close and he was forced to pull up. The Lancaster passed right beneath PA975 and, positioned low on the starboard side, its rear gunner opened fire from 100 yards. PA975's starboard inner engine burst into flames and the pilot corkscrewed to starboard to avoid further fire. The engine was quickly feathered and the offending Lancaster was not seen again.

The pilot, flight engineer and rear gunner of Lancaster PB241:X all simultaneously observed tracer coming towards them from the port side, and at the same level. The pilot turned to port and dived, losing 400 feet. The fighter, an Fw190, had dived in from the port bow, towards the tail of the Lancaster, effectively masking it from the rear guns, and the closing speed and break-away to port was too great for the gunner to follow. The mid-upper gunner did not see it at all and the crew was lucky to escape with only a cannon-shell hole in the port tailplane. This was the final battle of the raid for the much-harassed 7 Sqn crews.

Brest was attacked the same night by 324 aircraft and NE123, piloted by S/Ldr R.C. Chopping, was the only Lancaster lost. The following night the bombers went to Kiel, only to be frustrated by smoke screens laid to disrupt the bombing. The crews pressed home the attack, however, and caused serious damage to the city centre. PB180 did not come back. Coded MG-F, it took off from Oakington at 2003 hrs piloted by F/Lt William Smaill DFC RNZAF and crashed in the Baltic with the loss of all the crew: Smaill, F/Sgt Wooliscroft, P/O Fisher, P/O Baxter, P/O Butson and F/Sgt Godfray DFM. The crew was typical of many on the squadron at this time, being made up of men from all of the Commonwealth. Smaill's crew comprised one New Zealander, two Australians and four British members

The night of 26/27 August saw 372 Lancasters and ten Mosquitoes attack Kiel. The Germans put up a very successful defensive smoke screen, but despite this heavy damage was caused.

The following day 150 aircraft from Bomber Command, including 7 Sqn, carried out daylight attacks on flying-bomb sites, 7 Sqn going to Ouf en Ternois. On the night of the 29th/30th the bombers returned to Germany with a raid on Stettin. Four hundred and two aircraft took part in this raid for the loss of twenty-three Lancasters.

The squadron attacked V2 rocket stores at Lumbres in daylight on 1 September. W/Cdr Cox acted as deputy master bomber for 121 aircraft bombing Lumbres and La Pourchinte without loss. On the 3rd the targeting switched to airfields and 7 Sqn hit Venlo successfully. On the 5th 348 bombers went to Le Havre, which had been bypassed in the initial invasion assault, in the first of a series of heavy raids. Lancasters of 7 Sqn would attack the town on the 5th, 9th and twice on the 10th.

September saw German targets on the agenda again. Emden was attacked in daylight on the 6th with the loss of PB466:MG-Q. This was the last raid of the war on this town and the bombers were escorted to the target by Spitfire and Mustangs. PB466 was being flown by the master bomber, F/Lt Granville-Wilson DSO, DFC, DFM. The 23-year-old Irishman's Lancaster received a direct hit from flak and he was killed instantly. The navigator, Sgt D. Jones and the bomb aimer, Sgt E.R. Brunsdon were also killed. The rest of the crew escaped by parachute.

On 10 September Frank Leatherdale's crew were on their first marker op. 'We made our first flight as a marker when we attacked Le Havre in daylight. On this raid we had the squadron Commander, W/Cdr R. Cox, as pilot, while our skipper flew as second pilot. Also on this raid we took the squadron Bombing Leader, S/Ldr White, as our bomb aimer.'

The following day the crew took part in another daylight raid, this time to the synthetic oil plants at Kamen in the Ruhr. This was one of three areas bombed by three separate forces escorted by twenty-six squadrons of Spitfires and three each of Tempests and Mustangs. No German fighters were encountered and the plants at Kamen, clearly visible, were accurately bombed.

L to R: WO Fagan DFM (rear gunner), F/Lt Granville-Wilson DSO DFC DFM, killed in action 6 September 1944, and F/Lt W.F. Porteous DSO DFM*, killed in action 20 May 1944.
D. Cheetham

The next day we raided an oil refinery at Kamen in the Ruhr, when we again acted as a supporter, taking one 4,000 pound and sixteen 500 pound HE bombs. This was the first time I had seen the Ruhr in daylight and what a frightening sight it was! At night each AA shell appears just as a sparkle which is gone in an instant, but in daylight the smoke from each shellburst lingers in the air to join all the other bursts – so the sky appeared even more dangerous than it really was. On this attack our Lanc was hit in several places by flak splinters.

Some 992 bombers took part in this raid and attacked eight different German strongpoints. Each target was separately marked and accurately bombed. There were no losses from the attacking force. This raid was also the last flown by Fred Phillips and his crew – their sixth-fourth. Flight engineer Tom Jones recalls the sortie.

I vividly remember our last op together. On our return from Le Havre we approached base in a long shallow dive to beat up the runway. At 200 knots we thundered along the runway at zero feet to pull up hard at the far end, the G forces pulling the flesh out of our cheeks and the lower lids from our eyes. This manoeuvre was strictly forbidden, but surely, everyone must have felt on return from their last op the same jubilation and relief as the tension fell away. We had been a crew for a year, had flown 450 hours together and completed sixty-four ops without a rest period. We had done it, beaten the odds, and joined an exclusive club.

After landing, a mild rebuke from the tower, the grins on the faces of our ground crew were as broad as our own. We celebrated that night with the ground crew at the local inn at our expense as a token of our appreciation and gratitude. It was well worth the two-day hangover that followed.

Frankfurt was hit on the 12th/13th by 378 Lancasters and nine Mosquitoes, the squadron losing Lancaster NE126:MG-R, flown by F/Lt R.J.L. Banks. The city's firemen were away working in Darmstadt and the bombing caused severe destruction in the western areas. The bombers went to Gelsenkirchen in daylight the next day to bomb the Nordstern oil plant. Large explosions were seen through the smoke screen the Germans put out to try and spoil the bombers aim. Frank Leatherdale took part in this mission. 'After a night flight to Frankfurt we then found ourselves detailed to attack another oil refinery in the Ruhr at Nordstern, in daylight with a similar bomb load to that we dropped on Kamen. This time we were caught in a heavy flak barrage and our plane was hit in several places.'

Four hundred and ninety bombers of 1, 4, 6 and 8 Groups attacked Kiel on the night of 15/16 September and, in a highly concentrated raid, caused widespread damage to the old town and modern shopping centre. Lancaster PB431:D was making its way back from the target in clear, starlit skies, when the rear gunner, F/Lt W.E. Whiteman, saw an Me109 on the port quarter, attacking another Lancaster, which dived away to port. It immediately broke off its attack and spotting PB431 turned and attacked from 600 yards. Whiteman ordered a corkscrew to port and opened fire just before the fighter. The fighter's tracer passed well above the Lancaster, the pilot's aim probably thrown off by Whiteman's quick actions. The fighter then held off on the port beam, about 400 yards away, whilst the Lancaster continued to corkscrew. All the while Whiteman and the mid-upper gunner, F/Sgt

J.H. Lenaghan, poured bursts of machine-gun fire at it. Eventually the fighter broke away, probably having decided that this Lancaster's gunners were too alert for a successful kill.

On 23 September the crews were ordered to attack the Channel port of Calais. At this stage of the war the German army was trying to hold on to the Channel ports to deny their use as supply ports for the invading Allies. R.P. Todd's crew was to act as master bomber, which entailed marking the target and thereafter directing the bombing of the Main Force. For this operation they were allocated NE122:MG-V again, which had returned to the squadron from Bradwell Bay after undergoing extensive repairs during the last two months. This operation was not a complete success due to a series of mishaps. The squadron Operations Record Book noted:

The squadron provided three aircraft, Master Bomber, Deputy Master Bomber and one Backer Up to attack the Defence Area No. 9 at Calais. The Master identified the target by ground detail but shortly after was hit by light flak and the airspeed indicator was rendered u/s. He was unable to mark accurately and after failing to contact the Deputy gave orders to abandon the mission. This was carried out by the Backer Up but the Deputy Master Bomber failed to receive the message and took over as Master Bomber. The TIs were hit by flak on leaving the aircraft. This dispersed the majority, but the remainder fell one width south

Fred Phillips's crew, tour expired after sixty-four operations, in the doorway of Lancaster PA964:MG-K in September 1944. The crew survived but the Lancaster did not, going down on a raid to Buer on 6 October 1944. P. Jones

of the aiming point. The main force was then instructed to bomb centre of green TIs, which were situated in a semicircle, 250 yards radius, from the aiming point. Two aircraft followed these instructions but the remainder were not seen.

The role of NE122:V and its crew is recalled by navigator Richard Smith.

We arrived at the target area to find the cloud base was in the region of 1,500 feet. We flew across below the cloud to assess the situation and were met by intense and accurate light flak. The aircraft was hit several times, the flight engineer receiving a wound. Some of the flight instruments were rendered u/s.

The captain in his role of master bomber decided to call off the operation because the conditions due to cloud and flak opposition made accurate marking difficult. We circled the area for fifteen minutes giving the Main Force the agreed callsign for cancellation.

In view of the damage the aircraft had received the captain decided to jettison the bomb load and then land the aircraft at the emergency landing ground at Woodbridge, Suffolk. Woodbridge was equipped with all special fire fighting and crash gear and had a very wide and long runway. The place existed to receive aircraft which had been damaged on bombing missions.

As we approached to land at Woodbridge the controller warned to look out to avoid an obstruction on the runway. This was done and we noticed that the obstruction was a crashed American Liberator. We learned later that the crew had baled out over Holland and the Liberator had landed on Woodbridge runway. The crash services had hurried to the aircraft and found that there was no one on board. A most bizarre happening!

Paul Todd landed NE122:V safely if somewhat heavily and the crew were quickly out. We then saw that the pilot was still sitting in his seat. He was quickly assisted from the aircraft and only then were we aware that he had received a wound in the calf of his leg. His flying boot was badly cut. The boot was tightly strapped above the wound and the tight strap had served to staunch the blood, which would normally have flowed from such a bad wound. He had said nothing about this injury whilst circling the target cancelling the operation for fifteen minutes, flying to the jettisoning spot and landing the aircraft at Woodbridge.

Todd was taken away by ambulance to the RAF Hospital at Ely. He recovered from the wound but his operational career was over. The rest of the crew returned to Oakington, where the flight engineer was treated in sick quarters. The crew eventually teamed up with S/Ldr Davies DSO DFC, who had been posted in to commence his third tour.

Lancaster Mk IIIs PA964:MG-K and PB241:MG-X were lost on a daylight raid to the synthetic oil plants at Buer on 6 October. Bombing was accurate but nine aircraft were lost. P/O D. McRae, the captain of MG-K, and all of his crew survived to be taken prisoner. The crew of MG-X, under the command of F/O R.G. Beaune, all survived, with the exception of F/Sgt A.C. Davidson and Sgt W.A. McWilliam. Davidson was killed in the explosion of the bomber and McWilliam was shot and killed after having parachuted out. F/Lt Kenneth Milligan survived to become a POW. In November he was awarded the DFC after being recommended the previous August. The recommendation read:

This officer has completed thirty-eight operational sorties, all of them with the Pathfinder Force. Thirty-five of these sorties have been as Marker and the crew, of which he is a member, have on a great many occasions acted as Master Bomber. Flight Lieutenant Milligan, as Air Bomber, has always set his mind on the task in hand, and with utter disregard to self. His courage, skill and determination has set a fine example to the squadron.

Beaune was also quickly captured and interrogated following which he was sent to Stalag Luft 3 at Belaria. In January 1945, with the Russian advance the Germans moved the POWs to another camp, providing accommodation riddled with lice, fleas and bed bugs and a meal of watery soup once a day and bread made from sawdust. Liberated but held in the camps by the Russians in April 1945 Beaune escaped on 7 May and made his way to an American camp.

Jack Thornton joined the squadron as a pilot after completing a tour of operations with No. 115 Sqn. This was his first operation with the squadron.

Only seven of the squadron went. I was told to keep the chap doing the marking in sight and when we got over the target to get ahead of him and draw fire while he marked the target. So I did that and it was pretty hot. We lost two out of the seven. At that time 7 Sqn had a reputation for not losing any aircraft, so it was not a very good start for me.

Another view of the Phillips crew at the end of their tour of operations. Sgt Tom Jones, far left, looks less than happy to be tour expired in this shot! P. Jones

W/Cdr Cox came to the end of his tenure as CO and was replaced by W/Cdr D.M. Walburn DSO on 9 October. Another daylight raid was made on 12 October, this time to Wanne-Eickel, where the squadron lost Lancaster PB474:MG-L. S/Ldr B.C. Bennett and his crew were taken prisoner, with the exceptions of Sgt D. Parker and Sgt Richardson, who were killed, and Sgt N. Cardwell, who managed to return to the UK. Richardson was another of the squadron's 'old men' at 39. A direct hit on an oil storage tank early in the raid produced dense cloud and smoke which hindered later bombing and the refinery was not seriously damaged.

On 14/15 October the squadron targeted Duisburg and lost Lancaster PB357: MG-S, piloted by F/O C.N.C. Crawford. The attack on this target was designed to show the enemy the overwhelming air superiority held by the Allies. To that end a daylight raid was carried out by 957 bombers of Bomber Command on the 14th followed by 1,251 American bombers escorted by 749 fighters. This was followed up by the night raid by 1,005 aircraft, including PB357, the squadron's last loss of 1944. Nearly 9,000 tons of bombs were dropped on Duisburg in forty-eight hours. Heavy casualties and damage were inflicted.

On the night of 15/16 October, after a lay-off of three weeks, Richard Smith's crew was detailed to attack the naval base at Wilhelmshaven. They were using NE122: MG-V once again. Smith recalls the operation.

Another view of Fred Phillips and his happily tour-expired crew at Oakington in September 1944. Fred Phillips second from left. Tom Jones fourth from left. P. Jones

We took off for this night operation at 1730 hrs and immediately after take-off the main compass system went u/s. This meant that the H2S radar and the air position indicator could not be used. Davies decided that the operation would go ahead as ordered. The crew, in view of their previous two experiences in NE122:V, were not keen to go but could not object to the captain's decision.

The aircraft was navigated blind to the target using the basic compass and old-fashioned deduced reckoning and manual air plot. All was well! Almost precisely on estimated time of arrival we arrived and dropped our bombs and target indicators as ordered and returned to Oakington without any trouble. We never flew NE122:V again.

Jack Thornton flew on this operation carrying a new piece of equipment in his aircraft.

One night we went to Wilhelmshaven and we were carrying a new device. It was one of the most peculiar nights. There was this light cloud with an electrical charge in it and we had St Elmo's fire all around the windscreens and the guns. The new gadget consisted of two lights. I got a red light if I was predicted by flak and a green light if it was fighters [Radar prediction was the method used to offset the aim of Flak guns along the predicted track of the target aircraft]. *The St Elmo's fire was flashing all over and when the flak opened up, combined with the lightning it set both lights going like mad. The sweat was streaming off me. It put the fear of death into me. We did not know what was after us. I never used the gadget again.*

Not all of the squadron's aircraft were shot down or damaged by enemy action; on 23/24 October Lancaster NE122:V, which had been attacked by night fighters on 28/29 July, was again hit. This time the attack came from an unidentified, which damaged the front turret and both starboard engines. The crew were on the outward leg, close to the target area, when the pilot and bomb aimer saw the other Lancaster corkscrew across their nose from port to starboard, only 50 yards away. Suddenly the mid-upper gunner opened fire, putting a bullet through the front turret and two more into the starboard engine nacelles. The pilot of NE122 tried to read the code letters of the offending aircraft, but could not do so before it once again banked away.

A force of 771 aircraft attacked Essen in daylight on 25 October, bombing the target using sky markers as the area was covered in cloud. Frank Leatherdale had a close call on this trip.

On 25 October we were primary visual marker for a daylight raid in Essen. Once again we suffered several hits from flak splinters – one of which came up from below and passed right through my plotting table before going out of the roof. Had I not been standing behind our pilot at that moment I must inevitably have been hit, which would probably have stopped me ever fathering a child!

Two hundred and seventy-seven aircraft went to Walcheren to hit gun positions on the island on the 28th. Most of the bombing appeared to be successful. Frank Leatherdale's crew took part.

We acted as the deputy master bomber on a raid to destroy German coastal guns at Westkapelle on Walcheren Island. These guns commanded the Schelde estuary and were stopping our army from using the port of Antwerp, which was urgently needed to shorten their supply line. Again we were hit by flak, which caused us to shut down our port inner engine.

On 29 October the bombers went to Walcheren again, 358 aircraft attacking eleven different German positions. Visibility was again good and all of the targets were hit. Leatherdale flew on this operation, too.

The following day we returned to attack the same target, but this time we were made the master bomber for the raid. When flying at some 3,000 feet to assess the bombing we were fired upon by German machine-guns and light flak. Joe Hayes, our rear gunner, saw where this fire was coming from and shot back with the four .303 Brownings in his turret and had the satisfaction of seeing the German gunners run from their guns and dive into their shelter.

Frank Leatherdale's crew flew twenty-eight operations with the squadron, covering 17,329 miles and dropping 211,000 pounds of bombs. It is interesting to note that at this stage of the war the Allies had such overwhelming air superiority that they flew fifty hours, ten minutes on daylight operations and sixty hours, five minutes at night. They also flew forty-six hours, ten minutes on daylight training flights and a further two hours on night training. Frank Leatherdale, who retired from the RAF as a squadron leader with the DFC, comments:

AVM. Bennett, the AOC of 8 Group, insisted all PFF crews did. While we complained about it at the time, Bennett was quite right. Only by these means could we maintain our professional skills and it doubtless helped us to stay alive.

On the night of 31 October the crew of ND849:M was homeward bound from Cologne at 16,000 feet when the W/Op reported a Fishpond indication of an aircraft approaching from astern at a range of 2 miles. The rear gunner, F/Sgt Drury, spotted it and identified as an Fw189, as it closed to 1–½ miles astern and below. The mid-upper gunner, F/Sgt Lean, then picked it up at 1,000 yards and at 800 yards Drury ordered a corkscrew port, opening fire shortly afterward. Lean opened up at 500 yards, and the aircraft closed to 300 yards before breaking away without opening fire. This was a most unusual aircraft to see in the bomber stream at night as its main role was reconnaissance for ground troops. It is possible it was being used to report on the height and direction of the bomber stream, as the *Luftwaffe* used a number of different types for this purpose.

Whilst the gunners of ND849 were trying to shoot down the Fw189 the pilot of Lancaster PB490:B was watching tracer coming in at him from the port bow. At the time the aircraft was on 'George' the automatic pilot. Quickly disengaging, he dived to port and though neither of the gunners saw the fighter the mid-upper gunner, F/Sgt Lenaghan, loosed off a long burst in the general direction of the tracer to discourage any further attacks. The fighter was not seen then or later.

Jack Thornton took his crew to Gelsenkirchen in daylight on 6 November. Seven hundred and thirty-eight aircraft attacked the Nordstern synthetic oil plant; 514 bombed it before it became obscured by smoke, and the remainder bombed the town. Jack and his crew had a rough trip.

On my second tour, with PFF, I was hit by flak on nearly every trip. Most of the flak was predicted and I got hit nearly every time I went out. After one flight I had to have three engines changed when I came back. That was a particularly bad effort. It was a daylight raid. They sent us out, north of the Ruhr and then down the length of the Ruhr. It was a clear day. I was supporting, which meant we went in first to draw fire from the blokes carrying the TIs behind. I went in first and there was flak everywhere over Gelsenkirchen. Another pilot told me later he saw us in the lead, weaving all over, with flak all around and others following us. Out of nine aircraft following us seven were shot down [Bomber Command War Diaries record five losses on this raid]. The other pilot was flying the ninth aircraft carrying TIs. We both got away with it, but he was badly damaged too. When we got back we had to have three engines changed. One of them had burst into flames and another had been playing up.

Harold Lazenby joined the RAF in July 1939 and trained as a fitter IIE. In 1942 he volunteered for training as a flight engineer and joined 7 Sqn from Warboys in November 1944. Prior to joining the squadron he had completed thirty-six operations and a tour as an instructor at No. 20 OTU at Lossiemouth.

After arriving at Oakington and being settled in a barrack block I eventually reported to the flight engineer's office. The Flight Engineer Leader, F/Lt Whybray, then informed me that he was putting me in W/Cdr Alexander's crew. The crew were: W/Cdr Alexander DFC, pilot; S/Ldr Dawson DFC DFM, navigator; F/Lt Bentley DFC, bomb aimer; WO Denham, W/Op; F/Sgt Lazenby, flight engineer; F/Lt White DFC, rear gunner; and F/Sgt Dooley, mid-upper gunner.

The W/Op, Denham had been with W/Cdr Alexander for some time. The wing commander was much older than average aircrew. Denham told me that Alexander had been a pilot with Imperial Airways before the war and had over 5,000 hours and that he had a son of thirteen.

I first met W/Cdr Alexander and the crew on 12 November. Our duty was a cross-country exercise but it was not carried out, only flying one hour, twenty five minutes. Our next trip was on 15 November, a close-formation exercise. What purpose there was in the exercise I have no idea. After take-off the squadron formated behind a Mosquito and flew a course which finished up bang over Oakington. W/Cdr Alexander then contracted impetigo on his face and was therefore grounded. The Flight Engineer Leader then made me a spare engineer.

One of the most experienced navigators on the squadron at this time was F/Lt Victor Fowler. He was awarded the DFC on 1 December after being recommended for it in September when he had flown fifty-six operational sorties. His first sortie was a Gardening mission to the Friesian Islands. By the time of the recommendation he was well into his second tour and his latest sortie had been a five-hour trip to Kiel on 15 September. The recommendation read:

This officer has completed 56 operational sorties of which 21 have been in a Marker crew; 35 of these operations have been completed on this squadron. Flight Lieutenant Fowler is a navigator of a crew which has at all times accredited itself with distinction. This is in no small measure due to this officer's dogged determination, skill and devotion to duty. He has always shown a magnificent example to his crew by his complete disregard of danger and by his

7 Sqn group in late 1944. H. Lazenby

cheerfulness and determination. He has gained the complete confidence of his crew. He invariably sets his mind on the task in hand no matter how exacting the conditions, and by his exceptional ability and disregard of self have set a high standard to the squadron.

Another very experienced Squadron member, bomb aimer F/Lt John Corrigan was also awarded the DFC on the same day (he would later receive a Bar to this award whilst serving with the squadron). Between 10 April 1944, when he went on a sortie to Laon, until 5 July 1944, when he completed his fortieth sortie with a trip to Wizernes he had shown outstanding skill and determination. The recommendation for the award read:

This officer has completed 40 operational sorties, all of them with this squadron and sixteen as Air Bomber in a Marker crew. Under a calm and quiet manner, Flight Lieutenant Corrigan has a fine offensive spirit in action which inspires the utmost confidence in his crew. This officer has proved himself to be an outstanding member of a very fine crew and his splendid record and dogged determination has set a high example to the squadron.

The squadron crews went to Osnabruck on the night of 5/6 December in the first raid on this town since August 1942. It was only a partial success and only slight damage was caused. F/Lt Protheroe had to bring his damaged Lancaster back for a landing at the emergency airfield at Woodbridge.

By the end of 1944 the end of the war seemed to be in sight and the squadron enjoyed a fairly relaxed Christmas period. Jack Thornton recalls how difficult daylight raids into Germany at the end of 1944 could be.

By the end of 1944 we were doing daylights into Germany. There was not a lot of fighter opposition by then and we were getting fighter cover. One time my navigator told me we were ten minutes early, but in fact we were ten minutes late. The Main Force had overtaken us. When we discovered the mistake I put the nose down to make up the time. Instead of bombing from 20,000 feet we bombed from 10,000 feet and we brought four incendiary bombs home, from an aircraft above, in our petrol tanks. I could see them above me dropping 'cookies' and incendiaries. The 'cookies' were bloody big barrels and I could see them coming and avoid them, but the incendiaries were coming down like rain. Lucky it was daylight. The chap who did it had a lovely aiming point photo with me smack in the middle of it!

Harold Lazenby holds a great many memories of Oakington during the winter of 1944/45 and the run-up to the end of the war. After such a long period of time the dates, names and places of some of them have become a little faded in the memory but his recollection gives a vivid picture of what it was like to live and work on an operational bomber station at this stage of the war.

Once, when we returned from an exercise, Oakington was fog bound. W/Cdr Alexander made a perfect landing using the blind approach beam. It was the one and only time I landed in an aircraft that used the beam.

Towards the end of the war we went to Whittlesea bombing range for bombing practice. Each time the pilot called the range for permission to commence bombing all we received in reply was an orchestra playing 'In A Monastery Garden', so the Wingco said 'Sod it' and we went back to base.

When preparing to land W/Cdr Alexander would sometimes call up the rear gunner, F/Lt Richard White, and he would say, 'two little bumps, Dickie.'

The barrack blocks were centrally heated. The barrack rooms had polished wood floors. The NCO barrack rooms were very untidy. This was nothing unusual for an operational station. Aircrew were left without interference, doing their job was all that mattered.

The grass area at the rear of our barrack block had on it a considerable number of abandoned cars. It was like a breaker's yard, some being minus wheels and other parts. During the war a car could be acquired for a few pounds. The abandoned cars had either belonged to aircrew that had gone missing or had finished their operations and been posted. From October 1941 the basic petrol ration was abolished except for essential key war workers. Service personnel were excluded from the basic petrol ration. Any serviceman running his own car or motorcycle was probably using fiddled petrol or fiddled petrol coupons. I should also think that although many young men were flying aeroplanes they had never driven a car and probably had no driving licence.

Towards the end of the war, with victory in sight, aircrew were allocated petrol and some cars and motorcycles began to appear. If an airman was going on leave he would fill in a form stating his leave address, the make and horsepower of his car or motorcycle and its registration number. He would then be issued with petrol coupons to cover the journey to his leave address and back, the consumption of his vehicle having been calculated.

Lord Nuffield had a scheme whereby operational and ex-operational aircrew, by applying on a form when they went on leave, received for every day of their leave, five shillings. Under the scheme there were also hotels in various parts of the country where the airman could spend his leave if he so wished.

When I came to Oakington one of the ground staff fitters was Cpl Jack Harrison. We had both joined up in the summer of 1939 and had done our basic training at Padgate. Jack Harrison had done very, very well indeed to become a corporal tradesman. It could be long and arduous with trade tests where 80 per cent had to be achieved.

The sergeants' mess was comfortable with leather armchairs in the anteroom. There was also a snooker room and of course a bar. The food and dining facilities were good. There were washing and bathing facilities. There were also rooms above the mess, each room having two to four airmen. I moved into a room in the mess in the spring of 1945. I shared it with Gerry Dooley, our mid-upper gunner and another gunner, F/Sgt Fraser. Gerry Dooley came from Huyton Quarry, where his father, an ex-policeman kept a public house.

On nights or afternoons off it was usually into Cambridge. There was a bus in the evening and service transport was sometimes laid on. There was sometimes service transport to return or sometimes you might share a taxi, which seemed to run with no restrictions. You could also hitch-hike, depending on your luck. The pubs that were popular in Cambridge were the Criterian – this was a bit of a dive but always busy – the Barron of Beef, the Carpenter's Arms, the Blackamoor and the Eagle. The Eagle was kept by a tough-looking publican who looked like an ex-pugilist. On the ceiling in what appeared to be black paint were countless British and American squadron numbers and the names of airmen. There was also the Rose, which seemed a small, quiet pub, and the Prince of Wales, which was underground, more like a cellar. There were many cafés and teashops.

For dancing there was the Rex dance hall. There was a Rex cinema and the dance hall was part of it. There were also dances at the town or civic hall and the Dorothy Café.

One afternoon in the spring of 1945 I went into Cambridge on my own. In the late afternoon I went into a café for a meal. I was then joined by a young American airman (Cambridge was seething with Americans). The young airman was quietly spoken and well mannered. I think he must have concluded that I was a flight engineer and he then informed me that he was also a flight engineer, and after chatting for a while he then asked me how many operations I had done. I had done forty-five, which was nothing unusual at that stage of the war on a Pathfinder squadron. When I told the American I had done 45 he was absolutely dumbfounded and absolutely refused to believe me, no matter how I tried to explain. When we parted he still didn't believe it. All he kept saying was, 'How many, really?'

As the end of the war approached, on a Saturday night, if there was nothing on, we occasionally went to Histon, most of us on bicycles. We would go into the local pub, the Boot, and then on to a dance in the village.

213

The Ritual of the Greatcoat – when I was promoted warrant officer in December 1944 – I went to the stores for a warrant officer's uniform and greatcoat. As I had expected they did not have any. I then decided that I would get a new airman's greatcoat. It was said, though it may not have been official, that a greatcoat was supposed to last five years. My greatcoat was almost five and a half years old and was threadbare, so I considered I should have a new one. In order to get a new greatcoat a form had to be signed by an officer condemning the old one. I went into an office where I was confronted by a squadron leader. I saluted and explained what I wanted. That officer, whom I only ever saw the once, did a long and minute examination of that coat. I would never have believed it if someone else had told me about it. I was surprised he did not produce a magnifying glass! It was a long drawn-out, intensive examination. He finally held the coat up in front of a window and the light came through, which I think finally convinced him that it was just about worn out. Then, with some hesitation, he signed the form (BIG DEAL).

Bernard Elsworthy was a member of Ken Rawson's crew and together they completed forty-eight operations. He was trained as a WOp/AG at Yatesbury and Barrow and held his skipper in high regard.

One reason that Ken Rawson and crew survived forty-eight operations is that our Aussie pilot did not drink or smoke and was in excellent physical condition. Plus the fact that we were a well-disciplined crew who did not waste words when flying (no small talk!).

The most memorable op was to Essen on Christmas Eve 1944. We expected to return to base for the mess party and we had saved many goodies for this occasion.

With some other crews we were stranded at Woodbridge emergency airfield. They had some liquor and beer brought in and proceeded to finish it off to the point of intoxication. A brawl ensued – the sober ones retreated to the cold, damp Nissen huts for peace and rest and to await the bus that was to come and take us back to Oakington on Christmas Day, where the party commenced!

After the Christmas fiasco bombing trips seemed just routine, the highlight being kissing the ground when we landed after an op and having a good slug of rum to calm us down. Plus the 'flying meal' of eggs and bacon and the mushrooms we picked off the airfield on landing.

Jack Thornton took his crew out on the same operation.

We took off in thick fog and it was horrifying. When we briefed for it the visibility was about 10 yards. We went out to the aircraft expecting it to be scrubbed, but no. We taxied out to the end of the runway and I could not see across the runway. I took off keeping my eye on the edge of the runway. When we got to the intersection of the runways the edge disappeared then suddenly appeared again. We broke cloud at about 300 feet. We were the only PFF squadron to take-off. We didn't half get a warm reception over the target. We were damaged and landed back at Woodbridge. I remember landing at Woodbridge once, when the country was fogged out and about 500 aircraft landed there. We were landing four and five abreast. It was an amazing sight.

Drinking and brawling were only a couple of the ways that the heavily stressed aircrew relieved the pressure and it was common to find all kinds of bizarre behaviour and antics in the messes. Bernard Elsworthy remembers these days.

Aircrew on 7 Sqn were known for their exuberant antics, especially at mess parties, where someone would ride a motorcycle into the mess and around the corridors. I've seen a car being taken to pieces as a joke, wheels off and moveable parts piled high. Then there were the footprints across the ceiling in the mess, which also appeared in some Cambridge pubs. A really dangerous prank was the shooting, with a .38 revolver, of glasses off the antlers of the animal head wall trophies. These were some of the 'stress relieving' antics we indulged in.

There were other moments of light relief to be had during the winter of 1944/45, as Harold Lazenby recalls.

Richard 'Chalky' White was the rear gunner in W/Cdr Alexander's crew. I was the engineer. Being a warrant officer I did not see much of 'Chalky', but one thing that happened to him I remember quite well.
During the winter of 1944/45, aircrew could take a course of ultra-violet ray treatment. As far as I can recollect, the treatment room, with the ray lamp in the centre, was in station sick quarters, watched over by a medical orderly. Before entering the treatment room, you stripped to the waist and put on a pair of dark goggles. You then sat on this very low seat facing the lamp. I believe you started off with a two-minute exposure, which was increased by two minutes on each

Bernard Elsworthy's crew. L to R: Sid Robison, Jack Willie, Alex Stuart, Bernard Elsworthy, Ken Rawson, Andy Maitland, Alan Camlin and Sam Bowman. B. Elsworthy

subsequent session, up to a maximum of twelve minutes – which ended the course. The task of the orderly was to tell you when your exposure time was up and to record it.

One morning, after a session and just as I was leaving, 'Chalky' arrived for treatment. When I next saw 'Chalky', although in the middle of English winter, he looked as if he had fallen asleep in a deck chair, unprotected, on Brighton beach in the middle of June. He had a very, very red nose and face, both of which were peeling. He was quick to explain his appearance; the medical orderly had forgotten to tell him when his treatment time was up. Did old 'Chalky' curse that orderly!

On 30/31 December the Lancasters made the trip to Cologne/Kalk and bombed the Kalk-Nord rail yards and two passenger stations nearby. Two ammunition trains were blown up. This was Harold Lazenby's first operation, flying with F/O Thornton DFC. They took off at 1824 hrs as duty supporters. The presence of cloud caused difficulties for the Pathfinders and Lazenby recorded: 'It seemed a very quiet operation with slight heavy flak in the distance.'

Despite the difficulties of winter weather the squadron had managed 146 sorties during the month, and all for only one crew member wounded. The last day of the year saw W/Cdr Walburn replaced by W/Cdr D.A. Cracknell DSO DFC. Thus ended 1944.

CHAPTER SIX
JANUARY–SEPTEMBER 1945

January 1945 saw no let-up in the squadron's efforts, and Hanover was attacked on the 5th/6th, PB526 flown by F/O Friedrich failing to return. This was the first large-scale raid on this target since October 1943, with 664 aircraft. The bombs fell all over the city. The squadron was by now one of the Pathfinder Force's most experienced units, but even they could not compete with the poor weather of winter 1945 and many an operation was cancelled. When operations resumed many crews would return to report very little opposition. The Germans were being overwhelmed both by night and by day, but, the night fighters and flak were still deadly and the crews needed to maintain constant vigilance.

Bernard Elsworthy's crew bombed Munich on 7 January. It was their thirtieth operation.

A certain complacency came over many aircrews when they reached thirty ops and this was true with our crew when Munich was our thirtieth on 7 January 1945, after having bombed Nuremberg on the 2nd, on the 5th Hanover and Hanau on the 6th. It was followed by Dulmen on 14 January, a few days before my twenty-second birthday. This was probably the most active period and prepared us for the remaining sixteen operations and the end of the war – although we did not realize it at the time!

Some of the longer trips may not be memorable for any specific incident but have since made me wonder how we kept awake and alert considering the hours we took to have our flying meal, gather up our gear, go to the briefing room to check details of the raid we were on, assemble for the bus and then drive out to our dispersal to do the final check on our aircraft and equipment, plus the seven hours, ten minutes for Nuremberg, the seven hours for Munich, the seven hours, twenty-five minutes for Chemnitz on 14 February and again to Chemnitz on 6 March, taking eight hours, forty-five minutes because we flew over Berlin en route. Dessau followed the very next day and took eight hours, forty-five minutes in the air. When did we sleep or relax? Anyway we did survive these night trips!

Harold Lazenby went to Saarbrucken with F/Lt Thompson DFC on the night of 13/14 January along with 273 other aircraft. Bomber Command assessed the raid on the railway yards as extremely accurate and effective. Thompson's crew was duty visual centerer and Harold Lazenby recalls this trip. 'We were diverted to Tangmere due to low cloud at Oakington and the following day we flew back to Oakington. I should think half the force landed at Tangmere. We started our engines on the aircraft accumulators.'

Lazenby went to Zeitz with yet another pilot, F/Lt Ellis DFC, on 16/17 January as part of a force of 328 Lancasters from 1, 6 and 8 Groups. Ellis's crew were the duty blind markers for the raid. The target was the Braunkohle-Benzin synthetic oil plant. Much damage was caused to the northern half of the plant. Ten Lancasters were lost.

JANUARY 1945   7 SQDN.

Time carried forward :— 271·05 | 156·55

Date	Hour	Aircraft Type and No.	Pilot	Duty	Remarks (including results of bombing, gunnery, exercises, etc.)		Flying Times	
							Day	Night
		LANCASTER						
2·1·45	16·0	·7·	F/Lt MAWSON	WOP	OPS · NÜRNBURG · P.M.	M·22 27		7·10
5·1·45	705	·M·	F/Lt RAWSON	WOP	OPS · HANOVER · P.M	N·23 28		5·00
6·1·45	1520	·M·	F/Lt RAWSON	WOP	OPS · HANAU · N.C.	N·24 29		5·30
7·1·45	80·0	·L·	F/Lt RAWSON	WOP	OPS · MUNICH · N.C.	N·25 30		7·00
14·1·45	1730	·O·	F/Lt RAWSON	WOP	OPS · DULMEN · N.C.	N·26 31		5·15
17·1·45	1500	·L·	F/Lt RAWSON	WOP	BOMB DISPOSAL · F/A · CRAMER ·		2·15	
18·1·45	1030·	·N·	F/Lt RAWSON	WOP	ROUTE · 9 ·		1·50	

WEMBR O.C. 'B' FLT

SUMMARY FOR JANUARY. 45.
DATE · 10·2·45.
SIGNATURE · B/Sworthy

4·05 | 29·55

FROM MY LOG BOOK.

Bernard Elsworthy

TOTAL TIME ...275·10 | 186·50

Bernard Elsworthy's log-book entry for January 1945. B. Elsworthy

Operations were not the only trips, which had potential for danger, as Harold Lazenby recounts.

On 20 January 1945 we took off on a cross-country and fighter affiliation sortie. The pilot was F/Lt Tucker AFC. After take-off we went into thick cloud. The pilot did a fast climb up to 25,000 feet to climb out of it. We were diverted to Woodbridge but as we prepared to land the W/Op received a signal to return to Oakington. It was snowing and although snow collected on the wings it did not seem to affect the performance of the aircraft. The snowstorm was beginning to abate by the time we reached Oakington and we landed with no trouble. Two American B-17s landed just after us. The crews stayed overnight.

The bombers went to two targets on the night of 22/23 January: Duisburg and Gelsenkirchen. Jack Thornton took his Lancaster, along with 107 Halifaxes, twenty-eight other Lancasters and sixteen Mosquitoes to the latter. It was an area bombing raid and moderate damage was caused by the small force. No aircraft were lost. Thornton recalls the mission.

I was coned approaching the target and I was so close it was not worth weaving, as I would have had to go round again. I stayed in the cone and finished bombing. Of course, the fighters were waiting for us as we came out and as soon as I was clear one of them dived on me, but I evaded him. I put my nose down and there was another aircraft ahead of me. I was going so fast that when I turned to avoid him it turned out to be a Ju88. He did not catch me.

Daylight raids were better. They were not anything like as fearsome as night raids. You could see everyone around you. The only snag was that at night you were spread out more. Going over the target in daylight, everyone congregated together and nobody wanted to be on the outside, because of the fighters coming in. When you got over the target there were aircraft above you with their bomb doors open and aircraft on either side. That was the only thing I did not like about daylights. On PFF it was not so bad as you went in smaller groups.

On 28/29 January Bomber Command flew its largest mission to the city of Stuttgart. This was the last mission to this target; it had previously been attacked fifty-two times. This raid was split into two forces, three hours apart, the first attack by 226 aircraft, the remainder in the second force. Due to cloud cover the bombing of both forces was scattered.

Jack Thornton took his crew to the target on the twenty-second of twenty-six Pathfinder operations.

My twenty-second trip, to Stuttgart, was a bit dicey. I set out together with another bloke. We took off in daylight, though it was to be a night op. He and I were ahead of everyone else. We approached the target and, just as we made our bomb run, he was slightly above and ahead of me. Suddenly the flak opened up and he got a direct hit. He dove straight down on top of me. I just managed to swing clear of him and he missed us by inches. It was a very near thing.

On the night of 1/2 February F/Lt Steed DFC took his crew, including Harold Lazenby, to Ludwigshaven on a five hour, thirty minute sortie. They were duty blind markers for 382 Lancasters and 14 Mosquitoes. Bombs fell in many parts of the town and caused much damage. Lazenby recalls the operation. 'The thing I most remember about this operation is looking out at the other aircraft all around us as we headed out on our way. Much damage was caused and one of the Rhine bridges was hit and temporarily closed.'

Harold Lazenby went to Wanne-Eickel the next night with a pilot on his first Lancaster operation.

We took off in the dark. Someone had previously remarked for my benefit that the squadron leader [S/Ldr Allcock DFC] had done a tour on Whitleys at the early part of the war but that he had never taken a Lancaster off with a bomb load and as he insisted on taking the undercarriage up himself I was a little bit worried. But all went well with no trouble. However, according to the reports it was estimated that three-quarters of the bombs fell in open ground around a local coal mine. The attack was intended for the oil refinery but the area was cloud-covered. My own crew were with S/Ldr Allcock on this operation.

Another award came to a squadron member on 5 February when F/O Howard Gray, a Canadian, was awarded the DFC. Over the period of a year, between November 1943 and November 1944 he had flown forty-four sorties. He commenced his second tour of operations in the Pathfinder Force on 5 September 1944. The recommendation for the award had been submitted in November 1944 and read:

This officer is now on his second tour of operations, having completed in all forty-four sorties. Of these, sixteen have been completed in the Pathfinder Force, as a member of a Marker crew.

Flying Officer Sharp has always shown an utter fearlessness in the face of danger, his coolness, confidence and complete disregard for personal safety has gained the confidence of the crew of which he is a member, and his strong sense of duty is an example to the whole squadron.

On the night of 7/8 February 464 bombers struck the town of Goch on the Dutch/German border. F/O Wadham DFC was duty blind illuminator. Harold Lazenby went with him.

The attack was a prologue to the Canadians' advance into territory between the Meuse and the Rhine. Cloud base was at 5,000 feet over the target and as we approached the master bomber ordered crews to come below cloud. The pilot, F/O Wadham, then ordered me to drop the bombs. I had little time but I went down into the bomb aimer's compartment, quickly prepared, settled myself and called for bomb door open. We were descending fairly rapidly through cloud when ahead and through the cloud I could see green markers. So directing the pilot I released the bombs.

I had received some bombing instruction and practice at Warboys, but it was the one and only time that I bombed on operations. Some time later F/O Wadham and his crew went missing.

On the night of 13/14 February Bomber Command launched the infamous raid on Dresden. Some 805 bombers were dispatched in two separate raids, the second one led by 7 Sqn as the Pathfinders. In clear weather 592 Lancasters dropped more than 1,800 tons of bombs onto the target. Casualties are thought to have exceeded 50,000.

7 Sqn Gunnery Section at Oakington in 1945.

Lancaster PA978 was lost during the raid on Worms on 21/22 February. The captain, F/Lt Liddell, survived to return to the UK. Bomber Command mounted three large raids that night. Three hundred and seventy-three aircraft raiding Duisburg, 349 hitting Worms and a further 177 attacking the Mittelland Canal. No. 7 Sqn went to Worms on the only attack on this town. Thirty-nine per cent of the built-up area was destroyed by the bombers and the only firm devoted to war industry, making tank sprocket wheels, was destroyed.

Just after lunch on 23 February eleven crews were briefed at Oakington for that night's raid on Pforzheim. They were to be the markers and backers-up for a force of 367 Lancasters and thirteen Mosquitoes from 1, 6 and 8 Groups and a single Film Unit Lancaster. Final briefing was at 1445 hrs and the crews were driven to the flights at 1530. Soon they were off on the only area bombing attack of the war on this target. The bombing was carried out from only 8,000 feet and was highly accurate. The German authorities reported that over 17,000 people died in the raid, the third heaviest of the war after Hamburg and Dresden. The Lancasters returned to Oakington without loss. The following day five crews were briefed for a daylight raid on Kamen. W/Cdr Cracknell in PB489:MG-F was the master bomber, with W/Cdr Davies in ME360:MG-J as his deputy; the others were flying as visual centerers. Three hundred and forty aircraft took part in the raid. The aiming point was the synthetic oil plant at Bergkamen, just north of Kamen, and due to heavy cloud the force bombed on Oboe and H2S. In the report by the German authorities the oil plant is not mentioned but the loss of most of the town's churches and its hospital is. It was also reported that all of the public utilities failed and the townspeople had to 'go to bed when the chickens went, like our forefathers.'

The squadron took part in another daylight raid on 27 February. This time the target was Mainz and was attacked by 458 aircraft. Fifteen Lancasters left Oakington to find the target cloud-covered and the force dropped its bombs on sky markers. Severe destruction was caused to the central and eastern districts of the city in this, the last, heavy raid on Mainz.

On 1 March the squadron sent six Lancasters in support of the markers in a daylight raid on Mannheim. A total of 478 aircraft, from three groups, took part for the loss of three Lancasters. Encountering complete cloud cover, the target was marked with sky markers. The cloud hampered the attack and many of the bombs fell on nearby Ludwigshafen and surrounding villages. The squadron suffered no losses.

W/Cdr Alexander eventually returned fit to fly in March and Harold Lazenby carried out his first operation with him on 2 March, raiding Cologne. They were a duty visual centerer crew for this sortie, Lazenby's first daylight operation.

It was a beautiful sparkling morning. The British bombers were sent to attack German troops and armour which were concentrated in Cologne to oppose the American 1st and 3rd Armies, who were camped on the banks of the Rhine. Eight hundred and fifty-eight British bombers were dispatched. As we approached the target the cathedral stood out boldly and appeared undamaged. Another thing I remember was a Lancaster ahead of us blowing up in a huge black cloud.

This raid was one of two carried out on the city that day by Bomber Command. Among the 858 aircraft were six from the squadron acting as Pathfinders. Severe damage was caused. This was the last raid on Cologne by the RAF and four days later the Americans captured the city.

The Siegmar tank engine factory in Chemnitz was amongst the targets hit by a force of 760 aircraft on the night of 5/6 March. The squadron sent sixteen Lancasters as supporters and centerers in the marking force. The engine factory was destroyed, and much damage was caused to the centre and south of the city. There were no losses from the squadron, but nine 6 Group aircraft were lost in crashes after taking off in icing conditions and a further twenty-two were lost on the operation.

The town of Dessau was struck by a force of 526 Lancasters and five Mosquitoes on the night of 7/8 March. The squadron dispatched eleven bombers to this target for no loss. This was a two-target night for the squadron; a further six crews went to Heide to attack the Deutsche Erdoel refinery there, again with no loss. Twenty-three bombers were lost from both raids.

The following night it was the turn of much-bombed Hamburg again. The main target was the shipyards, which were building Type XXI U-boats. Sixteen crews from the squadron marked the target for a force totalling 312 aircraft but cloud cover caused scattered bombing and it was believed that little damage was done to the shipyards. The force did manage to sink the cruise liner *Robert Ley* during the attack.

Twelve crews led by W/Cdr Cracknell as master bomber went to Essen to mark the target for a force of 1,079 bombers in a daylight raid on 11 March. The target was completely covered in cloud and the squadron crews marked by Oboe-directed sky markers. The raid struck Essen a devastating blow and the American troops entered the city soon after. This was the last RAF raid on much-bombed Essen. Lancaster MG-O was flown by F/Lt Rawson as deputy master bomber and he returned with his rear gunner, Alan Camlin, injured.

Daylight raids were very much the order of the day during this period and the next morning the squadron navigators were briefed for a raid on Dortmund. This was followed shortly after by the wireless operator briefing and then the main brief for the remainder of the crews. By midday the buses were picking up the crews from the messes and transporting them out to the flights. Eleven crews lifted off from Oakington in a force of 1,108 aircraft and set off for the target. This was a record number of aircraft for a single raid and they dropped a record number of bombs – 4,851 tons – onto the cloud-covered city. Only two aircraft were lost and all of the squadron returned safely.

A daylight raid was mounted to Wuppertal/Barmen on 13 March by 354 bombers. Harold Lazenby was now permanently crewed with W/Cdr Alexander and on this sortie they were duty primary visual marker. Harold Lazenby recalls the difficulties encountered on this raid. 'The secondary target was bombed due to the bomb aimer's Perspex window icing up on the initial bombing run.' Thirteen crews took part in the raid on the cloud-covered target and most of the bombs fell to the east of the intended aiming point falling in the Barmen and Schwelm districts, causing much damage.

On the night of 14/15 March eleven crews went to Homberg in a force of 161 Lancasters, Halifaxes and Mosquitoes with the aim of blocking the transport routes for German troops making for the front lines. The attack was successful and all returned safely.

Canadian bomb aimer WO Jack Ross was awarded the DFC on 15 March 1945, having been recommended for the award in December 1944. He flew his first

Date	Hour	Aircraft Type and No.	Pilot	Duty	Remarks (including results of bombing, gunnery, exercises, etc.)	Flying Times Day	Night
					MARCH. 1945		
					7 SQDN. 2ND TOUR		
					Time carried forward :— 303·00 204·15		
		LANCASTER					
3·3·45		M	F/Lt Rawson	WOp	F/A BOMING.	3·10	
4·3·45		M	F/Lt Rawson	WOp	LOCAL FLYING	1·0	
5·3·45		L	F/Lt Rawson	WOp	ROUTE 14 F/A	3·10	
6·3·45		F	F/Lt Rawson	WOp	OPS- CHEMNITZ· BLIND-ILL 4·31 ×		8·45
7·3·45		X	F/Lt Rawson	WOp	OPS- DESSAU · VC M·33 37		8·45
8·3·45		M	F/Lt Rawson	WOp	OPS · HAMBURG · P.V.M. M·33 38		6·15
10·3·45		O	F/Lt Rawson	WOp	BOMING · ·	1·50	
11·3·45		O	F/Lt Rawson	WOp	OPS- ESSEN · DnB & M·34 39 R/G INJURED- ALLAN CAMLIN	5·00	
13·3·45		P	F/Lt Rawson ·	WOp	AIR · TEST	·40	
14·3·45		M	F/Lt Rawson	WOp	BOMBING · ·	1·15	
					16· 05 23· 45		
					TOTAL TIME ... 319· 05 228· 00		

Bernard Elsworthy's log-book for March 1945, showing the daylight raid on Essen, during which rear gunner Alan Camlin was wounded. B. Elsworthy

operation to Courtrai on 10 May 1944 and forty-six sorties later ended his tour with a raid on Essen on 12 December 1944. His recommendation read:

> This non-commissioned officer is on his second operational tour, having so far completed 17 of his 46 successful sorties on this squadron; he has on three occasions operated as a member of a Marker Crew. Of a quiet disposition, Warrant Officer Ross has nevertheless at all times shown a dogged determination to carry out his duties, and his high standard of efficiency as an air bomber helped materially in the success with which the crew of which he is a member have always operated. Always willing and cheerful, he has a complete disregard of personal safety and this has inspired the utmost confidence of his captain and the remainder of the crew.

Nos 4, 6 and 8 Groups sent 267 aircraft to Hagen on the night of 15/16 March for the loss of six Lancasters and four Halifaxes. The bombs were dropped in clear visibility, falling on the centre and eastern districts, causing severe damage. No. 7 Sqn Lancaster PB677:N, piloted by F/Lt Thompson, was on the way back to base, cruising at 12,000 feet, when the bomb aimer sighted a Lancaster on the port bow, about 800 yards away. Thompson altered course to port and the other Lancaster passed from port to starboard and in doing so opened fire. Thompson immediately dived away to port and lost it, but the Lancaster had suffered some damage though from the accurate fire of the offending aircraft gunner. The crew of PB677 were very annoyed by this attack as the visibility on the raid was excellent and they considered that a gunner could not have made an identification mistake in those conditions.

Hanau was struck by an area bombing raid on the night of 18/19 March by a force of 277 Lancaster's and eight Mosquitoes. The squadron provided sixteen crews as markers and supporters. The *Altstadt* was completely destroyed and over 2,00 people were killed for the loss of one Lancaster from the force.

Seventeen crews from the squadron took part in a daylight attack on Reckling-hausen on 20 March, led by W/Cdr Davies as master bomber and F/Lt Rawson as deputy master bomber. One hundred and fifty-three aircraft attempted to bomb the railway yards but the Pathfinder marking was spoiled by cloud and strong winds. Consequently the bombing was scattered. The squadron lost PB667:Q, captained by F/O Bacon, which crashed into the Schelde estuary on the return trip. All of the crew were killed. W/Cdr Alexander's crew took part. 'Pathfinder marking and the bombing was well scattered. Returned on three engines. Port outer shut down due to high temperatures caused by a coolant cock coming open.'

W/Cdr Alexander's crew followed this up with another daylight raid the next day acting as primary visual markers in Lancaster ME356:P. This time they went to Rheine in the company of 177 other bombers to attack the railway yards and surrounding town. Harold Lazenby recalls that the bomb aimer for this trip was F/Lt Taylor DFC DFM. 'Our task was to mark the marshalling yards at this important rail and road centre some 60 miles behind the German lines. It was a bright and sunny day. F/Lt Taylor was a very experienced bomb aimer and the marking was very accurate. W/Cdr Cracknell directed the bombing and the yards were left in complete chaos.'

A daylight attack was made on Hildesheim on 22 March. Twelve crews were given an early call at 0500 hrs and by 0600 hrs the navigators were being briefed on the route to the target. The crews were at the flights by 0800 hrs and took off shortly afterwards. Two hundred and thirty-five bombers dropped their loads onto the railway yards and surrounding built-up areas in the only major Bomber Command raid on this town during the war. Seventy per cent of the town was destroyed for the loss of four Lancasters.

A small-scale (by 1945 standards) raid was made on Hanover by 275 bombers from 1, 6 and 8 Groups on 25 March. Eight crews led by W/Cdr Davies in ME360:J, as master bomber, and F/Lt Butters in PB584:M as his deputy marked the target. Only one Lancaster was lost from the attacking force.

The next two raids planned were cancelled – the bombers were running out of targets as the ground troops advanced into Germany – and then on 31 March 469 aircraft went to Hamburg in a daylight raid to attack the Blohm & Voss shipyards. No. 7 Sqn provided thirteen crews for the marking force and a wide area of Hamburg and Harburg was damaged by the bombers, who dropped their deadly loads through cloud. W/Cdr Alexander, flying PB589:O, was duty visual centerer and Harold Lazenby saw his first jet fighter on this sortie.

After bombing, when leaving the target area, Me262 fighters appeared. They were the first jet aircraft I had ever seen. If my recollections are correct, we had a fighter escort, although I did not see it. When the Me262s appeared our pilot ordered the W/Op to stand by the Very pistol. A Lancaster about ½ mile or so ahead of us was attacked from the rear, twice, by the same Me262. I could see

S/Ldr Des Butters DFC* and crew. D. Cheetham

the exchange of fire but the Lancaster continued on its way as though undamaged. The German fighter appeared to fly a wide circle in order to make its attack and although it came fairly close to us on our port side we were ignored. As I remember, it was a rough-looking aircraft with no paint nor markings. As far as I can remember all 7 Sqn aircraft returned safely. However eleven aircraft, three of them Pathfinders were shot down.

One of the 7 Sqn Lancasters attacked by Me262s that day was PB489:F, flown by F/O Goody. The rear gunner, WO Black, sighted one of the jets at a range of 1,200 yards, four minutes after they had left the target. The jet approached from dead astern, slightly below and then slid out onto the starboard beam. At this point, F/Sgt Silver, the mid-upper gunner, ordered a corkscrew to starboard and opened fire. He continued to fire until the Me262 broke away at 800 yards. The jet pilot was not discouraged, however, and attempted to attack another Lancaster. PB489's W/Op, WO Hewitt, attempted to attract the attention of three escorting Mustangs by firing three red and one green Very cartridge and, luckily, they swept around the Lancaster to chase the jet off.

On 3 April the squadron was involved in an unfortunate attack on Nordhausen. Twelve crews set out in a force of 255 bombers to attack this target, which was thought to be a military barracks. Unfortunately the barracks was crammed with forced labourers from occupied countries and with concentration camp prisoners working on construction of V-weapons in a complex of underground tunnels. The bombing was accurate and many of the prisoners and forced labourers were killed.

The bombers were sent to Harburg on the night of 4/5 April. The target, the Rhenania oil plant, was easily identified and severe damage was caused. Lancaster Mk I NG229:S, captained by F/Lt Wadham, did not return, one of only three aircraft lost.

225

Oakington in March 1945.

WO Edward Coyne who had been awarded the DFC only the previous day was killed on this sortie. His citation for the award read: 'This warrant officer has completed, as air gunner, numerous operations against the enemy in the course of which he has invariably displayed the utmost fortitude, courage and devotion to duty.'

After a few days' break the squadron went to Hamburg on the night of 8/9 April. Eleven crews took part in a raid on the shipyards, bombing through partial cloud cover. The cloud caused the bombing to be scattered and six bombers were lost in this, the last, Bomber Command raid on the city. The following night sixteen crews went to Kiel to mark two aiming points in the harbour area. This was a highly successful raid, resulting in the capsize of the pocket battleship *Admiral Scheer* and damage to the *Admiral Hipper* and the *Emden*. The surrounding area was also severely hit. Only three Lancasters were lost in the raid, none from the squadron.

On 10 April the squadron went to Leipzig in daylight. Four Lancasters were sent to mark the target, which was the Engelsdorf and Mockau railway yards, and in clear weather the bombing was accurate. Bernard Elsworthy's crew, captained by F/Lt Rawson, acting as deputy master bomber, flew on this operation in Lancaster PB584:M.

We did a long daylight trip to Leipzig which took six hours, forty-five minutes and gave me the opportunity to see the other Lancaster bombers, the flak and we did report seeing a German jet fighter, which I think was an Me262. On night trips we usually only saw our other Lancasters when one was shot down in flames, or when one came too close for comfort, which was often. On one op our rear gunner shouted 'Down port!' just as a Lanc on fire was about to come down on top of our aircraft – a close call!

The squadron took part in a further operation this day. Crews were briefed for an attack on Plauen late in the afternoon and at 1730 hrs were transported to the flights for take-off. Ten crews marked the target for a force of 315 Lancasters and Mosquitoes from 1 and 8 Groups. The bombs fell on and around the railway yards in the north of the town. Over half of the town was destroyed.

The next day master bomber, W/Cdr Allcock led four of the squadron crews to Bayreuth to mark the railway yards for a force of Halifaxes from 4 Group and a few Lancasters and Mosquitoes. They were accurately bombed for no losses. By this time targets were drying up for Bomber Command and many smaller town and cities, which thus far had escaped the bombing came up on the target lists. Many of them were bombed to disrupt communications and reinforcements reaching the shrinking front lines of the beleaguered German armies.

Rear gunner Dennis Griffiths, photographed in his turret on 1 April 1945 just prior to a raid on Heligoland. D.J. Griffiths

1 April 1945. Rear L to R: Dennis Griffiths (rear gunner), Reggie? (mid-upper gunner), Brian Garner (pilot); Front L to R: Tommy Cleghorn (W/Op), Ray Barrow (bomb aimer), Pete Hunt (flight engineer). Hunt is holding a doll of P/O Prune made by the Station Commander's wife and won in a raffle. The doll was lost with maps etc. when the astro hatch blew out on a raid.
D.J. Griffiths

A large number of crews from the squadron, eighteen, took part in the raid on Kiel on the night of 13/14 April. W/Cdr Davies led the attack as master bomber and F/Lt Rawson was his deputy. Bernard Elsworthy was W/Op for Rawson and recalls:

Our first bombing op was on Venlo airfield, a daylight trip of three hours, twenty minutes, which remains in my memory as our first taste of being shot at and surviving. We were in the first wave of supporters for the markers. Our first night op was to Kiel docks; it was our fourth trip and took five hours, thirty minutes. Our forty-seventh op was also to Kiel when we were deputy master bomber helping to direct the raid – six hours on 13 April 1945.

This raid was directed at the port area and, though not very successful, managed to destroy an ammunition depot storing much need supplies for the Germans. Two Lancasters were lost from the force of 377 but all of the squadron crews returned safely.

The following night 500 Lancasters went to Potsdam, which was marked by fifteen crews from the squadron. The target was the barracks and railway yards. Severe damage was caused in the last major raid by Bomber Command on a German city. The squadron returned without loss and the force as a whole lost only one aircraft to a night fighter.

On 18 April 969 aircraft attacked the naval base, airfield and small town on the island of Heligoland. Twelve crews from the squadron marked the target. W/Cdr Alexander was the deputy master bomber, giving Harold Lazenby a grandstand view.

'What I remember about it is the great number of aircraft and, as we approached the island, looking down and seeing two ships leaving the island at high speed as they were both leaving a huge wake. The other thing I recollect was the huge cloud of pink dust over the island and I felt pity for those below.'

Bremen had been much bombed throughout the war and in the closing days it was bombed again, on 22 April, in daylight by a force of 767 aircraft. Sending a force in daylight to this target in earlier years would have been unthinkable, but now, with the Third Reich on its knees and with overwhelming air superiority, the force lost only two Lancasters. Fourteen 7 Sqn crews took part, led by W/Cdr Cracknell as master bomber. Harold Lazenby flew with W/Cdr Alexander in PB623:L.

If I remember rightly W/Cdr Cracknell was the master bomber for this operation. The raid was part of the preparation by the British for attacking Bremen. The bombing was on the south-eastern suburbs of the city where troops would attack two days later. The raid was hampered by cloud, smoke and dust from the bombing and because of the nearness of British troops the master bomber ordered the raid to stop after 195 Lancasters had bombed.

With the war almost over the squadron took part in its last bombing operation on 25 April. This was a daylight raid to knock out the coastal batteries on the Friesian island of Wangerooge, which controlled the approaches to Bremen and Wilhelmshaven. Four hundred and eight-two aircraft took part, ten from the squadron. Although the bombing, carried out in clear weather, was accurate, the gun emplacements, which were heavily protected by concrete, were hardly damaged and were in action again within hours. All of the squadron aircraft returned safely.

Throughout the war the aircrews were often shown great kindness by the local communities surrounding the airfields. Bernard Elsworthy recalls some of those at Oakington.

Patience Smith was one of the young girls who gathered at our dispersal fence at Oakington and gave us lucky charms and mementoes to take on ops. Many of the young girls took us to their homes where their parents shared their meagre rations with us and we sang songs around the old piano. It was the spirit and kindness of the local civilians around Oakington that helped maintain the morale of the young aircrew – they took us to their hearts and homes.

Operations planned for 26 and 27 April and 1 May were all cancelled. The next operations were of an entirely different nature – dropping supplies of food to the starving Dutch population, in Operation Manna between 29 April and 7 May. 'Cook's Tours' were also flown to show the ground staff the fruits of their labours. Seven crews took part in a supply drop on Rotterdam on 3 May and in addition to the normal crew complements twelve of the station staff were flown in the Lancasters. The following day seven more Operation Manna sorties were flown and once again thirteen ground staff went along for the ride. A truce had been arranged with the local German commander to allow these relief flights to take place and, though the crews were still wary of an attack, they were flown without incident or loss.

These were flown alongside Operation Exodus sorties, flying ex-POWs home from Brussels and later other occupied airfields between 26 April and 7 May, by which time the war in Europe had ended. On 7 May the squadron carried out another Manna operation, dropping food supplies on The Hague and Valkenburg airfield.

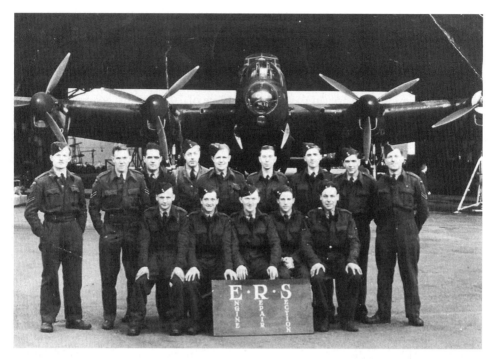

7 Sqn Engine Repair Section in 1945. 7 Sqn

Harold Lazenby took part in a Manna sortie on 1 May. 'The food dropping operation was in the Rotterdam area. Like everyone else on this operation, what I remember most is the thousands of people, some on roofs of buildings, waving anything they could lay their hands on. I have often wondered how many were hit by the sacks of food that were dropped.'

On 8 May 1945, VE Day, he took part in Operation Exodus.

This operation was bringing home POWs from a collection centre in Juvincourt. The POWs, some of whom had been prisoners for more than five years, were exhausted in mind and body and emaciated. They were a pitiful sight, but as excited as schoolboys to be going home. One POW, a Canadian Halifax bomb aimer, had been a prisoner for one year. The tail of his Halifax was knocked off by one of our own bombs. We brought back twenty-four POWs. An army staff sergeant was in the cockpit with me and as we reached the English coast our pilot shouted to him, 'What's that down there?' The staff sergeant looked and in a Cockney accent replied 'Southend Pier'. We landed at Wing. It was the only time we flew without parachutes. That night there was a big bonfire on the station. All the blackout curtains were burnt.

Lazenby did another Exodus sortie on 15 May. 'The main thing I remember about this is doing an overshoot at Wing with the twenty-four POWs on board. I have no idea what their thoughts must have been.'

During May 1945 P/O Eric Taylor, a Canadian air gunner with the squadron, was awarded the DFC. By the time of the award he had flown forty-six operations between 24 May 1944 and 2 February 1945. The recommendation for the award read:

7 Sqn Engine Repair Section on VE Day. 7 Sqn

This Warrant Officer has now done 46 operational sorties against the enemy; eighteen of these have been in the Pathfinder Force, all Marker trips. He has at all times shown an utter disregard for danger, while his cheerfulness, co-operation, unselfishness at all times, and undoubted skill as an Air Gunner have inspired a high standard of morale in his crew. Warrant Officer Taylor has always displayed a magnificent spirit of determination to give his best.

Two days after the war in Europe ended F/Lt John Corrigan, a Canadian bomb aimer serving with the squadron was awarded a Bar to his DFC. When awarded the DFC he had flown thirty-seven sorties and by the time of the recommendation for the Bar he had reached a total of sixty-eight. The text of the recommendation read:

This officer is on his third operational tour, having so far completed 68 sorties, all in the Pathfinder Force. He has on 48 occasions acted with a Marker crew. Flight Lieutenant Corrigan is an exceptionally good Air Bomber. His keenness and coolness in action against the enemy has set a fine standard of morale in the Flight Commander's crew with which he operates. Never at a loss to overcome difficulties, his steadfastness and determination to give his best at all times is highly commendable. He possesses courage of a high degree and cheerfulness under all circumstances. He has proved himself by showing a high degree of fearlessness, skill and initiative to be an outstanding member of a gallant crew.

A further Exodus sortie was flown on 24 May by sixteen crews bringing home POWs, many of who had spent many years in captivity. For the crews this was a very

The ground crew of 'A' Flt celebrate VE Day. Amongst those pictured: Jock Frazer, Paddy Lappin, Jean?, Dave (Aussie)?, Ron Marsh, Peggy (flying control)?, four WAAF and four more ground crew. 7 Sqn

satisfying way of ending the war in Europe, but the war was not over and the prospect of further operations against the Japanese was in the minds of many aircrew. W/Cdr Cracknell was replaced by W/Cdr K.H. Burns DSO DFC as CO on 5 June, as the plans for Bomber Command turned to other theatres.

The squadron's war was not over and they were earmarked for the Tiger Force, which began training for war in the Far East. They moved to Mepal, in Cambridgeshire, on 25 July to join this force and began intensive training. They also began to re-equip with Lancaster Mk I (FE). All was to come to nought, though, when the atom bombs were dropped on Japan and the Tiger Force was stood down. Reductions to peacetime levels soon followed and for 7 Squadron the long war was over.

Among the last wartime awards to the squadron was that of the DFC to F/O Robert Rhodes on 8 September 1945. He had been recommended for this award the previous April when he had flown thirty-three sorties. His first was a Gardening sortie in May 1944 and his last a trip to Kiel on 13 April 1945. The recommendation for the award read:

This officer, now on his second tour, has completed 33 operational sorties, of which twelve have been completed in the Pathfinder Force, all of them as Markers. Pilot Officer Rhodes always displays courage, skill and determination

S/Ldr George Harvey and crew, May 1945. This crew operated as a blind marker crew and flew Lancaster 'D for Dog'. L to R: F/O Bill Parnham (navigator), F/Lt Norman Wilkins (navigator/ radar), F/O 'Az' Azzaro (rear gunner), P/O Kevin Keogh (flight engineer), F/O Johnny Powell (W/Op), P/O Geoff Dyson (mid-upper gunner). S/Ldr Harvey in cockpit. D. Cheetham

in action without consideration of his personal safety. His strong devotion to duty, initiative and co-operation have contributed to a large extent to the success with which his crew operates.

The early days of peace were filled with a task which involved the return of many British troops from Italy to be demobbed. Operation Dodge involved the squadron flying to Bari in Italy from Mepal; between 15 October and 13 December 1945 they flew twenty-two sorties to bring the troops home.

During the war the squadron had flown 5,060 sorties, lost 157 aircraft and over 800 aircrew killed or missing. The squadron personnel received one CGM, one MC, one George Medal, thirty-five DSOs and six Bar, 327 DFCs and thirty-eight Bars, 139 DFMs and one Bar, one MBE and one Silver Star (US) – a remarkable record, and one which is remembered with pride.

CHAPTER SEVEN
THE SQUADRON POST-WAR

With the end of the war the squadron began to reduce to peacetime levels and many of the crews were transferred to Transport Command. It began to re-equip with the Lancaster Mk I(FE), though reduced in strength to ten aircraft.

The squadron moved from Mepal to Upwood in May 1946 and by early 1947 had a total personnel strength of only 105 of all ranks and trades. It was detached to Singapore for Operation Red Lion between January and March 1947. Four of the squadron's Lancasters carried out bombing sorties over Perak Island. In addition, the Lancasters also flew formation sorties with the Beaufighters of 45 Sqn, which involved flights to Madras, Bangalore, Calcutta, Colombo and return.

By mid-1947 the squadron was operating in a specialist role within Bomber Command. The task was sea mining, and trials of new techniques began in July 1947. It involved getting ahead of the naval force, with one Lancaster flying in front of the Main Force dropping Window to confuse the fleet radar. The Main Force would fly at between 500 and 4,000 feet, using radar to pinpoint the drop position. A drop accuracy of less than 200 yards was possible using this technique.

A mess party in 1946. Of note are the decorations made of Window foil strips. Front row, fourth from right, Dennis Griffiths; extreme left, Ace Pierson. D.J. Griffiths

Lancaster B Mk I (FE) TW892:MC-B at Shallufa in 1949. 7 Sqn

Lincolns replaced the Lancasters from September 1949 and by January 1950 the venerable Lancaster, which had served the squadron so well, was gone. After only a year operating the Lincoln the squadron won the Lawrence Minot Trophy for bombing. This competition had been established between the wars and recommenced after the Second World War. No. 7 Sqn had previously won the trophy nine times before the war.

Exercise Sunray found the squadron in Egypt in February 1953, flying out non-stop from Upwood. Returning in March it fell into the usual training routine and rounds of exercise before commencing formation-flying practice for the Queen's review of the RAF, which took place at Odiham on 15 June 1953.

By the end of 1953 the squadron had won another trophy, the Sassoon Trophy, for best photo-gunnery results and had taken part in trials of bomb fuses at Habbaniya in Iraq.

A detachment was sent out to Tengah in Malaya from January to October 1954 on counter-insurgency operations, carrying out the first bombing sorties on 20 January. The counter-insurgency sorties continued until 14 April, when No. 148 Sqn took over the duty. Four Lincolns remained on detachment until 15 October, taking

A 7 Sqn crew pose with their ground crew at Shallufa in 1951. The aircrew are L to R: Sgt Swain, Flt Lt R. Cunningham, Sgt P. Brown, Sgt G. Cooke, F/Sgt Curtis, Sgt B. Williams and R. Booth. R. Booth via 7 Squadron Association

A poor-quality, but still amazing, photograph of a 7 Sqn Lincoln being flown at extremely low level on only one engine. The photo was taken on Battle of Britain Day 1950. A. Gibson via 7 Squadron Association

part in combined operations with the other squadrons, until they finally returned on 15 October 1954.

April 1955 saw another victory in the Lawrence Minot Trophy, and throughout the year the squadron continued to train for it's anti-shipping mine-laying role. By now, however, the Lincoln was blatantly obsolescent in the new jet era and the squadron disbanded at Upwood in January 1956. It re-formed, equipped with the Vickers Valiant V-bomber, at Honington in October.

The Valiant was the first of the 'V' Bombers and the first issued to No. 7 Sqn was collected by the CO, W/Cdr Boxer, from No. 49 Sqn at Wittering. By the end of October the squadron had its full complement of Valiants and almost immediately the crews were put on standby for deployment on operations during the Suez Crisis; in the event they were not required.

With re-equipment the squadron continued to train for conventional bombing, but now included visual and radar nuclear bombing techniques in its inventory. In 1958 it detached to Malta for bombing exercises before returning to the routine of UK training. This was followed by success once again in the Sassoon Trophy in May 1960.

Lincoln RE397:U at RAF Upwood in 1952. via 7 Squadron Association

Lincoln RE301 over the Malay jungle. 7 Sqn

The Valiants moved to Wittering in July 1960 remaining there until October 1962, when the squadron again disbanded. During their stay at Wittering they were held on high operational readiness status as the Cold War was at its height during the period. Both the Berlin crisis and the Cuban missile crisis brought the crews to the brink, but luckily, in the end they were never scrambled. The reason for the squadron's disbandment was the discovery of serious metal fatigue in the Valiant main spar, and although a plan was mooted to re-equip with the Victor, it did not come to pass.

Lincolns RE301 and SX983 dropping bombs in the Ipoh area on 3 August 1954 during Operation Bold. The Lincolns were based at RAF Tengah from July to October 1954. 7 Sqn

It was eight years before the squadron re-formed at St Mawgan in Cornwall on 1 May 1970. It operated Canberras of various marks in the target facilities role in No. 18 Group. It operated Canberra TT Mk 18s fitted with the Rushton target towing system, comprising two winches, pylon mounted on the wings, which could stream a target on up to 5 miles of wire. The target itself looked similar to a missile and could be fitted with a flare system to make acquisition easier for the attacking aircraft or ship. The squadron had six Canberras on strength, all of which were maintained by civilian contractors Airwork Services Ltd.

Eventually the squadron would have ten TT Mk 18 and six B Mk 2s on strength, as well as two T Mk 4s for training. It carried out numerous detachments around the world, providing target facilities training and also maintained a semi-permanent

Lincoln RE348 of 7 Sqn with Lincolns of No. 1 Sqn RAAF after a strike in North Malaya in August 1954. 7 Sqn

Lincoln RE345 over the Yemen border in October 1955. 7 Sqn

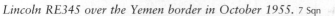

Another view of Lincoln RE345 in Yemen in 1955. 7 Sqn

The Squadron re-equipped with the Vickers Valiant at Honington on 1 November 1956. 7 Sqn

detachment at Kinloss to support the army missile ranges in the Hebrides. It was disbanded once more in 1981.

Re-formed as a support helicopter squadron at Odiham on 1 September 1982, equipped with the Boeing-Vertol Chinook HC Mk 1, the squadron crews took part in the Falklands War. The squadron has remained at Odiham since then and has taken part in operations in Lebanon, the First Gulf War, Bosnia, Kosovo, Sierra Leone and most recently Afghanistan and the second Gulf War. During this period it progressively re-equipped with the HC Mk 2 and HC Mk 3 versions of the Chinook. The crews were split into an Operations Flight and a Special Forces (SF) Flight during this period. The role of the SF Flight is shrouded in secrecy, but they were involved in numerous SAS operations during the first, and no doubt the second, Gulf War.

Throughout the 1980s and 1990s the squadron mounted numerous small detachments to Aldergrove in Northern Ireland in support of the forces there, providing airlift capability during rebuilding of border observation posts and working with army patrols and Royal Ulster Constabulary (RUC) units, particularly during the 'marching season'

In late 1990 Iraq invaded Kuwait and the RAF Support Helicopter Force was soon on standby to deploy to the region. The Chinooks of 7 Sqn were deployed in January 1991, with the SF Flight splitting off to carry out its own operations. The bulk of the squadron that remained was joined with the aircraft and crews of No. 18 Sqn from Germany to form the Chinook Squadron Middle East (CS(ME)). This provided all the airborne logistic support required by the British Army working alongside the Pumas of 33 and 230 Squadrons. The squadron began operations from a base at Al Jubayl in Saudi Arabia before moving out to a desert base close to Hafr Al Batin. This was followed by a second desert move, where they remained until the end of the war. The

No. 7 Sqn Valiants led the Queen's Birthday Flypast on 13 June 1957. 7 Sqn

7 Sqn Valiant WZ377 at Ikeja Airport in September 1960. 7 Sqn

Canberra TT Mk 18 WJ721 of 7 Sqn shows off its Rushton drogue target pods under the wings, along with the target-towing black/yellow striping. 7 Sqn

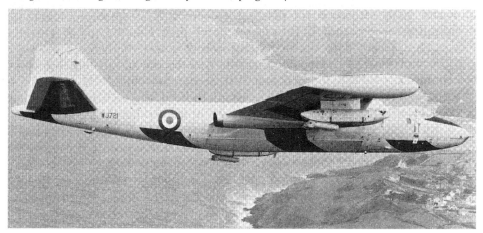

Canberra TT Mk 18 of 7 Sqn at high altitude showing off its yellow and black target-tug striping. 7 Sqn

A 7 Sqn Canberra of the Kinloss detachment in 1979. Author's collection

Chinook 'EZ' of 7 Sqn lifts from the deck of the RFA Reliant *during operations in the Lebanon in the early 1980s.* 7 Sqn

crews became extremely familiar with the road stretching out from Al Jubayl to the north-west, known as the 'Tap Line Road' as they daily flew its length transporting troops and supplies. Many sorties involved fourteen hour days flying from one desert grid to another, with little in the way of features to navigate by, relying on Global Positioning System (GPS) and Loran navigation systems. At the end of the war the squadron returned to Al Jubayl and thence to Odiham.

The crews were not to get much chance to recover and take leave before many of them were immediately detached to southern Turkey to provide humanitarian relief to the Kurdish refugees streaming across the northern Iraq border escaping the brutal regime of Saddam Hussein. Operating initially from Diyarbakir airbase and later a field site at Silopi and flying fourteen-hour days, the Chinook crews brought desperately needed food, medical supplies and shelter to the refugees, who were spread all over the southern Turkish mountains. The detachments stretched into the early summer months before all of the crews eventually returned to Odiham. Conditions in the region were extremely difficult and many of the squadron personnel had to contend with bouts of illness, including dysentery.

During 1995 elements of the squadron deployed to the former Yugoslavia to support the UN peacekeeping forces and by 1996 the squadron had crews and helicopters established at Divulje Barracks, Split, as part of the IFOR Multi-National Division. The task for the Chinooks was to transport troops, supplies and equipment to various up-country locations. The flights were so regular that they were dubbed the 'Bus Run' by the crews and troops involved. They were hardly routine trips though, as adverse weather and the ever-present risk of ground fire were constant risks. The

The squadron took part in many air displays with the Chinook during the 1980s and 1990s. This photo depicts one of the display crews at Mildenhall. L to R: F/Sgt G. Forbes, F/Lt A. Lewry, F/Lt M. Reeves, Sgt W. Hughes, F/Lt M. Niven, Sgt T. Thresher and F/Lt M. Fisk. M. Reeves via 7 Squadron Association

The Chinooks of 7 and 18 Sqns arrive at the docks in Al Jubayl in January 1991 for the first Gulf War. Author's collection

Chinook was a vital element in the force inventory during this period as the country was not suited to the use of large vehicle convoys. As well as supporting the troops the squadron got itself involved in the humanitarian side of the conflict with regular visit to a ruined school in Sipovo to deliver toys, games and footballs to the children of the area.

By the end of 1996 the squadron was involved in intensive tasking during the work-up training of the Joint Rapid Reaction Force, a UK-based force comprising elements of 5 Brigade, which was to be ready for immediate deployment anywhere in the world. In addition the squadron continued to provide support to No. 24 Brigade, which it had supported since the early 1980s. Also in 1996 it made a detachment to Switzerland in support of a multinational exercise. During the exercise the Chinook was used mainly to transport VIPs and high-ranking observers.

September 1999 saw the end of the squadron's involvement in Kosovo and Bosnia, with the return of the detachment, and by the end of the year the Chinook Wing at Odiham was in line for some major changes. No. 27 Sqn split into two with one part becoming No. 18 Sqn. No. 5 Flt of 7 Sqn was also hived off to join the remainder of 27 Sqn, leaving 7 Sqn with its HQ Flt, SF Flt and the engineering cadre to continue as a dedicated special forces squadron. It would eventually be incorporated into a Special Forces Wing, which included an Army Air Corps squadron, No. 657.

A Chinook delivers a container of spares to the squadron's first desert site outside Hafr Al Batin, followed closely but its own self generated dust cloud, which will shortly engulf everything in sight! Author's collection

245

Chinook ZA679 at 'Tranquillity Base', in full invasion markings, 25 February 1991. Author's collection

An air-to-air shot of a Chinook over the Iraqi desert, 2 March 1991. Author's collection

The combined Chinook Sqn Middle East (7 & 18 Sqn) crews, at 'Myrtle Beach', January 1991. Author's collection

Going home. Chinooks of 7 Sqn SF Flight and CS(ME) are prepared for loading onto cargo ships at Al Jubayl for the journey home, 10 March 1991. Author's collection

Whilst supplying the Kurdish refugees in southern Turkey and northern Iraq shortly after the Gulf War squadron crews operated a mix of OCU aircraft flown out from the UK and CS(ME). Desert-camouflaged Chinooks offloaded in Cyprus and were flown to Diyarbakir airbase. This OCU aircraft has the unit badge on the nose, 18 Sqn tailcode and the Union Jack, and was often flown by 7 Sqn crews! Author's collection

Offloading supplies from a Chinook on the Turkish-Iraqi border for Kurdish refugees. Author's collection

Two members of the Joint Helicopter Support Unit (JHSU) prepare to attach a pair of air portable fuel cells (APFC) to the underslung load hook of a 7 Sqn Chinook in 1996. The crew is F/Lt D. Curtis, F/Lt G. Drinkwater, F/Sgt T. Colley and F/Sgt S. Horton. via 7 Squadron Association

In 2000 the crews of the squadron were once again involved in conflict. This time Operation Palliser took them to Sierra Leone, where they supported ground troops successfully in the rescue of several British troops being held captive by rebel forces.

In early 2001 the squadron mounted a mountain-flying detachment to Norway and on return became heavily involved in trials with fitting skis to the Chinook in conjunction with the Rotary Wing Operational Evaluation Training Unit (RWOETU). The trials were considered to be very successful. Of course 2001 will be remembered for the outbreak of foot and mouth disease. Unfortunately the squadron's training area was badly effected and there were numerous no-fly areas to hamper the training routine.

By the end of 2001 the replacement for the Chinook HC Mk 2, the HC Mk 3, was being mooted for the squadron and a Mk 3 Fielding Flight was formed and sent out to the USA to carry out trials and testing of the type.

In 2002 the squadron became involved in one of the largest desert warfare exercises mounted for many years: Exercise Saif Sareea II in Oman. The crews, aircraft and equipment were flown out in the new RAF C-17 Globemaster II transport aircraft. On arrival in Oman the personnel moved into a massive tented city and the rebuild of the Chinooks was commenced. The exercise was going well when the events of 11 September unfolded in the USA and the detachment were recalled to the UK, arriving back in mid-October.

The squadron's next major event was its involvement in the second Gulf War, deploying to the region on 8 February 2003 and remaining in theatre until the ceasefire in April. Once again, due to the special forces operations being secret in nature, it will be some time before its part in this conflict is open to public scrutiny. At the time of writing the squadron is still involved in operations in Iraq and probably will be for some time to come.

The members of the squadron who served in the Second World War would be justly proud of the professional, dedicated young men, both air and ground crews, who serve on No. 7 Sqn today. The squadron is at the forefront of today's RAF operations and can still truly say that 'The Stars Led the Way'.

AIRCRAFT OPERATED BY NO. 7 SQUADRON

Armstrong Whitworth Whitley Mk II

Armstrong Whitworth Whitley Mk II K7244:LT-G. In 1938 this aircraft was based at Finningley with 7 Sqn. It was lost in a crash at Abersoch Bay whilst serving with No. 9 BGS on 19 February 1941. M. Barrass

K7226	To CLS [Central Landing School]
K7233	To 10 BGS
K7235	To 10 BGS
K7236	To 9 BGS
K7237	To 10 OTU
K7238	To 10 BGS
K7239	To 97 Sqn
K7240	To 10 BGS
K7241	Crashed into a house on approach to Finningley, 21 October 1938
K7242	To 9 BGS
K7244	To 9 BGS
K7245	To 2474M, December 1940
K7246	To 9 BGS
K7247	To 10 BGS
K7253	To 10 BGS

Armstrong Whitworth Whitley Mk III

Armstrong Whitworth Whitley Mk III. M. Barrass

K8962	To 58 Sqn
K8964	To 57 Sqn
K8965	To 58 Sqn
K8967	To 58 Sqn
K8968	Crashed on night approach to Finningley, 23 March 1939
K8969	To 58 Sqn

K8970	To 58 Sqn
K8971	To 58 Sqn
K8972	To 58 Sqn
K8973	To 58 Sqn
K8974	To 58 Sqn
K8975	To 58 Sqn
K8990	To 58 Sqn

Avro Anson Mk I

Avro Anson Mk I. M. Barrass

N5010	To RCAF, 11 March 1941
N5012	To 16 OTU
N5013	To 6 AONS [Air Observer Navigation School]
N5014	To 6 AONS
N5015	To 6 FTS [Flying Training School]
N5016	To 16 OTU
N5018	To 16 OTU
N5023	To 105 Sqn
N5025	To SFPP [Service Ferry Pilot Pool]
N5026	To 35 Sqn

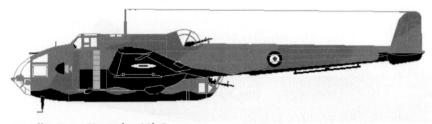

Handley Page Hampden Mk I. M. Barrass

Handley Page Hampden

L4041	To 16 OTU
L4042	To 16 OTU
L4138	To 16 OTU
L4139	To 16 OTU
L4140	To 16 OTU
L4155	Control lost on a training trip whilst practising change of pilot, spun in 5 miles east of Newark, 23 May 1939
L4156	To 16 OTU
L4157	To 16 OTU
L4158	To 16 OTU
L4159	Hit tree on approach to Upper Heyford whilst training, 6 November 1939

L4160	Force landed at Brackley airfield after engine failure, 29 March 1940
L4161	Dived into ground during a turn, Cockwood farm, near Finningley, 5 September 1939
L4162	To 14 OTU
L4163	To 144 Sqn
L4164	To 50 Sqn
L4165	To 144 Sqn
L4166	To 144 Sqn
L4167	To 144 Sqn
L4168	To 44 Sqn
L4169	To 16 OTU
L4170	To 16 OTU
L4176	To 16 OTU
L4190	To 16 OTU
P1260	Flew into Snaefell, Isle of Man in cloud whilst training, 1 January 1940
P1261	To 16 OTU
P1265	To 16 OTU
P1266	To 16 OTU
P2064	To 14 OTU
P4307	To 14 OTU
P4309	To 14 OTU
P4311	To 14 OTU
P4312	To 14 OTU
P4313	To 14 OTU
P4314	To 14 OTU
P4315	To 14 OTU

Short Stirling Mk I

L7605	
N3636:MG-A	Fell off jacks at Oakington and damaged mainplane strut, 7 August 1941

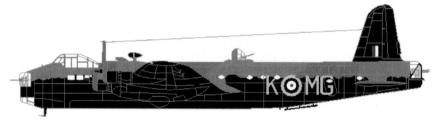

Short Stirling Mk I N3637:MG-K showing the revised colour scheme with special night (black) extended up the fuselage sides. M. Barrass

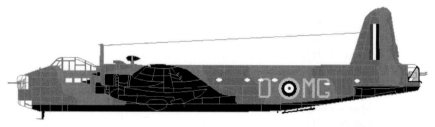

Short Stirling Mk I N3641:MG-D in the early colour scheme of 1941. Note lack of mid-upper turret in these early Mk Is. M. Barrass)

N3637:MG-K MG-G	To AFEE
N3638	To 15 Sqn
N3640	Hit by AA fire at 10,000 feet over Isle of Man, crashed at Hodge Branding, Kirkby Lonsdale, Lancs, 29 September 1940
N3641:MG-D	To 26 Conversion Flt
N3642:MG-E	To 15 Sqn
N3643	Crashed on fire after hitting HT cables returning from Rotterdam, 24 March 1941 at Hazelwood Common, Leiston, Suffolk
N3644:MG-H	To 15 Sqn
N3652	To 1651 CU
N3653	Failed to return from Brest, 3 March 1941
N3655:MG-R	To 1651 CU
N3663:MG-H	Failed to return from Berlin, 3 August 1941
N3664:MG-V	Failed to return from Hamburg, 30 June 1941
N3666:MG-Z	Severe structural damage caused by Bf110 attack on 28 August 1941, SOC [Struck Off Charge] 29 August 1941
N3668:MG-B	To 15 Sqn
N3669:MG-E MG-H	To 26 Conversion Flt
N3670	To 101 Conversion Flt
N3672:MG-M MG-U	Turned to avoid tractor when landing at Oakington and bounced, undercarriage collapsed when taxiing, 14 January 1942
N3677:MG-J	Failed to return from Berlin, 7 November 1941
N3679:MG-D	Belly-landed at Newmarket on return from Essen, 13 April 1942
N3680:MG-Y	Failed to return from Brest, 18 December 1941
N3700:MG-A	To 26 Conversion Flt, returned and then to 218 Sqn

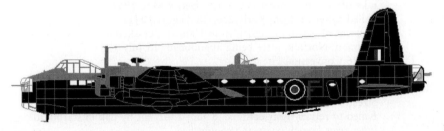

Short Stirling Mk I N3705:MG-F crashed in Holland on the night of 15/16 August 1942 and was salvaged by the Germans and returned to flying condition. M. Barrass

N3701	After a search flight over the North Sea, landed downwind in poor visibility at Oakington, hit an obstruction and the undercarriage collapsed, 2 December 1941
N3705:MG-R MG-F	Failed to return from a mining sortie off Borkum, 16 August 1942 Crash landed near Loevenstein Castle, Gorichem, Netherlands, repaired at Gilze Rijen and sent to the *Luftwaffe* test unit at Rechlin
N3706:MG-S	Failed to return from Bremen, 30 June 1942, believed ditched 50 miles off Cromer
N3708:MG-E	To 1657 CU
N3709:MG-K MG-S	Failed to return from Essen, 27 March 1942, crashed near Gendringen, Netherlands
N3710:MG-M	Failed to return from Stuttgart, 6 May 1942
N3716:MG-A	Failed to return from Mannheim, 20 May 1942
N3720	To 218 Sqn

N3727:MG-G	Failed to return from a mining sortie off Heligoland, 28 April 1942
N3750	Failed to return from Essen, 2 June 1942, crashed in North Sea off Holland
N3754:MG-O	Failed to return from Bremen, 26 June 1942
N3757	To 15 Sqn
N3760:MG-D	To 1657 CU
N3764:MG-J	Failed to return from Hamburg, 10 November 1942
N3765	To 1657 CU
N6001:MG-E	Failed to return from Hamburg, 30 June 1941
N6003:MG-S	To 26 Conversion Flt
N6004	To 15 Sqn
N6005:MG-F	To 26 Conversion Flt
N6006:MG-G	To 101 Conversion Flt
N6007:MG-Q	Damaged by Messerschmitt Bf109s and ditched in the North Sea, 28 June 1941
N6009	Crashed at 'Q' site at Stambourne, Essex returning from Cologne, 20 April 1941
N6010	Failed to return from Berlin, 11 May 1941
N6011	Failed to return from Berlin, 10 April 1941
N6012	Low approach on return from Hamburg, hit trees and crashed at Dry Drayton, Cambs, 3 May 1941
N6013:MG-A	Last seen circling dinghy on return from Borkum and being attacked by enemy aircraft, 1 July 1941
N6014	Landed in field at Wenhaston due to fuel shortage, the undercarriage collapsed 1 May 1941
N6017:MG-Z	Shot down by flak near Hardelot *en route* to Bethune, 10 July 1941
N6019	Crashed 1 mile north-east of Oakington after starboard outer cut on take-off and port outer cut at 100 feet, 9 May 1941
N6020:MG-B	Failed to return from Karlsruhe, 26 August 1941
N6022:MG-D	Ran out of petrol on return from Hanover, crashed at Newton Flotman, Norfolk, after being abandoned, 15 July 1941
N6032:MG-T	To 26 Conversion Flt
N6033:MG-T MG-W	Unable to locate airfield without W/T and in bad visibility on return from Hanover, engines cut due to fuel shortage and crashed in High Street, Northampton, 15 July 1941
N6034	Failed to return from Bethune, 8 July 1941, hit by flak in starboard inner over French coast and caught fire
N6035:MG-A	Failed to return from Berlin, 26 July 1941, crashed at Ouddorp, Holland
N6036:MG-Q MG-Y	To 214 Conversion Flt
N6037:MG-V	To 26 Conversion Flt
N6039:MG-Q	To 101 Conversion Flt
N6041:MG-H	Overshot at Oakington on return from bombing aerodrome south of Hanover, 15 August 1941
N6042:MG-T	Hit obstruction on runway at Graveley on return from Magdeburg, 15 August 1941
N6046:MG-Y	Failed to return from Berlin, 8 September 1941
N6048:MG-J	To 7 Conversion Flt then 1651 CU
N6049:MG-Z	To 26 Conversion Flt
N6073:MG-Y	Failed to return from Mannheim, 20 May 1942
N6074:MG-G MG-A	Ditched off Barmouth, North Wales, due to fuel shortage, 26 March 1942
N6075	To 101 Conversion Flt

N6085:MG-H	Shot down by a Ju88 near Bourn on return from Brest, 3 October 1941
N6087:MG-A MG-M	Struck telegraph wires when making forced landing near West Bluntisham, Cambs, due to port outer fire on return from Brest, 18 November 1941
N6089:MG-L	To 26 Conversion Flt
N6090:MG-Y	To A&AEE, returned, then to No. 15 Conversion Flt
N6091:MG-K	Failed to return from Berlin, 8 November 1941, crashed at Hekelingen, Holland
N6093	To 15 Sqn
N6094:MG-G	To 26 Conversion Flt
N6095:MG-K	Damaged by flak on Brest raid, 18 December 1941
N6104	To 1651 CU
N6120:MG-V	Port outer hit by flak from convoy 20 miles out in North Sea, overshot at Oakington and hit railway embankment, 17 January 1942
N6121	To 101 Conversion Flt
N6128	To 26 Conversion Flt
N6129	To 218 Sqn
N6300:MG-A	
R9143	To 149 Sqn
R9147	To 1651 CU
R9149:MG-S	Failed to return from Munich, 10 March 1943
R9150:MG-A MG-O	Failed to return from Turin, 30 November 1942
R9154:MG-F	Failed to return from Duisburg, 6 August 1942
R9156:MG-H MG-S	To 1665 CU
R9158	Landed at Manston due to fuel shortage on return from Nuremberg, overshot and collided with hangar, 29 August 1942
R9169:MG-Y	Failed to return from Hamburg, 10 November 1942
R9192	To 15 Sqn
R9193	To 15 Sqn
R9199:MG-F MG-T	Failed to return from Duisburg, 9 April 1943
R9249	To 1657 CU
R9251	To 1657 CU
R9252	To NTU [Navigation Training Unit]
R9255:MG-Q	Port outer hit by flak over Berlin and swung landing at Oakington, undercarriage collapsed, 28 March 1943
R9257:MG-C MG-E MG-R	To 1657 CU
R9258:MG-K	To 214 Sqn
R9259:MG-J MG-R	Failed to return from Mannheim, 7 December 1942
R9260:MG-O	Port outer backfiring after take-off for Hamburg, heavy landing made at Oakington when undercarriage collapsed after swing, 3 August 1943
R9261:MG-M	Failed to return from Stettin, 21 April 1943
R9262:MG-A	Failed to return from Munich, 22 December 1942
R9263:MG-D	Failed to return from Bocholt, 1 May 1943, shot down by night fighter and crashed near Akkerwoude, Holland
R9264:MG-L	Failed to return from Cologne, 3 February 1943, shot down by a night fighter and crashed at Hendrik Ido Ambacht, Holland
R9266:MG-J	Failed to return from Krefeld, 22 June 1943

R9267:MG-S	Belly-landed in a field at Hatley St George, Cambs, due to engine failure on a training flight, 14 June 1943
R9270:MG-S MG-Q	Failed to return from Nuremberg, 9 March 1943
R9272:MG-W	Failed to return from Krefeld, 22 June 1943, crashed at Gilze, Holland
R9273	To 1657 Cu
R9275:MG-Y	Failed to return from Frankfurt, 11 April 1943
R9277:MG-P MG-T	To NTU
R9278:MG-E	Failed to return from Stuttgart, 15 April 1943
R9280:MG-E	To BDU [Bombing Development Unit]
R9281:MG-V	Failed to return from Elberfeld, 25 June 1943, crashed in the North Sea near Holland
R9283:MG-Q	To 214 Sqn
R9284	To 214 Sqn
R9286:MG-C	Failed to return from Munster, 12 June 1943, believed ditched in North Sea
R9288:MG-P	To 214 Sqn
R9289:MG-F	To 214 Sqn
R9293:MG-F	
R9295	To 149 Sqn
R9296	To 149 Sqn
R9297:MG-P	To 7 Conversion Flt then 1657 CU
R9298	To 1651 CU
R9300:MG-L	To 7 Conversion Flt then 1657 CU
R9301:MG-Q	To 7 Conversion Flt then 1657 CU
R9305:MG-R	Failed to return from Lubeck, 29 March 1942, crashed near Hamburg
R9306	To 7 Conversion Flt then 90 Sqn
R9324	Failed to return from Essen, 17 June 1942
R9328:MG-A	Failed to return from Hamburg, 27 July 1942
R9331:MG-Y	Fast landing at Waterbeach caused overshoot, 14 July 1942
W7427	To 1657 CU
W7430	
W7433:MG-U	Failed to return from Stettin, 30 September 1941
W7434:MG-D MG-E	Undercarriage collapsed on heavy landing at Oakington on return from Hanover, 15 August 1941
W7435	To 15 Sqn
W7436:MG-D	Failed to return from Brest, 18 December 1941
W7438:MG-A	Failed to return from Duisburg, 28 August 1941
W7440:MG-W	To 101 Sqn Conversion Flt
W7441:MG-J MG-Y	Failed to return from Stettin, 30 September 1941
W7442:MG-M	To 1651 CU
W7443	To 15 Sqn
W7444:MG-G MG-L	Returned early from Bremen due to oxygen failure and undercarriage collapsed on heavy landing at Oakington, 31 October 1941
W7445:MG-V	Crashed onto a house after windscreen iced up during take-off at Oakington for Kiel, 15 November 1941
W7446:MG-S	Overshot at Oakington, brakes ineffective on wet ground and swung to avoid dispersal point causing undercarriage collapse, 18 November 1941
W7448:MG-Z	To 26 Sqn Conversion Flt
W7449:MG-J MG-M	To 214 Sqn

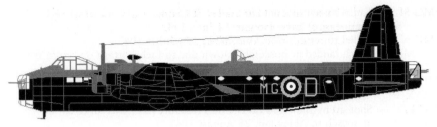

Short Stirling Mk I W7451:MG-D showing the reduced size squadron code letters, MG, used for most of the war. M. Barrass

W7451:MG-D	To 7 Conversion Flt then 218 Conversion Flt
W7454:MG-S	To 26 Sqn Conversion Flt
W7466:MG-B	Failed to return from Lubeck, 29 March 1942
W7467	Collided with 56 OTU Hurricane at Earith, 16 January 1942
W7468:MG-W	To 1651 CU
W7470:MG-U	To 7 Conversion Flt then 1657 CU
W7471:MG-J	Failed to return from Emden, 7 June 1942, crashed near Blija, Holland
W7472:MG-C	Failed to return from Emden, 21 June 1942, crashed in North Sea near Bergen, Holland
W7500:MG-B	Failed to return from Essen, 3 June 1942, crashed in the North Sea near Holland, probably shot down by a night fighter
W7501:MG-Z	Failed to return from Lubeck, 28 March 1942, crashed in North Sea north of Terschelling, Holland
W7504	To 15 Sqn
W7505	To 15 Sqn
W7517:MG-Z	To 1657 CU
W7520:MG-S	Failed to return form Mannheim, 20 May 1942
W7522:MG-G MG-K	To 1651 CU
W7529:MG-R MG-W	To 1665 CU
W7533:MG-G	Failed to return from Hamburg, 29 July 1942
W7539	Failed to return from St Nazaire, 28 June 1942., crashed in North Sea 40 km off Vlieland, Holland, probably shot down or after collision with Bf110
W7563	Tyre burst on take-off at Oakington *en route* to Bremen, swung and caught fire, 2 July 1942
W7564	Hit by flak over Maastricht, port inner u/s, port outer fell of and at English coast starboard inner cut, crash landed in field near Weeley, Essex, 11 September 1942
W7565	Failed to return from Hamburg, 29 July 1942, starboard inner failed, damaged by flak and shot down by night fighters
W7569:MG-D	Failed to return from Essen, 17 September 1942, crashed in the Ijsselmeer near Lemmer, Holland
W7574	To 1657 CU
W7579:MG-Y	Failed to return from mining Kiel Bay, 14 August 1942
W7581	To 1657 CU
W7616:MG-G	Failed to return from Frankfurt, 25 August 1942
W7617:MG-A MG-K	Failed to return from Stuttgart, 12 March 1943
W7620:MG-D MG-L	Failed to return from mining the Friesians, 6 November 1942
W7629:MG-Z	Failed to return from Duisburg, 6 September 1942

W7630:MG-M	Failed to return from Dusseldorf, 11 September 1942, crashed 1 mile south-east of Echt, Holland
W7632:MG-N	Failed to return from Munich, 22 December 1942
BF316:MG-M	Crash landed at Boscombe Down due to fuel shortage on return from Nuremberg, 29 August 1942
BF317:MG-D MG-X	Failed to return from Berlin, 28 March 1943
BF335:MG-E	Shot up by Ju88 and Fw190 on Frankfurt raid, port inner cut on approach to Abingdon, 25 August 1942
BF336:MG-Z	Failed to return from Frankfurt, 25 August 1942
BF339:MG-C MG-F MG-L	To 1665 CU
BF340:MG-A	To 1657 CU
BF342:MG-E	To 1657 CU
BF345:MG-H	To 1657 CU
BF354	To 1657 CU
BF358:MG-C	Failed to return from Munich, 22 December 1942
BF378:MG-W	To 15 Sqn
BF379:MG-D	Failed to return from Turin, 12 December 1942
BF387:MG-U	Failed to return from Hamburg, 10 November 1942
BF390:MG-A	Returning from mining off the Friesians, 30 miles south of track, was shot down by Great Yarmouth defences as it failed to identify itself, 21 October 1942
BF501:MG-N	To 218 Sqn
BF526	To 90 Sqn
BF532	To 90 Sqn
BK592:MG-M MG-F	Failed to return from Essen, 13 March 1943
BK602	To 75 Sqn
BK610	Crashed 1.5 miles east of Dungeness on return from Nuremberg, 9 March 1943, the mid-upper gunner baled out over Kent, rest of crew over Channel
BK621:MG-N	To 214 Sqn
EF361:MG-B	Failed to return from Dusseldorf, 26 May 1943
EF363:MG-G2	To 214 Sqn
EF364:MG-X	Failed to return from Hamburg, 30 July 1943
EF366:MG-L	Failed to return from Krefeld, 22 June 1943
EF368:MG-A	
EF369:MG-Z	Lost power on approach on return from Hamburg. Lost height and hit obstruction and crashed at Oakington, 28 July 1943
EF384	To 1665 CU
EF386	To 1657 CU
EF387:MG-D	Failed to return from Krefeld, 22 June 1943, crashed in Holland
EF388:MG-M	To 214 Sqn
EF390:MG-T	To 214 Sqn
EF392:MG-N2	Failed to return from Elberfeld, 25 June 1943, crashed in North Sea west of Zeeland, Holland
EF393:MGB MG-W	To 214 Sqn

Short Stirling Mk III

BK709:MG-F	Failed to return from Stuttgart, 15 April 1943
BK723:MG-E	To 90 Sqn

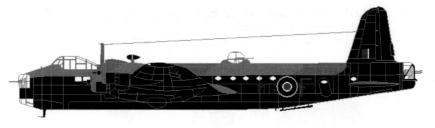

Short Stirling Mk III BK709:MG-F, which failed to return from Stuttgart on 15 April 1943.
M. Barrass

BK724:MG-I	To 214 Sqn
BK760:MG-X	Failed to return from Frankfurt, 11 April 1943
BK761	To 218 Sqn
BK769:MG-G	Failed to return from Stuttgart, 15 April 1943
BK773:MG-T	Failed to return from Dortmund, 5 May 1943, shot down by a night fighter and crashed in Ijsselmeer, south of Enkhuizen, Holland
BK779	To 90 Sqn
EE945	To 620 Sqn
EF401	To NTU
EF402:MG-N MG-Y	To 214 Sqn
EF406:MG-J	To 214 Sqn

Lancaster Mk I

ME438	SOC 2 June 1947.
NG229:MG-S	Missing, Harburg, 5 April 1945
NG249	SOC 22 May 1947
NN719	SOC 14 January 1948
NN725	SOC 22 May 1947
PA194	SOC 1 March 1949
PA267	SOC 30 November 1946
PA310	SOC 2 November 1946
PA331	Sold for scrap, 7 May 1947
PA384	To 148 Sqn
PA386:MG-A	To 214 Sqn
PA414:MG-G	SOC 20 October 1948
PA416	To French Aeronavale, June 1953
PA437:MG-C	Sold for scrap, 22 December 1948
PA449	To 214 Sqn
PB910:MG-B	SOC 12 March 1947
PB935	SOC 13 December 1946
PB955	SOC 15 January 1947
PB956	To CBE [Central Bomber Establishment]
PB961	To 49 Sqn, returned then SOC 5 November 1946
PB984	SOC 26 November 1946
PD223	SOC 28 January 1947
RA522	SOC 3 January 1947
RA567	SOC 22 March 1948
RA581	SOC 15 May 1947.
RF130	SOC 23 October 1946
RF133	SOC 2 November 1946
SW248	SOC 2 June 1947
SW265:MG-D	SOC 15 October 1946

SW269	SOC 22 May 1947
TW872	SOC 28 May 1948
TW873:MG-F	To 214 Sqn

Avro Lancaster Mk I (FE) TW892:MG-B operated by 7 Sqn at Shallufa during 1948–49.
M. Barrass

TW885	To 149 Sqn
TW892:MG-B	Sold for scrap 23 November 1950
TW895	To 148 Sqn
TW898	To 148 Sqn
TW908	To 148 Sqn

Lancaster Mk I (FE)

TW659:MG-D	Sold for scrap 29 August 1950
TW660:MG-F	To 35 Sqn

Lancaster Mk III

ED419	Missing, Essen, 13 March 1943
ED595:MG-Q	Missing, Wuppertal, 25 June 1943
ED971:MG-M	To NTU
EE119:XU-G	Failed to return from Berlin, 22/23 November 1943
MG-J	
MG-N	
EE129:MG-V	Missing, Berlin, 2 January 1944
MG-Y	
EE173	To 156 Sqn
EE175	To 83 Sqn
EE176	To 97 Sqn
EE177	To 156 Sqn
EE178	To 156 Sqn
EE179	To 97 Sqn
EE200:MG-A	To 166 Sqn
XU-K	
XU-X	
JA677:MG-S	To NTU
MG-U	

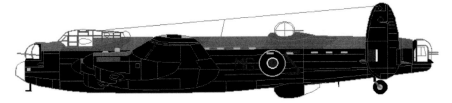

Avro Lancaster Mk III JA678:MG-S flown by S/Ldr Charles Lofthouse and shot down over Berlin on the night of 23/24 August 1943. The code letter 'S' is unusual in that it resembles a reversed 'Z'. M. Barrass

JA678:MG-S	Missing, Berlin, 24 August 1943
JA682:MG-D	Missing, Milan, 13 August 1943
JA685:MG-Z	Missing, Leipzig, 4 December 1943
JA693:MG-A	To 1667 CU
MG-J	
MG-W	
JA695:MG-A	
JA706:MG-C	Missing, Hanover, 9 October 1943
JA710:MG-N	Missing, Munchengladbach, 31 August 1943
JA712	To 83 Sqn
JA713:MG-V	Missing, Berlin, 4 September 1943
JA714	To 156 Sqn
JA715	To 97 Sqn
JA717:MG-B	Missing, Frankfurt, 23 October 1943
MG-C	
JA718:MG-T	Missing, Berlin, 29 January 1944
JA846	To 97 Sqn
JA849:MG-F	Missing, Hanover, 28 September 1943
JA850:MG-M	Missing, Milan, 15 August 1943
JA853:MG-L	Missing, Berlin, 17 December 1943
MG-R	
JA854:MG-X	Missing, Berlin, 4 September 1943
JA905:MG-K	Missing, Braunschweig, 15 January 1944
MG-V	
JA907:MG-U	Missing, Leipzig, 21 October 1943
JA911:MG-A	To 1653 CU
MG-N	
MG-Q	
MG-U	
JA917:MG-P	Missing, Hanover, 19 October 1943
JA929	Missing, Berlin, 4 September 1943
JA931	Abandoned out of fuel 10 miles north-east of Canterbury returning from Nuremberg, 11 August 1943
JA932:MG-M	Missing, Berlin, 24 November 1943
JA933:MG-R	
JA935:MG-O	Missing Braunschweig, 15 January 1944
JA936:MG-J	Missing, Munchengladbach, 31 August 1943
JA937:MG-H	Missing, Munchengladbach, 31 August 1943
JA962:MG-Q	To 582 Sqn
XU-W	
JA964:MG-D	Missing, Frankfurt, 23 March 1944
MG-P	
JA968:MG-H	
JA970:MG-N	Missing, Mannheim, 19 November 1943
JA971:MG-J2	Abandoned near Oakington returning from Berlin, 24 November 1943
XU-J	
JA978:MG-S	Overshot landing and hit tree, Waterbeach, 12 September 1943
JA980	To 405 Sqn
JB115:MG-G	Missing, Berlin, 23 November 1943
MG-S	
JB155:MG-L2	To 582 Sqn
MG-S	
JB175:MG-A	Missing, Leipzig, 21 October 1943
JB181:MG-V	Missing, Hanover, 9 October 1943
JB184:MG-V	Missing, Hanover, 23 September 1943

JB185:MG-X	To 1651 CU
MG-Y	
JB224:MG-B	Missing, Berlin, 16 February 1944
MG-W	
JB225:MG-V	Engine cut and undercarriage collapsed in forced landing at Swanton Morley, 29 September 1943
JB303:MG-F	Missing, Berlin, 27 November 1943
JB308:MG-B	Overshot landing at Oakington, 24 January 1944
JB313:MG-C	Missing, Aachen, 25 May 1944
MG-H	
MG-P	
JB317	To 156 Sqn
JB345:MG-V	To 582 Sqn
JB347:MG-V	Missing, Hanover, 19 October 1943
JB398:MG-C	Missing, Braunschweig, 15 January 1944
JB408:MG-A	Missing, Magdeburg, 22 January 1944
MG-U	
JB414:MG-Y	Missing, Berlin, 16 February 1944
JB417:MG-F	To 582 Sqn
JB455:MG-N	Missing, Lens, 16 June 1944
MG-P	
JB468:MG-A	Missing, Leipzig, 20 February 1944
MG-G	
JB475:MG-M	To 514 Sqn
JB480:MG-N	Missing, Berlin, 24 November 1943
JB488	To 83 Sqn
JB538:MG-G	Missing, Berlin, 24 November 1943
JB543:MG-J	Missing, Berlin, 17 December 1943
JB552:MG-K	Missing, Berlin, 17 December 1943
JB643:MG-M	To 12 Sqn
JB651:MG-K	Missing, Stettin, 6 January 1944
JB652	Damaged by a night fighter and abandoned 4 miles east of Halesworth, Suffolk, 21 December 1943.
JB653:MG-R	Missing, Le Mans, 20 May 1944.
JB656:MG-D	Missing, Berlin, 17 December 1943.
JB661:MG-L	To 300 Sqn
MG-T	
MG-Z	
JB671	To 97 Sqn
JB676:MG-K	Missing, Friedrichshafen, 28 April 1944.
JB677:MG-U	Missing, Berlin, 3 January 1944.
JB682:MG-A	Missing, Berlin, 2 January 1944.
JB684	To 405 Sqn
JB699	To 405 Sqn
JB717:MG-V	Missing, Berlin, 29 January 1944.
JB718	To 12 Sqn
JB719:MG-B	Missing, Karlsruhe, 25 April 1944.
JB722:MG-Q	Missing, Nuremberg, 31 March 1944.
MG-U	
JB731	To 97 Sqn
JB735	Crashed on take-off, Oakington, 24 December 1943.
JB911:MG-A	
LM690	SOC 21 May 1947
ME315	To 405 Sqn
ME356:MG-P	To 106 Sqn

ME360:MG-J	To 106 Sqn
ME369:MG-U	To 106 Sqn
ME370	To 405 Sqn
ME471	SOC 15 May 1947.
ND345	To 15 Sqn
ND347	To 405 Sqn
ND350	Crashed on overshoot at Feltwell, 31 March 1944.
ND353:MG-N	Missing, Dusseldorf, 23 April 1944.
ND354	To 83 Sqn
ND358	To 156 Sqn
ND365:MG-L	Missing, Berlin, 16 February 1944.
ND368:MG-U	Missing, Berlin, 21 January 1944.
ND387:MG-M2 MG-O	To 90 Sqn
ND395	To 83 Sqn
ND443:MG-L	Missing, Nuremberg, 31 March 1944.
ND445:MG-L MG-D	Missing, Berlin, 16 February 1944.
ND457:MG-F2 MG-O	Missing, Berlin, 25 March 1944.
ND460:MG-S MG-W	Missing, Normandy, 8 August 1944.
ND470:MG-S	Missing, Leipzig, 20 February 1944.
ND496:MG-T	To 44 Sqn
ND523:MG-X	Missing, Frankfurt, 23 March 1944.
ND557	Failed to return from Stuttgart, 15/16 March 1944.
ND581:MG-M	Missing, Berlin, 25 March 1944.
ND588:MG-Q MG-W	Missing, Duisburg, 22 May 1944.
ND590:MG-B MG-G	Missing, Coubronne, 24 June 1944.
ND592:MG-J	Missing, Laon, 23 April 1944.
ND693	To NTU
ND736:MG-D	Missing, Mont Couple, 20 May 1944.
ND744:MG-F	To 170 Sqn
ND750	To 582 Sqn
ND766:MG-P	Missing, Coubronne, 24 June 1944.
ND845:MG-C	Missing, Le Mans, 20 May 1944.
ND849:MG-M	To 152 Sqn
ND852:MG-D MG-G	Missing, Russelsheim, 26 August 1944.
ND860	To 460 Sqn
ND875	To 156 Sqn
ND897:MG-C	Missing, Siracourt, 29 June 1944.
ND899	To 582 Sqn
ND901:MG-B	Missing, Chambly, 2 May 1944.
ND906:MG-N	Flew into ground out of cloud, crashing at Ashby & Ledger Works near Church Lawford, 5 May 1944.
ND907	To 35 Sqn
ND912:MG-P	To 405 Sqn
ND916	To 35 Sqn
NE122:MG-V	To 1669 CU
NE123:MG-J	Missing, Brest, 26 August 1944.
NE126:MG-R MG-W	Missing, Frankfurt, 13 September 1944.

NE129:MG-G   Missing, Dreux, 11 June 1944.
NE356:MG-P

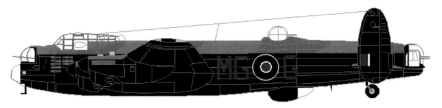

Avro Lancaster Mk III PA976:MG-G shown in March 1945. This aircraft was flown by F/Lt J.A. McCollah. Note the lightning flash and bomb log on nose and the reversion to full-sized squadron code letters. M. Barrass

NE496:MG-T	
PA964:MG-K	Missing, Buer, 6 October 1944.
PA975:MG-G	To 1660 CU
MG-H	
PA976	To TFU
PA978:MG-Z	Missing, Worms, 22 February 1945.
PA982	To 1660 CU
PA983	To 635 Sqn
PB118	To 1654 CU
PB123	To 35 Sqn
PB124:MG-H	To 106 Sqn
PB133	To 97 Sqn
PB148:MG-C	Missing, Sterkrade, 19 August 1944.
PB156	To 97 Sqn
PB179:MG-Q	To 279 Sqn
PB180:MG-F	Missing, Kiel, 27 August 1944.
PB212:MG-S	Damaged by flak over Hamburg and crash-landed at Bungay, 29 July 1944.
PB233	To 1660 CU
PB238	To 582 Sqn
PB241:MG-X	Missing, Buer, 6 October 1944.
PB287	To 635 Sqn
PB305:MG-K	To 106 Sqn
PB357:MG-S	Missing, Duisburg, 15 October 1944.
PB367	To 35 Sqn
PB371	To 9 Sqn
PB381:MG-S	
PB410	To 97 Sqn
PB420:MG-O	To 1660 CU
PB431:MG-D	To 1660 CU
PB435:MG-R	To 12 Sqn
MG-S	
PB437:MG-G	To 1660 CU
MG-W	
PB454:MG-J	To Middle East
PB466	Missing, Emden, 6 September 1944.
PB473	To 97 Sqn
PB474:MG-L	Missing, Wanne-Eickel, 12 October 1944.
PB481	To 5 LFS [Lancaster Finishing School]
PB487:MG-X	

PB489:MG-F	To 1660 CU
PB490:MG-B	To 12 Sqn
PB505	To 156 Sqn
PB513	To 405 Sqn
PB517	To 156 Sqn
PB526:MG-N	Missing, Hanover, 6 January 1945.
PB570	To 1669 CU
PB576	To 1667 CU
PB582:MG-T	
PB584:MG-M	To 1660 CU
MG-N	
PB587:MG-A	To 106 Sqn
MG-X	
PB589:MG-O	To 1660 CU
PB615	SOC 15 January 1947.
PB622:MG-C	To 106 Sqn
PB623:MG-B	To 106 Sqn
MG-L	
PB626:MG-E	To 106 Sqn
PB627	To 635 Sqn
PB667:MG-N	Crashed in Schelde Estuary returning from Recklinghausen, 20 March
MG-Q	1945.
PB677:MG-N	To 106 Sqn
PB679:MG-A	To ECFS [Empire Central Flying School]
MG-O	
PB680	To 635 Sqn
PB962	SOC 29 August 1947.
PB963:MG-O	SOC 29 January 1947.
PB964	SOC 15 January 1947.
PB965	SOC 17 June 1947.
PB966:MG-H	SOC 4 December 1946.
PB968	Converted to GR Mk III and to 236 OCU.
PB969:MG-Z	SOC 3 June 1947.
PB970	To CBE
PB975	SOC 19 September 1947.
PB976:MG-Z	SOC 4 September 1947.
PB977:MG-A	To CBE
MG-U	
PB979	To 49 Sqn, returned then SOC 4 September 1947.
RE130	SOC 20 August 1946.
RF215	SOC 25 March 1948.
RF236	To 1 Ferry Unit

Lancaster Mk VI

JB675:MG-O	To 405 Sqn then 635 Sqn, returned then to 76 Sqn.
JB713	To 405 Sqn
ND418	To 635 Sqn
ND673	To 635 Sqn

Lancaster Mk VII

NX691:MG-F	Sold for scrap, 21 August 1950.

THE OPERATIONAL RECORD

Raids Flown

3 Group	Stirling	167 bombing	11 minelaying
8 Group	Stirling	82 bombing	7 minelaying
8 Group	Lancaster	279 bombing	
Total		583 bombing	18 minelaying

Sorties flown

3 Group	Stirling	918
8 Group	Stirling	826
8 Group	Lancaster	3,316
Total		5,060

Losses

3 Group	Stirling	41 (4.5%)
8 Group	Stirling	37 (4.5%)
8 Group	Lancaster	87 (2.6%)
Total		165 (3.3%)

27 Stirlings were lost in non-operational crashes.

Claims to fame

- The first operational Stirling squadron
- The first squadron to use H2S operationally
- One of the original Pathfinder squadrons on formation of the force
- Suffered the highest percentage loss of all Stirling squadrons and the highest percentage loss in 8 Group
- Carried out more raids than any other 8 Group Lancaster squadron
- Suffered the third highest losses in Bomber Command

COMMANDING OFFICERS
1939–45

29 March 1939–27 November 1939	W/Cdr LG Nixon
28 November 1939–4 April 1940	W/Cdr AE Paish
7 August 1940–14 March 1941	W/Cdr PI Harris DFC
14 March 1941–31 March 1942	W/Cdr RH Graham DSO DFC
31 March 1942–9 April 1942	S/Ldr DJH Lay
10 April 1942–1 October 1942	W/Cdr BD Sellick DFC
2 October 1942–2 May 1943	W/Cdr CR Donaldson DSO DFC
3 May 1943–19 September 1943	W/Cdr HH Burnell
20 September 1943 –24 March 1944	G/Capt KR Rampling DSO DFC
25 March 1944–27 April 1944	W/Cdr WG Lockhart DSO DFC
28 April 1944–19 May 1944	W/Cdr JF Barron DSO DFC DFM
20 May 1944–8 October 1944	W/Cdr RW Cox DFC AFC
9 October 1944–31 December 1944	W/Cdr DM Walburn DSO
1 January 1945–4 June 1945	W/Cdr DA Cracknell DSO DFC
5 June 1945–20 January 1946	W/Cdr KH Burns DSO DFC

APPENDIX IV
SQUADRON BASES 1939–45

3 September 1936–31 August 1939	Finningley
1 September 1939–14 September 1939	Doncaster
15 September 1939–22 September 1939	Finningley
23 September 1939–4 April 1940	Upper Heyford
7 August 1940–1 November 1940	Leeming
2 November 1940–24 July 1945	Oakington
25 July 1945–May 1946	Mepal

APPENDIX V

NAMELESS CREWS

The crews in the following photographs all served with 7 Sqn but are presently unidentified. The author would be grateful for any information regarding these crews. You may contact the author through the publisher or by e-mail at thomasdocherty@tiscali.co.uk.

Lancaster crew – 1.

Lancaster crew – 2.

Lancaster crew – 3.

Lancaster crew – 4.

Lancaster crew – 5.

Lancaster crew – 6.

Lancaster crew – 7.

Lancaster crew – 8, with Lancaster JB185:MG-Y.

Lancaster crew – 9, all officers.

Lancaster crew – 10, all officers again. Note the lack of perspex central windscreen in the rear turret.

Lancaster crew – 11. Another 7 Sqn crew, all commissioned, posing in the crew entrance to a Lancaster.

Lancaster crew – 12.

GLOSSARY AND ABBREVIATIONS

AFEE	Airborne Forces Experimental Establishment
AONS	Air Observer Navigation School
AP	Armour Piercing (bombs)
ATA	Air Transport Auxiliary
A&AEE	Aeroplane & Armament Experimental Establishment
BDU	Bombing Development Unit
BGS	Bombing & Gunnery School
CBE	Central Bomber Establishment
Chiefy	Flight Sergeant
CLS	Central Landing School
Cookie	A 4,000 lb bomb
CU	Conversion Unit
DFC	Distinguished Flying Cross
DFM	Distinguished Flying Medal
Discip	Discipline
DR	Dead reckoning (navigation)
ECFS	Empire Central Flying School
Erk	A non-commissioned airman (groundcrew) below the rank of Corporal
ETA	Estimated Time of Arrival
Fishpond	Tail warning radar
FTS	Flying Training School
Gee	A navigation device used to accurately fix the bombers position over the target
GP	General Purpose (bombs)
GPI	Ground Position Indicator
HC	Heavy Case (bombs)
HCU	Heavy Conversion Unit
HF D/F	High Frequency Direction Finding
H2S	A downward and forward looking radar mapping and navigation device
IP	Initial Point
LFS	Lancaster Finishing School
LMF	Lack of Moral Fibre (Cowardice)
MC	Medium Case (bombs)
MF D/F	Medium Frequency Direction Finding
NTU	Navigation Training Unit
Oboe	A highly accurate navigation device
ORB	Operations Record Book
OTC	Officer Training Corps
OTU	Operational Training Unit
POW	Prisoner of War

Q Site	A dummy airfield designed to decoy enemy bombers
RCM	Radio Countermeasures
R/T	Radio Telephony
SFPP	Service Ferry Pilots Pool
SOC	Struck Off Charge
SWO	Station Warrant Officer
W/T	Wireless Telegraphy
Y Operator	Aircrew member whose role was to listen to and jam enemy transmissions

BIBLIOGRAPHY

Action Stations Vols 1, 2, 3, 5, 6, 7 and 9, Various authors (PSL, various dates)

Avro Lancaster – The Definitive Record, Harry Holmes (Airlife 1997)

Memoirs of a Wireless Operator 1938–1940, Ted Brightmore (Privately published)

Nothing Heard After Take-Off, 7 Squadron (The Lithoprint Company, Newquay)

The Berlin Raids, Martin Middlebrook (Penguin Books Ltd, 1988)

The Bomber Command War Diaries, Martin Middlebrook & Chris Everitt (Midland Publishing, 1996)

The Nuremberg Raid, Martin Middlebrook (Penguin Books Ltd, 1980)

The Stirling Bomber, Michael J.F. Bowyer (Faber & Faber Ltd, 1980)

1942 Offensive, Fred Mills (Privately published)

7 Squadron Association Newsletters

7 Sqn Operational Record Book, November 1938–April 1941

7 Sqn Operational Record Book, January 1942–May 1942

7 Sqn Operational Record Book, June 1944

7 Sqn Combat Reports, April 1944–March 1945

7 Sqn Daily Battle Order, April 1944 and February–May 1945

7 Sqn record of Photographic Flights, May 1941–January 1942

7 Sqn Night Photo Plotting Reports, September–November 1942

7 Sqn Order of Battle, 28 June 1943

7 Sqn Order of Battle, 24 May 1945

RAF Oakington Operational Record Book, October 1940–April 1941

RAF Oakington Operations Log Book, August–September 1944

ACKNOWLEDGEMENTS

All historical books are the sum of many parts: the research of the writer, the assistance of fellow historians, the reminiscences, papers and photographs of those who were there. I could not have written this book without the help of very many people and, in particular I wish to thank the following for their unstinting assistance. If I have omitted anyone I apologize.

Chris Allen
Ted Ansfield
Maurice Baird-Smith
Malcolm Barrass
Bob Baxter
David Beaune
Sgt Mark Bradley, No. 7 Squadron
   Historian
Margaret Broughton
Mary Catt
Clair Chalmers
Alan R Chambers
David Cheetham
Ron Claridge
Ernest Davenport
Peter Dunton
Les Ellingham
T.J. 'Jock' Elliot
Bernard Elsworthy
Tony Farrington
Geoff Garner
Ralph Graham
Hugh Halliday
Frank Haslam
Barry Hugo
Doug Humphery
H.E. Jacobson
Peter Jones
The late F/O Tom Jones DFC
Harold Lazenby
Frank Leatherdale
Jeff Lindsay
Errol Martyn
Ken Summers
Rob Thomas
Jack Thornton
Peter Van Gelderen

Members of No. 7 Squadron
   Association
Martin Middlebrook
Douglas Miller
Dennis Milne
John Moyles
Barrie Nancarrow
Geoff Negus
Gordon A. Paterson
P.K. Patrick
Ann Peters
Bill Peters
Graham Pitchfork
Bob Pointer
John Prentice
RAF Boy Entrants' Association
RAF Halton Apprentices'
   Association
Joe Raybould
Malcolm Reeves, Chairman of No. 7
   Squadron Association
Ann Reynolds
Harry W Rossiter
Robert J Rudhall
Mildred Watson Scales
Peter Scales
Jean Pierre Sleurs
Dave Smith
Richard H. Smith
Mary Smith
Gerry South
A. Speakman
Frank Stephenson
Stanley Warren
Oliver Wells
R.H. White
Fred Wills

The aircraft profiles are by Malcolm Barrass. You can find more profiles by Malcolm at his fine RAF historical website 'Air of Authority' at www.rafweb.org.

INDEX

PEOPLE